McCall's
NEEDLEWORK
In Colour

McCall's
NEEDLEWORK
In Colour

**By The Editors of
McCall's Needlework
& Crafts Magazine**

HAMLYN
LONDON·NEW YORK·SYDNEY·TORONTO

Published by
THE HAMLYN PUBLISHING GROUP LIMITED
LONDON · NEW YORK · SYDNEY · TORONTO
Hamlyn House, Feltham, Middlesex, England
© Copyright, 1964, by McCall Corporation
Copyright 1950, 1951, 1952, 1953, 1954, 1955, 1956,
        1957, 1958, 1959, 1960, 1961, 1962, 1963, by
        McCall Corporation
Revised edition 1967
Fifth impression 1973

Printed in Czechoslovakia by Svoboda, Prague
ISBN 0 600 024849
52003 / 5

Foreword

McCall's Needlework and Knitting in Colour is a carefully planned handbook to provide reference and inspiration for all who are interested in needle-craft. Some will find the book invaluable as a source for identifying and learning handicraft techniques. McCall's Needlework and Knitting in Colour, while covering the needlework field, gives special attention to the types of needlework of greatest interest to the needlewoman of today.

Our book is a "learn-and-make" book. There are instructions for each type of stitch illustrated. Some of the projects are easy enough for a child, while others are for the experienced and gifted needle-woman. Since this is a book for all who wish to learn, from children to adults, the items to make are chosen for their practical use as well as design. By following the step-by-step illustrated details with their written instructions, the student of needlework can proceed from the simplest embroidery stitches to the beautiful combinations of these stitches which are used to create the rich effects of crewel embroi-dery; or one can advance from casting on knitting stitches to learning intricate knitted patterns such as are used in Aran Isles and Scandinavian designs.

By presenting outstanding museum examples of both traditional and modern needlework, with the basic how-to for creating them, we hope to enable present day needlewomen to acquire the inspiration and knowledge she needs to create the museum pieces of the future!

During my twelve years as editor of the McCall's Needlework and Crafts publications, I have seen interest in all types of handwork increase: knitted and crocheted garments have become high fashion; well-known artists have switched from paint to yarn to create wall hangings of the highest artistic quality. As a result, needlework has sparked the imagination of decorators who often plan entire rooms around beautiful needlework pieces.

The material in this book has been compiled by the editors of the McCall's Needlework & Crafts publications. The following associate editors have assisted me and given their expert knowledge to the writing of sections in this book: Embroidery—Eleanor Spencer; Knitting, Crochet, and Tatting—Gena Rhoades; Quilts—Ellene Saunders.

NANINA COMSTOCK

Acknowledgements

The items chosen to feature in this book have been made from basic yarns, threads, and other materials readily available. We wish to express our gratitude to the following companies who have developed designs especially for our use, or have supplied us with materials: American Thread Co., The Artcraft Press, Emile Bernat and Sons C., Bernhard Ulmann Co., Columbia-Minerva Corp., D.M.C. Corp., John Dritz and Sons, Heirloom Needlework Guild, Inc.. Hero Mfg. Co., Lily Mills Co., A. & H. Shillman Co., Inc., Ralph C. Springer Co., Tuxedo Yarn Co., Walbead, Inc., Wm. E. Wright & Sons Co., and Yankee Homecraft Corp.

We are also indebted to The Metropolitan Museum of Art, The Newark Museum, The Cooper Union Museum, The Smithsonian Institution, and Museum of Fine Arts, Boston, for the photographs and information we obtained through their study departments and collections.

For the British edition we would like to express our gratitude to Miss Jean Kinmond of J. & P. Coats Limited and Mr James Norbury of Patons and Baldwins Limited and their departments for the invaluable assistance we have received from them. Curtains in frontispiece by courtesy of Arthur Sanderson & Sons Ltd.

Contents

PORTRAIT OF A LADY. ENGLISH XVII CENTURY. VICTORIA AND ALBERT MUSEUM.

1 Our Needlework Heritage

Since needlework has been from the earliest civilisations an important part of every culture, we have inherited a wealth of material from many sources. Our museums contain beautiful examples from this country and others in which the native needlework originated and developed. While the designs are strikingly individual and typical of both the area and the era of their origin, there is a worldwide similarity of the stitches and the basic techniques throughout history. Following are brief historical notes on typical ancient embroideries, the great interest in needlework which started in England as early as the 13th century, and the development of needlework which was strongly influenced by many European styles. More detailed information about the origin of each kind of needlework is given at the beginning of the chapter or section where it is featured.

ANCIENT EMBROIDERY

The origins of embroidery are lost in obscurity. The few examples of early Egyptian, Greek, and Roman embroideries often show fine strips of pure gold or other metals wound around a foundation thread of linen. These gold-covered threads were couched to the surface of the fabric to cover areas in a solid gold effect, or were used to outline coloured silk, wool, or linen embroidery. Also, there are rare examples of fabric appliqués which were used for wall hangings or to decorate garments.

Silk embroidery was developed in the Orient along with silk fabrics. The earliest Oriental garments of richly hued silks were embroidered with silk, metallic thread, or jewels. Seed stitch, chain stitch, outline stitch, featherstitch, and satin stitch were used, and tiny bits of metal similar to modern sequins were often added to the design. Mirror fragments were used in some of the embroideries of India, held in place by close chain stitching. Also in India, the Punjabs used a darning stitch to create fine all over ornamentation. Although European styles have changed through the centuries, Oriental designs and workmanship still follow the old traditions, colours, and designs.

When silkworms were first smuggled out of the Orient, they were cultivated in Italy and southern France. Fine silk fabrics, brocade, and velvet were made up into wall hangings or garments, all richly embroidered with silk floss and metal threads.

Embroidery and appliqué formed a part of the early wall decorations in European homes. Castles during the Middle Ages and up to the 17th century were built of stone, sometimes without mortar. Draughts blew through the walls unless hangings were used. One of the most famous early pictorial hangings is the Bayeux Tapestry, which is not a tapestry but an embroidery in wool on linen worked in outline, rope stitches, and laid work. It tells the story of the Norman conquest of England in the 11th century.

THE ENGLISH TRADITION

During the 16th century, Catherine of Aragon, the first wife of Henry VIII, introduced Spanish "black work" in England. Turkey tufting, which is believed to have been an imitation of Turkish carpets, was also popular in the Tudor Period. Elizabeth I and her cousin, Mary Queen of Scots, were both skilled needlewomen. Many embroideries of their time were done in wool or silk on a coarse linen similar to a very fine canvas with threads of an even count; this was called "canvas work." It was popular to make samplers or "exemplars" of the variety of stitches one could work on canvas. While many stitches were made, the most important one was tent stitch, the forerunner of needlepoint.

Another early form of embroidery in England was "needle worke cruell," which derived its name from the type of wool used, "a thin worsted yarn of two threads." This embroidery was worked on a linen background in various stitches. It reached its height of popularity during the early 17th century at the time of James I and is often called Jacobean work. Today the name "crewelwork" refers to embroidery of the same type as the early work. A very good example is shown on page 15.

Bed hangings of the 17th and 18th centuries, often worked in crewel, provided the sleeper with privacy and kept out cold night breezes. When heavy fabric was not available, several thicknesses of material were layered together and held with stab stitching, thus popularising the quilting technique.

EARLY EMBROIDERY IN AMERICA

American embroideries are descended from so many others that is is very difficult to know just where their individuality begins. For example, during the early 1700's they were making samplers similar to those being made throughout Europe at the time; crewel-embroidered bedspreads were closely related to the Jacobean designs being embroidered in England; needlepoint (then called "tent stitch") chair seats and pictures were as popular here as abroad. Most of the New England designs either came from or were strongly influenced by England.

Needlework teachers in the colonies not only sold imported designs but created their own in related subjects, colouring, and technique. An interesting example is the famous "Fishing Lady" of Boston worked in tent stitch (page 9). The exact origin of this design is not known; however, about eight different embroideries have been discovered which are very similar, using the same motifs arranged in different ways. It is believed that a key to the source of the designs is given by the following information which appeared in the Boston News-Letter for April 27/May 4, 1738, stating that there was "To be had at Mrs. Condy's near the Old North Meeting House; all sorts of beautiful Figures on Canvas, for Tent Stick; the Patterns from London, but drawn by her much cheaper than English drawing; All sorts of Canvas, without drawing; also Silk Shades, Slacks, Floss, Cruells of all Sorts, the best White Chapple Needles, and every thing for all Sorts of Work."

Early American crewel embroideries showed slight changes from those in England both in design and stitches, the most notable difference being the use of a modified Oriental or Roumanian stitch to replace the long-and-short stitch. The New England needlewoman found that she could conserve her crewel and still obtain a charming effect by executing this stitch so that she picked up with her needle only a few threads of linen ground, allowing most of the woollen threads to lie on the surface. Among interesting examples of early crewel embroidery in this country are the narrow

Pastoral Landscape with Fishing Lady, sometimes called "Boston Common," is an example of the embroidery which flourished in Boston during the 18th century. It is one of eight embroideries with a similar subject from the vicinity of Boston. The pieces are dated from 1743 to 1748. Detail at right, approximately actual size, illustrates size of stitch used in canvas work of this period.

Birds, Beasts and Flowers is a detail from a colourful crewel—embroidered petticoat border made in New England, 1725 to 1750.

9

COURTESY OF THE NEWARK MUSEUM, NEWARK, NEW JERSEY

Innocence and Friendship is a typical "mourning piece", embroidered with silk floss and chenille on silk. Background is painted, cottage roof is actual straw. A broad margin of black glass surrounds the elaborate picture, worked by Mary P. Paul, of Philadelphia, in the late 18th century.

COURTESY OF THE COOPER UNION MUSEUM, NEW YORK

Sampler shows a combination of simple cross–stitch letters with a rich floral border of flowers, foliage, and a pineapple in satin stitch, stem stitch, and French knots. It was embroidered by Eliza J. Benneson, 1835.

The Caswell Carpet, made by Zeruah Higley Guernsey Caswell, is one of the best–known large–scale embroideries. Squares worked in tambour stitch were joined to make the $12' \times 13\frac{1}{2}'$ carpet. It is recorded that two young Patawatomi Indians who lived with Zeruah's family while attending Castleton Medical College worked on the carpet, designing the two squares marked with their initials. This impressive embroidery was completed in 1835, after two years' work.

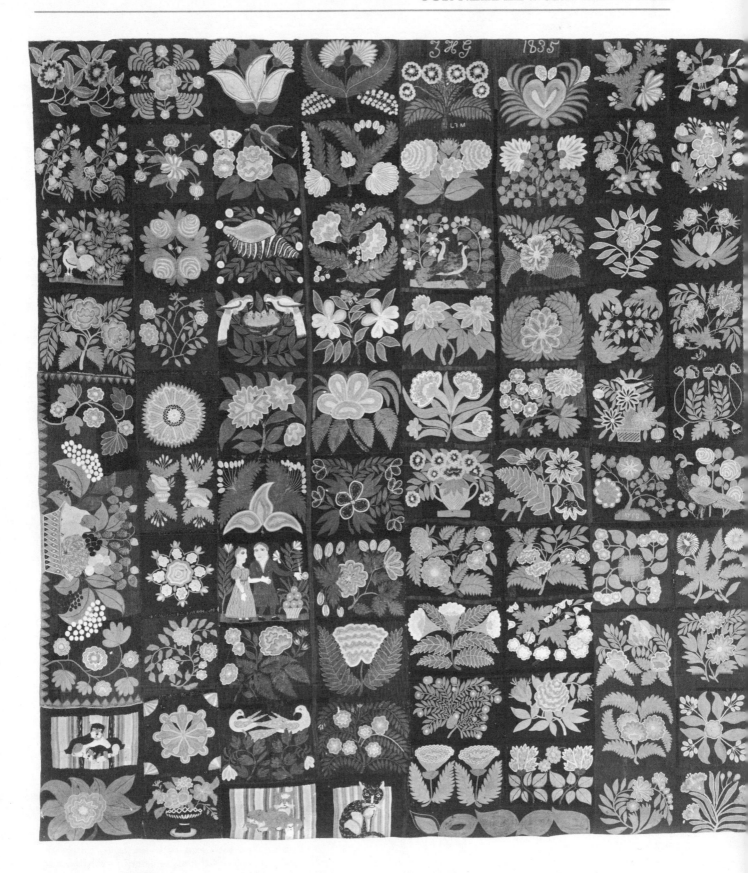

THE METROPOLITAN MUSEUM OF ART, NEW YORK, GIFT OF KATHERINE KEYES, 1938, IN MEMORY OF HER FATHER, HOMER EATON KEYES.

embroidered bands running around the hemlines of petticoats. These designs are less formal than the English, and sometimes the borders showed landscapes with beasts and buildings, as well as floral ornaments. (See page 9.)

Many of the crewel designs were worked in native dyed wools. The early settlers who found it expensive to import yarns from England had to depend on their own inventive ability, and a number of colours used by them were discovered by accident or through experiment. Many a New England colonist raised her own indigo plants and boasted the possession of an indigo tub in the rear kitchen. Here lambs' wool was tinted various shades of blue. Attempts were made to match the Canton blues of the chinaware from the Orient, and crewel embroideries worked in these shades were called "Blue and White Work."

Instruction in embroidery was part of the education of every well brought up young girl in America. Their samplers varied according to the part of the country where they were made.

The young girls of New England were apt to combine only a few simple stitches, using them for a small picture, a flower border, and an alphabet. There might also be a rather lugubrious verse along with the embroiderer's name and date of working.

Many of the samplers made by the early Pennsylvania Dutch settlers are long narrow strips of linen in a fairly open mesh. These show drawnwork and a variety of quite complicated stitches.

Samplers from various parts of the country were genealogical charts, with sturdy trees, each branch labelled with the names and dates of each ancestor.

An interesting type of embroidery sprang up from the teaching of the Moravian sect. These people migrated from Moravia in central Europe and settled in Bethlehem, Pennsylvania, in 1740. The art of embroidering memorial samplers (see page 42) was taught in their schools. Later, this kind of embroidery became a fad in other areas, with less morbid subjects, such as ships and pastoral scenes. These pictures were a combination of a tinted satin background and silk embroidery in a variety of stitches.

In the early 1800's the alphabet samplers became more elaborate and often had rich floral borders requiring skilful workmanship. (See page 10.)

While young girls were making their samplers, there was a great deal of embroidery being done for practical use in the home. Cross-stitch was worked on canvas to produce large carpets. Chairs and benches were upholstered with canvas worked in Bargello or flame stitch (see page 40). Turkey work was used as an upholstery fabric, for bed covers and rugs.

Popular in Europe at this time, and widely used here, was a kind of embroidery called "tambour." This is an embroidered chain stitch worked with a fine needle resembling a crochet hook. The Caswell carpet (page 10) is a unique example.

A practical use of needlework by the settlers of New England, New Amsterdam, Virginia, and the

COURTESY OF THE NEWARK MUSEUM, NEWARK, N. J.

Detail of appliquéd and embroidered quilt made by Emiline Dean Jones, about 1835.

Carolinas was quilt making. Among early quilts we find beautiful all-white examples—some puffed with padding (see page 107), some embroidered with heavy white cotton cord, and others worked with wicking, thus giving us the name "candlewicking" (see page 108).

The art of quilt making has continued through many stages. During the Revolutionary era, flower sprays were cut from French toile and appliquéd on the backgrounds; combinations of appliqué, patchwork, and quilting depicted patriotic emblems or the other interests of the maker. The uncounted number of patchwork designs which appeared in the 19th century were inspired by almost anything from a "duck's foot" to a "log cabin." Some of the more intricately designed quilts were often highly personalised, as is shown by a representation of the family homestead in the centre of the quilt detail on page 12.

Just as white quilts were popular in the 18th century, so were other types of "white work." This term applies to white embroidery in general, which was greatly influenced by the French; some of the best examples come from Louisiana. It is interesting to note that the tambour stitch used to embroider the Caswell carpet was equally popular in white work for embroidering dainty veils, shawls, and collars of fine net. Interest in white work continued until about the middle of the 19th century.

While original native quilt designs and the French-inspired white work were a part of every trousseau, it was Berlin work which dominated the 19th century. This kind of embroidery had been called "canvas work" during the 15th and 16th centuries, but in the early 1800's it received the name "Berlin work" because the patterns originated in Berlin. These patterns, drawn

COURTESY METROPOLITAN MUSEUM OF ART, NEW YORK

Unusually well–designed example of Berlin work, with sculptured and beaded accents.

EMBROIDERY IN THE 20th CENTURY

During the last quarter of the 19th and first quarter of the 20th century needlewomen did a great deal of knitting, crocheting, and tatting. They also made embroidered antimacassars, bureau runners, doilies, and other household linens, known as "fancy work." Designs were available stamped on material, as perforated patterns, or as hot iron transfers. They were used for both white work and embroidery in silk on linen using Kensington stitch in the realistic colours of flowers and fruits.

Starting in the 1920's there was a revival of interest in crewel embroidery and needlepoint. Most of the designs were copies of old pieces and were used to upholster both antique furniture and reproductions. At the same time many needlewomen embroidered unique designs which were created to their specifications by artists who either painted the needlepoint designs on canvas or made perforated patterns to stamp the designs on linen.

Today there is an ever-increasing demand for unusual and well designed needlework patterns. Top artists not only design for other needlewomen; they themselves are literally painting with yarns, creating articles and wall hangings which are museum pieces. Right now we are in the most exciting period of all needlework history. We have a vast heritage of handwork techniques, a limitless variety of yarns and other materials with which to work, and the needle arts are recognised by museum authorities as fine arts media of the 20th century.

on "paint paper" or painted on canvas, often copied celebrated pictures to be worked in needlepoint, using silk, then beads, and finally the brightly-coloured Berlin wool. Other characteristic subjects were birds, flowers, and arabesque motifs in bold colour. The Berlin type of design was prevalent during the Victorian era, and was adapted to a variety of embroidery techniques. See afghan, facing page 16.

Poppy: late 17th century COURTESY VICTORIA AND ALBERT MUSEUM

2 Embroidery

From time immemorial women have embroidered on clothing, accessories and linens to accent their intrinsic qualities or add new interest. One of the great advantages of the art is that it can be as simple or as complex as the needleworker cares to make it. Many of the basic stitches are the heritage of assorted cultures and are centuries old. To these have been added variations and new techniques eminently suited to today's functional and exciting use of colour and design.

Whether you choose to make a line-for-line copy of a design, adapt it with modifications, or create an entirely new piece of work, you will find that embroidery offers something for everyone with an eye for beauty.

Crewel Embroidery

Crewelwork, or Jacobean embroidery, became fashionable first in the 17th century, and expressed the extravagant taste of the time for richly-embroidered decorations. Early designs, which customarily featured exotic flowering trees combined with birds and animals, resulted from an exchange of ideas between Asia and Europe. Although the first crewel embroidery was worked in shades of one colour, generally blue or green, later designs sometimes used varied and brighter colouring; greens and blues still predominated.

The exotic Tree of Life was, and is, the most popular basic design. An elaborate example is the hanging shown below from the Metropolitan Museum of Art. The odd thing about these trees is that a single trunk with its many branches will carry a wide variety of flowers and fruits. Even the leaves vary in shape. Thus crewel embroidery gives you a chance to express your individual design ideas since the kind of forms you use is limited only by your own imagination.

Swirl the trunk gracefully up the centre of the area, decreasing its diameter as you get to the top of the tree. At the base of the trunk embroider satin stitch scallops of brown and green to represent earth and grass; spot with flora and fauna.

TREE OF LIFE DESIGN
COURTESY METROPOLITAN MUSEUM OF ART, NEW YORK

Embroidery Stitches

All basic embroidery stitches are easy. What may appear to be a difficult, complicated work is often the result of a well thought-out combining of several basic stitches to produce a richly-embroidered piece.

This is especially true in crewel embroidery which can be as varied as you choose—from confining it almost exclusively to long and short stitch, to using all the stitches presented here.

The more familiar you are with these basic stitches, the greater the excitement you can derive from developing your own combinations.

For practising the stitches you will need embroidery wools or thread, a linen or linen-like textured fabric, and embroidery needles which are available in sizes 1 to 10. An embroidery frame is optional, but it is often preferred to enable you to keep your stitches even and smooth.

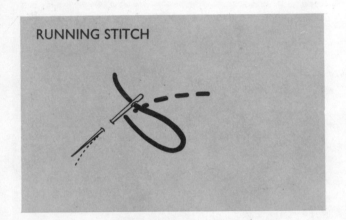

RUNNING STITCH

RUNNING STITCH Worked along a line that is either straight or curved. It consists of evenly spaced stitches even in size. It may have variations with one stitch longer than the others placed at even intervals. It may be used for a flower stem, or to form veins in leaves. It may fill in an open area with an all over design of many rows.

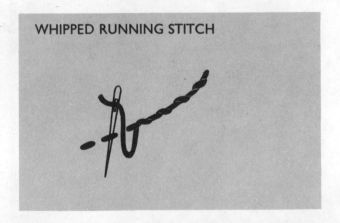

WHIPPED RUNNING STITCH

WHIPPED RUNNING STITCH A combination of two stitches. First the running stitch is completed with evenly spaced stitches. Then the blunt pointed needle is threaded with contrasting colour and worked through the stitches without going through the fabric. This gives the effect of a twisted cord.

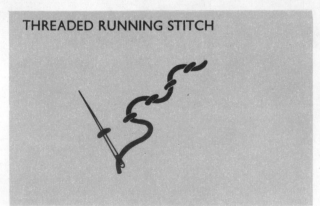

THREADED RUNNING STITCH

THREADED RUNNING STITCH Another variation. The running stitch has a second thread worked through in a wave by passing the blunt pointed needle first through the right of one stitch then through from the left of the next stitch. This differs from the twisted stitch in which the second thread is always passed through from the right to the left.

Lovely afghan or carriage robe from the Victorian era has designs cross-stitched on an afghan-stitch crochet background, rich fringe. The insignia in the lower left corner indicates it may have been made for a clergyman.

STRAIGHT STITCH   May be made as single stitches here and there in a design, or separated straight stitches in a ring or semi-circle to form a flower. It may be made in various lengths and in clusters, but each stitch is always separated from the others.

STRAIGHT STITCH

BACKSTITCH   Short stitches are placed end to end for a slim outline. This may be used alone for stems or borders, or to outline solid areas. The stitches just meet in the row, but the thread is carried under the fabric for twice the distance. Work from right to left, and carry the thread along the outline.

BACKSTITCH

THREADED BACKSTITCH   Made in the same way as the threaded running stitch. A second colour is worked in and out of the stitches of the backstitch without piercing the fabric. A third colour may thread through to make loops on the opposite side as well. See dotted lines in illustration.

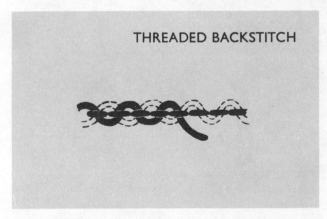

THREADED BACKSTITCH

COUCHING   Lay thread to be couched across fabric. Use an embroidery frame. With the same colour or a contrasting colour of thread, take small stitches at even intervals over the laid thread. Couching can be used solidly for special effects on small areas.

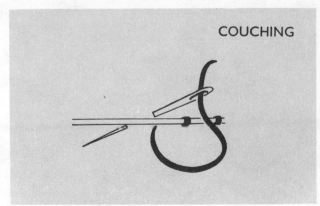

COUCHING

Contemporary version of crewel work, left, is a Penelope Jacobean design cushion, 'Peregrine'. From Needlecraft book N54.

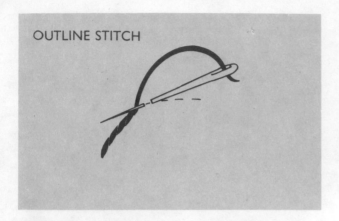

OUTLINE STITCH   Bring needle up through fabric. With thread to left of needle, insert needle a short distance away and on the line and bring needle out again on the line. This stitch makes a fine line and is used around edge, for veining and detail lines.

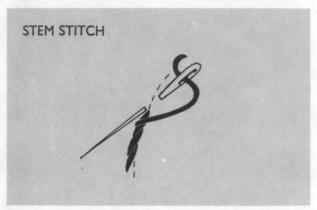

STEM OR CREWEL STITCH   This differs from outline stitch in that the thread is held on the opposite side of the line; the needle is inserted to the right of the line and brought up to the left of the line, making a thick outline. This stitch may be used as a filling by working rows along side of each other.

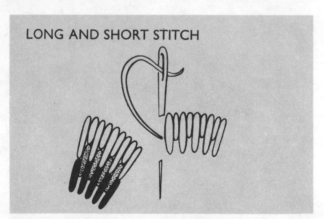

LONG AND SHORT (KENSINGTON) STITCH   Used to fill areas solidly, and shade colours. The first row is alternating long and short stitches, as shown. Following rows are stitches of equal length, worked at ends of short and long stitches. Regularity of the following rows depends on shape to be filled. Start at outer edge and work towards centre or downwards, keeping stitches generally in the same direction. Plan the stitches in an area so they fill it naturally and gracefully; it is helpful to mark with pencil the direction of some of the stitches. Shade colours into each other in rows.

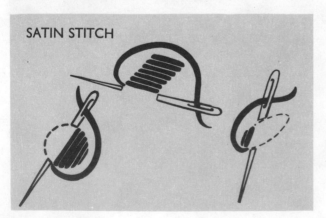

SATIN STITCH   Straight stitches worked side by side, usually slantwise, to fill small areas. For straight areas, work slantwise from top to bottom; for small circles, work centre long stitch vertically first, then fill each side; for leaf shapes, work diagonally, starting at left edge.

SATIN STITCH LEAF When area is large, divide into sections; work separately, changing direction of stitches for each section. Keep neat, firm outline and smooth, parallel stitches.

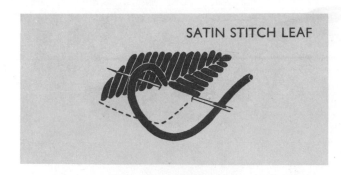

OPEN LEAF STITCH Start at base, left of centre. Insert needle on opposite margin part way up, bring out at base, right of centre. Continue as shown, alternating from side to side.

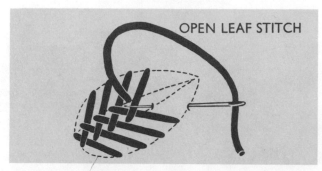

FISHBONE STITCH Starting at point, work as shown, slanting each succeeding stitch more until correct angle is obtained. Try with two needles and two shades of the same colour.

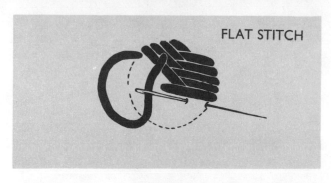

FLAT STITCH Work in similar manner as shown for small leaves and petals. For larger areas, work bands of stitch side by side, interlocking bands at sides to resemble braid effect at centre.

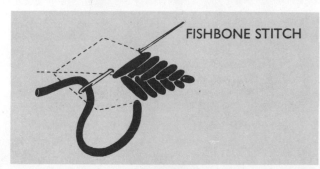

LAZY DAISY STITCH A popular stitch for making flower petals. Bring thread up at base of petal, hold loop with thumb and anchor it with a small stitch. Work lazy daisy petals in a ring with base of each close, for a round flower. May also be used as a filling stitch by scattering lazy daisies at random.

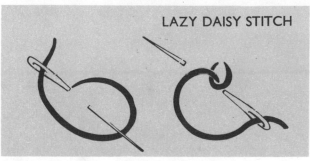

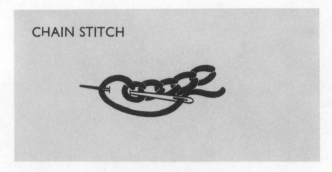

CHAIN STITCH   Worked from top down. Bring needle up through fabric; hold loop with thumb and insert needle again at same place. Bring needle up a short distance away with thread looped under needle; repeat. Use for heavy outlines or as a filling, making rows of chains follow the outline of shape being filled.

CHAIN WITH BACKSTITCH, WITH COUCHING Make backstitch down centre of chain; or couch down on one side of chain as shown, using another colour of yarn.

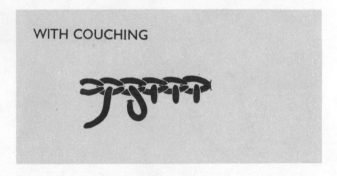

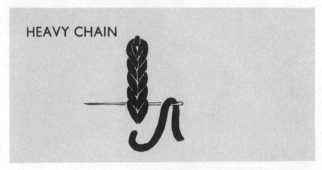

HEAVY CHAIN   Start with a small vertical stitch; then make a small loop through stitch, without picking up the fabric. Continue making loops under the second one above.

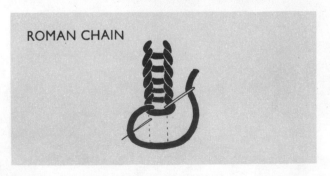

ROMAN CHAIN   Made in a similar manner to regular chain, except that the loop ends are wide apart. Keep the width of the loops even and make them close together.

DOUBLE CHAIN Use when a broader border decoration is desired. This is done in same way as regular chain stitch except that the needle is angled from right to left, then from left to right as shown.

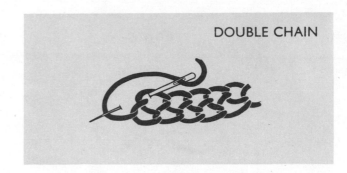

DOUBLE CHAIN

BUTTONHOLE STITCH Worked from left to right. Bring needle up through fabric. Holding thread under left thumb, form a loop; then pass needle through fabric and over the looped thread; repeat.

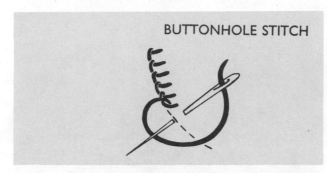

BUTTONHOLE STITCH

CLOSED BUTTONHOLE STITCH Made in same manner as above, but with stitches close together. May be used to make scalloped edges as shown, or to fill an area by working several touching rows.

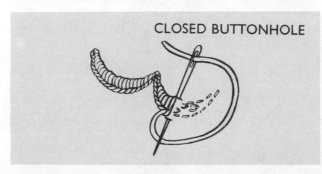

CLOSED BUTTONHOLE

HERRINGBONE STITCH Worked between two lines. Bring thread up through lower line, insert needle in upper line a little to the right and take a short stitch to the left. Insert needle on lower line a little to the right and take a short stitch to the left. May be used for thick stems, or to connect two solid areas for softening effect.

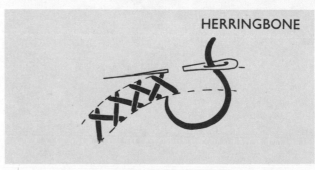

HERRINGBONE

COUCHED HERRINGBONE First make herringbone stitch. Then touch down with separate thread in contrasting colour, if desired, where stitches cross.

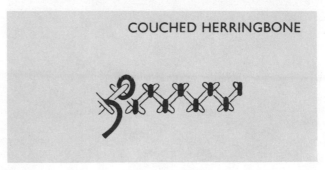

COUCHED HERRINGBONE

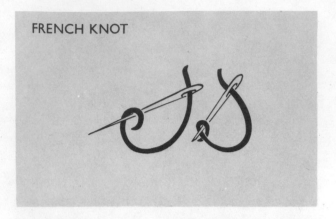

FRENCH KNOT Bring thread up through fabric. Wrap thread over and under needle, crossing beginning thread; insert needle in fabric close to where it came up. Thread may be used double to produce larger knots if desired.

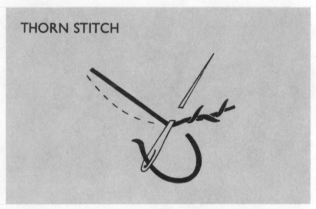

THORN STITCH Work in an embroidery frame. First lay a long thread across area. Take diagonal stitches from side to side to hold long thread in position as shown. Used for some stems to produce a special effect.

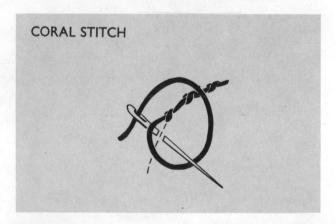

CORAL STITCH Work from right to left. Bring thread up through fabric and hold with thumb. Take a small stitch across line, under and over thread. Pull up thread to form a small knot; repeat. May be used for fine stems.

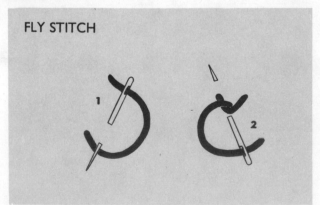

FLY STITCH Similar to lazy daisy stitch, but the ends of the loop stitch are widely separated. Make a small backstitch to anchor the centre in place, bringing needle up in position for next stitch. Can be used as a scattered space filler where a simple, textured background is desired.

FEATHERSTITCH Worked along a single line out-line with the needle slanted to touch the line. Placed first to the right, then to the left and so on alternately each time, the thread is passed under the needle for a buttonhole loop. This is similar to the chain stitch, but the loop is open, not closed. The branches may be kept all even with each stitch the same length, or they may be varied in length.

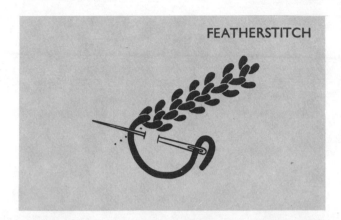

FEATHERSTITCH

CLOSED FEATHERSTITCH Worked along a double outline, with the needle kept erect along that line instead of being pointed towards the centre. The same method of alternating the stitches from right to left is used as in plain featherstitching, but each stitch is taken at bottom of the stitch above.

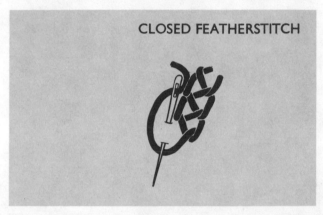

CLOSED FEATHERSTITCH

STRAIGHT FEATHERSTITCH Formed in the same way with a double guideline and perpendicular stitches, but the ends of the thread do not meet the stitch above.

STRAIGHT FEATHERSTITCH

There are many fancy variations of featherstitching. Two stitches may be taken at each side before al-ternating the side. This forms Double Featherstitch. Or three stitches may be taken to form Treble or Triple Featherstitching. A definite scallop or zigzag may be used as a guide in featherstitching.

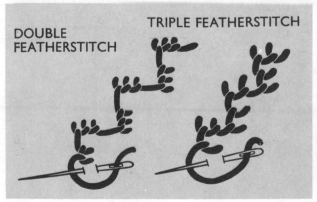

TRIPLE FEATHERSTITCH

DOUBLE FEATHERSTITCH

Embroidery : filling stitches

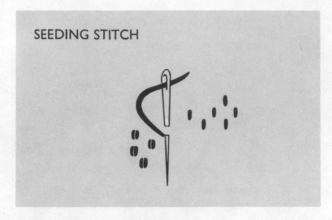

SEEDING STITCH   Take two small stitches side by side, or one small single stitch. Scatter over area to be filled, alone or combined with other stitches.

DIAGONAL FILLING Take stitches diagonally across area to be filled, in opposite directions. With contrasting colour of thread, take short stitches across diagonal stitches where they cross, proceeding diagonally from top left to bottom right as shown.

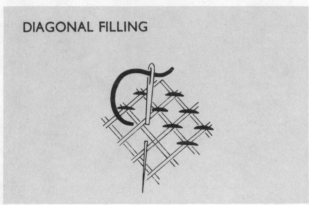

STAR FILLING   Work an upright cross, then a diagonal cross. They all are held together with a small cross worked over centre of large crosses. May be used in combination with other stitches as filling.

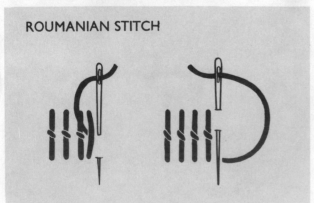

ROUMANIAN STITCH   May be used as a solid filling by making rows of stitches close together; or for borders or spot decorations. It is made in two steps. One long stitch is fastened in the centre with a short couching stitch as shown in the diagrams.

ORIENTAL STITCH   Since satin stitch is very popular in Oriental embroideries it is natural that one variation should be so named. This stitch is used to cover a fairly large area. Long floating threads of satin stitch are first placed vertically over the area. Another thread is then laid across them and held in place with short anchoring stitches spaced equally, as in couching. These anchoring stitches may match or contrast in colour. The couched threads may also be laid across the background threads diagonally.

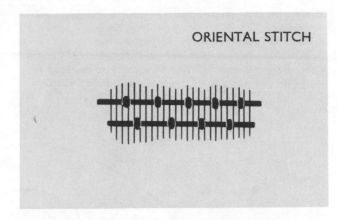

ORIENTAL STITCH

TRELLIS AND CROSS   Take long stitches across area to be filled in, horizontally and vertically. Where stitches cross, work a small cross in same or contrasting colour of thread. French knots are sometimes worked in centre of squares.

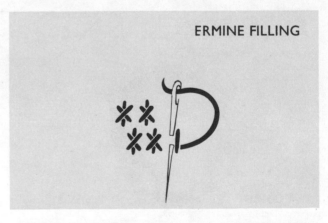

TRELLIS AND CROSS

ERMINE FILLING   Take an upright stitch. Bring up needle to right of upright, nearly at bottom; insert needle near top at left of upright. Bring needle out at left near bottom and insert at dot on right, near top. Use in rows. alternating spacing to fill area.

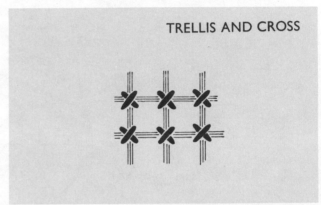

ERMINE FILLING

FAGGOT FILLING Take four or five stitches close together across fabric. Tie the stitches together at middle with two small stitches through fabric and around stitches to make a bundle.

FAGGOT FILLING

Embroidered Ornaments

These gay tree ornaments may also double as useful pincushions. They are embroidered with a variety of stitches detailed elsewhere in this section. Use Coats 'ANCHOR' Tapisserie Wool and six-strands Clark's 'ANCHOR' Stranded Cotton to embroider the bind for which we give the actual-size pattern and the directions.

The other ornaments may be traced from the photographs on page opposite 32 then enlarged on 1″ squared paper as explained on page 244. The embroidery can easily be copied from the photographs using 'ANCHOR' Tapisserie Wool for the bold sections and 'ANCHOR' Stranded Cotton in varying strands for the remainder.

STITCH KEY

- • — SEQUIN

- ——— OUTLINE STITCH

- ＞〰 ✳ STRAIGHT STITCH

- – – – – BACKSTITCH

- +++++ COUCHING

- ✕✕✕✕ THORN STITCH

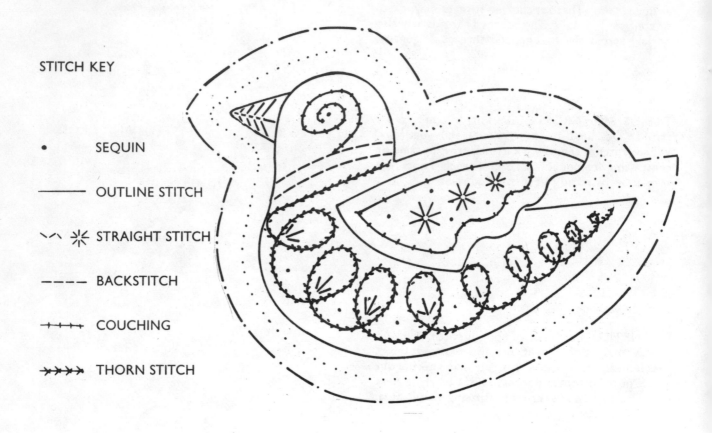

EQUIPMENT: Embroidery needles. Pencil. Tracing paper. Carbon paper. Scissors.

MATERIALS: Scraps of heavy cotton fabric or felt in green, blue and red. Coats Satinised No. 40 to match. Cotton wool or Kapok for stuffing. Coats 'ANCHOR' Tapisserie Wool: 1 skein each 013, 0161, 0163, 0203, 0205, 0295, 0402 and 0403. Clark's 'ANCHOR' Stranded Cotton: 1 skein each Kingfisher **0161**/483, Laurel Green **0210**/576, Buttercup **0295**/960, **0402**/White and **0403**/Black.

Sequins: assorted colours. All purpose glue. 1 Milwards 'Gold Seal' chenille needle No. 19 (for Tapisserie Wool). 1 each Milwards 'Gold Seal' crewel needles Nos. 5, 6 and 7 (for stranded cotton 6, 3 or 4 and 2 strands respectively).

DIRECTIONS: Trace pattern, including all embroidery details. Using carbon paper, mark pattern on double broadcloth; mark embroidery details. Cut out double fabric for design on dot-dash line. Dotted line is seam line.

Embroider design on one fabric piece, following embroidery stitch key which indicates the stitch to use for each part of design. Plain solid line is outline stitch. Use tapisserie wool and stranded cotton in colours shown, or use your own colour combinations. Leave second fabric piece plain.

When embroidery is complete, stitch the two fabric pieces together on seam line with right sides facing and leave an opening for turning. Turn right side out and press. Stuff firmly with cotton. Turn in edges of opening and sew closed inconspicuously. Glue on sequins at single dots on pattern. Sequins may be sewn on, topping each with a seed bead.

Embroidery : on ticking

This attractive and amusing embroidery technique was worked out using stripes of ticking as guidelines.
The stitches illustrated below: Chain Stitch, Blanket Stitch, Chevron Stitch, Open Cretan Stitch, Couching, Stem Stitch, are especially suitable, see pages 30–31.

Use bold, bright colours to embroider household articles, or personal items like the spectacle case. For articles that will receive frequent washing make sure that the wools or thread used are colourfast. Remember, also, not to embroider over the seam allowance.

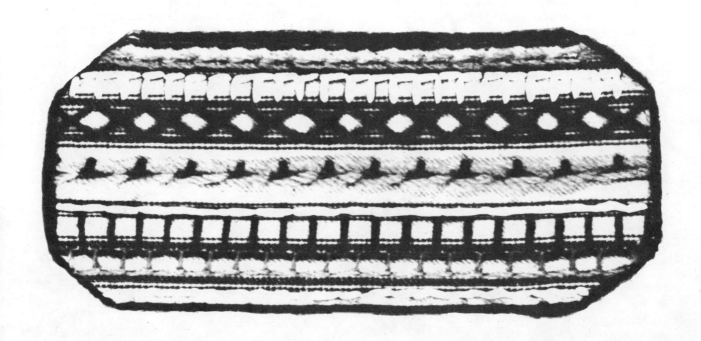

SPECTACLE CASE

MATERIALS: Clark's 'ANCHOR' Soft Embroidery or Clark's 'ANCHOR' Stranded Cotton (Use 6 strands); 1 skein each Canary Yellow **0291**/490; Flame **0334**/807; **0402**/White and **0403**/Black.

Two pieces of ticking and two pieces of bright cotton (for lining), 7″×4″. Cut off corners diagonally about ¾″ in from tip.

1 Milwards 'Gold Seal' chenille needle No. 19 (for Soft Embroidery) or 1 Milwards 'Gold Seal' crewel needle No. 5 (for Stranded Cotton).

Stitches used, from top to bottom: Chain Stitch (Black), Chain Stitch (Flame), Blanket Stitch (White), Chevron Stitch (Black, 2 rows), Open Cretan Stitch (Black) laced with (Yellow), Couching (Yellow), Blanket Stitch (Black), Couching (Black and Yellow Laid Threads together) Couched (Yellow), Stem Stitch (White), Couching (Yellow).

Embroider both pieces of ticking. Turn under seam allowances on all pieces (turning under seam allowances on lining slightly more than ½″). Hem linings to inside of ticking pieces. Whipstitch ticking pieces together along sides and across one end. Finish with braided, twisted or crocheted cord: whipstitch cording to all edges.

Embroidered Flower Prints

The three flower pictures shown on the opposite page were embroidered in so few simple stitches that even a beginner can enjoy making them. Cut linen 8″ by 11″ for each picture. Choose one of these flower designs or pick your own from china, a chintz design or a flower print.

If the design is the right size trace it as it is. We chose flower sprays 6½″ to 8″ long. See actual-size details at left. Draw your outline in this simple way on a piece of tracing paper or drawing paper. Use Scotch tape to fasten linen and drawing on a windowpane; with drawing underneath trace outline with medium soft pencil. Or place carbon between linen and paper, with paper uppermost and draw over design with a hard pencil.

Choose simple stitches as here. We used outline stitch and slanted satin stitch for stems. Kensington stitch shades the petals of the Wild Rose.

The enlarged details at the left show the stitch treatments for the Thistle and for the Buttercup.

Make your flower prints a sampler of all the stitches you know. Have fun experimenting with different stitches to see how lifelike you can make the flowers appear by relating the stitches to the form and texture of the flower.

MATERIALS: Clark's 'ANCHOR' Stranded Cotton:
Wild Rose: 1 skein each Rose Pink **050**/402, **052**/403, **054**/404; Rose Madder **059**/754, Laurel Green **0209**/575, **0211**/577 and Moss Green **0267**/790.
Thistle: 1 skein each Violet **096**/412, **0101**/415; Almond Green **0262**/957 and Muscat Green **0279**/947.
Buttercup: 1 skein each Laurel Green **0211**/577; Parrot Green **0255**/463; Canary Yellow **0291**/490 and Flame **0332**/629. Use 4 strands throughout.
1 Milwards 'Gold Seal' crewel needle No. 6.

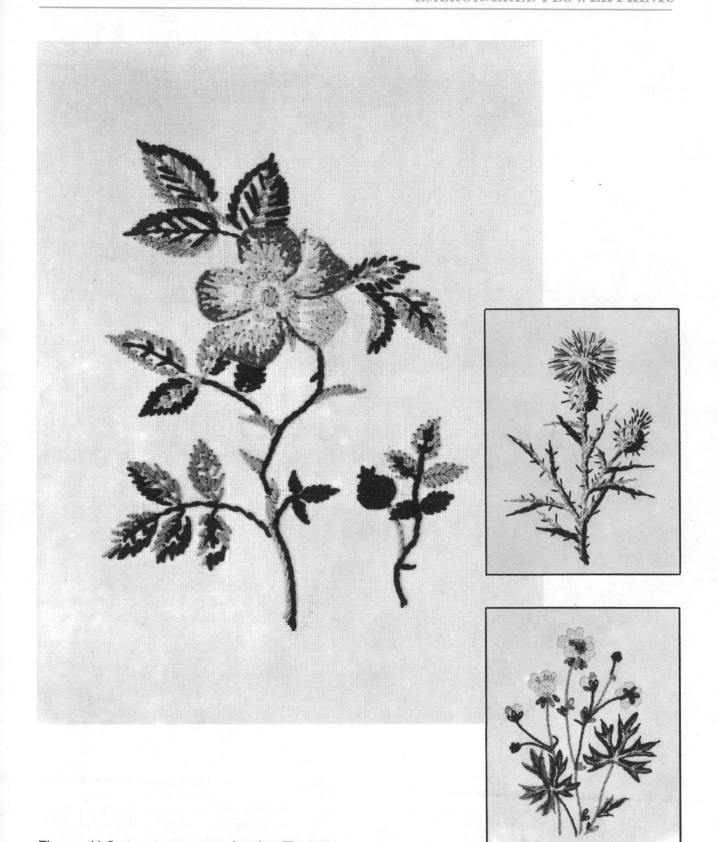

Three wild flower pictures to embroider. The Wild Rose is in actual size so you can trace it. Patterns for Thistle and Buttercups are on opposite page.

Embroidery : border stitches

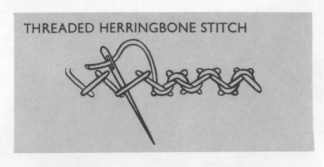

THREADED HERRINGBONE STITCH

THREADED HERRINGBONE STITCH   Created by running contrasting thread through the zigzags of the herringbone stitch without going through the fabric beneath. Diagram shows method of looping the thread around the crossed ends of the stitch.

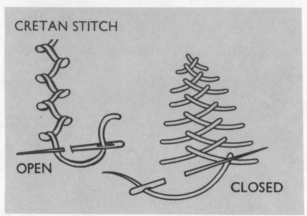

CRETAN STITCH

OPEN   CLOSED

CRETAN STITCH   Made with the needle turned towards the centre of the row, and the zigzags worked back and forth from right to left alternately as in catch stitch. **Closed Cretan Stitch** simply involves setting the stitches closer together. They may be closed up tight if desired in the same way as in closed chain stitch.

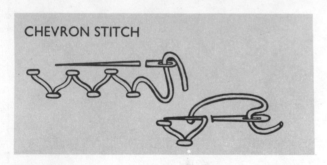

CHEVRON STITCH

CHEVRON STITCH   Involves herringbone stitch with a second step at each diagonal end. This consists of a perpendicular stitch marking each end.

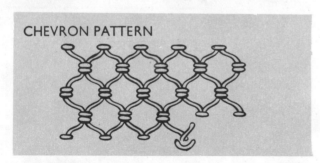

CHEVRON PATTERN

CHEVRON PATTERN   Is an all over area of chevron stitch simply consisting of repeated rows of the stitch. Each end stitch can be elaborated with repetition, or it may be worked out with a contrasting colour stitch to resemble smocking.

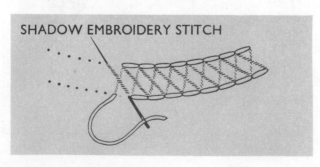

SHADOW EMBROIDERY STITCH

SHADOW EMBROIDERY STITCH or CROSSED BACKSTITCH   On the right side of the work this stitch resembles two rows of backstitch and on the wrong side it looks like a closed herringbone stitch. Slant the needle and take a backstitch, bring it out above and to the left; then work the line above in same manner. Work on sheer materials for shadow effect.

Embroidery : edge stitches

BLANKET STITCH A quicker stitch made in the same way as buttonhole stitch, but more widely spaced. This may be used on a raw edge of material that will not ravel, or on a turned edge of other fabric. The hem turn should be basted in place first, then the stitches placed over the width of the hem, and close enough together to hold it firmly in place. These two stitches are often used in appliqué work. For a most decorative effect vary the depth of the stitches of either buttonhole stitch or blanket stitch. These edgings may be done in varied colours, or a single colour. See diagram of two variations, one a pyramid border, and one a sawtooth border.

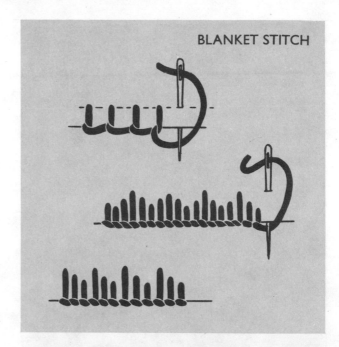

BLANKET STITCH

CLOSED BLANKET STITCH Forms tiny inverted V's all along the edge. The needle is slanted to the left as shown in the diagram for the first stitch. The next stitch starts at the top of the same stitch and slants towards the right, taking up a bit of the lower edge to hold it firmly in place. Alternate stitches 1 and 2 all across the edge.

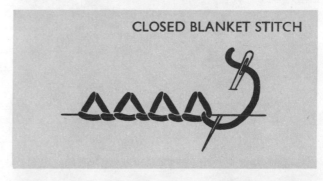

CLOSED BLANKET STITCH

CROSSED BLANKET STITCH Worked on the same premise of alternating angled stitches but the tops of the stitches cross instead of joining at the top.

CROSSED BLANKET STITCH

KNOTTED BLANKET STITCH Worked in two steps. First a loosely worked blanket stitch is formed. Then with the stitch still free from the fabric the needle is passed through the loop again to form a knot.

This stitch or any of the above edge stitches may be used on knitted garments to form an edge finish, and may be substituted for a crocheted edge finish. In delicate yarns or embroidery thread it is very useful for baby garments.

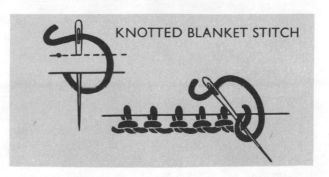

KNOTTED BLANKET STITCH

Embroidery : raised wool

FLORAL SPRAY MADE BEFORE CIVIL WAR.
COURTESY SMITHSONIAN INSTITUTION, WASHINGTON

You can create a lovely flower picture of your own like the museum piece right which is an example of shaded wool embroidery in a raised effect. If you hesitate to use your own design, choose a flower picture and sketch in on a dark coloured fabric with chalk or dressmaker crayon. Place the fabric in an embroidery frame and work in Anchor Tapisserie Wool, crewel. In this embroidered piece, the multicoloured flowers and leaves are worked mostly in satin stitch, with some petals and leaves stitched on top of others. Other stitches used are stem stitch. French knots and lazy daisy stitch. See detail, below, of satin stitch petals and French knot centre. Add seed beads and embroidery details in stranded cotton.

SATIN STITCH PETALS
FRENCH KNOT CENTRE

Embroidery : tufted wool

DETAIL, DECORATED TABLE COVER.
COURTESY SMITHSONIAN INSTITUTION, WASHINGTON

This is also from an original museum design. The detail at the right is part of a black broadcloth table cover.

To embroider a similar tufted design, outline the flower pattern on dark fabric with chalk or crayon. Embroider the stems first in outline or stem stitch. Then start with the larger flower at the centre. Tuft the area by sewing with turkey work loops as shown in detail.

TURKEY WORK LOOPS

Start with unknotted yarn end on front of work and make a small anchoring stitch. Loop yarn above needle and take another small stitch as shown, holding the loop; then with yarn below needle take another small stitch to anchor the loop. Continue placing each stitch close to preceding stitch. Shade the colourings as you work. Complete the tufting of a petal or the whole flower, then shear off the loops, cutting parts shorter than others to give a rounded, realistic form to the pile.

COURTESY VIETNAM HANDICRAFT DEVELOPMENT CENTRE'. DESIGNER, KEN J. UYEMURA OF RUSSEL WRIGHT ASSOCIATES. EMBROIDERED ORNAMENTS, SEE PAGE 26

Canvas Work: colours and textures

The two examples below were worked on canvas with 10 meshes to the inch in 'ANCHOR' Tapisserie Wool.

The first sample is oblong cross-stitch with back stitch. Cross-stitch loops are worked between some rows of cross-stitch. Coats 'ANCHOR' Tapisserie Wool: 1 skein each 0148, 0168, 0205, 0308 and 0325. 1 Milwards 'Gold Seal' tapestry needle No. 19.

The second example is a checkerboard design of cross-stitch loops and couched needlepoint squares.

Use double 'ANCHOR' Tapisserie Wool, lay yarn in rows, diagonally across the canvas to form a square; couch yarn using double wool in another colour and working in a diagonal needle point stitch. Work alternate squares in cross-stitch loops.

MATERIALS: Coats 'ANCHOR' Tapisserie Wool: 1 skein each 0147 and 0148.
1 Milwards 'Gold Seal' tapestry needle No. 19.

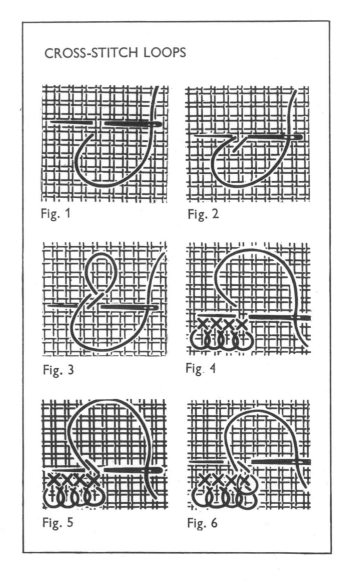

CROSS-STITCH LOOPS

Fig. 1

Fig. 2

Fig. 3

Fig. 4

Fig. 5

Fig. 6

Starting at upper right, make first half of cross and pull yarn tight, Fig. 1. Take next stitch above cross, Fig. 2, and form loop ¼" long while completing cross, Fig. 3. Work across in this manner from right to left. For next row, turn work and work as shown in Figs. 4, 5 and 6, holding loops below work.

Canvas Work: needlepoint

There are conflicting opinions as to the terms describing needlepoint. The differences may result from the fact that needlepoint has come down to us from various countries und in various stitches. Briefly, needlepoint is embroidery on canvas; the most common stitch is half of a cross-stitch which is also called "tent stitch".

Needlepoint-tapestry is an often used expression which shows the relation of needlepoint to the tapestry designs of the middle ages. This is especially true when the needlepoint is worked in an upright Gobelin stitch which gives the effect of a woven tapestry.

This early work was done on a loosely-woven material like coarse linen. Later, canvases were made especially for the purpose—both in single thread canvas, or with threads arranged in pairs to make "double thread canvas". The double thread canvas was often worked in needlepoint combining the fine petit point stitch, used for detailed shading, with gros point used for large flat design areas. To make this combination, the double thread canvas was "split"; that is, the meshes opened with a needle or pin to form a single thread canvas for working in petit point.

As with all other forms of embroidery it is very difficult to give exact dates, and even places where the technique originated. Canvas work dates back to the sixteenth century, but reached its peak during the late seventeenth and early eighteenth centuries. Needlepoint was extremely popular in Colonial America where it was used for pictures, as an upholstery fabric, and for fashion accessories.

During the Victorian era, Berlin work came into popularity. It is often characterised by brilliant worsteds and combinations of geometric and floral designs. The majority of the designs were developed as hand-painted patterns on squared paper, especially made for copying in needlepoint or cross-stitch on canvas. The best of these designs came from Berlin, thus naming it.

The current revived interest in needlepoint started to gain momentum during the late twenties and continues to increase in popularity with the evergrowing interest in handicrafts. Designs are available in department stores and shops all over the country, although there is a growing number of needlepoint enthusiasts designing original pieces in a large variety of stitches.

HOW NEEDLEPOINT DESIGNS
ARE SOLD

Embroidered Centres The majority of imported needlepoint pieces have the centre already worked, with only the background left to be filled in. Needlepoint pieces with the designs already worked were formerly planned primarily for dark backgrounds, such as maroon and black. Today, the lighter, modern furniture requires lighter backgrounds and many new designs are being planned for these colours.

Tramé Pieces The design has yarn laid in long stitches across the canvas in the exact pattern. The colours used in tramé patterns are approximately the colours to be used in working the piece in needlepoint. The needlepoint is worked over the long laid stitches following the correct colour arrangement. This helps to pad the piece, and is easy to follow.

Painted or Tinted Pieces These are becoming more available in department stores as well as in speciality shops. The design is painted directly on the canvas in colours approximating the colours to be used in working the needlepoint. You can paint your own designs on

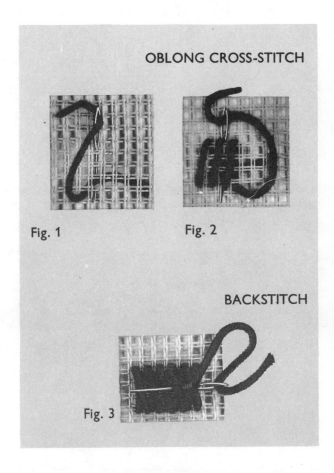

OBLONG CROSS-STITCH

Fig. 1   Fig. 2

BACKSTITCH

Fig. 3

Work from left to right over four horizontal meshes of canvas and one vertical mesh, Fig. 1. Work back crossing stitches, Fig. 2. Make a backstitch, Fig. 3, over centre of each cross-stitch and between rows of cross-stitch.

needlepoint canvas, using oil paints mixed with benzine.

Charted Designs Many designs for pictures and other needlepoint pieces are available in chart form. Following a chart, a design may be worked on any size canvas mesh desired to produce a large or small piece. Each square on the chart represents a stitch in the canvas.

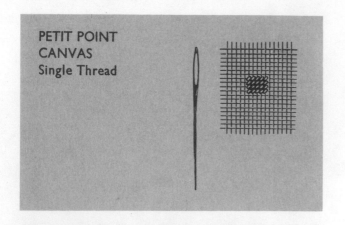

PETIT POINT
CANVAS
Single Thread

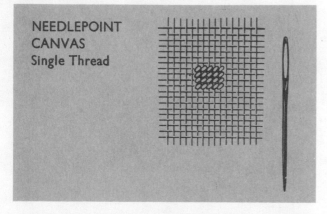

NEEDLEPOINT
CANVAS
Single Thread

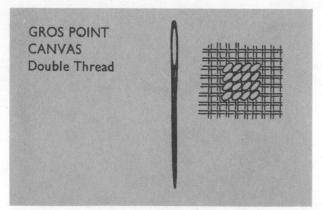

GROS POINT
CANVAS
Double Thread

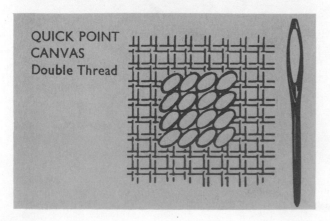

QUICK POINT
CANVAS
Double Thread

Needlepoint is the general term for an embroidery stitch used to cover canvas, as well as for the embroidered piece. When this stitch is worked on canvas 20 meshes to the inch or smaller, it is called petit point. When worked on 16 to 18 to the inch mesh, it is called simply needlepoint. On 9 to 11 to the inch mesh, it is called gros point. Larger meshes, such as 5 to the inch, have been used in the past for making rugs and are sometimes referred to as large gros point. However, we have coined a name for this larger stitch. We call it quick point.

YARNS TO USE WITH DIFFERENT CANVASES

In general you can use one strand of crewel wool or split tapestry wool on canvas 18 to 23 meshes to the inch. Use two strands of crewel wool on 13 to 16 mesh canvas. Use one strand of tapestry wool on 9 to 13 mesh canvas.

It is possible to combine in one needlepoint piece crewel wool, tapestry wool and rug wool, provided sufficient strands of the finer yarns are used to balance the weight. This is done only when special colours are unobtainable in the correct yarn. Other yarns may be used if they have a tight, firm twist. However, care must be taken in the choice. For example, knitting worsted is not suitable for needlepoint, because the twist is not firm enough, and it wears thin from constant pulling through the canvas.

NEEDLES A blunt tapestry needle is always used. Needles range in size from fairly fine to the large rug needles. Sketches on this page show sizes.

STITCHES What stitch should be used? First, there is the half cross-stitch. This just covers the canvas with practically no yarn at the back. (See details on p. 35.) This stitch does not cover the canvas as well as the continental stitch or the diagonal stitch. The half cross-stitch is practical when working a picture or areas which will not receive hard wear; it is a yarn-saver since almost all the yarn appears on front of canvas.

Three methods of working basic needle-point stitch

HALF CROSS-STITCH Start at upper left corner of canvas. Bring needle to front of canvas at point that will be the bottom of first stitch. The needle is in a vertical position when making stitch (see detail). Always work from left to right; turn work around for return row. Catch yarn ends in finished work on back.

The needle is always in a vertical position when making the stitch.

CONTINENTAL STITCH Start design at upper right corner. To begin, hold an inch of yarn in back and work over this end. All other strands may be started and finished by running them through wrong side of finished work. Details 1 and 2 show placement and direction of needle; turn work around for return row. Always work from right to left. Finish design, then fill in background.

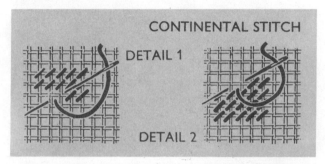

Detail 1 shows starting a new row below finished portion. Detail 2 shows starting a new row above finished portion.

DIAGONAL STITCH Begin by tying a knot at end of yarn and putting needle through canvas to back, diagonally down from upper right hand corner of work. Never turn work; hold it in the same position.

Step 1: The knot is on top. Bring needle up at A, down through B and out through C. **Step 2:** Needle in D, out through E. **Step 3:** Needle in F, out through G. **Step 4:** Start next row in at H and out through I.

You are now ready to work from the Big Diagram. Each stitch is drawn on Big Diagram with a blunt and a pointed end. Put needle in at pointed end, out at blunt end.

Stitch No. 5 is your next stitch. It extends from space 1 to A. Complete stitches to 10 on diagram in numerical order to finish diagonal row. Stitch No. 11 starts next row diagonally upwards.

After starting row going up, needle is horizontal. Needle slants diagonally to begin new row down, as in Step 1. Going down, needle is always vertical, as in Step 2; and again, when the last stitch is made, the needle slants diagonally to begin next row up, Step 3.

Work as far as knot; cut knot off. All other strands of yarn may be started and ended by running them through finished work on back. Work background to design; the work design. Fill in remaining background.

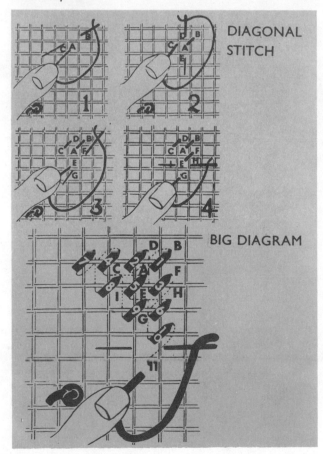

Advantages of the two preferred stitches

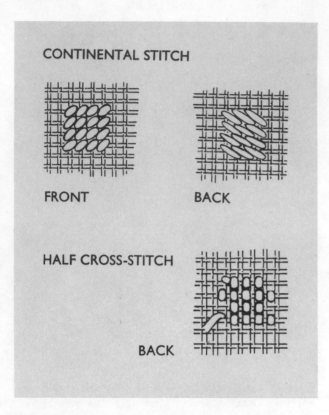

CONTINENTAL STITCH

FRONT   BACK

HALF CROSS-STITCH

BACK

The continental stitch is the one most promoted. It uses more wool than the half cross-stitch; however, it covers the canvas on both front and back (see detail). As a result, the finished piece is more attractive and the wearing quality is increased. The slight padding on the back makes it durable and practical for upholstery pieces.

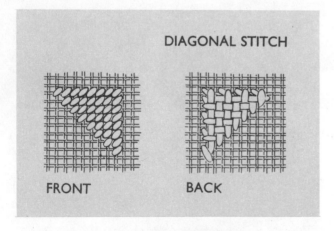

DIAGONAL STITCH

FRONT   BACK

The diagonal stitch, contrary to popular belief, does not use more wool than the continental stitch. It uses the same amount. This stitch covers the canvas and reinforces it, as it is actually woven into the canvas, and works up into a strong embroidered piece (see detail).

Blocking

Cover a wooden surface with brown paper and mark on this the size of canvas, being sure corners are square. Place needlepoint, right side down, over guide and fasten with drawing pins placed ½″ apart near edge of canvas.

Wet thoroughly with cold water; let dry. If work is badly warped, restretch, wet and dry again. If yarn is not colourfast, apply salt generously to back of needlepoint before wetting.

More stitches on canvas

Needlepoint offers a variety of other interesting stitches, ranging in texture from the ribbed effect of upright Gobelin to the elegant Florentine stitches. For footstools and chair seats these can be used instead of tent stitch for backgrounds and borders to make handsome tone-on-tone fabrics or to form a brilliant pattern in two or more colours.

Details on this page show finished work actual size, as well as the method of working upright, wide, and encroaching Gobelin stitches.

 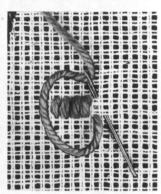

UPRIGHT GOBELIN STITCH

UPRIGHT GOBELIN STITCH   Working from bottom to top, take upright stitch over two horizontal double threads. Continue across from left to right, placing stitches immediately next to one another. Rows are begun in same way as for other needlepoint stitches.

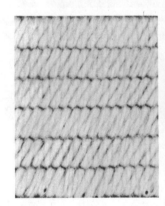 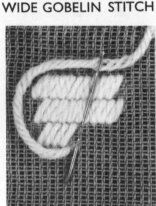

WIDE GOBELIN STITCH

WIDE GOBELIN STITCH   This stitch is slightly slanted as it is worked over two vertical and three horizontal meshes of the canvas. Work across from right to left. Turn canvas upside down to work next row in same manner.

ENCROACHING GOBELIN STITCH

ENCROACHING GOBELIN   This stitch is worked over five horizontal and one vertical mesh of canvas and is just slightly slanted. Start the second row only four meshes below and work as before over five horizontal meshes, thus making the encroaching stitch. This stitch fills areas very quickly.

Other stitches on canvas

HUNGARIAN STITCH

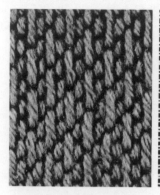 

HUNGARIAN STITCH Work upright stitches over two, four and two double threads, making a diamond shape. Skip one vertical mesh, continue across from left to right. Dovetail succeeding rows, alternating contrasting colours or using one shade.

STEM STITCH

STEM STITCH Work diagonal stitches from top to bottom, over four meshes of canvas each way, making each stitch one mesh below. Work the second row in diagonal stitches in opposite direction. When diagonal stitches are completed, work backstitch in another colour of yarn between the diagonal rows.

CHECKERBOARD STITCH

CHECKERBOARD STITCH Work diagonal stitches left to right over one, two, three, four, five, four, three, two, one double threads, forming a square. Make other squares in same way, alternating direction of stitches and changing colour, if desired.

JACQUARD STITCH

JACQUARD STITCH From left to right, work diagonal stitches over two double threads, taking six stitches down and six across, continue row for desired length. Next row, work over one double thread, make same number of stitches, arranged in the same way.

RICE STITCH

RICE STITCH or CROSSED CORNERS CROSS-STITCH Work cross-stitch over two double threads. Using crewel wool in contrasting colour, take diagonal stitches over each arm of crosses, having the stitches meet in space between crosses.

FERN STITCH

FERN STITCH Work rows from top to bottom. The first half of stitch is worked over two meshes of canvas each way; the second half is also worked over two meshes of canvas each way, to the opposite side of centre stitch with needle coming out again one mesh below the beginning stitch.

STAR STITCH

STAR STITCH Each star consists of eight stitches all meeting in the centre. Each star should be worked the same way. Work over two meshes of canvas for each stitch of star, bringing needle down through centre mesh each time and working around to complete star. Backstitch may be worked around the completed star.

MOSAIC STITCH

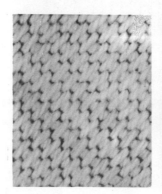 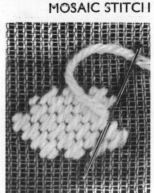

MOSAIC STITCH Consists of long and short stitches taken alternately in diagonal rows. Work over one and two meshes of canvas. In each succeeding diagonal row a short stitch is worked into a long stitch and a long stitch into a short one.

Florentine work

Chair covered with Bargello work.

Florentine, Bargello, or Hungarian work is of ancient origin and was generally used for covering cushions. Later it came into use for upholstery fabric and such personal items as handbags. It is also known as Flame Embroidery, because of the distinctive zigzag patterns which characterise this work. Traditionally, several shades of one colour are used to give a soft and gradual ombre effect, but for a more striking effect, several different colours may be combined in one design. The work consists of perpendicular stitches which can be made all the same length, or in combination of long and short perpendicular stitches, covering from two to six meshes of the canvas. The canvas used is usually single thread, 18 meshes to the inch. Depending on the colour combinations and stitch arrangements, various effects are obtained which give names to the patterns, such as diamond, skyscraper and sawtooth.

Bargello stitch is easily worked from a graph pattern. Work the first row in peaks, following chart below; starting at the centre, work to right and then left to finish row and establish the pattern. For succeeding rows, follow first row, in long or short stitches as indicated on chart, until all the surface is covered. Fill in the corners of the design to completely cover the area.

A Bargello design may be carried out for chair upholstery to cover both seat and back as shown. It is advisable to plan the colour scheme and work a small section of one seat to determine how much yarn will be required. Suppose you are working the chair seat and back shown here. Outline areas on your canvas to correspond with seat and back of chair. Work one-quarter of the back and determine how much yarn you used. Then purchase enough to cover that area, multiplied by the number of times necessary to cover all of back and seat, before continuing with the work.

MATERIALS: Coats 'ANCHOR' Tapisserie Wool: 0381, 0334 and 0313. Work from first row of chart in order:— brown, yellow and flame.
1 Milwards 'Gold Seal' tapestry needle No. 19.

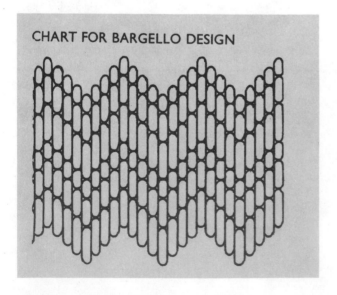

CHART FOR BARGELLO DESIGN

How to cross-stitch

Cross-stitch is easy to do and attractive whether used for ornamenting clothes, for monogramming, or for home decoration. Cross-stitch pieces are often worked on linen in six-strand of 'ANCHOR' Stranded Cotton. Several different ways to do the stitch are described and illustrated on this page. All yield equally good results if care is taken to make sure that the strands of thread or yarn lie smooth and flat. Secure the end of your thread on the wrong side by running it under the work.

In working cross-stitch over a stamped transfer (Method A), work across all stitches in each row from left to right before crossing back in the other direction. Be sure crosses touch. Details 1 and 2.

Method B shows the design following the mesh of coarse fabric such as monk's cloth. Here the design may be worked from a chart without a transfer pattern simply counting each square of equal size for one cross-stitch.

Method C shows a checked material used as a guide for the cross-stitch design. Here the corners of the blocks are guidelines.

Method D illustrates the use of round thread linen or sampler linen. The threads may be counted, and each cross-stitch made the same size. For instance in the illustration a 3-thread square is counted for each stitch. This same method was used for many of the Victorian pictures, with the design stitched on coarse canvas or stiff scrim mounted on a needlepoint frame. The design may be painted on the canvas or outlined with crayon.

Method E is illustrated in the larger picture at the right. Here Penelope canvas, or cross-stitch canvas, is basted to the fabric on which the finished design is to be shown. The design is then worked counting threads as shown, and making the crosses over the threads. When design is completed the bastings are removed and the threads of the canvas drawn out, leaving the finished design on the fabric. This canvas is available in several size meshes. Choose the finer sizes for smaller designs, larger sizes for coarser work in yarn.

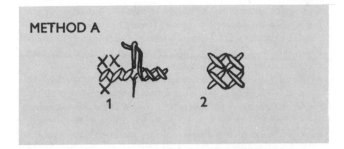

METHOD A

1   2

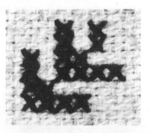

METHOD B

METHOD C

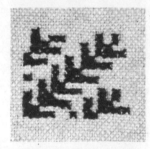

METHOD D

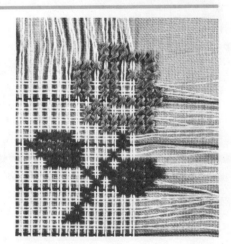

METHOD E

Making a cross-stitch sampler

Few gifts as happily combine challenge and fun for the giver with an assured welcome from the receiver as individual samplers do. Design your sampler either around the particular hobby or interest of the recipient, or plan a special-occasion sampler for a bridal couple, or a friend's baby. These samplers are easily worked on even mesh linen, or by using Penelope canvas as a guide. Some suggestions for details suitable for such samplers are shown in chart form on page 43. Some of the designs may be worked in a single colour, while others combine two or three colours. The alphabet of cross-stitch block letters on page 52 may be used in combination with the motifs given here.

Other samplers similar to the old one shown here are to be found in museums in various parts of the country. Your public library may have books illustrating old samplers, parts of which you can copy or trace to work out your design.

On the right are a few motifs which may be used in cross-stitch samplers. Each symbol represents a different colour. Other designs may be found in cross-stitch booklets, or evolve your own on graph paper.

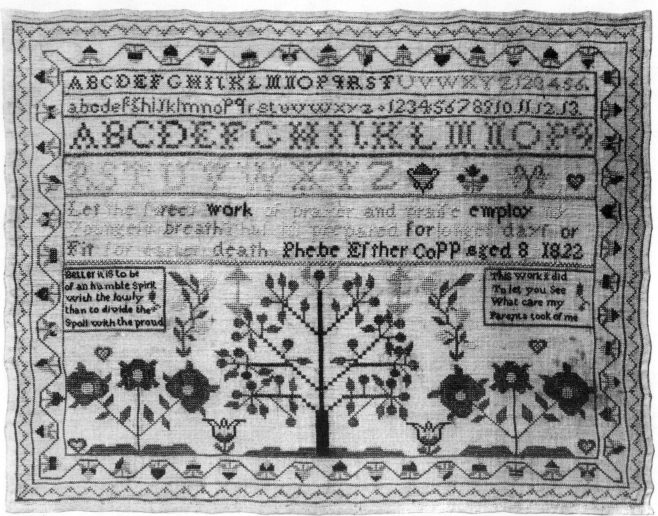

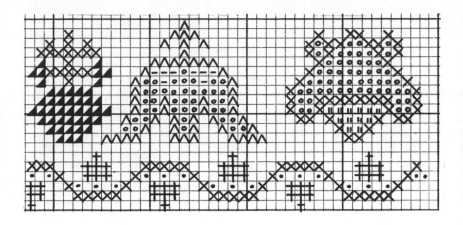

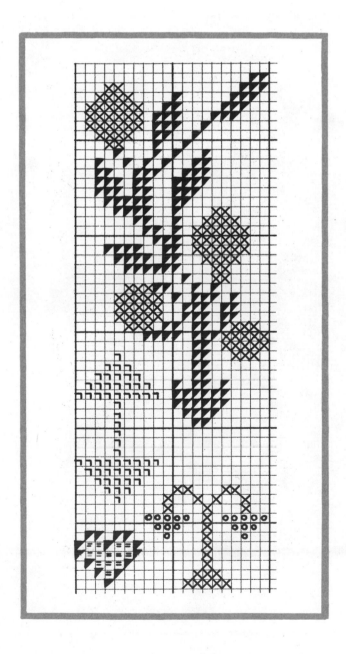

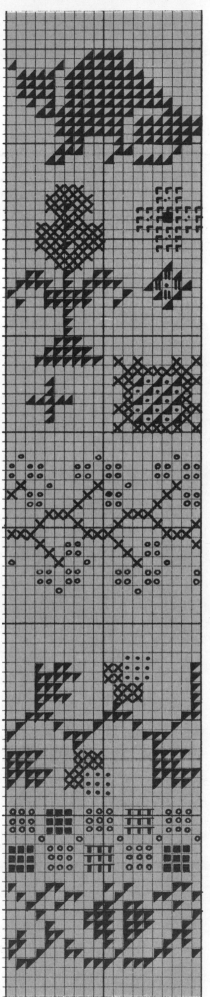

Cross-stitch on gingham

Checked gingham fabric offers an easy guide for working cross-stitch designs. Each cross is worked within a check of the gingham with the ends of crosses at corners of the check. Gingham comes in many sizes of checks, from four to the inch to 10 to the inch or more. For big bold designs, use four to the inch. For most designs, however, you will find that gingham with 8 checks to the inch is easiest to work on. Many designs are worked out especially for gingham and in some of these the embroidery is to be done in the white checks of the fabric only. However, almost any cross-stitch design can be followed, utilising all of the checks of the gingham. The apron below has a daffodil design in yellow and green Stranded Cotton on green-and-white checked gingham.

GENERAL DIRECTIONS: Gingham with checks 8, 9 or 10 to the inch is most suitable for working these cross-stitch designs. When working on 10 checks to the inch, use three strands 'ANCHOR' Stranded Cotton in the needle. On 8 checks to the inch, use six strands in the needle.

Cross–stitching is usually done on the white checks of gingham only. But for a more solid look, or special design, the dark checks are utilised also. Place gingham in an embroidery hoop to obtain even stitches and prevent pulling of thread. Work bottom stitch of crosses all in one direction, then complete crosses with top stitches all in opposite direction (see stitch detail on this page).

Follow charts in working cross-stitch designs. When the design is all one colour, an X symbol is used on the chart. If more than one colour is used, X is used for one colour and various symbols used for the other colours.

You may find embroidering easier if you first mark the designs in hard pencil on the gingham, following charts.

APRON: MATERIALS: Clark's 'ANCHOR' Stranded Cotton: 4 skeins each Canary Yellow 0289/488 and Parrot Green 0257/780. Use 6 strands throughout. Gingham with 9 or 10 checks to the inch, 3/4 yard, 35″ wide, Coats Satinised No. 40 to match. White rickrack. 1 Milwards 'Gold Seal' crewel needle No. 5 (for the embroidery).

DIRECTIONS: Cut gingham for skirt, 29″ wide and 22 1/2″ long. Cut two ties, 3 1/2″ × 28″. Cut waistband, 3 1/2″ × 16 1/2″. Cut pocket, 5 1/4″ × 6″. Embroider designs across bottom of skirt, leaving 2 1/2″ for hem and a margin below design as desired. Embroider daffodil design in yellow and green; wide border in white with white rickrack sewn between rows of crosses. Sew on other rickrack as shown. Fold waistband in half lengthwise as guide for placing border. Embroider border across waistband near fold; sew on rickrack underneath border. For pocket, embroider border along one shorter edge for top, about 2″ from edge.

Make 1/4″ hems at sides of apron skirt and 2″ hem at bottom. Gather top edge in to 16″. Stitch one long edge of waistband to skirt top, with embroidered side of band and right side of skirt facing. Fold waistband in half to back, turn in edge and sew to skirt. Turn in raw ends of waistband. Hem both long edges and one end of ties. Stitch raw ends of ties in waistband.

For pocket, make a 1 1/4″ hem at top. Turn in 1/4″ all around remainder of pocket. Stitch to apron, 3 1/2″ down from waistband and 6″ in from side.

CROSS-STITCH DETAIL

x = Canary Yellow **0289**/488
/ = Parrot Green **0257**/780

DAFFODIL APRON CHART

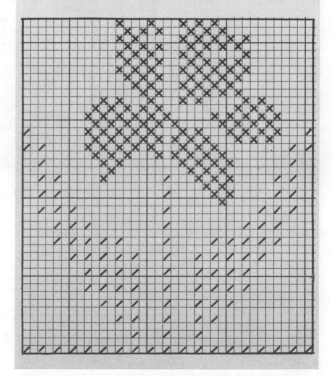

BORDER FOR DAFFODIL APRON

Cross-stitch variation on gingham

A combination of cross-stitch and straight stitches produces medallion-like designs to work on checked gingham. Medallions in other shapes and other arrangements can be used to make an endless variety of designs. A chart is given below, showing the cross-stitches and straight stitches. This was used to make one of the pot holders shown on the opposite page. Make your own designs on graph paper to embroider on such household items as tablecloths, place mats, curtains.

MEDALLION POT HOLDER - MATERIALS: For each pot holder, checked gingham with 8 checks to the inch, 14″ square. Cotton batting, or other padding, 7″ square. Clark's 'ANCHOR' Stranded Cotton **0403**/Black. Coats Satinised No. 40. I Milwards 'Gold Seal' crewel needle No. 5 (for the embroidery) 1″ plastic ring.

DIRECTIONS: Cut two pieces of gingham 7″ square. From remainder of gingham, cut 1″ wide strips diagonally across fabric; place one strip across another at right angles and stitch together diagonally from the end of top strip to end of bottom strip to make a continuous piece. Sew bias strips together until piece is long enough to fit around gingham.

On one gingham square embroider medallion design following chart, below. Work straight stitches connecting crosses as indicated on chart. With right side of bias strip facing right side of embroidered square and raw edges matching, stitch bias strip all around square with $1/4$″ seam; ease strip around corners and join ends by turning in edge of one end and sewing to square under opposite end. Place padding between gingham squares with right sides out and baste together. Quilt through all three thicknesses with tiny running stitches in a diamond shape, outlining embroidered motifs. Turn bias strip to back of pot holder; turn in raw edge and slip-stitch in place. Sew ring at corner.

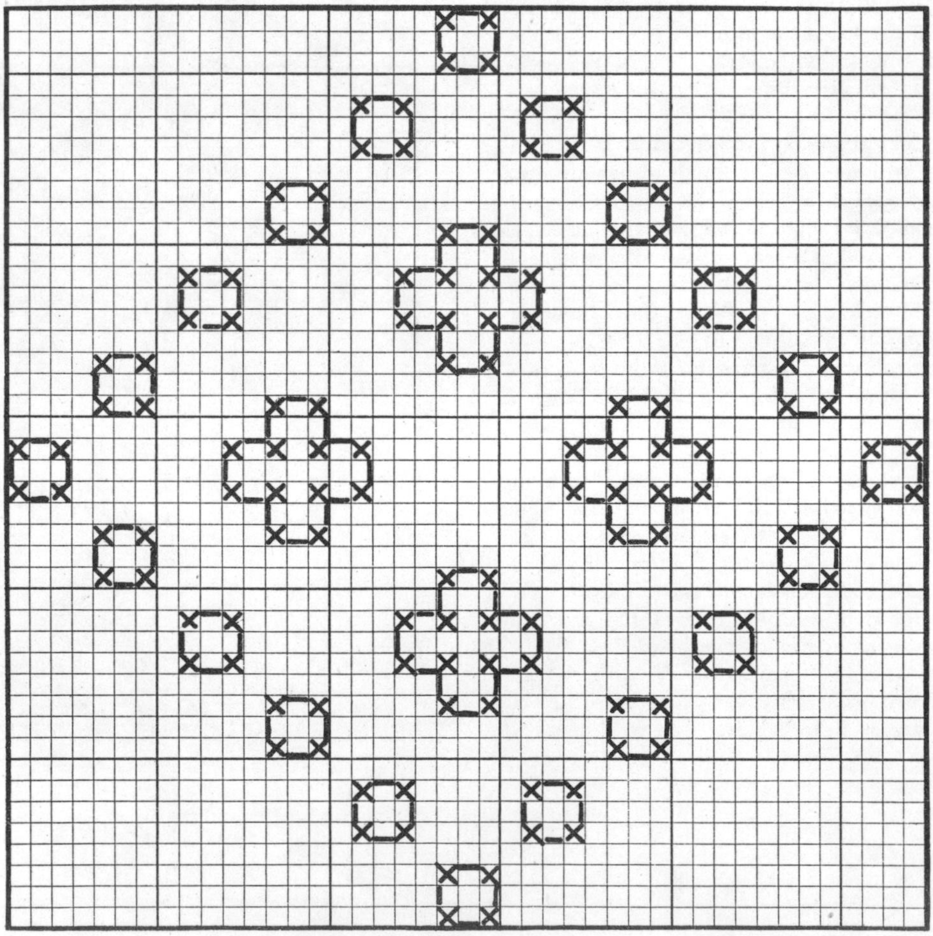

CHART FOR MEDALLION DESIGN

Gingham with eight checks to the inch was used to make this simply designed apron and the pot holder. Directions are given on opposite page for making a pot holder with self-bound edges and embroidering it.

The apron shown on this page can be made by following the fabric quantities and making up instructions for the apron on page 45. The design is similar to the pot holder and the same chart may be used.

Assisi Embroidery

Assisi work, named for the Italian village of its origin, is a very distinctive type of needlework. Traditionally it is done on pale ivory linen and embroidered in red, blue, and black, or a combination of two colours. Simplicity of design is important to show the true characteristics of this technique. At its inception, as now, the designs were worked from charts and embroidered by counting the threads of the linen.

The design is first outlined with a running stitch or straight stitches and worked back again in the same way to fill in between the first line of stitches. This is called Holbein Stitch and when finished resembles Back Stitch. See stitch detail below. The background is then filled in solidly with cross-stitch, leaving just the design area open. The cross-stitch must be done very carefully, counting an equal number of threads vertically and horizontally for each stitch, and making all stitches even. Work first half of all crosses in one direction and the second half all in opposite direction. After the Assissi work is completed, narrow borders can be added in cross-stitch and straight stitch in simple repeat patterns.

MATERIALS: Clark's 'ANCHOR' Stranded Cotton: Terra Cotta **0340**/816 and **0403**/Black. Use 4 strands. Work the Cross Stitch in Terra Cotta and the Holbein Stitch in Black. Evenweave fabric with 28 threads to 1 in. Work each stitch over 4 threads of fabric. 1 Milwards 'Gold Seal' tapestry needle No. 23.

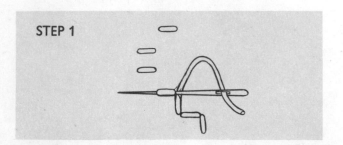

STEP 1

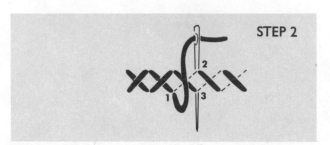

STEP 2

48

On the opposite page is shown a delightful needlepoint chair seat 'Montacute'. Full working instructions are in Coats Sewing Group Book No. 1007.

Monogramming

Your monogram should be very personal. Whether you wish to monogram apparel or household linens, choose a style of letter which you think best expresses your own tastes and the sort of social life you lead. A few alphabets are given on the following pages. When you have chosen one, trace the letters, enlarging or reducing them, by following the square method. (See Index).

TABLE LINEN. A dinner cloth should be monogrammed at apposite ends or opposite right hand corners above the area that hangs down 12″ to 15″ over the side of the table. If centred it should be above the table setting. Use only one monogram for a lunch cloth, or tea cloth, and place that similarly. Monograms on place mats may be arranged perpendicularly or horizontally at the left hand side. Or they may be centred above the plate position. For napkins the marking should correspond to the treatment of the cloth or mat, but be smaller in size. Some prefer a single initial on the napkin. Always place the initials on the dinner napkins so the base of the initial faces the corner. Then when each adjoining side is folded under for correct service the monogram will be upright parallel with the fork.

LINENS for the trousseau are monogrammed with the maiden name, with the surname initial centred. For a married woman the three initials used are her first name, maiden surname and married name with the marriage surname larger and in the centre. If the three initials are the same size, and placed either perpendicularly or horizontally, then the married surname comes last.

SHEETS are monogrammed in the centre of the turnover just above the hem. Pillowcases may be monogrammed in the centre of the area just above the hem or towards the top of the case to one side.

TOWELS are usually monogrammed at the centre just above the hem, so that when folded the monogram will appear a few inches above the hemstitched hem, or the decorative border of terry cloth towels.

HANDKERCHIEF monograms, or monograms for lingerie or men's shirts are usually quite small in size, and should be embroidered with finer thread, or a single strand of 'ANCHOR' Stranded Cotton.

On the opposite page is shown an unusual teacloth with ice crystal motifs. Full working instructions are in Cross Stitch Book NO. 441.

SATIN STITCH may be done by hand, or by machine. In either case you will find it essential to use an embroidery hoop to hold the work firm while working. After the design for the letters has been transferred or drawn in outline with dressmaker crayon, set the frame in place. For hand embroidery use two or three strands of Clark's 'ANCHOR' Stranded Cotton or Clark's 'ANCHOR' Coton a Broder No. 18.

The first step in hand embroidering a monogram is the underlying padding. This is used to give the work the richly rounded effect so desirable. Use slightly heavier embroidery thread than the covering thread. Outline each letter with running stitch, carrying this thread just inside the stamped outline, having a short stitch on the wrong side with a longer stitch on the right side, Detail 1. Then fill in the area inside this outline with the same stitch. Or use chain stitch, Details 2 and 3.

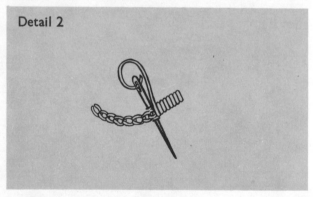

Detail 1

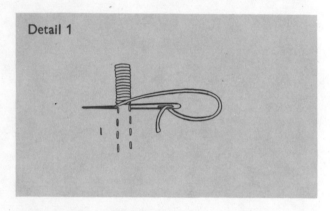

Detail 2

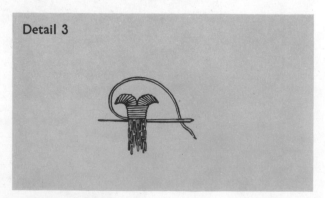

Detail 3

You are now ready to add the surface covering. Thread needle with the other thread, and work over the padding placing the needle exactly through the fabric right on the stamped outline. Each stitch should be even in length, and placed just a thread apart each time. The closer the spacing of the stitches the smoother the finished effect will be. If your letter has a formal swirled end or a shaped curve such as in a C or S turn the stitches gradually to fit the curve. In a corner such as in an E or an M the turn may be more abrupt. The stitches may either swing gently out in a fan or may be tapered into each other in a mitre.

CHAIN STITCHING (See Index) may be used for informal linens used daily. These may be script instead of block letters and may be a first name in lieu of a monogram.

OUTLINE STITCH may also be used for such individual markings. It may be used alone, or in combination with the chain stitch, or to outline a monogram of French knots. It is often of another colour forming a shadow outline along one side of the lettering, or carried all around.

FRENCH KNOTS (See Index) are particularly suitable for working a monogram on bath towels. The raised quality looks well with the tufts and makes an effective monogram. These should be worked quite large for the utmost effectiveness.

CROSS-STITCH MONOGRAMS may be used on linen towels, and are particularly suitable for small guest towels or fingertip towels. The monogram is usually simple block letters set in line. Follow the usual directions for working cross-stitch, making all the slanting stitches in one direction first, then adding the cross top stitch in the other direction. You may work these over Penelope cloth mesh, then pull out the threads.

The letters on the left and those on the following page can be traced and used in the size drawn or they can be enlarged or decreased in size by copying on graph paper with larger or smaller squares.

Several ways of arranging monograms from these script letters are shown here, incorporating decorative motifs as well. These monograms are planned for satin stitch. However, if a very large monogram is desired, the letters may be filled in with rows of chain stitch.

Embroidery: openwork

Openwork, also called punch stitch, is sometimes mistakenly called drawn work, although no threads are drawn from the fabric. The reason for the name punch stitch is that a large three-sided punch needle is sometimes used when working on coarse fabric. This needle separates the threads of the fabric, making an open space. A punch needle is not necessary, however. A regular needle may be used, but a much thicker one than for ordinary embroidery.

Openwork is used mainly for backgrounds and filling spaces. It can be done as shown in the samples below in oblong or square spaces, or used as borders. Designs can be worked out in bold geometric fashion, working diagonally and straight. Since the threads are not drawn, it can also be worked in circles and curved lines, as in intricate fruit, flower and leaf shapes. This work often is used in combination with other embroidery to fill open areas of a design.

Loosely woven linen is best to use, as the threads must be counted and each stitch taken over the same number of threads, usually four. However, fine linen or lawn, or even satin may be used. Thread should be strong, a little finer than the material, and usually the same colour.

The four-sided square is made in four steps and worked horizontally. On the back of the work cross-stitches are formed in the process of making the blocks. For a diagonal row, work the top and one side stitch for length desired; then work back with the bottom and other side stitch to complete the squares. As each stitch is taken, the thread is pulled tightly, thus accenting the holes.

Because the needles used are large and have big eyes, you may find it easier to tie the end of the thread to the needle eye when working. Pull thread tight after each stitch. Bring thread to front of fabric, count up four threads, insert needle at this point and bring out again at beginning point. Insert needle again at top of stitch and bring out four threads to left and four threads down, Step 1. Insert needle in beginning hole and bring out in hole four threads to left. Insert again at beginning stitch and bring out four threads up and four threads to left, Step 2. Insert needle four threads to right in hole of first stitch, bring out in hole to left. Insert again in hole to right and bring out four threads to left and four threads below, Step 3. Complete square with two stitches in same manner as before, as shown in Step 4. Continue making squares for length desired. Turn work to make next row, and work in holes of previous row.

STEP 1

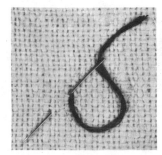

STEP 2

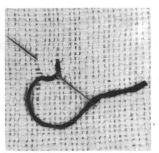

STEP 3

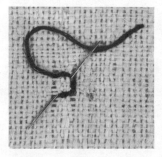

STEP 4

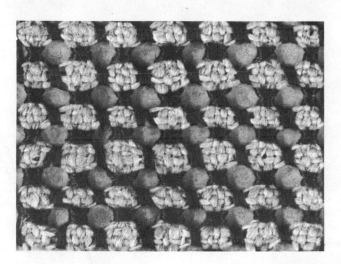

Cutwork or Richelieu Embroidery

The illustration above is an example of a design executed in round and oval eyelets, and is sometimes called Madeira work. The eyelets are all beautifully worked in overcast stitch, with satin stitch leaves and dots. The photograph is actual size and can be traced and worked on squares of fine linen, or used as corner motifs.

An actual-size detail at left shows typical contemporary cutwork in a rose pattern, as used on a tablecloth. Here the embroidery is almost completely buttonhole stitch, with details of satin stitch and outline stitch. Clark's 'ANCHOR' Coton a Broder No. 18, Clark's 'ANCHOR' Pearl Cotton No. 8 and Clark's 'ANCHOR' Stranded Cotton (2–3 strands) are suitable threads for Madeira work and cutwork.

PUNCHED EYELETS may be made up to $\frac{1}{4}''$ in diameter. Use an embroidery stiletto or a knitting needle to pierce the hole in the fabric after marking the placing of each. Outline with running stitch to support the buttonhole stitches before punching the holes. Then whip edges with close overcasting, or buttonhole. If desired, shaded eyelets may be made with one side more narrowly edged than the other. The buttonhole loop may be at the outside of the petal if desired. See small oval shape thus formed.

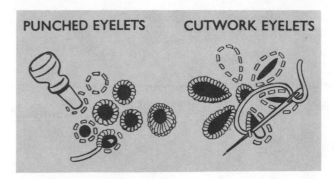

CUTWORK EYELETS are made as in diagram i. e. the centre slashed and snipped to fit after the outline has been reinforced with tiny running stitches. As the edge is buttonholed or whipped the fabric is held back to the running stitch outline.

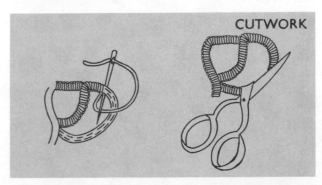

CUTWORK in other shapes or larger areas is made in the same way. The design is outlined in running stitch for reinforcement. Use small pointed embroidery scissors to cut the necessary slashes as you sew the outline areas with buttonhole stitch or overcast whipping. Trim off extra fabric after the edges are sewn. If the area to be cut out is rather large, make ladders of several strands of embroidery thread crossing from side to side before cutting away the fabric underneath. These ladders are covered with buttonholing.

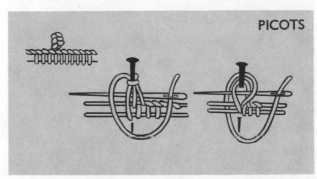

PICOTS may be used to decorate these ladders or the edge detail. To form such picots loop several strands of thread and buttonhole them, or make a French knot part way along the bar.

THE METROPOLITAN MUSEUM OF ART.
PURCHASE, ROGERS FUND, 1908.

HEDEBO This form of cutwork embroidery has many variations. The open areas may be round, oval, or of various shapes. The edges are first finished with buttonhole stitch, then ladders of thread worked across the opening in various angles. These are then worked over and over with the twist, sometimes interlaced with a modified spiderweb design. This Danish work is interesting for the advanced needleworker.

Drawn Work: hemstitching

PLAIN HEMSTITCHING

FIG. 1

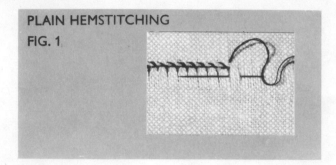

FIG. 2

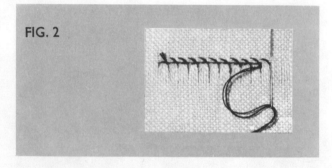

FIG. 3

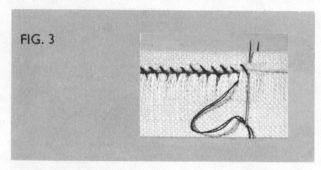

FIG. 4

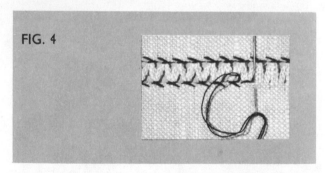

FIG. 5

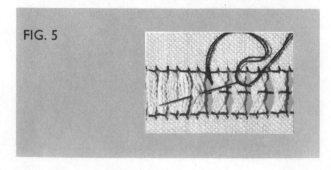

Drawn work describes those kinds of embroidery in which some of the warp or weft threads are drawn from the fabric; the remaining threads are pulled together with a fine needle threaded with a matching or contrasting colour. Illustrations are examples of drawn work used to finish hems and make borders. Directions are given on these pages for plain hemstitching with zigzag and twisted thread variations, and for Italian hemstitching which makes a more elaborate border. Suitable fabrics for hemstitching vary from the finest linen to burlap. Threads, too, can be widely varied.

GENERAL DIRECTIONS: Any linen or cotton fabric with a plain weave may be used for hemstitching. To draw out threads, insert a pin under one thread near edge of fabric and pull it up; then carefully draw the thread from fabric all the way across. Try to ease it out without breaking it. Hemstitching is done on wrong side of fabric, from left to right.

Plain Hemstitching: Draw out two or three threads across fabric, depending on its coarseness. Secure thread at left edge of drawn section without making a knot by taking a few stitches over end of thread. Put needle under next three or four upright threads of drawn section from right to left (Fig. 1). Pull thread taut, insert needle in second row of threads above drawn section (Fig. 2) and pull thread tight. Continue across, as in Figs. 1 and 2, always picking up same number of threads. Secure thread at end. Bottom edge of drawn section may be hemstitched also as shown in Fig. 4.

A hem may be made at same time hemstitching is done. Turn fabric over twice, to make hem desired width, and baste. Draw out threads just below edge of hem. Starting at left, hemstitch as in Figs. 1 and 2, inserting needle in 2nd row of threads above and through bottom edge of hem (Fig. 3.) Repeat these two steps across, catching hem edge and picking up same number of threads each time.

For a more decorative border (Fig. 4), pull out about eight threads and work across in same manner as Figs. 1 and 2, picking up six threads at a time. To hemstitch lower edge of drawn section and make zigzag design, pick up first three threads only, then continue across, picking up six threads at a time (Fig. 4).

To make twisted groups of hemstitched threads (Fig. 5), pull out 10 or more threads and work plain hemstitching evenly at top and bottom of drawn section, picking up four threads at a time. Turn work over to right side, secure thread at right-hand edge in middle of drawn section. Pick up second group of threads at left section. Pick up second group of threads at left with needle pointing from left to right. Bring this group of threads over and to the right of first group by inserting needle under first group and turning it to the left, keeping second group on needle. Continue across in same manner, always picking up second group of threads first.

Italian Hemstitching: This is based on the same two steps as plain hemstitching, except in the second step, the needle points downwards instead of upwards, unless otherwise stated.

To make border shown in Fig. 6, baste hem. Draw out two threads just below hem, skip three threads, draw out next two threads, skip three, etc., for desired width. Make first row of hemstitching, picking up four threads at a time. With needle pointing downwards for second step, insert needle in hem first, two threads up from fold, then through all thicknesses and out at drawn section. Continue across in same manner. To make succeeding rows, insert needle in space between groups of threads of preceding row (Fig. 6).

A wide decorative border, the right side of which is shown in Fig. 7, is worked as follows: Baste hem. Draw out two threads just below hem, skip three threads, draw out ten threads, skip three threads, draw out two threads Work first two rows of hemstitching as shown in Fig. 6, picking up four threads at a time. On next row, fasten thread at base of wide drawn section and work a row of plain hemstitching as in Fig. 4, picking up eight threads at a time. On last row, fasten thread in last drawn section and work a row of hemstitching like second row, inserting needle in space between groups of threads and at base of groups.

To make border in Fig. 8, baste hem. Draw out ten threads just below hem, skip four threads, draw out two threads, skip four threads, draw out ten threads. Work first row as for Fig. 6, picking up nine threads at a time. Turn work around. Work second row along other edge of same drawn section, picking up three threads at a time and inserting needle in second row of threads above. Turn work around. Work third row in narrow drawn section, picking up three threads at a time and inserting needle in second row above. Turn work. Make fourth row in same drawn section along other edge in same manner. Turn work. Make fifth row in next wide drawn section, picking up three threads at a time and inserting needle in second row of threads above. Turn work. Make last row along other edge of wide drawn section, picking up nine threads at a time and inserting needle in second row of threads above. Be sure that nine-thread groups are in line with groups in first drawn section.

Many other decorative borders may be made by combining examples above and drawing out different numbers of threads.

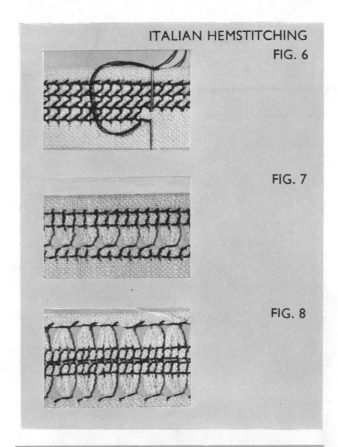

ITALIAN HEMSTITCHING

FIG. 6

FIG. 7

FIG. 8

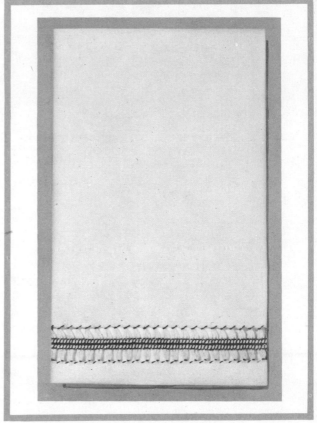

The border of a white linen towel is worked in green. Spaces between thread clusters give the design lightness.

Drawn Work: needleweaving

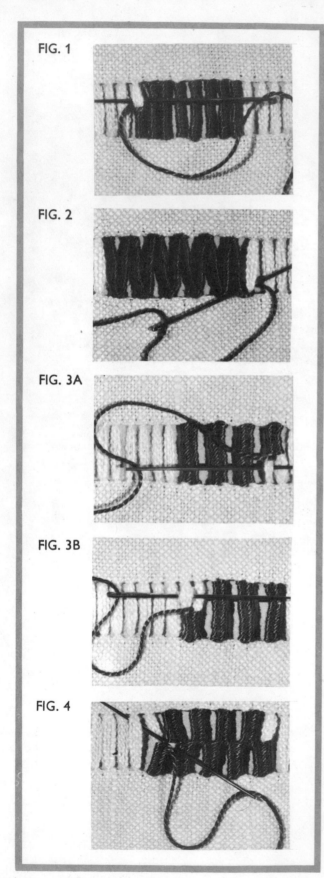

FIG. 1

FIG. 2

FIG. 3A

FIG. 3B

FIG. 4

Needleweaving has been a favourite in many countries for centuries. This technique of drawing threads from a fabric and then replacing them by weaving a design over the remaining threads is ideal for working colourful borders on linens. Here we give designs done in a thread heavier than the threads removed, thus producing an enriched, constrasting texture. These heavier threads of Clark's 'ANCHOR' Pearl Cotton No. 5 or Clark's 'ANCHOR' Stranded Cotton (6 strands) are woven with a tapestry needle, following simple repeat patterns on charts. The designs are striking when worked in strong colours, more subtle when done in white.

GENERAL DIRECTIONS: Choose coarse or fine linen or other fabrics from which threads can be drawn easily. Use Clark's 'ANCHOR' Pearl Cotton No. 5 or 6 strands of Clark's 'ANCHOR' Stranded Cotton and a tapestry needle for weaving.

Draw out enough threads to make desired border. Both edges of the drawn section should be hemstitched first (see Index). Use thread to match fabric for hemstitching. Take an equal number of vertical threads in each stitch (usually 3, 4 or 5) according to weight of fabric being used. Then do needleweaving on right side of fabric over and under each group of threads divided by hemstitching—never split these groups. Always be sure that weaving threads are close together so they cover vertical threads of drawn section.

To begin work, fasten end of thread by placing it along first group of threads and working over it. To end off, run needle back into weaving for about four rows and cut thread close to work.

Practise the following six basic formations before starting to work borders on opposite page.

Vertical Bars (Fig. 1): Fasten thread at lower right and work closely around first group from bottom to top. End off thread. Make each bar separately in same way.

Zigzag Bars (Fig. 2): Fasten thread at bottom right and work one vertical bar, but not do end off. Work two stitches around first bar and next group of threads at same time, then work down 2nd group of threads. Work around bar just completed and next group of threads at same time. Continue in same way.

Double Bars (Figs. 3A and 3B): Fasten thread at lower right, weave under first group of threads and over 2nd group (Fig. 3A). Then weave under 2nd group and over first group (Fig. 3B). Continue weaving closely under and over first and 2nd groups from bottom to top. End off thread. Make each double bar separately.

Broken Double Bars (Fig. 4): Fasten thread at lower right and weave double bar same as above, halfway up drawn section; then weave under first group, over 2nd and under 3rd. For 2nd half of bar, weave over 3rd group of threads and under 2nd, then back over 2nd group and under 3rd. Continue weaving over and under 3rd and 2nd groups to top. End off thread. Start next broken bar at bottom, weaving 3rd and 4th groups of threads halfway up and continuing to top on 4th and 5th groups. Work across in same manner. First bar is finished by working to top.

Alternating Blocks (Fig. 5): Fasten thread at lower right, weave under first group of threads, over 2nd group, under 3rd, over 4th. Then weave back under 4th, over 3rd, under 2nd, over first. Continue weaving in this manner halfway up drawn section. Then weave under first group, over 2nd, under 3rd, over 4th, under 5th, over 6th. Weave back under 6th, over 5th, under 4th and over 3rd. Continue weaving to top on 3rd, 4th, 5th and 6th groups of threads. Fasten off threads. Start next block at bottom on 5th, 6th, 7th and 8th groups of threads and weave halfway up. Then weave on 7th, 8th, 9th and 10th groups of threads to top. Continue across in this manner. Finish first 2 groups of threads as a double bar.

Pyramids (Fig. 6): Fasten thread at lower right, weave under and over first 8 groups of threads and back under and over to first group. Weave back and forth for one-quarter depth of drawn section. Then weave over and under one group less of threads on each side (6 groups) for 2nd quarter of depth. Weave under and over one less group on each side (4 groups) for 3rd quarter of depth. Weave over and under 2 centre groups for last quarter, to top of drawn section. End off thread. Start next pyramid upside down at bottom of drawn section. Weave under and over 2 groups of threads for first quarter; over and under 4 groups for 2nd quarter; under and over 6 groups for 3rd quarter; over and under 8 groups for last quarter. End off thread. Continue across in same way.

Many interesting designs can be made with these basic formations.

FIG. 5

FIG. 6

Shown from top to bottom: Narrow Border of Triangles is worked in Clark's 'ANCHOR' Pearl Cotton No. 5: Cobalt Blue **0134**/511, **0129**/592 and Gorse Yellow **0302**/443. Medium Border of Vertical Diamonds in Geranium **08**/734 and Cobalt Blue **0134**/511, and Wide Border of Reverse V's in Grass Green **0242**/497 and **0245**/500. Milwards 'Gold Seal' tapestry needle No. 21.

Teneriffe Embroidery

This type of embroidery involves the same technique as for needleweaving. However, no threads are drawn from the fabric for Teneriffe. Long straight stitches make the web or spoke and then you work over and under these long stitches to weave the design. It is a simple matter to use checked gingham as the background to form an even outline for your design. Form designs of squares, triangles, diamonds and circles, using the checks of the gingham as a guide for placing the long straight stitches. The apron and pot holder below show Teneriffe used as a border.

Teneriffe apron and pot holder

MATERIALS: Gold-and-white checked gingham with 4 checks to the inch, 1⅛ yards, 36″ wide. Coats Satinised No. 40. Clark's 'ANCHOR'. Pearl Cotton No. 5, two balls each Emerald **0229/731** and Kingfisher **0161/483**. Milwards 'Gold Seal' tapestry needle No. 21. Bone ring, 1″. Terry cloth, 6¾″ square.

DIRECTIONS: Apron: Keeping selvages at sides, make skirt 36″ wide and 22½″ long. Turn up a 4″ hem; press, but do not sew. Make Teneriffe border following directions below. Gather top edge of skirt to measure 16¾″. Cut waistband 17¼″ long and 5″ wide. Fold in half lengthwise. Turn in long edges and ends. Insert gathered top edge of skirt between halves of waistband and stitch across. Cut two ties each 27″ long and 5″ wide. Stitch ¼″ hems on both long edges and one end of ties; fold end over to adjacent side and stitch together forming triangle. Repeat for other tie end. Make a tuck in raw end of each tie and insert in ends of waistband; stitch across.

Cut pocket 8″ wide and 9″ deep. Make design across top following directions below. Press sides under ½″ and bottom edge ¼″. Make 2″ hem along top. Stitch pocket to skirt 5″ below bottom edge of waistband and 3¾″ in from right side.

Pot Holder: Cut two pieces of gingham each 9″ square. Follow weaving directions below for border. With right sides together and squares matching, stitch along three sides making 1″ seams. Turn to right side and insert terry cloth padding. Fold in remaining edges and stitch together. Make a few small stitches through all thicknesses to secure.

With blue, single crochet (see Index) closely around bone ring and sew to one corner of pot holder.

To Weave Teneriffe Design: For apron, start design at right corner of third square in from right edge and 4½″ up from pressed hem. With green, make three straight stitches for bottom triangle web as shown at point A on chart. Each square on chart represents a check on gingham. Bring thread to front of gingham at bottom of triangle and weave design as shown in Fig. 1; run needle over and under spokes of web, working back and forth to fill spokes. Do not pull thread too tightly: push rows of threads down towards point to fill closely. At top, bring needle to back of work and fasten. Work top triangle in same way. With blue, make centre web on four squares of gingham, starting each of eight stitches from centre, between the two triangles as illustrated in chart. Starting at centre of web, loop around each spoke of web as shown in Fig. 2; work around web twice. Work next triangles and centre wheel reversing colours. Repeat straight across apron to complete border, ending with green triangles and blue web.

For pocket, begin design 4½″ up from 9″ edge and ½″ from 8″ edge. Work design across as for apron until it measures about 7″ across, beginning and ending with blue triangles.

For pot holder, make design on one piece only. Begin in right corner of 13th square in from left edge and 6th square up from lower edge. Starting at point A on chart, work with green as for apron. Then reverse colours moving to the left. For corners, follow chart and work the two outside corner points with green and the centre web with blue; work the two inside corner points with blue. Repeat design, alternating colours, except for corners, around entire pot holder; make corners all the same.

Chart for working design shown on apron. Each square represents one check of gingham fabric.

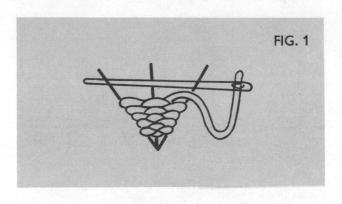

FIG. 1

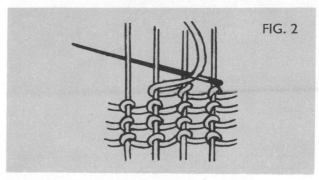

FIG. 2

Hardanger Work

Hardanger work is based on the square blocks of cut-work. This is done on coarse even mesh linen with the threads drawn and cut away in blocks as each motif is worked. The cross threads are used as a basis for stitches woven through to form sturdy ladders. The adjoining areas are decorated with satin stitch blocks or open blocks after the edges of the openings have been whipped with straight even stitches. Designs for this work should be kept to the block forms typical of Norwegian embroidery. This embroidery is most effective for luncheon sets.

Suitable thread for this type of work is: Clark's 'ANCHOR' Pearl Cotton No. 5 for all Kloster blocks and Clark's 'ANCHOR' Pearl Cotton No. 8 for all bars and fillings.

1. Kloster block of five stitches worked over four threads of linen.

2. Designs are made up of combinations of these blocks turned in different directions.

3. Kloster blocks in place, centre ready to be cut.

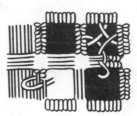

4. Typical block of open Hardanger showing drawn threads with blocks cut away. Weaving or darning stitches worked through the ladders and over and over edge stitching. Spider stitch worked in open block.

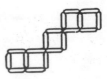

5. Open block worked in outline running stitch similar to Holbein stitch.

A DETAIL OF A DESIGN FOR A TABLECLOTH FROM COATS SEWING GROUP BOOK NO. 896.

Faggoting

The technique of joining fabric pieces with a decorative stitch to produce an open, lacy effect is called faggoting.

Almost any material can be used, but silk, satin, linen and cotton are best.

Seams can be joined by faggoting them together, or a much more ambitious project—a blouse, for example—can be produced by faggoting strips of material to each other.

These stitches are also most useful for joining a false hem to a skirt, and can look most effective on hand-made underwear or on children's garments.

To do the decorative stitch, use:

Clark's 'ANCHOR' Pearl Cotton No. 5 or 8 or Clark's 'ANCHOR' Stranded Cotton (2–6 strands depending on weight of fabric).

The edges of the fabric to be joined are first hemmed by slip-stitching neatly. The two pieces of fabric are then basted to a piece of stiff paper, leaving the desired amount of space between. The space may vary for different pieces, but must be kept constant on one article. The tension of the embroidery should be kept even throughout. When the faggoting is completed, clip the basting and remove it from the paper.

The sample on this page shows the two most familiar stitches—Trellis and Twisted Bars—plus Sheaf Stitch, Grouped Buttonhole and Knotted Insertion Stitch.

Vary them as you wish after you have done a little experimenting with the ones shown here.

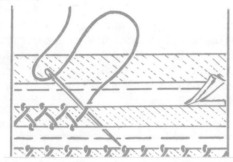

TRELLIS STITCH Similar to Open Cretan Stitch worked on the edge of two pieces of fabric.

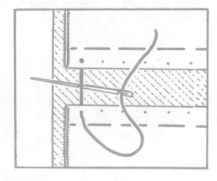

TWISTED BARS First make a straight stitch from bottom to top between the two fabrics.
Sample above shows actual-size faggoting done with double thickness of bias tape between embroidery.

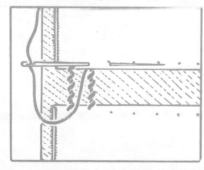

Next, overcast the bar from top to bottom to fill the space neatly and evenly. Start next bar to left.

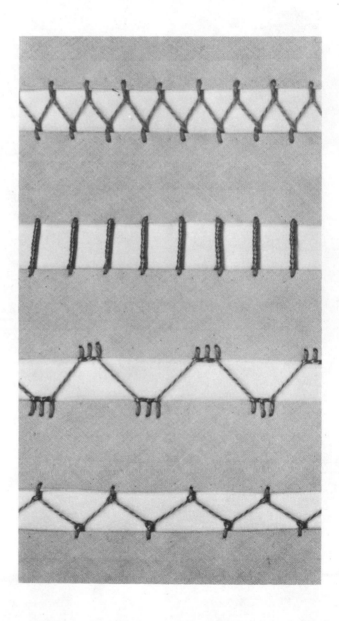

Sample above shows actual-size faggoting done with double thickness of bias tape between embroidery.

Embroidery on Net

Net or tulle with hexagonal meshes is used for the background of this embroidery and is worked in a manner so it resembles the fine old pillow laces. The embroidery may be done in a simple darning stitch, or more elaborately by using a variety of stitches. Some stitch details are shown on these pages. Combine them to make your own designs on net. The embroidery can be done with a fine thread to make a dainty lace, or you may use heavier threads or yarn. The net should be of a good quality so that the meshes will not break while being embroidered. Use a needle with a blunt tip and darn in ends of threads to start and finish. Never make knots because they show. You may draw your design on stiff paper and tack the net to this as a guide for embroidering. Or you may want to follow a pattern by counting the mesh of the net. You may find it easiest to outline your design first with a simple running stitch, then embroider in any stitches desired.

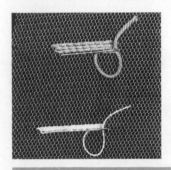

DARNING This is worked in rows back and forth, going over and under one mesh for each stitch, or more, depending on embroidery thread being used. The top detail shows a fine yarn being darned. In this detail three rows of darning are put alternately over and under each mesh. The second detail shows a heavy yarn being used with just one row through each mesh of the net.

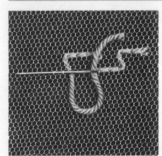

OUTLINING This is merely a running stitch worked over and under each mesh to outline a design. To fasten the embroidery thread, fold it over on back of work and embroider over it. Run the end back into the embroidery to finish off a thread.

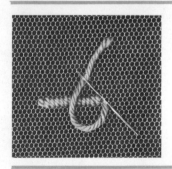

OVERCASTING To overcast, the embroidery thread is worked over two or more meshes of net solidly. When using a fine thread at least two stitches should be made over each mesh to fill; for a heavier yarn, make just one stitch over each mesh.

The sampler at left is a simple geometrical design, using many of the stitches shown.

OPEN BUTTONHOLE STITCH This is worked just the same as buttonhole stitch on any fabric. Make one buttonhole stitch in each mesh of the net. Can be worked horizontally, vertically or diagonally and in fine or coarse thread.

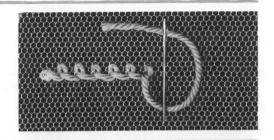

CLOSED BUTTONHOLE STITCH This is the same as open buttonhole stitch except that a number of stitches are worked over each mesh to fill solidly. This stitch is normally used when working with a fine thread.

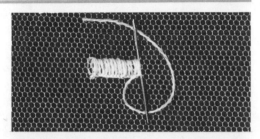

COUCHED BUTTONHOLE If a design is first outlined, this is the way buttonholing would be done. When working by the counting method, first run a single thread in and out of the meshes to the desired outline. Then work buttonholing over the outline.

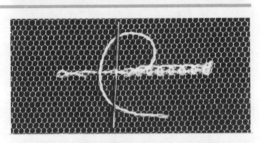

EYELET ROW This is worked in two rows back and forth. Work in and out of each mesh of net, going below and around one side of first mesh, then above and around one side of next mesh. Continue across row in this manner, then work back around the same meshes to complete the eyelets.

STEM AND EYELET First darn a single line for the stem, then work completely around one mesh for eyelet. Alternating the darning, work around eyelet again and down stem.

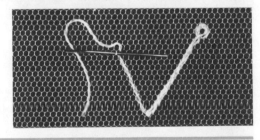

STAR When using a fine embroidery thread, two stitches should be taken for each arm of star; with a heavier yarn, make one stitch for each. Take stitches over two meshes or more, down through centre mesh and out at next diagonal, horizontal, or vertical row of meshes. Continue around in this manner to make a star with six evenly spaced arms.

Smocking : English

Smocking is easy to do when you have mastered the simple stitches which are based on the familiar embroidery stitches, such as outline stitch and backstitch, together with a kind of whipped stitch. These are combined with fullness introduced either by gathers set before the smocking is begun, or by following pattern dots. You may smock with a transfer pattern as your guide, or create your own design.

There are two methods of smocking—English smocking for which the material is gathered in pleats first and regular smocking in which the gathers are made as the pattern is followed.

The best fabric to use for smocking is one with a firm weave and even grain. Cotton poplin, chambray, piqué and gingham are popular. Patterned fabrics such as squared and striped materials provide their own guide lines, as do also such materials as dotted Swiss and dimi-

ty. Use 'ANCHOR' Stranded Cotton (3–6 strands) to embroider, carrying out the design in a single colour, in two, three or four colours, as you wish, and as the pattern recommends. If the garment is washable, make sure that you use washable, colourfast thread, as quoted above.

For every inch of finished smocking, about $2\frac{1}{2}$ inches of fabric is required.

Rows of dots are marked on the back of the fabric, $\frac{1}{4}''$ apart. There are transfer patterns of rows of dots which can be stamped on to the fabric with a hot iron. There are also machines that will gather the fabric evenly for English smocking. After the marking is done each row of dots is gathered on the wrong side forming uniform pleated folds. The smocking is then worked on the right side of the material by using stitches described and shown here.

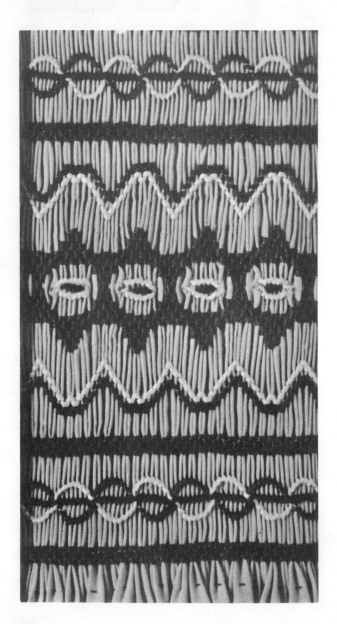

First mark centre of smocking area with a vertical contrasting basting thread. Pull up gathering rows (about 3 at a time) so material to be smocked is slightly smaller than the desired finished size. Fasten threads.

Smocking is now worked on the right side of material, using four strands of six-strand cotton. Starting at left-hand edge and working from left to right, pick up the top of each pleat of material, following instructions for desired smocking design. Gathering threads are removed after smocking.

TO SMOCK: Gather stamped dots with contrasting sewing thread as in Fig. 1. To start, bring needle up between first and second pleats, then insert needle again, picking up first pleat (Fig. 2).

Cable Stitch: With thread below needle, pick up next pleat and pull up. (Fig. 3). With thread above needle, pick up next pleat and pull down (Fig. 4).

Outline Stitch: With thread above needle, pick up each pleat across (Fig. 5).

Two-Step Wave: With thread below needle, pick up first pleat as in Fig. 3. With thread below needle, pick up next pleat ($\frac{1}{2}$ step up and) pull up (Fig. 6). With thread below needle, pick up top pleat and pull up (Fig. 7). With thread above needle, pick up next pleat and pull down. With thread above needle, pick up next pleat ($\frac{1}{2}$ step down) and pull down (Fig. 8). With thread above needle, pick up bottom pleat and pull down (Fig. 9). With thread below needle, pick up next pleat, pull up.

Three-Step Wave: Begin same as two-step wave (Figs. 6 and 7). Then continue in same manner up one more step. With thread above needle, pick up next pleat and pull down. With thread above needle, work down three steps in same manner as two-step wave.

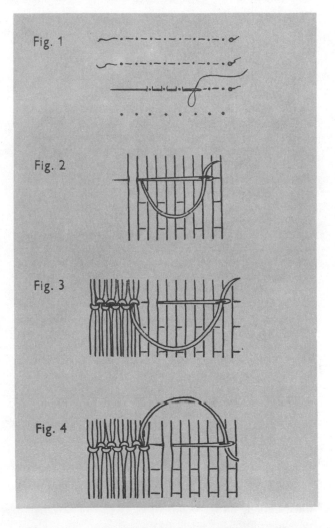

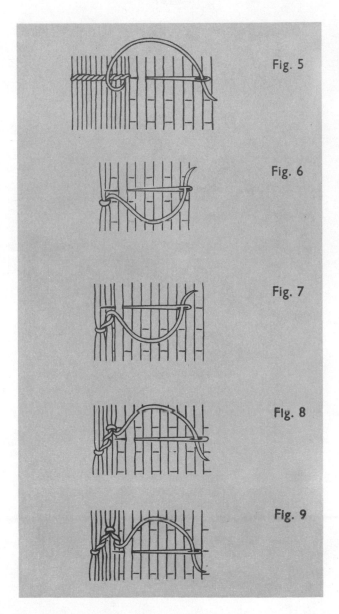

On the left-hand page are two fine examples of English smocking. You will note the even, deep-pleated appearance of the gathers which is the characteristic of this type of smocking—noted for its elasticity.

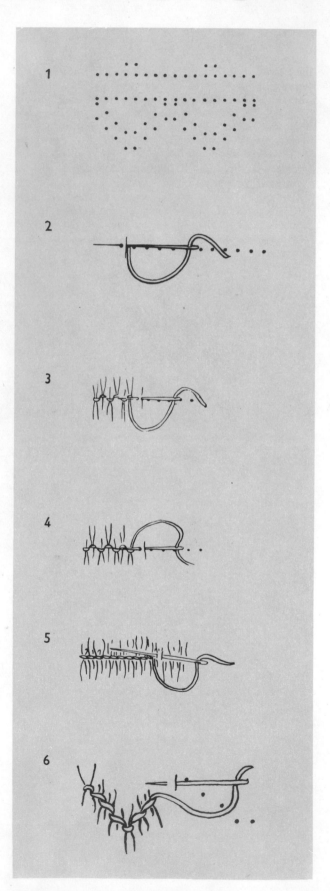

The regular method of smocking is based on picking up dots arranged in a pattern as they are given in McCall's Transfer Patterns. Following these dots, which are stamped on right side of material, forms the smocking pattern, and pulls the material up into tiny pleats or folds. In regular smocking, the needle picks up the dots and the stitch covers them. In English smocking, the needle picks up the top of the gathered pleats.

The cable stitch, outline stitch and wave stitch are done in the same manner as for English smocking. There are also two more stitches in regular smocking, the honeycomb or seed stitch and diamond or chevron stitch.

The fabric to use for regular smocking and the embroidery cotton are the same as for English smocking. After marking the smocking dots on the right side of fabric, either with a hot iron transfer, or by hand, start smocking (Fig. 1), on right side, working from left to right.

CABLE STITCH The thread passes alternately above and below the row of dots, gathering in the fold of fabric with each stitch. Figure 2 shows the first stitch with the needle facing from right to left, taking up a fold of fabric. The next two dots are then joined on the next stitch taken with the thread below the needle. Figure 3. The thread is passed above the needle and the needle passes through the next two dots gathering them together. Figure 4. Continue along the entire row.

OUTLINE STITCH With the needle always pointing to the left, adjoining dots are gathered with the thread always below the needle point. This is often used above or below a smocked section as a finish. Figure 5.

WAVE STITCH Designs often call for two step wave or three step wave. This describes the number of descending or ascending steps in the design. For this stitch use dots similar to those shown in Figure 1 left. There should be 6 dots for a three step wave. Knot thread, bring needle up to right side of material between first and second dots. Insert needle again, nearer the first dot, and bring up through first dot, pick up second dot having thread above the needle, and pull down together. With thread above needle pick up third dot. Keep thread above needle for 2nd, 3rd, 4th and 5th dots, but have thread below the needle for 6th, 7th, 8th dots, and the 1st dot of next wave. Pull up each time as in Figure 6. Continue along row in this way with thread above the needle when working down the wave, and below the needle when working up the wave.

HONEYCOMB OR SEED STITCH: This design is worked out with two or more rows of dots. Make a knot in the end of the thread and bring to the surface through 1st dot of top row. Join with dot 2 in anchoring stitch or buttonhole loop stitch. Pass under the fabric to dots 2 and 3 of row below, drawing them together. Pass thread under fabric again to upper row gathering together next 2 dots. Then alternate working up and down all the way across the rows of dots. This pattern is often worked out for deep areas using 4 or more rows of dots for the pattern. Figure 7.

DIAMOND OR CHEVRON STITCH This pattern is worked in the same way as the honeycomb stitch except the thread carries along the right side of the material instead of under the fabric to follow the folds of the fabric. Figure 8.

SHAPING YOKE OR COLLAR Sometimes you may wish to use your transfer pattern around a neck, to make a shaped yoke, or to form a curved collar line. To do this, carefully slash the transfer edges at even intervals and pin it together to form the desired shape. Then pin or baste to the material and press as for a straight transfer. Figure 9.

HOW TO PRESS SMOCKING You may press the smocking sections by steaming before making up the garment. Use a wet piece of thin fabric to make full steam when using the ordinary iron. If the finished work is narrower than desired it may be widened by pulling the smocking over the iron as if pressing flat, by pressing with the pleats from the top downwards.

Actual-size details of honeycomb smocking show a straight band and typical pointed design.

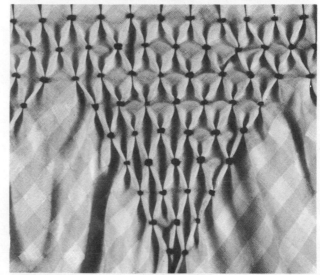

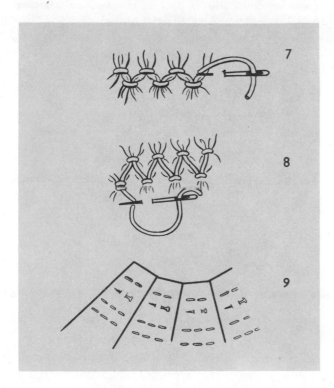

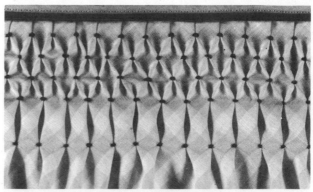

A typical example of a smocked yoke done in regular smocking. Practical and charming on children's clothes.

Smocking : lattice

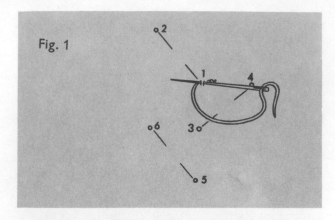

Fig. 1

Worked on corduroy and velvet, this kind of smocking is particularly suitable for making decorative pillows. Done by means of dots systematically placed on the wrong side of the fabric, the smocking produces deep, bold pleats on the right side of the fabric. If you wish, you may use satin or antique satin instead of napped fabric. Lattice smocking is easy to do, once you have learned the basic steps, and the smocking works up very quickly. Hats, handbags and even curtains may also be made in this type of smocking, using any fabric suited to the article.

Transfer patterns are made by McCall's for stamping the smocking dots used, but you can mark your own if you like. Use buttonhole twist, heavy-duty sewing thread or nylon sewing thread in the needle. Knot end of thread. All smocking is worked on wrong side of fabric. Stitches will not show on right side after smocking pleats are formed. After dots are marked on wrong side of fabric, start smocking at upper left. To pick up dots insert needle into fabric to right of dot and out through left side of same dot. Thread is carried from dot to dot on working side of fabric. Pick up dot 1 and make a second holding stitch as shown in Fig. 1. Then pick up dot 2, go back to first dot and pick up again as shown in Fig. 2. Pull dots 1 and 2 together and knot securely, Fig. 3. Pick up dot 3, then with thread above needle, slip needle under the thread between dots 1 and 2 as shown in Fig 4, pulling thread tightly at dot 3 to form knot. Be sure to keep fabric flat between dots 1 and 3. Pick up dot 4, then go back and pick up dot 3 again as shown in Fig. 5. Pull dots together and knot securely. Pick up dot 5 as shown in Fig. 6, slip needle under thread between dots 3 and 5 and knot as in Fig. 4. Continue down row of dots in this manner, starting with Fig. 2 and picking up dot 6 next.

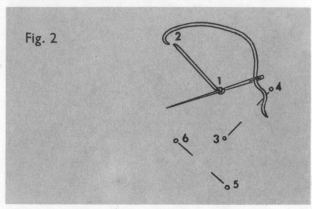

Fig. 2

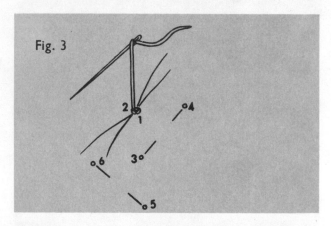

Fig. 3

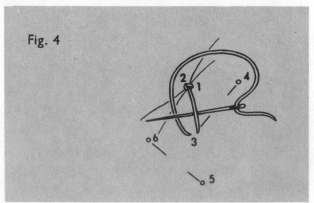

Fig. 4

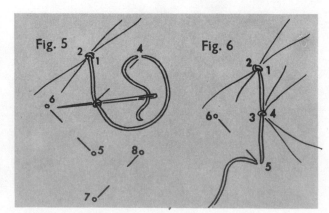

Fig. 5   Fig. 6

Lattice-smocked cushions made of rich materials can give a note of elegance to most surroundings.

CUSHIONS ARE McCALL'S PATTERN No. 2467

Smocking : on gingham

This is a fascinating and quick way to do smocking in the well-known honeycomb stitch. By working on gingham with one-inch square checks, you produce not only the classical honeycomb pattern, but an interesting light and dark effect when the gingham squares are brought together. This fabric smocking is particularly suitable for such useful household items as cushions. The stitch is easy to master and the large checks of the gingham are simple to follow. A puffy pineapple smocking can be produced in a similar manner by pulling the checks together in symmetrical instead of alternate rows. Smocking can also be done on plain material by using a transfer pattern to stamp guide dots on the fabric. Variations of the honeycomb smocking can also be done by leaving free rows, which form flat pleats, between smocking rows.

The illustration below shows a gingham cushion and a bolster of plain fabric, both smocked in the honeycomb stitch. The chair back and seat cushion are another example of honeycomb smocking on gingham, with pressed pleat ruffles formed by the smocking.

Honeycomb smocking stitch on gingham

Woven gingham with one-inch square checks is used for the smocking. To determine the amount of material required for honeycomb smocking, measure width of area to be smocked and allow double that amount of fabric. After measurements are taken, add seam allowances and hems as required. Use mercerized knitting and crochet cotton, or for a bolder effect and contrast, use six-strand embroidery cotton, the full six strands in needle. Smock on right side of gingham.

To start, make a knot in end of thread. To pick up corners of gingham checks, take a small stitch through fabric at corner of check. Thread is pulled up on right side only, and is kept flat between stitches on wrong side.

Bring needle up one inch in from upper and right edges, at lower right corner of a medium-tone check. See Fig. 1. Pick up lower left corner of same medium-tone check, Fig. 1. Pull thread up and take another stitch, bringing corners together so that two dark checks meet, Fig. 2. Insert needle through fabric as in Fig. 3, bring it out at lower right corner of next medium-tone check, keeping thread flat on wrong side. Secure with another stitch taken in same corner, Fig. 4. Pick up lower left corner of same check and pull thread up, bringing the two dark checks together. Take another stitch to hold as shown in Fig. 6. Insert needle to wrong side as in Fig. 3 and continue across row to one inch from left side.

To make next row, bring needle up through fabric at lower right corner of second light check. Pick up lower left corner of same light check, Fig. 7. Pull up thread and take a stitch to hold, Fig. 8, bringing the two white checks together. Insert needle through fabric as in Fig. 9 and bring it out at lower right of next light check, keeping thread flat. Secure with another stitch and continue across row as for previous row. Repeat these two rows alternately. The margin of fabric across top and bottom naturally falls into pleats which can be tacked and used as ruffle. If pleated ruffle is desired at sides, separate pieces of gingham must be cut and pleated and seamed to sides.

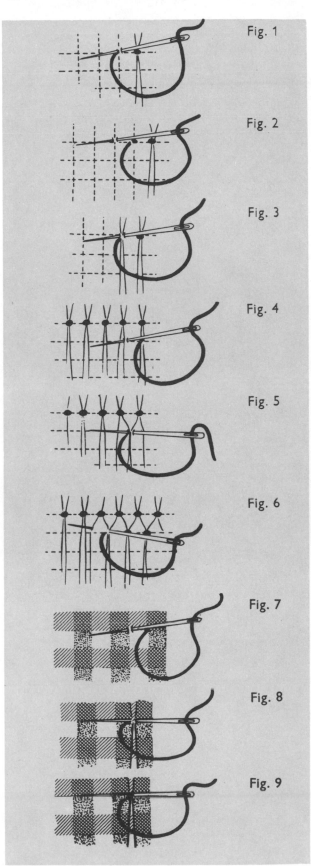

Fig. 1

Fig. 2

Fig. 3

Fig. 4

Fig. 5

Fig. 6

Fig. 7

Fig. 8

Fig. 9

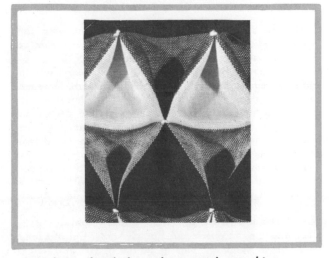

Actual-size detail shows honeycomb smocking.

Appliqué

Appliqué is a very decorative embroidery done by laying pieces of fabric on a background fabric and stitching them in place. Its appeal lies in the colourful effect that can be obtained by using a variety of fabrics both print and plain to form the designs. In most cases embroidery stitches on the appliqué pieces are used to define and accent the design. But for the most part embroidery can be kept to a minimum, since the appliqué pieces themselves are the chief decorative element.

Almost any material can be used for the background. Choose a fabric to suit the design and effect you want to achieve. A fine, matching thread can be used to sew the appliqué piece to the background, or an embroidery thread in a contrasting colour may be used, if the appliqué is to be attached with decorative stitches. Appliqués are used on household linens, wearing apparel, quilts, and to make pictures for framing.

For the appliqué pieces themselves, many kinds of fabric may be used, but they should have a firm weave so a clean edge will be left after the pieces are cut. A cotton fabric like broadcloth is easiest to work with, but other materials such as linen, taffeta, velvet, cretonne and similar fabrics are also suitable. Several kinds of fabrics can be combined in one piece of work.

The best and most accurate method to use for appliquéing is to mark the complete design first on the background fabric. Then make a pattern piece for each part of the design. Taking each pattern piece in turn, mark the outline on the appliqué fabric, and mark a seam allowance all around the piece, usually ¼″ wide. Next, machine stitch on the design outline for a neat turning edge as shown in Fig. 1. Then cut out the appliqué on outer seam allowance line as shown in Fig. 2. For a smooth edge, clip curved edges and corners, then turn in seam allowance just inside machine stitching as shown in Fig. 3, and press. Pin the appliqué in place on the background and slip-stitch in place with tiny stitches as shown in Fig. 4.

If a decorative edging is desired on the appliqué piece, it can be topstitched in matching or contrasting colour, or whipped in place. Or use a buttonhole stitch around the piece with stitches close together or spaced. Appliqué pieces may also be machine stitched in place, using a zigzag stitch either widely spaced, or closed for a satin stitch edge. A chain stitch may be used to embroider an appliqué to background.

Fig. 1

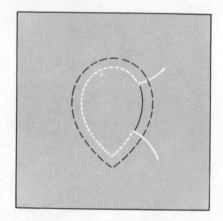

Fig. 2

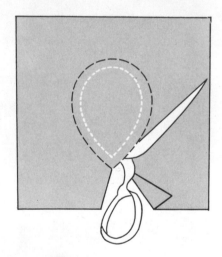

Fig. 3

Fig. 4

On the right is the pattern for reproducing the Blue Appliqué Picture, opposite page 88. To enlarge it to actual size, mark off a paper 21″×15″ in 1″ squares. Transpose the lines in each square on to your 1″ squares. Make a separate pattern for each appliqué piece and add $\frac{3}{16}$″ seam allowance all round each. Carefully trace the complete design on to cream colour linen background. Cut appliqué pieces from cotton broadcloth in colours shown in picture. Slip-stitch appliqué pieces to proper place on background putting down pieces first that appear underneath others. Embroider details with Clark's 'ANCHOR' Stranded Cotton: Indigo 0127/535, Azure 0155/460, Grass Green 0244/499, 0246 and 0402/White. Use 6 strands. Work in outline stitch, running stitch, lazy daisy, satin stitch and French knots. Cut out long wide green stems on bias of fabric, in straight strips. These can then be curved and sewn in position.

San Blas 'Appliqué'

Indian women on the picturesque San Blas Islands off Panama have a unique way of embroidering colourful blouses or "molas". The method used, which might be called "reverse appliqué", creates designs more by cutting out than by adding fabric. San Blas women start a blouse design with four or five thicknesses of cotton cloth—each layer a different, brilliant colour—orange, red, green, blue—bottom layer sometimes black. Photos 1 to 3 on p. 77 illustrate cutting-away technique to reveal different colours and thus bring out the designs. The over all shape of the main design, such as a bird, is cut and edges sewn under; then the wing, tail

and other large sections of design are treated in a similar way. Occasionally pieces of fabric are sewn on top, as in classic appliqué, to bring out small details (4), or a few embroidery stitches are added.

The designs reveal the ingenuity and imagination of these clever Indian women who copy from nature, from canned goods' labels—anything at all that interests them. Letters of the alphabet often appear with complete disregard for their meaning!

The cloth used for the blouses, usually from England, is paid for with coconuts—the currency of San Blas. See "mola" designs below.

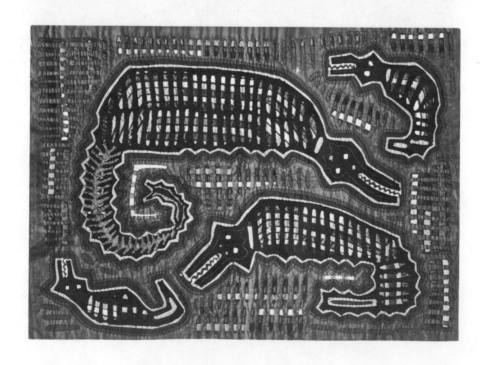

How to do San Blas (reverse) appliqué

The reverse appliqué technique involves sometimes as many as five or six layers of fabrics all in different colours.

Parts of the top layers are cut away to reveal the colour below. If a central motif is to be used, the arrangement of the layers must be carefully planned before starting.

You may have to cut through one, two or three layers at once to get to the colour desired for some parts of the design.

But if the colours are arranged well, it should not be necessary to cut through more than one layer at a time. It is also possible to arrange pieces of different colours of fabric under only some parts of the design. To experiment with this type of appliqué, try using only three layers of fabric, and then using some small two-layer appliqués in open spaces.

As you become more skilled you will want to include animals and figures in your design, and try to achieve an interesting three-dimensional effect.

Embroidery may be used in simple stitches but should only accent the design. It should never detract from the strong, basic quality of the appliqué. In turning under edges of the fabric always use a slip stitch and matching thread.

The illustrations show steps of reverse appliqué.

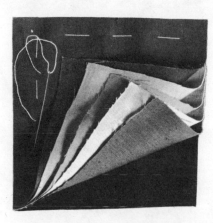
1

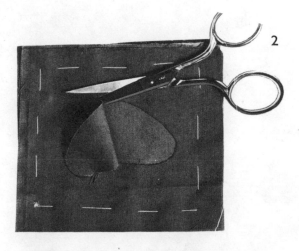
2

After number of colours and arrangement have been decided, baste fabrics all together around edge and also diagonally across to hold them securely.

To reveal the first colour under top layer, cut away a portion of top fabric in design desired, using a pair of sharp embroidery scissors.

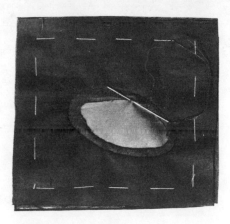
3

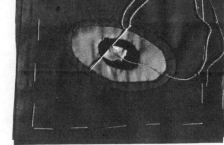
4

Clip the edge of fabric to be turned under on all curves or corners and turn in 1/8″. Using matching sewing thread, slipstitch edge to layer below.

Small appliqués of another colour may be added in one layer as shown above, or in two layers or more using same technique of cutting out to reveal colour.

Felt appliqué

For easy-to-do appliqué, use felt pieces. Since this material does not fray or ravel there is no need to turn the edges under. The pieces are merely pinned in place and slip-stitched to the background. Felt appliqués may be held in place while sewing by applying a few dabs of glue. In keeping with the feeling of felt appliqués, a heavy, textured fabric should be chosen for the background.

Burlap and most upholstery fabrics, for example, make attractive backgrounds for wall hangings. To add interest to the appliqués, use yarn embroidery alone or with rickrack.

Coloured wools for the embroidery combine well with felt appliqué; and sequins and beads can be effectively added for eyes of animals, stamens of flowers etc.

A chart for making the wall hanging is given above. Enlarge it to actual size by copying it on paper ruled in 1″ squares.

A McCALL'S NEEDLEWORK & CRAFTS MAGAZINE FEATURE.

Felt appliqués on a burlap background, designed for a modern setting, are especially suitable for a play room. The foam rubber-filled cushions double as game boards. The wall hanging is red burlap with white felt appliqués and wool yarn embroidery, with bits of white rickrack (flower outlines and base of plants). It was backed with white cotton fabric. The play cushions are also burlap with white felt appliqués and yarn embroidery. They are made with boxing and a zipper and white ready-made welting.

Sewing Machine Embroidery

These entrancing cats are worked directly on the background fabric with a hand-operated sewing machine described as "by way of being an antique, so giving the interesting hoppity-hoppity line." However, you can duplicate these results without owning an antique machine.

This is an ideal type of embroidery for a sewing machine that does only straight stitching. The tension is loosened and a large stitch is used. A zigzag machine may be used, but a little experimenting will have to be done to produce this stitch effect. Using a purely inspirational approach the cats can be stitched "freehand" on tailor's canvas or linen, adding detail and ornamentation ad lib. Or enlarge the drawings below to use as patterns.

Creative readers will want to try original work in the same technique. For those who admire the whimsical results but lack their designer's light touch, we offer on the opposite page directions for embroidering and matting these pictures.

Detail shows wavy stitch line, which adds charm to the finished effect.

The chart below for the two cats and the stars is to be enlarged on ½″ squares to make actual size. Enlarge patterns on tracing paper, which is used in the process of doing sewing machine embroidery.

Sewing machine cat picture

MATERIALS: Pencils. Tracing paper. Ruler. Scissors. Sewing, beading, and embroidery needles. Clark's 'ANCHOR' Machine Embroidery Thread No. 30 to match felt. Clark's 'ANCHOR' Stranded Cotton: **0403**/Black; **0402**/White. For fabric background, tailor's canvas or linen in white or eggshell; size specified below. Felt: dark grey or black for bodies, blue for eyes, contrasting colour for flowers. Gauze or net in a contrasting colour.

DIRECTIONS: Enlarge the patterns by copying on tracing paper ruled in ½" squares. When working the machine-stitched portions, if your machine does only straight stitch, use loose tension and longest possible stitch; if your machine does zigzag stitch, experiment to find a point part way between a straight stitch and a narrow zigzag stitch which approximates line shown in stitch detail opposite.

To make cats and flowers, pin paper patterns for cats to 5" × 9" piece of felt; cut out the two cats. Pin or baste cats in position on 10" × 14" fabric background, and machine stitch twice around each. Hand-embroider noses, mouths, whiskers, and eye outlines, using black stranded cotton (3 strands) and straight stitches. Define eyes by adding felt pupils, seed beads and a few stitches in white stranded cotton between pupil and outline of eye.

Stitch star flowers ad lib to fabric background; three sample shapes are shown on pattern. For each flower, use a circle of felt as a centre and a larger gauze circle in a contrasting colour over it.

Backing Pictures: To back finished picture, cut white cardboard 3" smaller all around than background fabric. Turn 1½" of background fabric over cardboard on all sides and glue.

Matting Picture: To mat picture, cut a mat-frame of desired size from mounting board. Cut an opening for picture ¼" smaller all round than cardboard-backed picture. To support picture in cutout opening, glue narrow strips of mounting board around edge of opening on back of mat-frame; place picture in position face down on mat-frame to gauge exactly where to place these strips. Build up thickness of mat-frame at outer edge so it equals thickness of inner edge: cut four long strips of mounting board and paste completely around back edge of mat-frame.

From mounting board or heavy cardboard, cut a backing same size as mounting board mat-frame. Place picture in position face down on mounting board mat-frame. Apply glue to built up strips. Press the backing firmly in place and allow to dry.

Zigzag sewing machine embroidery

The automatic sewing machines of today have brought a new embroidery art into the home. With the side-to-side swing of the needle, many interesting designs for borders and monograms can be produced in addition to the usual zigzag. Entire pictures can also be created.

Some machines move the fabric back and forth while they stitch from side to side.
A wide variety of interesting stitchery can be done on an automatic machine, and the manual accompanying it will explain this in detail.

Enlarged detail of machine embroidery shows satin stitch outlines and appliqués.
Below are patterns for butterfly wings and bodies, to be enlarged on 1″ squares.

1 RED   2 YELLOW   3 DARK YELLOW
4 GREEN   5 DARK GREEN   6 TURQUOISE
7 BLACK

The silk butterflies shown on the opposite page can be done on a semi-automatic machine, a fully automatic one, or by using a zigzag attachment on a straight stitch machine. The zigzag stitch is worked very closely to produce satin stitch lines and dots to outline and accent the segments of the butterfly wings and bodies.

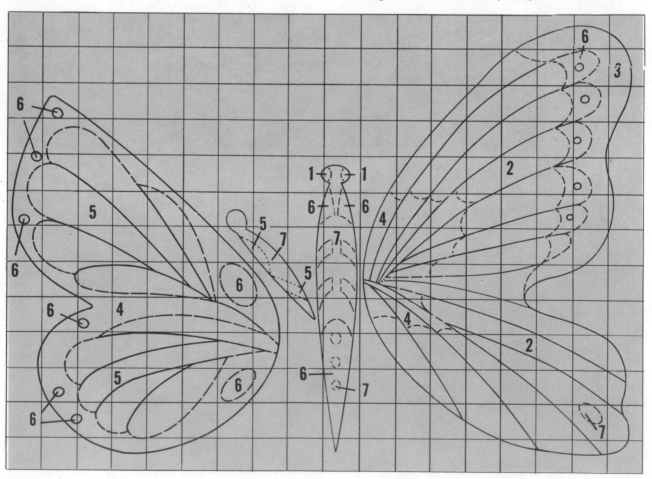

Exotic hued silks are used to make these machine embroidered appliqué butterflies. Wings are interlined and wired for support. The larger of the two butterflies shown here is about 12½″ high. Make several in different sizes and see how well they adapt themselves to a wall grouping.

MATERIALS: Silk fabric, various colours. Clark's 'ANCHOR' Machine Embroidery Thread No. 50:- 1 reel each red 469, Yellow 488 and 445, Green 462 and 776, Turquoise 875 and Black. Heavy Vilene. Medium wire. Tracing paper. Hard and soft pencils. Pins. Small, pointed scissors. Automatic zigzag sewing machine.

DIRECTIONS: Enlarge patterns on opposite page for wings and bodies by copying on tracing paper ruled in 1″ squares.

With soft pencil trace along lines of pattern on wrong side. Pin background silk on Vilene. Using pattern as a guide, pin pieces of different colours of silk as indicated on pattern to top of background silk (dash lines show outline of appliqué pieces, solid lines are stitching lines). Cut appliqué pieces a little larger than sizes on pattern. (If background colour is darker than colour of appliqué, place a piece of Vilene between them to ensure true colour of appliqué.) Now pin pattern securely, right side up, on silk, being sure pattern matches placement of appliqué pieces, and all edges of silk and Vilene are secure. With hard pencil, trace around pattern on appliqué outlines and stitching lines to transfer design to silk. Remove pattern, cut away excess fabric and Vilene around butterfly, leaving a 1″ margin.

With a straight stitch, sew by machine around all solid lines and dash lines to hold silk in place. Trim off silk close to outside line of appliqués (leave extra fabric around butterfly). Set machine for satin stitch and stitch along straight stitching lines, changing width of stitch as you go to form solid lines of varying thickness. Do not satin stitch around outside of butterfly. When all designs inside butterfly have been satin stitched, pull ends of threads through fabric to back and tie. Lay a contrasting colour of silk on back of Vilene, pin in place. Following first straight stitching on front of butterfly (outline), satin stitch around outside. Trim away excess silk and Vilene close to stitching. Make bodies in same manner.

For each butterfly, make an extra plain wing in darker colour for shadow effect. Sew appliquéd wing to matching plain wing at body section; tack body to wings.

FINISHING: To stiffen wings, cut a tiny hole with small, pointed scissors at back of butterfly near inside edge of wing, about ¾ of the way from top, in silk only. Carefully insert wire in hole between silk and Vilene and push wire around top of wing and down other side to opposite point; bend wire to fit outline of wing. Bend a length of wire in half and shape into antenna; paint black. Tack antenna to back of butterfly body.

Huck embroidery

This type of embroidery gets its name from the fabric it is worked on, which is huck towelling, a textured fabric with the raised threads on both front and back. Huck embroidery is actually short for huckaback, and is also known erroneously as Swedish weaving. It can be done with six-strand cotton, pearl cotton, fine wool yarn, or other kinds of embroidery threads. The technique is simply running the thread under the pairs of raised threads on the wrong side of the huck. There are three main types of stitches, shown on this and the two following pages. A blunt needle is used so the pairs of threads can be picked up easily without going through the fabric.

Knots should not be used; weave ends back into the same row of embroidery. Huck weaving can also be done on the right side of the fabric where prominent raised single threads appear. This method would be used if the length of the fabric was required. The pairs of raised threads on the back of the fabric are used across the width of the huck.

You can centre a design on huck by starting the first row at the centre and working to each side. If you are not centring the pattern, start at lower right corner and work across to left.

Bag is worked in basic stitch shown in enlarged detail.

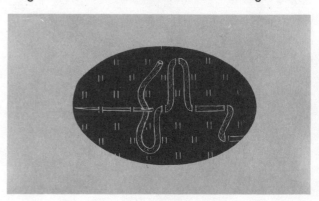

RED HUCK BAG

MATERIALS: ¾ yd. red huck towelling 17″ wide. ¼ yd. lining material 36″ wide. Clark's 'ANCHOR' Stranded Cotton: Amber Gold **0307**/733 (use 6 strands) and Grey **0401**/420 (use 1 strand). 1 yd ¼″ gold braid. Coats Satinised No. 40 to match fabric. Milwards 'Gold Seal' Tapestry Needle No. 21.

DIRECTIONS: Work design on wrong side of huck under pairs of prominent threads.

To Cut: For bag front and back, cut 2 pieces 9½″ across huck and 6″ deep. For heading, cut 2 pieces 8″ across huck and 5½″ deep. For boxing strip around sides and bottom, cut 1 piece 3½″ across huck and 19″ long. Round off the 2 bottom corners of front and back pieces.

To Embroider: This design does not have to be centred, but it will be easier to begin the first row of front and back pieces at bottom in the centre, ¼″ from lower edge, and work to both sides since bottom edge of front and back is curved and border design runs off material. With single strand of yarn in needle, work complete repeat border across huck following chart. Then start next border directly above with bottom of design going through same threads as top of first border design. Work 3 complete borders on front and back pieces. On boxing strip, work a wide border on right side of huck under single prominent threads, starting at lower right-hand corner with 3 top rows of chart; work all the way across. Then directly above, work one complete border across. End with first 3 rows of chart worked above complete border.

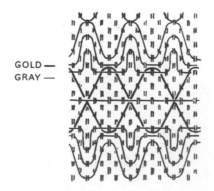

GOLD —
GRAY —

Chart shows one repeat of all over design of bag.

To Assemble: With embroidered sides together, baste boxing to sides and bottom of front and back pieces with ¼″ seams. Clip seam allowance at curves and stitch. Hem side edges of 2 heading pieces and fold in half lengthwise. Turn under top edges of bag and, centring headings, stitch one heading to inside of bag front and one heading to inside of bag back. About 1″ from folded edge of heading make a line of stitching across front and back for casing. Turn under and hem ends of boxing and raw edges at top of bag.

Cut a front, back and boxing from lining material, same as huck pieces, and stitch together. Place inside of bag with wrong sides of lining and bag together. Turn in raw edges of lining and blind stitch at bottom of heading. Make a 1″ tuck at ends of boxing on inside and tack. Run gold braid through casing twice around. Stitch ends of braid together. Pull cords of braid out on each side of bag to close top.

HOT-PLATE MAT

SIZE: 6″×8¾″.

MATERIALS: Red cotton huck towelling, 8″×11″, with 7½ pairs of prominent threads to the inch. Clark's 'ANCHOR' Pearl Cotton No. 5: 0402/White. Milwards 'Gold Seal' Tapestry Needle No. 21. Unbleached muslin. 14″ of round elastic. One piece heavy cardboard, ¼″ thick, or 2 pieces of thinner cardboard. White rick-rack. Coats Satinised No. 40 (White).

DIRECTIONS: Entire mat is worked on every other row of pairs of prominent threads.

Work on wrong side of huck. Draw an oval 7½″ wide x 10½″ long on huck with prominent pairs of threads parallel to 10½″ length. Starting at lower right hand, embroider straight lines across with pearl cotton. Start squirrel design (see chart) about 2½″ from right side and 3″ from bottom, working straight lines of stitches on each side of design to edges of material. After completing squirrel, continue embroidering across in straight lines until work is completed. If coarser huck is used, squirrel design will be larger and must be centred on oval accordingly.

When embroidery is finished, make huck oval into slipcover as follows: Cut a bias strip of muslin 3″ wide and about 24″ long to fit around edge of huck for casing. Hem both ends. Fold muslin in half lengthwise and stitch both raw edges to edge of huck oval with ¼″ seam. At opening of muslin insert elastic with safety pin and pull all the way through casing to other end of opening. Overlap elastic ends and stitch. Cut cardboard oval 6″×8¾″. Put slip cover over cardboard. Centre rickrack around edge, sew on.

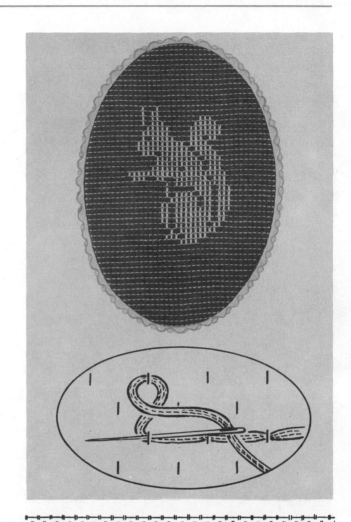

Squirrel design made into an oval table mat and worked entirely in the figure eight stitch as shown in detail above. Follow chart to make squirrel motif with straight rows of thread filling in background.

Huck Embroidery

CHILD'S APRON

MATERIALS: Turquoise huck towelling with seven pairs of prominent threads to the inch, a piece 17″ wide and 15″ long. Clark's 'ANCHOR' Stranded Cotton: 2 skeins Grey 0401/420 (use 6 strands). Coats Satinised No. 40 to match fabric. Turquoise grosgrain ribbon 1″ wide, 1½ yards. Milwards 'Gold Seal' tapestry needle No 21.

DIRECTIONS: Place huck flat, with pairs of prominent threads vertical; cut off a 2″ wide piece across huck for waistband. Cut off end of waistband to make it 10½″ long.

Using full six strands of embroidery cotton in needle, weave six plain rows across waistband, leaving ½″ seam allowance above and below. Turn in ½″ all around waistband and baste.

For skirt of apron follow chart below. Embroider design across skirt, starting 2¼″ from bottom.

If there are no selvages at sides of huck, make ¼″ hems; make a ¼″ hem across bottom. Gather top of skirt in to 9½″. Baste waistband across gathers. Place grosgrain ribbon along back of waistband with even lengths at sides for ties. Stitch waistband to ribbon around all sides.

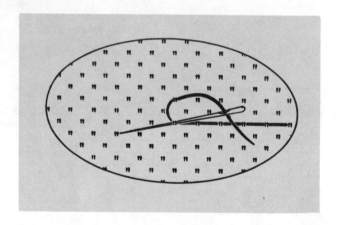

The looped stitch shown in detail on the left is worked in same manner as figure eight stitch. Embroider design, and fill in the background with straight rows of thread. The family of cats, below, is an especially appropriate design for a child's apron.

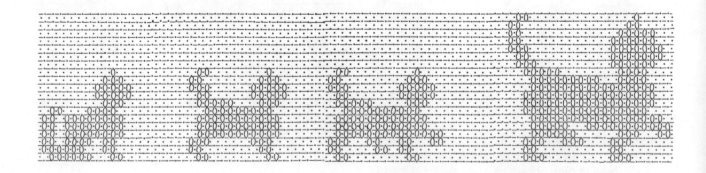

Other fabrics for Huck embroidery

Huck-style weaving done on a variety of smooth textured fabrics opens up possibilities for designing many new patterns. The basic huck weaving stitch is used, with stitches being taken through the material, picking up a few threads of the fabric pattern to form the design. A wide range of effects can be achieved by using different materials—checks, dots, tiny-patterned fabrics. All designs shown are worked in 'ANCHOR' Stranded Cotton (6 strands).

General directions, here and on opposite page.

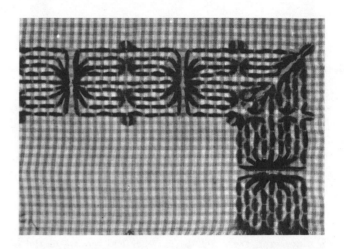

GENERAL DIRECTIONS: The technique used here for embroidering designs on various fabrics is basically the same as huck weaving. However, since the fabrics are generally smooth and have no raised threads to work through, the stitches are taken through the material, picking up a few threads of a dot, check or pattern for each stitch. In huck weaving, the stitches are taken through raised threads and not through the huck fabric. The embroidery thread between these tiny stitches forms the design. Good fabrics to use are diagonal or square checks, dotted Swiss or other dotted cottons, fabric with very close patterns in even or alternating lines, waffle piqué or monk's cloth.

Any huck weaving border chart can be used to embroider designs on checked fabrics, dotted Swiss, piqué, or other tiny-patterned material. On checked fabric like gingham, for instance, every other check represents one stitch as shown on the chart. On fabric with a pattern of smaller checks, every fourth check would represent one stitch. To work on dotted Swiss, use each dot, just as on the charts, because the dots are placed in the same position as the pairs of prominent threads on huck. On waffle piqué, the stitches go through the raised threads of the piqué, but not through the fabric, just as in regular huck weaving.

The border with the corner, top right, is done on a fabric which looks like huck, but has no raised threads. Therefore, each stitch goes through the fabric.

One advantage of using patterned fabrics, rather than huck, is that because there are no vertical raised threads to work through, the stitches can be made in any direction. Therefore corners can be turned and designs worked both horizontally and vertically. Design

Detail shows huck weaving stitch used for all designs on these pages. Stitch goes through fabric, picking up the background check of the material as basis of pattern. It is interesting to note that the same design worked on two different fabrics produces different effects. On dotted Swiss fabric, the design is large and graceful. It is bolder and more striking worked on a fabric of small checks.

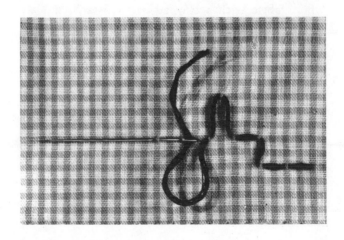

your own corners to go with a straight huck weaving design.

The size of the finished design will vary depending on the size of the checks or dots of fabric used. When working on a two-coloured check, the design can be made small and compact by working first row of stitches in each check of one colour across and next row of stitches in alternate checks of other colour in next row. To enlarge design work stitches in alternating squares of one colour for the first row and in alternating squares of other colour in next row. On one-colour checks, work first row of stitches in every other square and second row of stitches in alternate squares of next row. Dotted fabrics usually have rows of alternate dots, but the size of the design will vary with the spacing of the dots. When planning a definite size for an article such as a place mat, there will be more or less repeats of the border design around all sides depending on the size of checks or spacing of dots in the fabric. Work the repeats of design and corner as nearly as possible to size planned.

Since it is difficult to determine the exact size to cut fabric for finished article with corner motifs, it is best to leave the fabric uncut until the first row of weaving is done. Begin weaving at lower right-hand corner of fabric. Follow the bottom row of chart from corner repeating design along side to next corner, turn chart and work corner. Continue around all sides or as many sides as required.

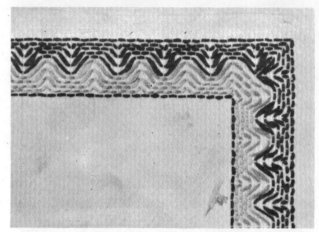

Fabric with a diagonal checked pattern can also be used. Here, as with regular checks, every other check, or more, would be skipped, depending upon the size of the checks. Small checks are shown above. A border with corner was worked on a white fabric with a tiny all-over pattern, similar in appearance to huck. The same design looks quite different (below) when worked on a checked gingham fabric.

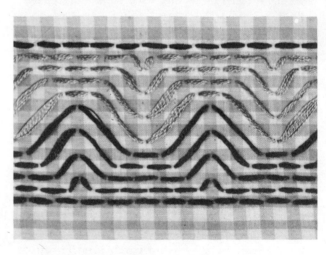

An appliquéd picture done in shades of blue with appliqués of cotton broadcloth slipstitched to a linen background. Note the touches of embroidery in outline stitch, running stitch, straight stitch, lazy daisy stitch and satin stitch. A pattern is given on page 75 for reproducing this picture. Framed size, 18" x 24".

Appliquéd Quilt

During the late 18th century American quilts featuring intricate appliqués were made, but it was not appliqué as we think of it today. Motifs were carefully snipped from imported English chintzes and elegant French toiles—flowers, garlands, and birds—rearranged on a background, and stitched down to form lovely "picture quilts".

By 1850, appliquéd quilts using fabrics in shapes other than those suggested by prints had been developed and popularised. It is interesting to note, however, that flowers and birds continued to be a favourite theme for appliqué.

The Garden Bouquet appliquéd quilt shown here was adapted from a beautiful old quilt. See how to copy an old quilt, Page 92.

Many articles not ordinarily thought of in connection with huck weaving can be made in attractive designs on huck fabric. The baby blanket and stole shown above combine a number of stitches and are worked to cover the huck completely. The outer portion of the baby blanket was worked in pink baby wool on pink huck fabric, while the centre portion was done in white yarn. The stole, embroidered on white huck with green and gold metallic cotton thread, has long fringes at both ends.

Beading: Fabric pictures

Unique pictures to accent a room can be created by stitching coloured glass beads on fabric. Sprinkle bead highlights on large design areas; use beads for colour outlines, and enrich details with clusters of beads. Add depth by padding the wrong side of the printed fabric with absorbent cotton, and quilting on a backing. Beading instructions, together with details, are given below.

Many of today's printed fabrics—designed and sold primarily for other purposes—are eye-catching enough to be used as framed pictures. Some have individual motifs within squares or circles which can be cut apart to make small pictures. Others with a large central motif, even though surrounded by smaller designs, can be scissored to make most attractive pictures, as does the flower print opposite page 97.

The best kind of fabric to use for beading pictures is polished cotton. Large yardage departments carry designs suitable for any room in the house, from game room to nursery. All can be beaded to add richness.

Use either crystal glass seed beads, or opaque glass seed beads, depending on the kind of design being beaded. Small bugle beads, which are oblong, can be added if they suit your design. All these beads come in a great variety of colours, which can match or contrast with the colour of the fabric design.

Before cutting the fabric, study it carefully to determine the best part to use for your picture, and be sure there is enough fabric left around it for mounting on a backing.

Some parts of the design will demand to be filled solidly with beads, while others call for only a sprinkling or an outline of beads. (See detail of bird's head, above.) Use a beading needle and fine thread and sew each bead on separately as shown in the beading details at right. Leaf veins and flower petal edges can be outlined in beads of a deeper tone than the fabric. Try using black or white beads as accents.

If you wish to pad any areas of your picture—individual flowers or figures, for instance—you will need a backing of thin material, such as lawn. Pad the area on back of picture sparingly with absorbent cotton and pin the backing to the wrong side of the picture to hold the padding in place. Then, with thread to match the area and a fine needle, take tiny running stitches around the padded area to make it look lightly puffed.

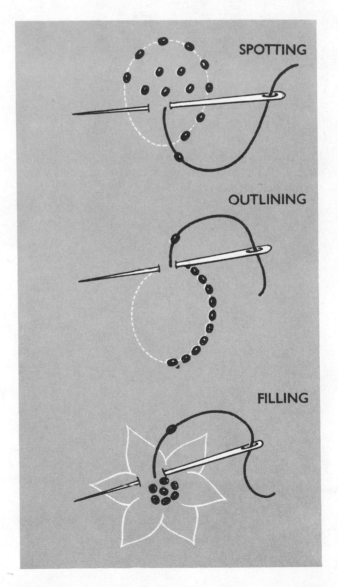

SPOTTING

OUTLINING

FILLING

This well-designed monogram for a knitted garment utilises seed beads, bugle beads, sequins and pearls for massive effect.

Combine seed and bugle beads with sequins for flattering and inexpensive glamour in your wardrobe. You can add chic to hostess slippers or an evening bag by sewing on pearls, sequins or rhinestones. Add them to a collar or combine them to make a bold, handsome monogram similar to the one shown here. Turn a sweater of simple design into an after-five favourite by couching metallic thread to make a flower stem with glittering jewel flowers. Directions given below.

HOW TO ATTACH A SEQUIN: To hide the stitch bring thread up through centre of fabric and sequin, taking care to have the right side uppermost. Pass thread down to back of fabric and up through for next stitch as shown in Fig. 1. Thread a sequin on, and take a backstitch along the same line as shown in Fig. 2. This causes the sequins to overlap and thus hides the stitches. Continue around the outside of any area, then fill in the centre.

TO ATTACH SEQUIN WITH BEAD IN THE CENTRE: Bring thread up through fabric and centre of sequin, then pass through the bead, then carry the thread down through the centre of the sequin again. The bead acts as an anchor to hold the sequin in place. Pass needle through fabric to adjoining space for next sequin and bead, and repeat steps 1, 2 and 3 in Fig. 3.

TO SEW ON BEADS, PEARLS OR SMALL SHELLS: Pearls, round or faceted beads and some shells have two holes opposite each other. Choose a needle slim enough to slide through without splitting the bead and sew on with backstitch. Coats Satinised thread is recommended. Make each stitch just long enough to match the length of the bead. They will thus lie close together on the fabric. An alternate method is to string the beads or pearls and couch on with a second thread. Fig. 4.

Bugle beads are sewn on in the same manner, passing the thread through the hole in the bead as in Fig. 5 or stringing them to couch the strand to the fabric as in Fig. 4.

RHINESTONES OR FLAT FACETED JEWELS have a slot at the back, with sometimes another crossing it. Bring thread up through the fabric and pass through the slot at the back, sewing twice to fasten it firmly.

In sewing beads or sequins on fragile material or on sweaters, place a piece of firmer fabric or crisp muslin underneath to act as a stay support. A transfer design may be marked on tissue paper. Baste tissue in position on right side of material and sew the sequins along design through tissue, material and backing. When finished, tear tissue away close to edge of sequins.

Another method for sewing a bead design on a sweater is to stamp the design on organdie and baste it to right side of sweater. Then the beads are sewn in position through organdie and sweater with backstitch. When completed, cut away organdie.

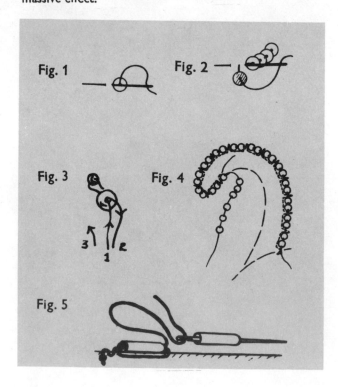

Fig. 1   Fig. 2

Fig. 3   Fig. 4

Fig. 5

3 Quilts

English and Dutch settlers brought quilt-making to America, where it developed into one of the greatest areas of folk art.

The earliest bed covers had prepared homespun backgrounds, pieced, embroidered, or appliquéd. The now rare wool-on-wool coverlets were worked in hooking or a combination of hooking and coarse needlework on wool blanketing. During the 18th century, motifs were cut from patterned chintzes, arranged to form new designs, and appliquéd in place. Simple mosaic patchwork grew into multi-block designs.

The old-time quilting bee was not only a party with a purpose, but a social event as well. Often girls would put their finished quilt tops away until the day friends were invited to a quilting bee—the equivalent of a formal engagement announcement! It was a charming custom for the bride's friends to stitch one block each to make up a "Bride's Quilt," using the best available materials and the finest needlework. They are a valuable source of information about the fabrics and needle arts of their times, and serve as inspiration to today's quilt designers. For quilts are still a favourite project of America's needleworkers, individually and in groups, and are one of the most popular items in art needlework departments.

Copy an Old Quilt

The Garden Basket Quilt is a lovely combination of popular quilt-making techniques: piecing, appliqué, embroidery, and quilting. The nine baskets are pieces of red and green triangles and form a part of a square block with appliquéd and embroidered flowers. These colourful blocks are set diagonally with white blocks.

quilted with Princess Feather wreaths. An appliquéd and embroidered flowering vine encircles the quilt top; a cable-pattern quilted border establishes the line for the scalloped edge.

Patterns and directions for this quilt are on the following pages. Shown in colour opposite page 104.

Above is a diagram showing one quarter of the Garden Basket Quilt, with placing for all appliqué, embroidery, and quilting. Note that diagonal quilting lines of border radiate at the corner.

Garden basket quilt

SIZE: Approximately 80″ × 80″.

EQUIPMENT: Tracing paper. Heavy paper. Cardboard. Ruler. Pencils. Tailor's chalk. Scissors. Needles. Quilting frame.

MATERIALS: Cotton fabric, 36″ wide, such as muslin, percale, cambric, calico, broadcloth, in the following amounts: 5¾ yds. white for quilt top; 6 yds. white for quilt lining; ⅜ yd. red. 1½ yds. light green for basket pieces and appliqués. Clark's 'ANCHOR' Stranded Cotton: Geranium 09/735, 013/831, Carmine Rose 045/839, Canary Yellow 0288/487, Amber Gold 0307/733, Grass Green 0240/496, 0242/497, 0245/500 and Kingfisher 0161/483. Use 6 strands throughout. Coats Satinised No. 40 to match fabrics. 1 Milwards 'Gold Seal' crewel needle No. 5 (for the embroidery). Cotton batting. Quilting thread.

DIRECTIONS: To Make Basket Blocks (Make nine: finished size, 10″ square): Using tracing paper and sharp pencil, trace patterns on pages 94-95, matching indications carefully to make one complete pattern. On back of tracing, go over lines with soft pencil. Place tracing, right side up, on cardboard and go over lines with sharp pencil to transfer.

Cut a piece of tracing paper exactly 10″ square. Place over cardboard pattern with bottom right point of basket at side edge of tracing paper. Trace all lines of basket (not flowers or quilting lines). Place ruler along each side edge of basket tracing; draw line straight up from each side of basket to edge of tracing paper. Block is now divided into its component pieces: one large 5-sided piece at top for flower embroidery and appliqué, eight triangles and one 4-sided piece for basket, two strips at sides of basket, and one triangle below.

Make cardboard patterns of these pieces (only one triangle for basket and one side strip are needed). Basket pieces are cut from red and light green fabric; all other pieces are white. Place cardboard patterns on wrong side of fabric, allowing ½″ between patterns. Mark around patterns lightly with pencil. Cut pieces ¼″ outside markings for seam alowance. Sew pieces together with running stitch to form 10½″ blocks (¼″ seam allowance on all sides). Press pieced sections with seams to one side; open seams weaken construction.

Go over lines on original tracing to make extra dark. Tape tracing to window pane; tape pieced fabric block in place over tracing. With sharp pencil, mark all embroidery and appliqué lines.

Use original tracing to make cardboard patterns for appliqués (two large red flowers at sides, and light green leaves). Cut appliqué pieces from fabric, allowing ⅛″ for turning under. Sew appliqués (see Index) to blocks. Next, work embroidery, following colour key. Work stems in outline stitch, flowers in satin stitch and long and short stitch. Dotted lines on flowers indicate

BORDER PATTERN

KEY

PINK
MEDIUM RED
DARK RED
LIGHT YELLOW
GOLD
LIGHT GREEN
DARK GREEN
LIGHT BLUE
— VERY LIGHT GREEN
---- DIVISIONS IN EMBROID
--- QUILTING STITCHES
— SEAM LINES
ALSQ LEAVES AND BUD
VERY LIGHT GREEN

Three embroidery stitches for Garden Basket Quilt:
Long and short, Satin, and Outline.

dividing lines between groups of stitches. Work satin stitch around edges and at centre of left appliquéd flower.

To Cut and Join Quilt Top: Cut 10″ square piece of cardboard. Place on wrong side of white fabric; mark lightly around. Cut fabric block 1/4″ outside markings; cut four. Cut cardboard pattern in half diagonally; cut eight white fabric triangles from pattern in same manner as blocks. Cut cardboard triangle in half; cut four small white fabric triangles.

Trace "Princess Feather" quilting design, on page 96. Turn paper to complete pattern. Transfer to white fabric squares, triangles as for Basket Blocks.

Assemble centre of quilt top, following placement of blocks and triangles as shown in diagram for quarter of quilt top, on page 92.

Make cardboard pattern of stylised flower motif, p. 96. Place on quilt top as indicated in diagram and mark lightly with pencil. Transfer small vine motifs on Basket Blocks.

Borders: Measure one side of assembled quilt top. Cut two strips that length and 18″ wide (cut 36″ wide fabric in half lengthwise). Sew strips to sides of quilt top. Cut two strips 80″ × 18″ for top and bottom borders. Sew to quilt top. Press seams.

To Embroider and Appliqué Serpentine Border: Enlarge the border pattern on page 93 to actual size by copying on heavy paper, 20″×8″, ruled in 1″ squares.

First, plan placement of long curved appliquéd vine around border. Centre of pattern is centre of border. Repeat design to corners. Dotted lines across vine on pattern indicate corners. Pin paper pattern to border and, using longest stitch in sewing machine and no thread, stitch through vine. Repeat around border. Go over with tailor's chalk. Cut 1″ bias strips of light green fabric; fold in edges 1/4″ on each side; appliqué strips over markings.

Placement of floral designs can be planned in same manner by perforating as many lines as necessary to place appliquéd leaves and embroidered flowers and stems. (Work same as for Basket Block.)

Continued on page 98

Actual-size pattern for quilt block used diagonally in Garden Basket Quilt. Follow directions for using pattern. Colour key indicates colours to be used for pieced basket, embroidery and for appliqué.

PRINCES FEATHER QUILTING DESIGN   REPEAT AROUND TO MAKE COMPLETE CIRCLE

FLOWER MOTIF QUILTING DESIGN

HANGING IS A McCALL'S NEEDLEWORK & CRAFTS MAGAZINE LEAFLET No. 619 N. B

The hen in the wall hanging, in smart decorator colours exemplifies the bold, primitive feeling of the San Blas art. Here six layers of fabric are used and the hanging is backed with one of the colours. A few lines of embroidery were added in outline stitch to accent the feathers and feet of the hen. The small appliqués in cutout spaces are in two and three layers. See page 76.

BEADING: FABRIC PICTURES, SEE PAGE 89 A McCALL'S NEEDLEWORK & CRAFTS MAGAZINE FEATURE.

CABLE QUILTING DESIGN FOR BORDER

To Mark Border for Quilting: Transfer quilting lines of Cable-pattern Border, page 97, and Leaf motifs, below, in same manner as appliquéd vine, using sewing machine and tailor's chalk, following diagram on page 92.

Note that diagonal quilting lines of border radiate at the corner. To plan corner, continue line formed by bottom edge of quilt blocks straight out for 4″. Make a dot at this point. Mark inner edge of cable-pattern border every $\frac{1}{2}$″. Radiate quilting from dot to half-inch marks on cable-pattern border until lines are parallel to quilting on sides.

To Line and Interline Quilt: Cut and sew lining material to make lining same size as top. Place inter-lining over lining; smooth out all wrinkles and creases. Baste together with long basting stitches, starting at centre and sewing towards edge on all sides. Lay top over interlining and smooth. Then baste all three layers together through centre horizontally, vertically, and diagonally. Baste near edges.

Quilting: Quilt in hand, or use a quilting frame. With quilting needle and thread, quilt Princess Feather, Flower, Leaf, Small Vine on Basket Blocks, and Cable-pattern Border motifs. In addition, quilt around lines of embroidery and quilt diagonal lines on border.

To Finish Edge: Cut scalloped edge $\frac{1}{2}$″ beyond outer quilting line. Buttonhole-stitch around edge with white embroidery cotton, or bind edges with bias binding tape.

LEAF QUILTING DESIGN

Patchwork Quilts

Patchwork has been practised by industrious needle-women ever since the first piece of cloth wore out, but not until the middle of the eighteenth century was it developed into the fine household art we know it to be. The diamond patch quilt is considered a patchworker's highest achievement. Before sewing them together, all the many pieces of coloured cloth are cut into regular diamond shapes, and then worked into the design.

It requires accurate piecing so that the finished quilt will lie perfectly flat and even.

Below: Harvest Sun's eight-point star is known by many names—Star of Bethlehem, Lone Star, Star of the West, Rising Sun, and others. The dividing squares are blue, brown, and a rose floral stripe. Tan, blue, red, and brown prints predominate in the border

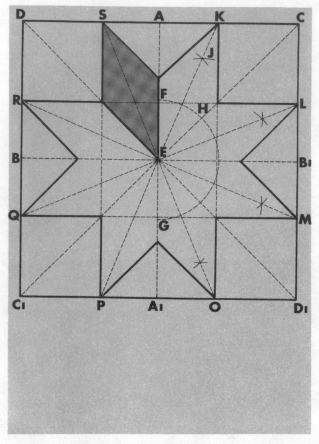

To make diamond pattern in Harvest Sun, cut from paper a square the size of desired centre star (8″ in quilt shown). Quarter, draw diagonals with dotted lines. Compass on centre (E), draw arc FG. With compass on F, then H, bisect angle at J. Repeat three times more on arc. Draw lines through bisection points and centre (E) to opposite side. For star points, draw horizontal and vertical lines RL, QM, SP, KO; draw diagonal lines RO, SM, KQ, LP. (Coloured areas are pattern pieces.)

GENERAL DIRECTIONS: Cut master pattern pieces of thin cardboard; place on wrong side of fabric. Squares and oblongs must be cut with weave; diamonds and right-angle triangles need two sides on straight of goods.

Mark around edges on wrong side with hard pencil. Cut patches ¼″ outside pencilled lines (seam allowance). Hold the patches firmly in place, face to face; seam together with small running stitches on pencilled lines.

If the problem of sharp points and true meeting of seams proves difficult, cut from firm paper patterns exact size and shape of master pattern. Fit firm paper within pencilled lines on wrong side of fabric patch and baste ¼″ seam allowance back over edges of paper. Whip patch pieces together with small over-and-over stitches. It will not matter if stitching goes through the paper; it can be removed as work progresses.

Press pieced sections with seams to one side; open seams weaken construction. When sewing blocks together, make sure all strips are even with one another. They must form a continuous line.

HARVEST SUN: Each of eight star points contains nine diamond patches, four dark and five light. Piece each point separately, then join four points for each half. Join halves, bringing all points together in centre. Light and dark colours alternate in concentric circles. Stars are joined with squares and half-squares. Nine star units, three to a row, comprise body of quilt. Large squares (equal to four corner ones) and half-squares (equal to two, oblong in shape) fit into spaces made by nine pieced stars placed point to point. Smaller squares (size of corner square) fit diagonally into remaining spaces. The border is made of twenty-four pieced diamond patches, six to a side, placed point to point. The same diamond unit and arrangement is repeated as in points of star. For background and to even off border, patches half the size of pieced diamonds are fitted into spaces. Strips of calico, two inches wide, enclose border; four patches fill each corner. Baste quilt top, interlining, and lining together and place in frame. Quilt diagonally in both directions across each square, spacing about ¾″ apart. (Lines may be marked with ruler and white chalk pencil.) Trim edges around quilt and finish with a bias binding in colour preferred.

The evolution of patchwork

The very first pieced quilts were arranged in a crazy quilt or hit-or-miss style, but quilt makers were soon trimming the shapeless scraps into uniform shapes. Hexagons were found to be especially adaptable in making one-patch quilts, and were used in the beautiful early "Mosaic" quilts. Another one patch-design, "Tumbler" contrasts light and dark colours for a cheerful effect.

Next developed was the two-patch design, with diagonally-cut squares or rectangles creating the first true quilt block. "Birds In The Air" is such a pattern. A well-known variation of it, and an example of a four-patch design, is "Flock of Geese". In "Broken Dishes",

triangles are arranged in a four-patch block, then four of these are four-patched again.

The fundamental "Nine-Patch" is simply one block divided into nine equal squares. Variety is achieved by different arrangements of the dark and light squares, or by division of the individual squares. The old "Shoo Fly" pattern illustrates this, while even more intricate variations can be seen in "Duck and Ducklings" (known also as "Hen and Chicks").

Careful colour placement and a greater variety of shapes resulted in more elaborate quilts.

By combining squares and diamonds of different shades, the effect of piled cubes is achieved in "Pandora's

MOSAIC

TUMBLER

BIRDS IN THE AIR

FLOCK OF GEESE

BROKEN DISHES

NINEPATCH

SHOO FLY

DUCK AND DUCKLINGS

THE EVOLUTION OF PATCHWORK

Box." (The same shapes in another shade arrangement produces "Heavenly Steps.") "World Without End" is more complicated in effect because colours are reversed in, alternate blocks, although the shapes are simple triangles, squares, diamonds.

Light and dark squares with circular pieces cut out of corners and transposed create the very popular "Drunkard's Path" and "Steeplechase". "Rob Peter and Pay Paul" seems to "rob" a light square to piece a dark, and vice versa; actually the patches must be larger to allow for seams.

Contrasting rectangles around a central square form the "Log Cabin". Arranging the pieced blocks to form squares, stepping stones, or stairs results in three "different" quilts. No border is used.

A great favourite with experienced quilt makers is the deceptively simple "Double Wedding Ring." Using many different prints for the small wedge-shaped blocks which form the "rings," it is actually an involved arrangement of wedge, square, and melon shapes.

Perhaps the most difficult patchwork quilt is the "Clam Shell" because of its curved shapes. The effect can be obtained by overlapping circles, but traditionally it is made from shell-shaped patches in alternately light and dark rows.

PANDORA'S BOX

WORLD WITHOUT END

STEEPLECHASE

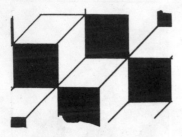

DRUNKARD'S PATH

ROB PETER AND PAY PAUL

LOG CABIN

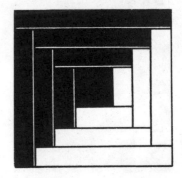

DOUBLE WEDDING RING

CLAM SHELL

Hawaiian Quilts

The first Hawaiian quilting bee took place in Honolulu harbour aboard the brig Thaddeus, when the wives of the New England missionaries gave the Hawaiian women their first sewing lesson. The Hawaiians learned how to sew small pieces together, Yankee fashion, using material from the ragbags which provident missionary ladies had brought with them. It was not long, however, before they adapted the quilting technique to their own circumstances. Since they had worn only grass skirt and flower leis, they had no ragbag resources! Thus they cut their quilting patterns in one large piece from material bought new.

The Hawaiians drew upon their environment for inspiration, just as every other quilt maker has done, and the quilts reflect the beauty of the Islands. The original colours were turkey red on white, known as the "pai ula" or red pattern. The second development was cool green on white, used especially to depict waterfalls, leaves, and trees. Red and yellow were traditionally royal colours, because of the colours of the magnificient old feather capes, so red and yellow became favourite quilt colours.

The design is created in the same manner as for the Snowflake Bride's Quilt, except that only one large central motif is used.

Appliqué the design and a border (if desired) to loosely woven cotton background material, line the quilt with cotton batting, and add the backing material. Devise a pattern of quilting that utilises the curves and lines of the central motif.

Above: A Bride's Quilt, always a welcome wedding present. This one is appliquéd of printed cottons on white blocks. No two of the prints are alike, but they all have the same soft red background. A block in the bottom row is inscribed, "Priscilla Halton's Work, 1849."

Left: Patterns for the lacy "snowflake" designs are made by folding a square of paper in half, then in quarters, and in eighths. Using sharp scissors, cut the folded paper as shown, being careful not to cut into the folds. Cut a variety and select the best ones.

The Garden Basket Quilt, a great favourite of other days, is featured here for ambitious and expert needle-workers to reproduce. This beautiful old quilt was made in New York State around 1835, and is unique in its delicate wool embroidery. See page 93

Homespun Blue Bedspread

Adapted from the heavy English Jacobean work of the same period, the American designs were airier and simpler to embroider—and more appropriate for today's interiors, too!

This Homespun Blue bedspread is typical of the old crewel designs, and is worked in comparatively inexpensive six-strand embroidery cotton rather than the traditional crewel wools.

Crewel embroidery worked in blue-dyed lamb's wool on creamy homespun linen coverlets and valances decorated many an early colonial bed. New England homes often had an indigo tub in their rear kitchens, in which wool was tinted in a great variety of blue tones, inspired perhaps by the lovely Canton blues of the newly-arrived Oriental chinaware.

AN EXAMPLE OF A JACOBEAN HOMESPUN BLUE BEDSPREAD.

Corded coverlet with trapunto roses

EQUIPMENT: Tracing paper. Pencil. Carbon paper. Heavy paper for patterns. Scissors. Needles.

MATERIALS: Two white fabrics, one with a fairly firm weave and the other more open (for lining): about 4½ yards each. (Amount will vary, depending upon width of bed and of fabrics.) Cording, about 40 yards. Absorbent cotton. Clark's 'ANCHOR' Stranded Cotton: 0402/White (use 3 strands for quilting). Coats Satinised No. 40 for making up. 1 Milwards 'Gold Seal' crewel needle No. 6 (for quilting). Bias binding, about 8 yards.

DIRECTIONS: Top: Cut fabrics for coverlet and lining the same length and width as top of bed, plus ⅝" all around for seams. Baste pieces together. Draw diagonals at 6" intervals on lining. Quilt as directed page 107 for Italian or Corded Quilting.

Overhang: Measure one side of coverlet top. Cut two strips each of top and lining fabrics, that same length and 18" wide. Baste pieces together and sew to sides of coverlet top. (For a more finished seam, use welting.) Measure width of coverlet, including overhang on each side. Cut one strip each of top and lining fabrics that same length and 18" wide. Baste pieces together and sew across foot of coverlet and overhang pieces.

Trace pattern for rose, opposite. Using carbon paper, transfer to heavy paper; make several such patterns, so that you can keep designs clean and clear. Transfer one rose centred diagonally to each corner area, on underside of overhang. Space and trace other roses as desired for size of bed. Quilt as directed for Trapunto or Padded Quilting on page 107.

Gentle scallops may be cut at edge of overhang to emphasize rose designs, or overhang may have a straight edge.

Finish coverlet by binding outer edges.

Trace actual-size pattern for Trapunto Rose. Cross-line indications are guides for placing squarely on coverlet overhang and for enlarging or reducing (see Index) if desired for other purposes.

TOP

Above: Quilted White Coverlet made by Maria Kellogg
and her sister as a gift for their mother, Lydia Bouton
Kellogg, circa 1805.

Raised Quilting

Raised quilting uses two layers of fabric but no inter-lining. (If it is to be used for warmth, such as in a robe or quilt, a lining and interlining are added after quilting is completed). There are two methods of doing this quilting. One is Trapunto quilting, in which the design areas are outlined with stitching and stuffed with cotton to make a puff padding. The other method is Italian quilting, in which two rows of stitching are used and a cotton cord or heavy wool yarn is drawn between the rows of stitching to make a raised line. The directions for both methods are given below.

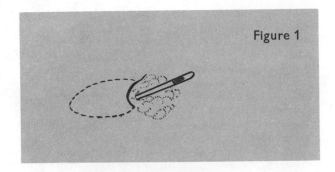

Figure 1

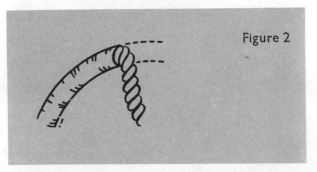

Figure 2

It is best to use designs consisting of small areas, as a large area cannot be padded evenly. Baste together muslin for backing and a fabric such as silk for the top. Mark the design on the muslin backing. Outline all sections of design to be padded with small running stitches through both thicknesses, using matching thread. When design is completely outlined, pad each area separately. To pad, snip a tiny opening in muslin and stuff the area firmly with cotton, using a steel crochet hook or blunt end of a large needle (Fig. 1). Care must be taken to keep padding smooth and even.

Baste together muslin for backing and silk satin, or taffeta fabric for top. Mark design on muslin in double lines. (If cording is to be used for the padding, buy the cord first and plan the double rows of stitching to be spaced just far enough apart to hold cord firmly.) Working on the wrong side, stitch each line, using a fine running stitch through both thicknesses of fabric. When stitching is complete, run cord or heavy yarn through channels made by the double stitching, using a bodkin or large, blunt needle (Fig. 2). Take care not to catch top fabric or go through it, but keep padding in channel. (If using wool yarn, be sure sufficient yarn is used to raise design so it stands out well. It may be necessary to run yarn through channels a second time.) At angles or sharp curves, bring needle out on back, leave a small loop, and insert needle into channel again through same hole and continue (Fig. 3). This will prevent pad-ding from shrinking and pulling when washed.

The work can be done from the right side, if de-sired, and the stitching may be done by machine. Using a thin fabric such as organdie or lawn for the top and bright-coloured yarn for padding produces a lovely soft colouring in the design. (Be sure to use colourfast yarn.)

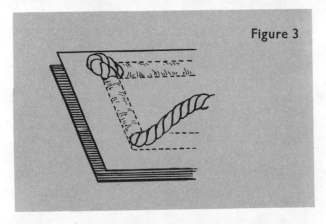

Figure 3

Right: Detail from a coverlet, showing types of raised quilting. Trapunto quilting is used for fruit and leaf areas; Italian quilting makes lines of basket and stems.

Candlewicking

Candlewick embroidery, first used in colonial days to decorate bedspreads, is truly American in origin. In its early period, it was always worked with natural cream-coloured candlewick cotton—from which it took its name—on an unbleached background. At times during its development the French knot and backstitch were used in the embroidery; now the stitch generally associated with this work is a simple running stitch, clipped between stitches to form tufts. White-on-white is still popular, although other colours are also used. Curtains, pillows, bath mats and robes, as well as the traditional bedspreads, feature candlewicking. (Commercially produced chenille fabric closely resembles hand-tufted candlewicking).

Candlewick cotton is a thick, loosely twisted multi-ply yarn; the background fabric should be firm but rather loosely woven, such as unbleached muslin, and not preshrunk—so that washing will tighten to secure candlewicking in fabric. Special candlewicking needles or large-eyed darning needles are used. A candlewicking needle has a thick shaft, large eye, and may be curved or slightly widened at the point. Double-eyed needles are used for extra-large, thick tufts.

Almost any kind of design is suitable, from flowers and scallops to geometric straight-line designs. Candlewicking may outline the design, fill in some areas, or cover the background solidly.

Mark the pattern and work on the right side.

Thread a long length of candlewick cotton in the needle, pulling ends even so thread is double. To start, pick up a few threads of fabric on right side and draw candlewick through until a short end remains as a small tuft. Make even running stitches about ½″ apart, picking up only a few threads with each stitch, and leaving cotton between stitches loose. End with cotton on right side of fabric, clipping off to make small tuft. When stitching is completed, clip cotton at centre between each stitch. The cut strands of cotton fluff up, making tufts. If stitches are taken close together,

tufting will be in a continuous line; to spot tufts, space the stitches further apart and trim tufts to size.

Shrinking fabric to hold tufts securely is the finishing touch in candlewicking. If a washing machine is used, wash in warm, soapy water for at least twenty minutes. If washing by hand, let soak for three or four hours. Shake out; do not squeeze or wring. Hang in the sun to dry—if it is a windy day, so much the better. Lightly brush tufts before they are quite dry to fluff them. Do not iron a candlewick spread—the crinkly look is characteristic.

This beautifully designed bedspread is a handsome example of candlewick embroidery as it was done in 1825, when the tufts were often left uncut. Then, as now, the eagle of the Great Seal of the United States was a favourite motif of needleworkers.

THE METROPOLITAN MUSEUM OF ART. GIFT OF JANE A. EVERDELL, IN MEMORY OF CORNELIA AUGUSTA CHAPMAN EVERDELL, 1923.

Quilting and Tufting

After the quilt top is finished, it is quilted or tufted. This serves the practical function of holding the layers of fabric and padding together, as well as providing additional decoration.

To prepare for quilting, spread the quilt top out carefully, face down, on a large, flat surface. Arrange wadding on top and tack at intervals. Add lining and smooth in place. Pin the three layers together, then baste at intervals of about 6″.

Select your quilting design carefully to suit the top. If you plan to follow the design of the piecing or appliqué, work from the right side. If there is a pattern to be drawn or transferred on to the lining, then work from the wrong side. The designs shown here are some of the more popular and some of the easiest ones to do. They should be enlarged to three or four times the size shown (see Index, "Enlarging or Reducing Designs"). Border designs are to be traced around the outside, with all over quilting in the centre.

Quilting designs can be marked in several ways. Probably the simplest method is to make perforated patterns. Trace the pattern on wrapping paper and machine stitch along lines of the design, with the machine needle unthreaded. The design is marked on the quilt by laying the perforated pattern on the quilt lining, rough side down, and rubbing stamping powder through the perforations.

Quilting can be done in hand or using a quilting frame. If a frame is used, sew top and bottom edges of quilt to fabric strips attached to long parallel bars of frame. Sew securely with several rows of stitches, using strong thread, so that quilt will not pull away from frame when stretched taut.

The quilting stitch is a short even running stitch. There are two methods of making it. One is done in two separate motions, first pushing the needle down through the three thicknesses, then pushing it up again close to first stitch. One hand is always held under the quilt to guide the stitch; stitches should be of equal length on both sides. The second method is to take two or three little stitches before pulling needle through, holding quilt down at quilting line with thumb of one hand. (Tape this thumb to prevent soreness.) If you are a beginner, practise quilting a small piece in an embroidery hoop to find the easiest and best way for you to work.

The usual quilting needle is a short, sharp needle— No. 8 or 9—although some experienced quilters prefer a longer one. Coats Satinised No. 40 (White) or Clark's 'ANCHOR' Stranded Cotton 0402/White. Use 2–3 strands, according to weight of fabric. Start quilting midway between the long parallel bars of frame, and sew towards you. To begin, knot end of thread. Bring needle up through quilt and pull knot through lining so it is imbedded in interlining. To end off, make a single backstitch and run thread through interlining.

If you wish to tuft rather than quilt, use several layers of wadding between the top and the lining. Mark evenly spaced points on the top surface with tailor tacks or pins. Thread a candlewick needle with candlewick yarn, or use a large-eyed needle with double knitting wool. Using thread double, push needle from top through layers to back, leaving thread end on top. Push needle back up again to surface, about ¼″ away. Tie yarn in firm double knot. Clip ends to desired length (at least ½″) to form tuft.

Simple quilting designs, to be enlarged three or four times size shown here.

4 Knitting

The origin of knitting is lost in the mists of antiquity. The earliest knitters were probably a nomadic race living in the desert palaces of North Africa. They knitted tent flaps whose decorative colour patterns formed part of the magic that surrounds their lives. The knitted symbols on the flaps were supposed to frighten away the evil spirits.

The shepherds tending their flocks — the fishermen watching their nets, formed the background to the historic development of the knitters' craft, and the fishermen have left us a magnificient legacy in the traditional sweaters of the ports where they laboured, known as 'bridal shirts'.

Knitting was carried to the Mediterranean countries by the early Phoenician traders and had firmly established itself in England by the reign of Edward IV, as an Act passed at that time imposed a tariff on knitted sleeves imported from France.

Knitting was a man's craft until towards the end of the sixteenth century when the economic changes, that were to lead to the industrial revolution three centuries later, changed the whole background of family and social life.

From roughly the year 1600 women commenced knitting in the home, and children in the poor houses and charity schools were forced to knit for as long as sixteen hours a day.

The craft has a very rich heritage. Rural communities in all parts of the world have enriched and enhanced the craft with their traditional stitches and colour patterns, some of which are included in the garments in the following pages.

JAMES NORBURY

Knitting Needles and Accessories

**COMPARABLE TABLE OF AMERICAN
AND ENGLISH NEEDLE SIZES**

ENGLISH NEEDLES

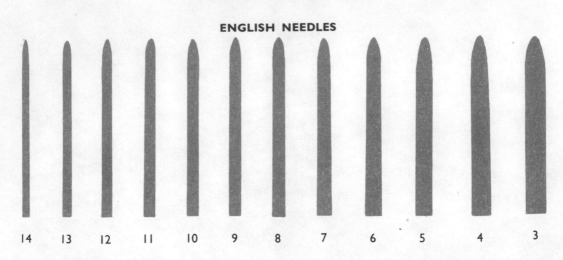

14   13   12   11   10   9   8   7   6   5   4   3

AMERICAN NEEDLES

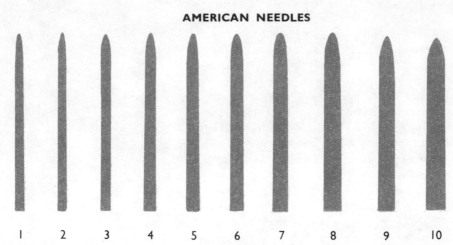

1   2   3   4   5   6   7   8   9   10

Comparison of English and American sizes of needles with corresponding numbers above each other.

BRITISH.   1   2   3   4   5   6   **7**   8   9   10   11   12   13   14

AMERICAN.   8   9   10   11   12   13   14

Sets of four steel needles numbered as British.

16   15   14   13   12   11   10   9   **8**   **7**   6   5   4   3   2   1

Pairs of needles numbered as Continental.

No. 7 is the same size in each method of numbering.

The Boatneck Pullovers shown opposite get their distinction from "Swedish Weave" stripes which are made by weaving in yarn as you knit. For directions, see page 174

Knitting needles with single points are sold in pairs and are made in a wide variety of substances and in selecting them the knitter should look for a needle that has a smooth finish and short tapered points. It is advisable when buying needles to make sure that the size is clearly marked on the needle itself and to always check the size of your needle carefully before commencing any piece of work.

Needles with points at both ends are sold in sets of four and are generally used for knitting in rounds for socks, mittens, and gloves. They are always used in the neckbands of sweaters when there is no back or front opening in the garment.

Circular needles, that some knitters prefer for skirts and dresses, are available in most standard sizes and in lengths varying from 9—36 inches. In using a circular needle the knitter has to be very careful in maintaining a correct tension; as when the stitches move off the point to the finer part of the circular needle it is very easy to tighten up the stitches and this produces an uneven fabric.

Among the accessories that every knitter ought to have in her work box are stitch-holders, cable needles and a knitting needle gauge to check the size of her needles if she's doubtful as to whether they are the correct ones to use for any particular piece of work. A tailor's inch tape, that is re-inforced with metal for 3 or 4 inches along the end, will be found the best type to use when measuring pieces of knitted fabric.

Never put your knitting away without finishing the row you are working on, because if you leave it in the middle of a row you may find unevenness in the fabric when your work is completed. If you are going to have to put it away for some time, do not leave the stitches on the needle but slip them on to a length of coloured wool, placing them back on the needle again when you are ready to carry on with the piece of fabric you are knitting.

Knitting Lesson for Beginners

There are only two basic stitches in knitting; a KNIT stitch and a PURL stitch, all patterns are simple variations on these two stitches. The first thing a knitter must do is cast on the number of stitches stated in the instructions on which she is working. After you have finished each piece of the knitting it is necessary to cast off the stitches so that the fabric will not unravel. On the following pages, step by step instructions with illustrations and directions of how to cast on, how to knit, how to purl and how to cast off are given.

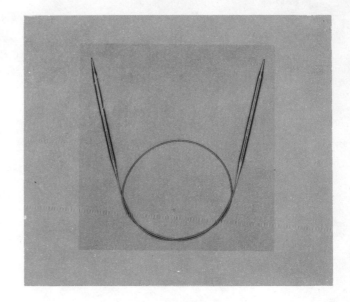

Circular needles, illustrated on the right, are available in most standard sizes, and in lengths varying from 9—36 inches.

A Novelty Stitch Pullover to make for a young miss depends on tone-on-tone for its unusual effect. Make the sweater and hat following the instructions on page 175.

TO CAST ON WITH ONE NEEDLE

1. For the practice piece of fabric you are going to knit you will need a ball of Patons Double Knitting and a pair of No. 8 Beehive knitting needles.

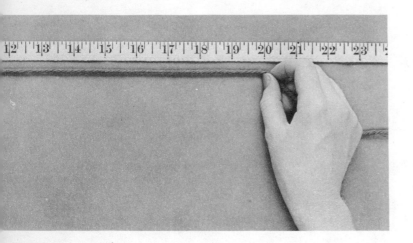

2. Measure off 20 inches from the end of the wool to cast on 20 sts.

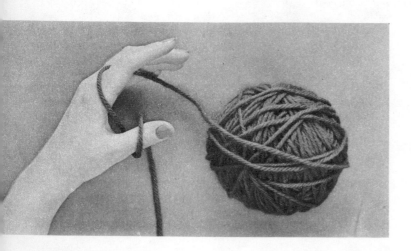

3. Bring end of wool from ball over left index finger. Bring other end of wool under and over the thumb.

4. Holding needle in right-hand insert point of needle from left to right through the loop on the thumb.

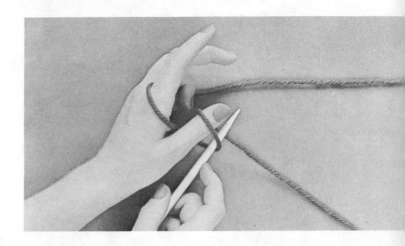

5. Hold both strands of wool with three fingers of left-hand. Insert point of needle under strand on index finger.

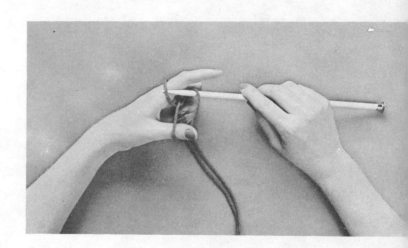

6. Bring the strand towards you and through loop on thumb. Remove thumb from loop.

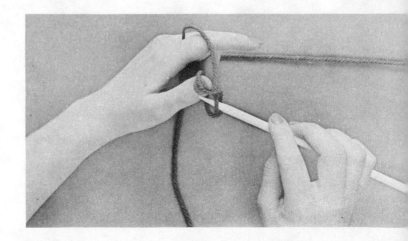

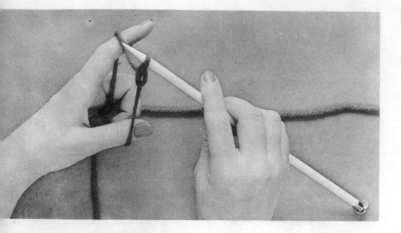

7. Place thumb under strand of wool nearest to you. Pull gently until slip knot is close to needle.

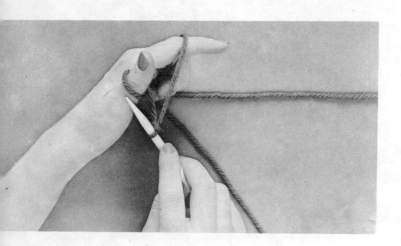

8. With thumb back, bring needle to front of thumb and to left of strand of wool, thus forming a loop on thumb.

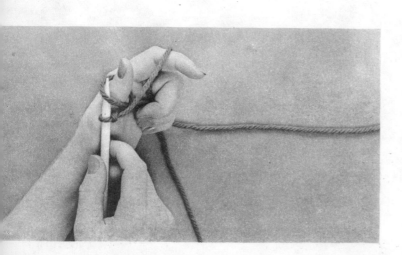

9. Holding both strands of wool, insert point of needle from left to right through loop on thumb.

10. Pick up strand on index finger, pass through loop on thumb, removing thumb at the same time.

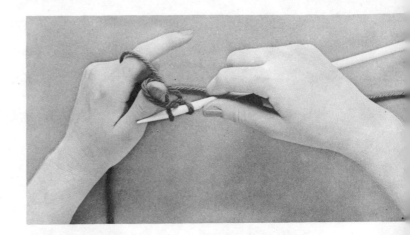

11. Place thumb under front strand as before and tighten second stitch so that it lies close to the first stitch on the needle.

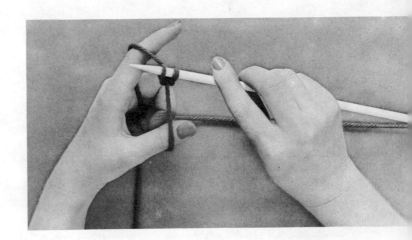

12. Repeat these actions until you have cast on 20 stitches. Place the casting-on needle in the left hand.

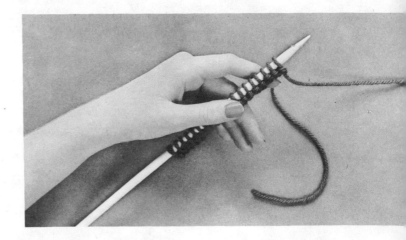

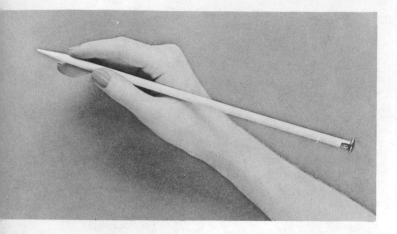

HOW TO KNIT A STITCH

13. The needle with which you are going to knit is held in the right hand in the same way in which you hold a pencil.

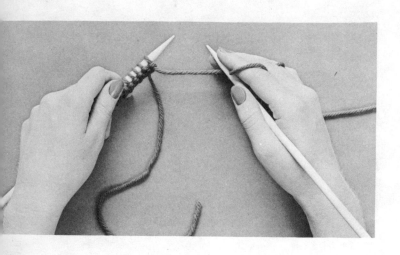

14. Wrap wool over index finger of right hand, under middle finger, over third finger and under little finger. Do not hold the wool tightly as it must pass smoothly and easily through the fingers when you are knitting the fabric.

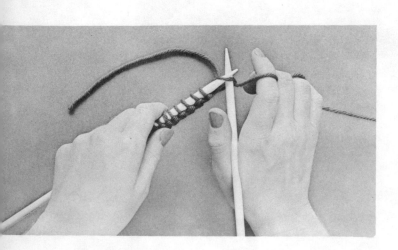

15. To knit the first stitch, insert point of right-hand needle into the front of stitch on the left-hand needle from left to right.

16. The point of the right-hand needle now lies behind the point of the left-hand needle, bring wool under and over the point of the right-hand needle.

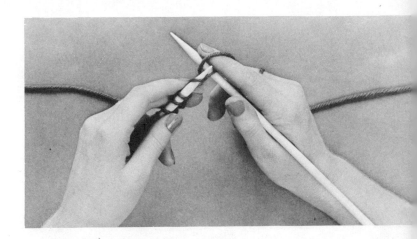

17. Bring point of right-hand needle down and under the left-hand needle to the front, thus drawing loop on right-hand needle through stitch.

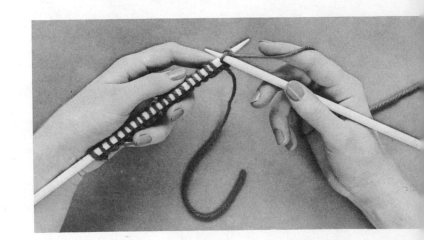

18. Slip the stitch, through which you drew the wool, off the left-hand needle. You have now knitted one stitch.

19. Insert the point of the right-hand needle into the point of the next stitch, and repeat the actions as before thus knitting the second stitch. Knit off the remaining stitches in the same manner.

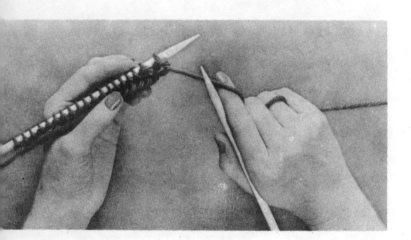

20. When row is finished turn work round, place it in the left hand and knit another row in the same manner.

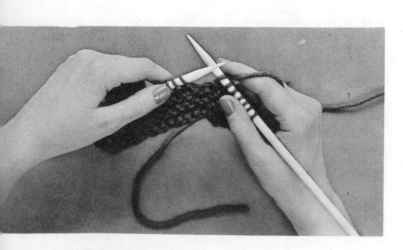

21. Continue knitting rows of stitches thus forming plain knitting, usually called Garter Stitch. The fabric as you can see from the photograph has a ridged surface.

TO PURL

22. Bring the wool to the front of the right-hand needle.

23. Insert point of right-hand needle from right to left through the front of the first stitch on the left-hand needle.

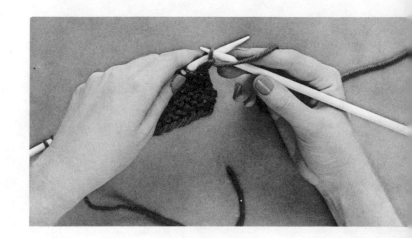

24. Bring wool back between the points of the needles, then bring it down under the point of the right-hand needle to the front of the needle.

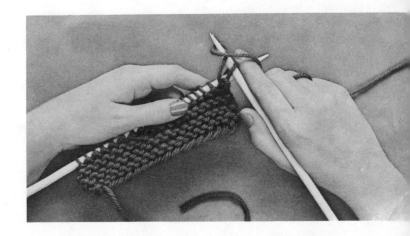

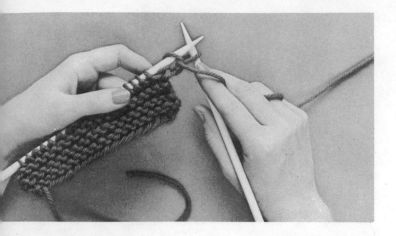

25. Bring the point of the right-hand needle back through the first stitch. The point of the right-hand needle is now behind the point of the left-hand needle.

26. Slip the loop through which you drew the wool off the left-hand needle. One purl stitch is on the right-hand needle.

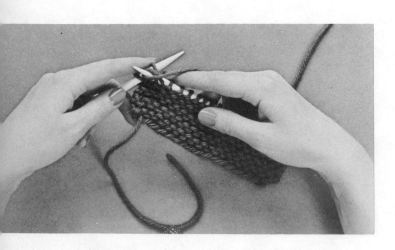

27. Continue across the row until you have purled off all the stitches. By working in alternate rows of purl and knit you produce Stocking Stitch. The fabric on the photograph shows the reverse side of stocking stitch.

28. Using two No. 8 Beehive needles and Patons Double Knitting, cast on 22 sts. Work 30 rows, knitting the first row and purling the second row, continuing in this manner until the 30 rows are completed. You will have now produced a 4-inch square of Stocking Stitch as the tension of Double Knitting on a size 8 needle is $5^{1}/_{2}$ stitches and $7^{1}/_{2}$ rows to one square inch measured over stocking stitch (see page 126).

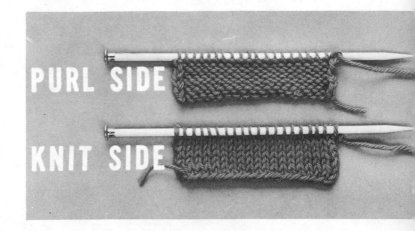

HOW TO CAST OFF

29. Knit the first two stitches. Insert the point of the left-hand needle from left to right through the front of the first stitch (second stitch on the right-hand needle).

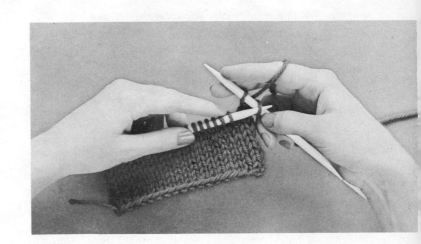

30. Lift the first stitch over the next stitch and over the point of the needle. One stitch has been cast off.

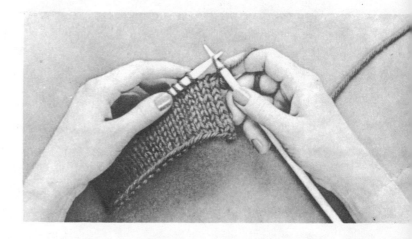

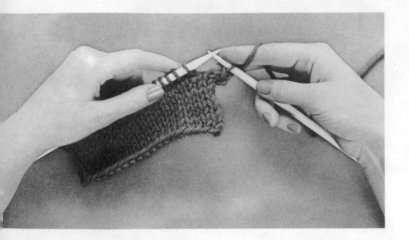

31. You will now have one stitch on the right-hand needle. Knit the next stitch on the left-hand needle. There are now two stitches on the right-hand needle again.

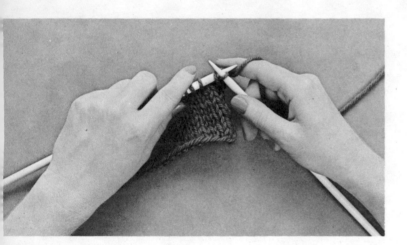

32. Once again lift the first stitch over the second stitch and off the right-hand needle. Two stitches have now been cast off.

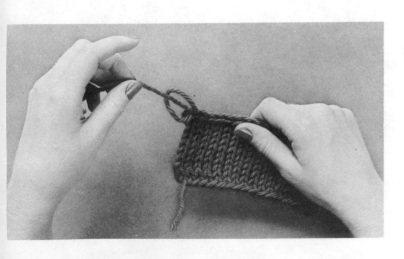

33. Continue working in this manner until all the stitches are cast off. When they are all cast off one stitch will remain on the right-hand needle. Cut off the wool, draw the end through the loop and draw up the loop.

OTHER METHODS OF CASTING ON STITCHES: The most simple one-needle method is illustrated and the working method shown in diagrams 1–5 below.

Fig. 1. Make a slip loop and place it on the point of the needle.

Fig. 2. Loop wool round left thumb.

Fig. 3. Insert needle in loop.

Fig. 4. Remove thumb.

Fig. 5. Pull wool to tighten stitch formed on needle.

The thumb method of casting on is shown in diagrams 6 and 7. Commence with a slip loop leaving a length of wool at the end allowing one inch for each stitch to be cast on. If for example you are casting on 50 stitches you will need a length of 50 inches before the loop. Hold needle with slip loop in the right hand. * With short end of wool make a loop on left thumb, then by bringing wool up around thumb from left to right (Fig. 6), insert the point of the needle in the loop from left to right (Fig. 7) bring wool from ball, under and over the needle, draw through loop on the thumb, tighten the short end with the left hand, from * until the required number of stitches have been cast on.

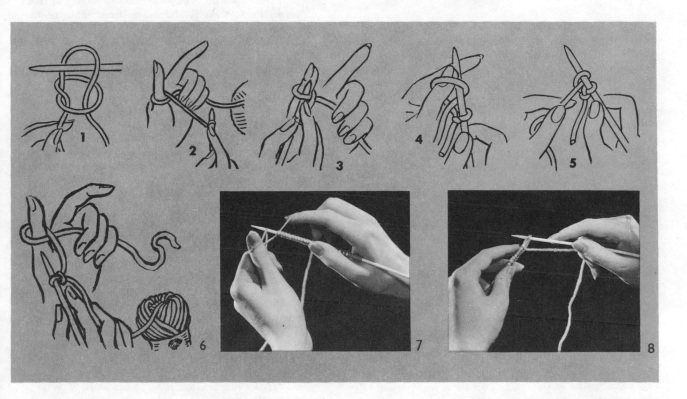

THE TWO NEEDLE METHOD OF CASTING ON: Make a slip loop over the left needle. * Pass point of right-hand needle through loop from left to right, wrap wool under and over point of right needle. Draw wool through loop and transfer loop on right needle to left needle by inserting point of left needle to loop from right to left (Fig 8). Repeat from * until required number of stitches have been cast on.

Whatever method of casting on you are using it is essential to maintain a loose edge otherwise you will find there is no elasticity in the cast on edge and this is essential in all knitted garments.

THE RIGHT WAY TO CAST OFF: Casting off is usually worked in the pattern stitch of the fabric used in the garment. That is, each stitch to be cast off is worked in the same way as it would be in the pattern. Unless you are told in the knitting instructions you are using "to cast off tightly" or "to cast off loosely," the cast-off edge should be the same tension as the knitting. The easiest way to cast off tightly is to use a size finer needle than the one you are working on. The easiest way to cast off loosely is to use a size larger needle than the one you are working on.

A SIMPLE GUIDE TO KNITTING TERMS:

Inc.—Increase one stitch by knitting into the back and then into the front of the next stitch before slipping the stitch off the needle.

M. 1.—Make one by picking up the loop that lies between the stitch just worked and the following stitch, place the loop on the left-hand needle and knit into the back of the loop.

The other principle is worked in three different ways:

W. fwd – Wool forward and consists of taking the wool over the point of the right-hand needle before continuing the pattern.

W. R. N.—Wool round needle and is generally used between two purl stitches. The wool being taken round the point of the right-hand needle before continuing in pattern.

Sl.—Slip a stitch. This is done by slipping the point of the right-hand needle through the next stitch on the left-hand needle as though to purl a stitch and then drawing the stitch off the left-hand needle.

K. 2 tog.—Knit two together by slipping the point of the right-hand needle through the next 2 stitches over the left-hand needle and knitting them as though they were one stitch.

P. 2 tog.—Purl two together by slipping the point of the right-hand needle through the next 2 stitches on the left-hand needle as though to purl them and purling off the two stitches together.

P. S. S. O.—Pass slip stitch over. This abbreviation is used where you are going to pass a slip stitch over one or more stitches as directed in the pattern.

K.—knit; **P.**—purl; **K. B.**—knit into back of stitch; **P. B.**—purl into back of stitch; **st.**—stitch; **sts.**—stitches **sl.**—slip; **sl. 1 P.**—slip 1 purlwise; **W. fwd**—wool forward; **W. ft.**—wool front-bring wool to front of needle; **W. b.**—wool back-take wool to back of needle; **w. r. n.**—wool round needle; **y. r. n.**—yarn round needle; **w. o. n.**—wool on needle; **p. s. s. o.**—pass slip stitch over; **tog.**—together; **t. b. l.**—through back of loops; **inc.**—increase; **dec.**—decrease; **beg.**—beginning; **alt.**—alternate; **rep.**—repeat; **patt.**—pattern; **ins.**—inches; **incl.**—inclusive; **O.**—No stitches, rows or times; **M. 1.**—Make 1; **M. 1P.**—Make 1 purlwise by picking up loop that lies between stitch just worked and following stitch and purling into back of it; **C. 2F.**—Cable 2 Front by working across next 4 sts. as follows:—Slip next 2 sts. on to cable needle and leave at front of work, knit next 2 sts., then knit 2 sts. from cable needle; **C. 2B.**—Cable 2 Back as C. 2F. but leave sts. at back of work in place of front; **C. 3F.**—Cable 3 Front by working across next 6 st. as follows:—Slip next 3 sts. on to cable needle and leave at front of work, knit next 3 sts., then knit 3 sts. from cable needle; **Tw. 2.**—Twist 2 by knitting into front of 2nd st., then front of first st. on left-hand needle and slipping 2 sts. off needle together; **Cr. 1B.**—Cross 1 Back by slipping next st. on to cable needle and leaving at back of work, K. B. 2, then P. 1 from cable needle; **Cr. 2F.**—Cross 2 Front by slipping next 2 sts. on to cable needle and leaving at front of work, P. 1, then K. B. 2 sts. from cable needle; **ch.**—chain; **s. c.**—single crochet.

MULTIPLE SIZES OF ONE DESIGN: Where instructions are given for the same garment in several sizes the first figure refers to the first size and the figures in round brackets ( ) to the following sizes. Care must always be taken to check that you are using the right set of figures in the bracket for the size you are knitting from the instruction.

JOINING IN THE WOOL: It is always advisable to join in new wool at the beginning of the row. Tie the end of the new ounce of wool with a slip knot round the end of the ounce of wool you have completed using, draw the slip knot up to the point of the needle and continue working with the new ounce of wool. When the piece of the garment you are making has been completed, run in the ends along the edge of the fabric before making up the garment.

Tension is a word that terrifies the majority of knitters and yet it is a word that signifies the correct number of stitches and rows to a square inch of knitted fabric, thus controlling the size and shape of each piece of the garment. To check your tension for any design, first of all look at the number of stitches stated to the inch, if the number stated is 5 stitches on No. 6 needles, using a size 6 needle and the same wool you are going to make the garment in, cast on 20 stitches, $20 \div 5 = 4$ inches. If the row tension is $6\frac{1}{2}$ rows work 26 rows in stocking stitch. $26 \div 6\frac{1}{2} = 4$ inches. Lightly press the square of fabric and when you measure it, it should be exactly 4 inches.

If you want to check the tension of the piece of fabric on the garment you are knitting, lay the fabric on the table. Place an inch tape along a row of stitches and mark one inch on the inch-tape with two pins, count the number of stitches between the two pins and this will give you the number of stitches you are working at to the inch. To check the row tension lay the inch tape from the top to the bottom of the fabric, mark one inch with pins as before and count the number of rows between the pins, this will give you the number of rows you are working to the inch. If your tension is too loose try a size finer needle, if your tension is too tight try a size coarser needle.

GAUGE: All knitting directions for garments include a stitch gauge. The stitch gauge gives the number of stitches to the inch with the yarn and needles recommended in the pattern stitch of the garment. The directions for each size are based on the given gauge. The gauge (or tension) at which you work controls the size of each finished piece. It is therefore essential to work to the gauge given for each garment if you want the garment to fit. To test your gauge, cast on 20 or 30 stitches, using the needles specified. Work in the **pattern stitch** for 3″. Smooth out your swatch and pin it down. Measure across 2″ and place pins 2″ apart as shown. Count number of stitches between pins. If you have **more** stitches to the inch than directions specify, you are knitting too tightly; use larger needles. If you have **fewer** stitches to the inch, you are knitting too loosely; use smaller needles.

Most patterns give a row gauge too. Although the proper length of a finished garment does not usually depend upon the row gauge (directions usually give lengths in inches rather than rows), in some patterns it is important to have the proper row gauge too.

TO PICK UP DROPPED STITCH: Use a crochet hook. In stocking stitch, from knit side of work, insert hook through loop of dropped stitch from front to back of work, hook facing upward. *Pull horizontal thread of row above stitch through loop on hook; repeat from * to top.

TO UNRAVEL KNITTING: When it is necessary to undo work and then pick up stitches again, remove needles from work. Rip down to row of error. Rip this row stitch by stitch, placing each stitch (as if to purl) on a fine needle. Then knit these stitches on to correct size needle.

TO PICK UP AND KNIT STITCHES ALONG EDGE: From right side of work, insert needle into edge of work, put yarn around needle, finish as a knit stitch. When picking up on cast-off or cast-on edge, pick up and knit 1 stitch in each stitch (going through 2 loops at top of each cast-off stitch). On front or side edges, pick up and knit 1 stitch in each knot formed on edge of each row.

TO CHANGE FROM ONE COLOUR TO ANOTHER: When changing from one colour to another, whether working on right or wrong side, pick up the new strand from underneath dropped strand. This prevents a hole in your work. Carry the unused colour loosely across back of work. Illustration shows wrong side of work with light strand being picked up under dropped strand in position to be purled.

TO COUNT STITCHES WHEN CASTING OFF: At the beginning of a row, when directions read 'cast off 7 sts,' knit 2 stitches; 1 insert left needle under first stitch on right needle and lift it over the second stitch. This is 1 stitch cast off. Knit 1 more stitch and repeat from *

MEASURING YOUR GAUGE

CHANGING COLOURS

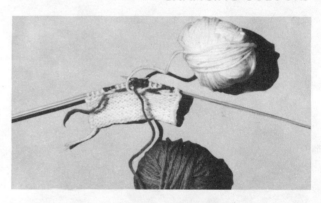

6 times-7 stitches cast off (8 stitches have been knitted to cast off 7 stitches but 1 stitch, already knitted, is on right needle).

When casting off within a row (as for buttonholes), knit the required number of stitches to point of casting off, then knit next 2 stitches to cast off first stitch. Cast off required number of stitches (1 stitch is already knitted after cast-off stitches). When directions read 'knit until 7 sts after cast-off stitches,' this means to knit 6 more stitches or until there are 7 stitches after cast-off stitches.

TO INSERT MARKERS: When directions read 'sl a marker on needle,' put a small safety pin, paper clip, or commercial ring marker on needle. In working, always slip marker from one needle to another. To mark a row or stitch, tie contrasting thread around end of row or stitch.

TO MEASURE WORK: Spread piece on flat surface to required width, measure length at centre.

WORK EVEN: This term means to work in same stitch without increasing or decreasing.

THE LEFT-HANDED KNITTER: Knitters who are left-handed often wonder whether they need use a different technique to the ordinary right-handed person. The answer is "No". In following the diagrams showing the method of knitting in the earlier pages of this book,

all you need to remember is that all the actions in the diagrams carried on by the right-hand are carried on by the left-hand, while all the left-hand actions are performed by the right-hand. The method of casting on, of knitting and purling are identical once this change over of hand positions has been mastered.

If you are still finding the diagram difficult to follow, then place a mirror along the lower edge of the diagram and you will find that the reflected diagram in the mirror has automatically reversed the right-hand method diagram in the book to left-hand method diagram for the left-handed knitter.

INTERCHANGEABILITY OF WOOLS: The Paton's Wools recommended throughout this section of the book are obtainable all over the United Kingdom.

If for any reason you desire to substitute the wool stated for some other wool or yarn, the important thing is to check the tension of the new yarn as it must knit to the same tension as the one specified if the garment you are knitting is to be the correct size when it is completed.

Unless you are an expert yourself, and have a basic knowledge of how to design hand knitted garments, you will be well advised not to try and alter the instructions to suit a different type of wool altogether than the one used in the original garment. In the range of Paton's Wools and Yarns the following list shows you the wools and yarns that knit to the same tension. In some cases the yardage to the ounce varies, that means you may need more or less of the wool or yarn you are substituting for the one specified for the design you are knitting.

3-PLY

WOOLS—PATONS BEEHIVE 3-PLY, Patonised, PATONS PURPLE HEATHER 3-PLY. Wool and Nylox = PATONS 3-PLY NYLOX.
SYNTHETIC YARN—PATONS 3-PLY BRILLIANTE 100 % BRI-Nylon.

4-PLY

WOOLS—PATONS BEEHIVE 4-PLY, Patonised, PATONS PURPLE HEATHER 4-PLY.
Wool and Nylon = PATONS 4-PLY. NYLOX.
SYNTHETIC YARN—PATONS 4-PLY BRILLIANTE 100 % Bri-Nylon. PATONS IOI COURTELLE 4-PLY SOFT KNIT

DOUBLE KNITTINGS

WOOLS—PATONS TOTEM Double Crepe, PATONS DOUBLE KNITTING, PATONS MOORLAND Double Knitting.
SYNTHETIC YARN—PATONS BRILLIANTE Double Knitting 100 % Bri-Nylon. PATONS IOI COURTELLE DOUBLE CREPE, PATONS 101 COURTELLE DOUBLE KNITTING.

Pattern for the woman's two tone sweater in double-knitting wool, illustrated on the left, is on page 147

Knitted Pattern Stitches

1. BASIC K. 2, P. 2 rib (Multiple of 4 + 2)

1st row— * K. 2, P. 2, rep. from * to last 2 sts., P. 2.
2nd row— * P. 2, K. 2, rep. from * to last 2 sts., K. 2.
These 2 rows form the rib pattern.
Variations on Ribbed Patterns are worked by following the above principle, but increasing the number needed in the rib, for example:—For a K. 3, P. 3 rib, cast on a multiple of 6 + 3 and work as K. 2, P. 2 above, substituting 3 for 2 throughout the 2 rows of the instruction.

BASIC K2, P2, RIB

2. BRIOCHE RIBBING

Cast on a multiple of 2.
1st row— * W. fwd., sl. 1 purlwise, K. 1, rep. from * to end.
2nd row— * W. fwd., sl. 1 purlwise, K. 2 tog. (the sl. st. and w. fwd., of previous row), rep. from * to end.
Rep. 2nd row to form the pattern.
To cast off omit the w. fwd. and work a P. 1, K. 2 tog. action all across the sts. as you cast them off.

BRIOCHE RIBBING

3. EMBOSSED RIB PATTERN (multiple of 4 + 3)

1st and every row— * K. 2, P. 2, rep. from * to last 3 sts., K. 2, P. 1.

EMBOSSED RIB

4. EMBOSSED SLIP STITCH PATTERN (multiple 6 + 5)

1st row—K. 5, * sl. 1 pur.wise, K. 5, rep. from * to end
2nd row—P. 5, * sl. 1, P. 5, rep. from * to end.
3rd row—As 1st row.
4th row—P.
These 4 rows form the pattern.

EMBOSSED SLIP STITCH

MOSS STITCH

5. MOSS STITCH

Cast on an odd number of sts.
1st and every row— * K. 1, P. 1, rep. from * to last st., K. 1.

DOUBLE MOSS STITCH

6. DOUBLE MOSS STITCH (Multiple of 4 + 2)

1st row— * K.2, P.2, rep. from * to last 2 sts., K.2.
2nd row— * P.2, K.2, rep. from * to last 2 sts., P.2.
3rd row—As 2nd row.
4th row— * K.2, P.2, rep. from * to last 2 sts., K.2.
These 4 rows form the pattern.

GARTER STITCH RIB

7. GARTER STITCH RIB (multiple of 5 + 2)

1st row—K.
2nd row— * K.2, P.3, rep. from * to last 2 sts., K.2.
These 2 rows form the pattern.

GIRLS WING PATTERN

8. GIRLS WING PATTERN (multiple of 7 + 1)

1st row—P.1, * K.6, P.1, rep. from * to end.
2nd row—K.1, * P.6, K.1, rep. from * to end.
3rd row—P.1, * K.2, sl.2 purlwise, K.2, P.1, rep. from * to end.
4th row—K.1, * P.2, sl.2, P.2, K.1, rep. from * to end.
5th row—P.1, * sl. next 2 sts. on cable needle, leave at back, K.1, K.2 sts. from cable needle, sl. next st. on cable needle, leave at front, K.2, K. st. from cable needle, P.1, rep. from * to end.
Rows 2–5 form the pattern.

SIMPLE CABLE RIB

9. SIMPLE CABLE RIB (multiple of 11 + 5)

1st row—P.5, * K.6, P.5, rep. from * to end.
2nd row—K.5, * P.6, K.5, rep. from * to end.
3rd to 10th row—Rep. 1st and 2nd rows 4 times.
11th row—P.5, * sl. next 3 sts. on cable needle, leave at back, K.3, K.3 sts. from cable needle, P.5, rep. from * to end.
12th row—K.5, * P.6, K.5, rep. from * to end.
Rows 3 to 12 form the pattern.

CABLE AND RIB

10. CABLE AND RIB (multiple of 12 + 2)

1st row—* K.2, P.2, K.6, P.2, rep. from * to last 2 sts., K.2.
2nd row—* P.2, K.2, P.6, K.2, rep. from * to last 2 sts., sts., P.2.
3rd to 6th row—Rep. 1st and 2nd rows twice.
7th row— * K.2, P.2, sl. next 3 sts. on cable needle, leave at front, K.3, K. 3 sts. from cable needle, P.2, rep. from * to last 2 sts., K.2.
8th row—As 2nd row.
These 8 rows form the pattern.

PLAITED CABLE STITCH

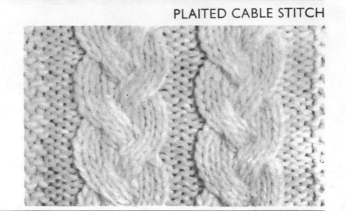

11. PLAITED CABLE STITCH (multiple of 12 + 3)

1st row— * P.3, K.9, rep. from * to last 3 sts., P.3.
2nd row— * K.3, P.9, rep. from * to last 3 sts., K.3.
3rd row— *P.3, sl. next 3 sts. on cable needle, leave at back, K.3, K. 3 sts. from cable needle, K.3, rep. from * to last 3 sts., P.3.
4th row—As 2nd row.
5th and 6th rows—As 1st and 2nd.
7th row— * P.3, K.3, sl. next 3 sts. on cable needle, leave at front, K.3, K. 3 sts. from cable needle, rep. from * to last 3 sts., P.3.
8th row—As 2nd row.
9th and 10th rows—As 1st and 2nd.
Rows 3 to 10 form the pattern.

DOUBLE CABLE PATTERN

12. DOUBLE CABLE PATTERN (multiple of 12 + 4)

1st row— * P.4, K.8, rep. from * to last 4 sts., P.4.
2nd row— * K.4, P.8, rep. from * to last 4 sts., K.4.
3rd to 6th row—Rep. 1st and 2nd rows twice.
7th row— * P.4, sl. next 2 sts. on cable needle, leave at back, K.2, K. 2 sts. from cable needle, sl. next 2 sts. on cable needle, leave at front, K.2, K. 2 sts. from cable needle, rep. from * to last 4 sts., P.4.
8th row—As 2nd row.
These 8 rows form the pattern.

MOCK CABLE PATTERN

13. MOCK CABLE PATTERN (multiple of 8 + 3)

1st row—P.3, * K.2, P.1, K.2, P.3, rep. from * to end.
2nd row—K.3, * P.2, K.1, P.2, K.3, rep. from * to end
3rd row—P.3, * K. into front of 2nd st. on needle, then knit into front of 1st st., slip both sts. off needle, P.1, K. into front of 2nd st. on needle, K. into front of 1st st. on needle, slip both sts. off needle, P.3, rep. from * to end.
4th row—As 2nd row.
These 4 rows form the pattern.

BASKET PATTERN

14. BASKET PATTERN (multiple of 10 + 3)

1st row— * K.3, P.7, rep. from * to last 3 sts., K.3.
2nd row— * P.3, K.7, rep. from * to last 3 sts., P.3.
3rd and 4th rows—As 1st and 2nd.
5th row—P.5, * K.3, P.7, rep. from * to last 8 sts., K.3, P.5.
6th row—K.5, * P.3, K.7, rep. from * to last 8 sts., P.3, K.5.
7th and 8th rows—As 5th and 6th.
These 8 rows form the pattern.

HERRINGBONE PATTERN

15. HERRINGBONE PATTERN (multiple of 7 + 1)

1st row—(Wrong side), P.
2nd row— * K.2 tog., K.2, M.1 by placing point of right-hand needle behind the left needle, insert point of right-hand needle from top, down through st. below next st., K. this stitch, then K. stitch above, K.2, rep. from * to last st., K.1.
3rd row—P.
4th row—K.3, * M.1, K.2, K.2 tog., K.2, rep. from * to last 5 sts., M.1, K.2, K.2 tog.
These 4 rows form the pattern.

BLACKBERRY PATTERN

16. BLACKBERRY PATTERN (multiple of 4 sts)

1st row—(Right side) P.
2nd row— * K.1, P.1, K.1 in next st., P.3. tog., rep. from * to end.
3rd row—P.
4th row— * P.3 tog., K.1, P.1, K.1, in next st., rep. from * to end.
These 4 rows form the pattern.

HONEYCOMB STITCH

17. HONEYCOMB STITCH (multiple of 2 + 1)

1st row—(Right side) P.
2nd row—P.
3rd row—K.1, * w.fwd., sl.1, K.1, p.s.s.o., rep. from * to end.
4th row—P.
These 4 rows form the pattern.

HONEYCOMB BRIOCHE STITCH

18. HONEYCOMB BRIOCHE STITCH (multiple of 2 sts.)

1st row—(an increase row) K.1, * w.ft., sl.1 purlwise, K.1, rep. from * to last st., K.1.
2nd row—K.1, w.ft., * sl.1 purlwise, w.r.n., P.2 tog., rep. from * to last st., K.1.
3rd row—K.1, P.1, * sl.1 purlwise (the w.r.n. of previous row), P.2, rep. from * to last 3 sts., sl.1 purlwise, P.1, K.1.
4th row—K.1, * P.2 tog., sl.1 purlwise, w.r.n., rep. from * to last 4 sts., P.2 tog., sl. 1 purlwise, K.1.
5th row—K.1, w.ft., * sl.1 purlwise (the w.r.n. of previous row) P.2, rep. from * to last st., K.1.
Rows 2 to 5 form the pattern.

RIDGE PATTERN

19. RIDGE PATTERN.

1st row—K.
2nd row—P.
3rd and 4th rows—As 1st and 2nd.
5th row—P.
6th row—K.
7th and 8th rows—As 5th and 6th.
These 8 rows form the pattern.

FANCY RIDGE PATTERN

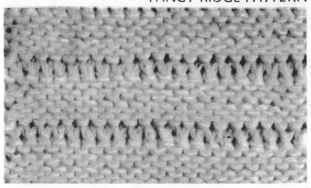

20. FANCY RIDGE PATTERN (odd number of sts.).

Rows 1 to 6—K.
7th row— * K.1, w.fwd., rep. from * to last st., K.1.
8th row— * K.1, drop w.fwd. of previous row, rep. from * to last st., K.1.
These 8 rows form the pattern.

LACE DIAMOND PATTERN

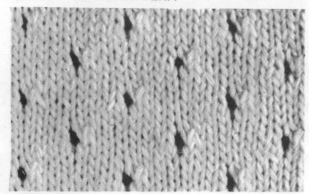

MINIATURE LEAF PATTERN

STRIPED LACE PATTERN

LACE EYELET PATTERN

21. LACE EYELET PATTERN (multiple of 8)

1st row—K.
2nd and every alt. row—P.
3rd row— * K.6, w.fwd., K.2 tog., rep. from * to end.
5th row—K.
7th row—K .2, * w.fwd., K.2 tog., K.6, rep. from * to last 6 sts., w.fwd., K.2 tog., K.4.
8th row—P.
These 8 rows form the pattern.

22. MINIATURE LEAF PATTERN (multiple of 6 + 3)

1st and every alt. row—(Wrong side) P.
2nd row—K.1, * w.fwd., K.3, w.fwd., sl.1, K.2 tog., p.s.s.o., rep. from * to last 2 sts., K.2.
4th row—K.1, * w.fwd., sl.1, K.1, p.s.s.o., K.1, K.2 tog., w.fwd., K.1, rep. from * to last 2 sts., w.fwd., sl. 1, K.1, p.s.s.o.
6th row—K.2, * w.fwd., sl.1, K.2 tog., p.s.s.o., w.fwd., K.3, rep. from * to last st., K.1.
8th row—K.1, * K.2 tog., w.fwd., K.1, w.fwd., sl.1, K.1. p.s.s.o., K.1, rep. from * to last 2 sts., K.2.
10th row—K.5, * w.fwd., sl.1, K.2 tog., p.s.s.o., w.fwd., K.3, rep. from * to last 4 sts., w.fwd., sl.1, K.2 tog., p.s.s.o., w.fwd., K.1.
Rows 3 to 10 form the pattern.

23. STRIPED LACE PATTERN (multiple of 11 + 3)

1st row- * K.3, w.fwd., sl.1, K.2 tog., p.s.s.o., w.r.n., P.2, w.o.n., sl.1, K.2 tog., p.s.s.o., w.fwd., rep. from * to last 3 sts., K.3.
2nd row—P.6, K.2, * P.9, K.2, rep. from * to last 6 sts., P.6.
3rd row—K.6, P.2, * K.9, P.2, rep. from * to last 6 sts., K.6.
4th row—As 2nd row.
These 4 rows form the pattern.

24. LACE DIAMOND PATTERN (multiple of 10 sts).

1st and every alt. row (Wrong side) P.
2nd row—K.3, * w.fwd., sl.1, K.2 tog., p.s.s.o., w.fwd., K.7, rep. from * ending last rep. K.4.
4th row—K.2 tog., K.2, * w.fwd., K.1, w.fwd., K.2, sl 1, K.1, p.s.s.o., K.1, K.2 tog., K.2, rep. from * to last 6 sts., w.fwd., K.1, w.fwd., K.2, sl.1, K.1, p.s.s.o., K.1.
6th row— * K.2 tog., K.1, w.fwd., K.3, w.fwd., K.1, sl.1, K.1, p.s.s.o., K.1, rep. from * to end.
8th row—K.2 tog., * w.fwd., K.5, w.fwd., sl.1, K.1, p.s.s.o., K.1, K.2 tog., rep. from * to last 8 sts., w.fwd., K.5, w.fwd., sl.1, K.1, p.s.s.o., K.1.
10th row—K.1, w.fwd., * K.7, w.fwd., sl.1, K.2 tog., p.s.s.o., w.fwd., rep. from * to last 9 sts., K.7, w.fwd., sl.1, K.1, p.s.s.o., (1 extra st.).
12th row—K.1, * w.fwd., K.2, sl.1, K.1, p.s.s.o., K.1, K.2 tog., K.2, w.fwd., K.1, rep. from * to end.
14th row—K.2 tog., * w.fwd., K.1, sl.1, K.1. p.s.s.o., K.1, K.2 tog., K.1, w.fwd., K.3, rep. from * ending last rep. K.2 (extra st. discarded).
16th row—K.2, * w.fwd., sl.1, K.1, p.s.s.o., K.1, K.2 tog., w.fwd., K.5, rep. from * ending last rep., K.3.
These 16 rows form the pattern.

25. LEAF PATTERN LACE STITCH (multiple of 12 + 1)

1st and every alt. row—(Wrong side) P.

2nd row— * K.1, w.fwd., sl.1, K.1, p.s.s.o., K.7, K.2 tog., w.fwd., rep. from * to last st., K.1.

4th row— * K.1, w.fwd., K.1, sl.1, K.1, p.s.s.o., K.5, K.2 tog., K.1, w.fwd., rep. from * to last st., K.1.

6th row— * K.1, w.fwd., K.2, sl. 1, K.1, p.s.s.o., K.3, K.2 tog., K.2, w.fwd., rep. from * to last st., K.1.

8th row— * K.1, w.fwd., K.3, sl.1, K.1, p.s.s.o., K.1, K.2 tog., K.3, w.fwd., rep. from * to last st., K.1.

10th row— * K.1, w.fwd., K.4, sl.1, K.2 tog., p.s.s.o., K.4, w.fwd., rep. from * to last st., K.1.

12th row—K.4, K.2 tog., * w.fwd., K.1, w.fwd., sl.1, K.1, p.s.s.o., K.7, K.2 tog., rep. from * to last 7 sts., w.fwd., K.1, w.fwd., sl.1, K.1, p.s.s.o., K.4.

14th row—K.3, K.2 tog., K.1, * w.fwd., K.1, w.fwd., K.1, sl.1, K.1, p.s.s.o., K.5, K.2 tog., K.1, rep. from * to last 7 sts., w.fwd., K.1, w.fwd., K.1, sl. 1, K.1, p.s.s.o., K.3.

16th row—K.2, K.2 tog., K.2, * w.fwd., K.1, w.fwd., K.2, sl. 1, K.1, p.s.s.o., K.3, K.2 tog., K.2, rep. from * to last 7 sts., w.fwd., K.1, w.fwd., K.2, sl.1, K.1, p.s.s.o., K.2.

18th row—K.1, K.2 tog., K.3, * w.fwd., K.1, w.fwd., K.3, sl.1, K.1, p.s.s.o., K.1, K.2 tog., K.3, rep. from * to last 7 sts., w.fwd., K.1, w.fwd., K.3, sl.1, K.1, p.s.s.o., K.1.

20th row—K.2 tog., K.4, * w.fwd., K.1, w.fwd., K.4, sl.1, K.2 tog., p.s.s.o., K.4, rep. from * to last 7 sts., w. fwd., K.1, w.fwd., K.4, sl.1, K.1, p.s.s.o.

These 20 rows form the pattern.

26. SHELL LACE PATTERN (multiple of 11 + 6)

1st and all odd rows (Wrong side) P.

2nd row—K.1. * K.1, w.fwd., K.2, sl.1, K.2 tog., p.s.s.o., K.5, w.fwd., rep. from * to last 5 sts., K.1, w.fwd., K.2, sl.1., K.1. p.s.s.o.

4th row—K.3, * w.fwd., K.1, sl. 1, K.2 tog., p.s.s.o., K.4, w.fwd., K.3, rep. from * to last 3 sts., w.fwd., K.1, sl.1, K.1, p.s.s.o.

6th row—K.4, * w.fwd., sl.1, K.2 tog., p.s.s.o., K.3, w.fwd., K.5, rep. from * to last 2 sts., w.fwd., sl.1, K.1, p.s.s.o.

8th row—K.1, w.fwd., K.3, * sl.1, K.2 tog., p.s.s.o., K.2, w.fwd., K.1, w.fwd., K.5, rep. from * to last 2 sts., sl.1, K.1, p.s.s.o.

10th row—K.1, w.fwd., K.3, * sl.1, K.2 tog., p.s.s.o., K.1, w.fwd., K.3, w.fwd., K.4, rep. from * to last 2 sts., sl.1, K.1, p.s.s.o.

12th row—K.1, * w. fwd., K.3, sl.1, K.2 tog., p.s.s.o., w.fwd., K.5, rep. from * to last 5 sts., w.fwd., K.3, sl.1, K.1, p.s.s.o.

These 12 rows form the pattern.

27. ALL OVER LACE PATTERN (multiple of 6 × 3)

1st row—K.2, * w.fwd., sl.1, K.1, p.s.s.o., K.1, K.2 tog., w.fwd., K.1, rep. from * ending last repeat K.2.

2nd row—P.

3rd row—K.3, * w.fwd., sl.1, K.2 tog., p.s.s.o., w.fwd., K.3, rep. from * to end.

4th row—P.   These 4 rows form the pattern.

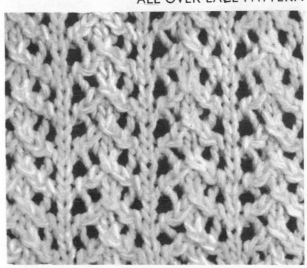

BACKSTITCHING SEAMS

WEAVING VERTICAL SEAMS

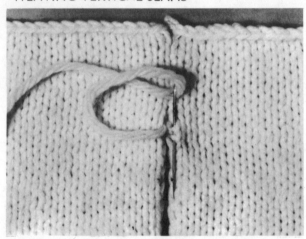

WEAVING STOCKING STITCH

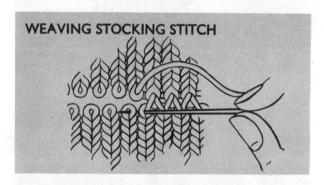

DUPLICATE STITCH

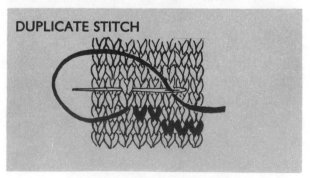

FINISHING STITCHES

TO SEW SEAMS WITH BACKSTITCH: Most seams should be sewn with backstitch. Pin right sides of pieces together, keeping edges even and matching rows or patterns. Thread matching yarn in tapestry needle. Run end of yarn through several stitches along edge to secure: backstitch pieces together close to edge. Do not draw yarn too tight. See illustration.

TO SEW IN SLEEVES: Place sleeve seam at centre underarm and centre of sleeve cap at shoulder seam. Ease in any extra fullness evenly. Backstitch seam.

TO WEAVE SEAMS TOGETHER: Straight vertical edges, such as those at the back seam of a sock, can be woven together invisibly from the right side. Thread matching yarn in tapestry needle. Hold edges together, right side up. Bring needle up through first stitch on left edge. Insert needle down through centre of first stitch on right edge, pass under 2 rows, draw yarn through to right side. Insert needle in centre of stitch on corresponding row of left edge, pass under 2 rows as before, draw yarn through to right side. Continue working from side to side, matching rows. Keep seam flat and elastic.

TO WEAVE TOP EDGES OF STOCKING STITCH: Two equal top edges of stocking stitch can be joined by an invisible seam. In this case, the stitches are not cast off, but are kept on the needles or stitch holders until they are ready to be woven. Thread yarn in tapestry needle. Lay the two pieces together so that the edge stitches match. Draw up yarn in first stitch of upper piece, inserting needle from wrong side; insert needle from right side in first stitch on lower piece, bring up through next stitch on lower piece, from wrong side. Draw up yarn, * insert needle from right side in same stitch as before on upper piece, bring up through next stitch on upper piece from wrong side. Draw up yarn, insert needle in same stitch as before on lower piece. Repeat from * until all stitches are joined.

DUPLICATE STITCH: When an additional colour is desired for a small area it is advisable to work it in with duplicate stitch rather than to knit it in. Thread a tapestry needle with yarn of contrasting colour and work as follows: Draw yarn from wrong side of work to right side through centre of lower point of stitch. Insert needle at top right hand side of same stitch. Then holding needle in horizontal position draw through top left hand side of stitch and insert again into base of stitch to left of where needle came out at start of stitch. Keep yarn loose enough to lie on top of work and cover knitted stitch.

Body measurements

How to Take Measurements

Directions for the knitted and crocheted items on the following pages are based on body measurements given in the tables on this page.

To take body measurements for men's, women's, and teens' sizes, measure around fullest part of chest or bust (with bra), natural waistline, and fullest part of hip. Find the column of measurements in the tables which approximates the measurements taken. Necessary allowance has been made in the directions for the proper fit of each garment according to style, stitch and yarn type. The blocked, or finished, bust measurement of the knitted or crocheted garment is given with the directions.

To take body measurements for children's sizes, measure around fullest part of child's chest over underwear, holding tape comfortably, neither snugly nor loosely. Find the chest measurement in table. Other measurements in table will help you decide whether your child differs in build from the average so that adjustments can be made easily as you work. Children's garments are designed for a casual, easy fit and allow for a child's growth. The chest, or breast, measurement, not the child's age is your guide in choosing the correct size to knit. This is the most important measurement in fitting a child's knitted garment. Shoulders are in proportion to chest.

Adjusting to Larger and Smaller Sizes

To make a garment one size larger than given in directions, add the number of stitches equalling 1″ to both back and front for a pullover, 1″ to back and ½″ to each front for a cardigan or jacket, 2″ to a skirt. Subtract the same number for a smaller size. When stitch is a repeat pattern, add or subtract the number of stitches equal to one or more multiples.

There is a ½″ difference across back and front at shoulders for each women's size, 1″ for each men's size. To obtain desired width at shoulders, decrease more or less stitches at armhole shaping, dividing evenly between armholes. There is a ¼″ difference at wrist and ½″ at underarms for each size.

The length of sweater, jackets, dress waists, and sleeves is changed by adding or subtracting required number of inches before armhole is reached.

MEN AND WOMEN

	Depth of Armhole			
Bust or chest	Raglan	Set in Sleeve	Sleeve Seam	Length
32″	8″	7″	17″	24½″
34″	8½″	7¼″	17″	25″
36″	9″	7½″	17½″	25½″
38″	9½″	7¾″	17½″	26″
40″	10″	8″	18″	26½″
42″	10½″	8¼″	18″	27″

BABIES AND CHILDREN

		Depth of Armhole			
Age	Chest	Raglan	Set in	Length	Sleeve seam
Birth — 6 months	18–19″	4½″	3¾″	9″–10″	4¾″–5″
6 months — 1 year	20″	5″	4″	10″	5″–6″
12–18 months	21″	5¼″	4″	10½″	7¼″
18 months — 2 years	22″	5½″	4¼″	11″½	8″
2–3 years	22″	5¾″	4½″	12½″	9″
4–5 years	24″	6″	4¾″	13¼″	10¾″
6–7 years	26″	6½″	5″	15″	12½″
8–9 years	28″	7″	5½″	16¼″	13½″–13¾″
10–11 years	30″	7½″	6″	17½″	15″–15½″

Classic Waistcoat

This classic waistcoat features knitted-in pockets.

MATERIALS: 8[9, 10] oz. PATONS PURPLE HEATHER 4-ply. Two No. 12 BEEHIVE needles or QUEEN BEE and two No. 14 QUEEN BEE needles. Four stitch-holders. Six buttons.

MEASUREMENTS: To fit 36[38, 40] inch chest. Length, 19½[20,20½] ins.

SIZES: The figures in square brackets [ ] refer to the medium and large sizes respectively.

TENSION: 8 sts. and 10 rows to one square inch on No. 12 needles, measured over stocking stitch.

BACK Using No. 12 needles, cast on 120[128,136] sts.

Proceed in stocking stitch, inc. 1 st. at both ends of every 6th row until there are 140[148,156]sts.

Continue on these sts. until work measures 9 ins. from cast-on edge.

Shape armholes by casting off 5 sts. at beg. of next 8 rows.

Dec. 1 st. at both ends of every alt. row until 92[100, 108]sts. remain.

Continue until work measures 9½[10,10½)ins. from commencement of armhole shaping.

Shape shoulders by casting off 7[8,9]sts, at beg. of next 8 rows. Cast off 36 sts.

POCKET LININGS (2) Using No. 12 needles, cast on 28 sts.

1st row. — K.4, turn.
2nd row — Sl. 1, P.3.
3rd row — K.8, turn.
4th row — Sl. 1, P.7.

Continue in this manner working 4 sts. more on every K. row until all sts. are worked.

Continue until work measures 3 ins. from beg. measured at longest side.

Slip sts. on to a stitch-holder.

RIGHT FRONT Using No. 12 needles, cast on 60[64,66] sts.

1st row — K.4, turn.
2nd row – Sl. 1, P.3.
3rd row — K.8, turn.
4th row — Sl.1, P.6, inc. 1 st. in last st.

Continue in this manner working 4 sts. more on every K. row and inc. 1 st. at front edge as on 3rd row on every 4th row from previous inc. until 6 more inc. have been worked at front edge and all sts. are worked on one needle (68[72,76]sts.).

Continue on these sts. inc. 1 st. at side edge on every 6th row until work measures 1¾ins. from beg., finishing at end of a P. row.

Work Pocket Top as follows: —

K.24, slip these sts. on to a stitch-holder, cast off 4 sts., K. to end. Still inc. at outside edge on every 6th row as before, continue casting off 4 sts. on K. rows on every alt. row until 28 sts. **in all** have been cast-off, finishing at side edge. Slip second set of sts. at side edge on to a stitch-holder and leave.

Break off wool.

With right side facing, rejoin wool, K. across 24 sts. from stitch-holder, slip 28 sts. of Pocket Lining on to left-hand needle (52 sts.). Work 11 rows on these 52 sts.

Next row — K.52, K. across sts. on remaining stitch-holder.

Continue in stocking stitch still inc. on every 6th row at side edge as before until there are 78[82,86]sts.

Continue on these sts. until work matches Back to armhole shaping, finishing at side edge.

Next row — Cast off 5, P. to end.

Next row — K. 24, cast off 4, work to end.

Complete Pocket as before, **at the same time** cast off 5 sts. at armhole edge on next and every alt. row as before until 3 more sets of 5 sts. (**4 in all**) have been cast off at armhole edge, then dec. 1 st. at armhole edge on every alt. row until 4 dec. have been worked at armhole edge, finishing at front edge (54[58,62]sts.). Complete Pocket Top, **at the same time shape neck** by dec. 1 st. at front edge on next and every following 4th row until Pocket Top is completed.

Continue dec. on every 4th row at front edge until 28[32,36] sts. remain.

Continue on these sts. until work matches Back to shoulder shaping.

Shape shoulder as on Back

POCKET LININGS (2) Using No. 12 needles, cast on 28 sts.

1st row — P.4, turn.
2nd row — Sl.1, K.3.
3rd row — P.8, turn.
4th row — Sl. 1, K.7.
Complete as Pocket Linings for Right Front.
LEFT FRONT Using No. 12 needles, cast on 60[64,68]sts.
1st row — P.4, turn.
2nd row — Sl.1, K.3.
3rd row — P. 8, turn.
4th row — Sl.1, K.6, inc. 1 st. in last st. at front edge.
Continue in this manner to match Right Front until there are 70[74,78]sts., finishing at end of a K. row.
Work 3 rows.
Next row — K. to last 5 sts., cast off 3, K. to end.
Next row — P.2, cast on 3, P. to end.
Working Pocket Tops to match Right Front and placing Pocket Linings as on Right Front **noting** that the 1st row of the pocket top is a P. in place of a K. row, and working buttonholes 2 ins. apart until 5 buttonholes **in all** have been worked, complete to match Right Front, reversing armhole, neck and shoulder shapings.
BORDER. Using No. 14 needles, **knit up** 36 sts. along back of neck, K.5 rows. Cast off.
With right side facing, commencing at edge of neck, using No. 14 needles, **knit up** 3 sts. for every 4 rows along front edge of Right Front and 1 st. in each st. along lower edge.

K. 5 rows.
Cast off.
Work Left Front Border to match.
Using No. 14 needles, **knit up** 120[128,136]sts. along lower edge of Back.
K. 5 rows.
Cast off.
Using No. 14 needles, **knit up** 28 sts. along top edge of Pocket.
K. 5 rows.
Cast off.

ARMBANDS (2) Using a fine back-stitch seam, join shoulders of Back and Fronts.
Using No 14 needles, **knit up** 178 [184,190]sts. round armhole.
K. 5 rows.
Cast off.

TO MAKE UP With wrong side of work facing block and press lightly using a warm iron and damp cloth. Flat-stitch Pocket Linings into position on wrong side, Pocket Tops on right side. Flat-stitch top edge of border to edge of border at back of neck. Using a flat seam for Border and a fine back-stitch seam for remainder, join ends of Armbands and side seams. Work buttonhole-stitch round buttonholes. Attach buttons. Press seams.

Striped slip-over

MATERIALS: 3 [3, 4] oz. Dark, 3 [4, 4] oz. Light, 3 [4, 5] oz. Medium, PATONS DOUBLE KNITTING or PATONS TOTEM Double Crepe. Two No. 8 and two No. 6 BEEHIVE or QUEEN BEE needles, set of four No. 9 QUEEN BEE needles with points at both ends. Two stitch-holders.
MEASUREMENTS AND TENSION as Striped Cardigan Page 141.
SIZES: The figures in square brackets [] refer to the medium and large sizes respectively.
BACK: Work as Striped Cardigan, do not cast off, but slip 22 [24, 26] sts. on to a stitch-holder.
FRONT: Work as Back of Cardigan until 40 [44, 48] sts. remain at raglan shaping, finishing at end of a 1st row.
Next row — P. 15 [16, 17], P. next 10 [12, 14] sts. on to a stitch-holder and leave.
Proceed on **each** group of sts. as follows:
Still dec. at armhole edge on every alt. row as before,

at the same time dec. at neck edge on next and every alt. row until 5 dec. have been worked at neck edge. Continue dec. at armhole edge **only** as before until all sts. are worked off.
SLEEVES: Using No. 9 needles in place of No. 8 for K.1, P.1 Cuffs, work as Cardigan on page 141.

TO MAKE UP: Omitting ribbing, block and press on wrong side using a warm iron and damp cloth. Using a flat seam for ribbing and a fine backstitch seam for remainder, join side and sleeve seams, stitch Sleeves into position matching shapings, stitching 5 rows at top of Back to centre of cast-off sts. at the top of Sleeve.

NECKBAND: Using set of No. 9 needles and Dark, **knit up** 66 [68, 70] sts. round neck including sts. from stitch-holder.
Work 7 rounds in K.1, P.1 rib. Cast off in rib. Press seams.

Striped cardigan

MATERIALS: 3 [3, 4] oz. Dark, 3 [4, 4] oz. Light, 3 [4, 5] oz. Medium, PATONS DOUBLE KNITTING or PATONS TOTEM Double Crepe. Two No. 8 and two No. 6 BEEHIVE or QUEEN BEE needles. Five buttons. Two press studs.

MEASUREMENTS: To fit 26 [28, 30] inch chest. Length, 16½ [17¼, 18¾] ins. Sleeve seam, 11 [12½, 13½] ins.
SIZES: The figures in square brackets [] refer to the medium and large sizes respectively.

TENSION: 5 sts. and 6½ rows to one square inch on No. 6 needles, measured over stocking stitch.

BACK: Using No. 8 needles and Dark, cast on 64 [68, 72] sts.
Work in K.1, P.1 rib for 1 [1¼, 1½] ins.
Change to No. 6 needles and proceed in stocking stitch as follows: (2 rows Dark, 2 rows Light, 2 rows Dark, 10 rows Medium) 3 times, 2 rows Dark, 2 rows Light, 2 rows Dark. Break off Dark and Medium.
Work 5 [5, 9] rows in Light.
Using Light for remainder of Back, **shape raglan as follows:**
** Next row — Cast off 2, P. to last 2 sts., cast off 2. Break off wool.
Rejoin wool and complete raglan thus:
1st row — K.1, K.2 tog., K. to last 3 sts., K.2 tog.t.b.l., K.1.
2nd row — P.
Rep. these 2 rows until 22 [24, 26] sts. remain, finishing at end of a dec. row. Work 5 rows more on these sts. Cast off.

RIGHT FRONT: Using No. 8 needles and Dark, cast on 32 [34, 36] sts.
Work as Back to cast-off row at armhole shaping.
Next row — Cast off 2, P. to end.
1st row — K. to last 3 sts., K.2 tog. t.b.l., K.1.
2nd row — P.
Rep. these 2 rows until 18 [20, 22] sts. remain.
Still dec. at armhole edge on every alt. row as before, **at the same time shape neck** by casting off 6 [7, 8] sts. at beg. of next row, then dec. 1 st. at neck edge on next and every alt. row until 4 dec. **in all** has been worked at neck edge.
Continue dec. at armhole edge **only** on every alt. row as before until all sts. are worked off.

LEFT FRONT: Work as Right Front to cast-off row at armhole shaping.
Next row — P. to last 2 sts., cast off 2.

A pair of raglan-sleeved sweaters for the younger set. Both the cardigan and slip-over are worked from the neck down in contrasting stripes. For instructions see pages 139 and 141

1st row — K.1, K.2, tog., K. to end.
2nd row — P.
Complete to match Right Front, reversing shapings.

SLEEVES: Using No. 8 needles and Dark, cast on 40 [42, 44] sts.
Work in K.1, P.1 rib for 2 [2¼, 2½] ins., inc. 1 st. at end of last row (41 [43, 45] sts.).
Change to No. 6 needles, inc. 1 st. at both ends of 9th row following and every following 10th [10th, 12th] row until there are 51 [53, 55] sts.
Proceed in stocking stitch in following order of stripes: 0 [6, 8] Medium, (2 Dark, 2 Light, 2 Dark, 10 Medium) 3 times, 2 Dark, 2 Light, 2 Dark.
5 [5, 9] rows in Light.
When the 5 [5, 9] rows in Light have been completed, work as Back from ** to **, then rep. 1st and 2nd rows until 9 sts. remain, finishing at end of a dec. row. Cast off.

TO MAKE UP: Omitting ribbing, block and press on wrong side using a warm iron and damp cloth. Using a flat seam for ribbing and a fine back-stitch seam for remainder, join side and sleeve seams and stitch Sleeves into position matching shapings, stitching 5 rows at top of Back to centre of cast-off sts. at top of Sleeve.

NECKBAND: Using No. 8 needles and Dark, **knit up** 73 [75, 77] sts. round neck.
1st row — * P.1, K.1, rep. from * to last st., P.1.
2nd row — * K.1, P.1, rep. from * to last st., K.1.
Rep. these 2 rows twice more, then 1st row once. Cast off in rib.

LEFT FRONT BAND: Using No. 8 needles and Dark, cast on 9 sts.
1st row — K.2, (P.1, K.1) 3 times, K.1.
2nd row — (K.1, P.1.) 4 times, K.1.
Rep. these 2 rows 1 [2, 3] times more.
Next row — Rib 3, cast off 3, rib to end.
Next row — Rib 3, cast on 3, rib to end.
Continue in this manner working a buttonhole on every 25th and 26th rows from previous buttonhole until 5 buttonholes **in all** have been worked. Work 2 [2, 4] rows after last buttonhole. Cast off in rib.
Omitting buttonholes, work Right Front Band to match.

TO COMPLETE MAKE UP: Flat-stitch Front Bands into position. Attach buttons. Stitch press studs to top of Front Bands. Press seams.

An all over raised motif and doubled V neckline vary this classic pullover. See pattern on page 146.

In these comfortable cardigans, back, fronts and sleeves are worked separately from the bottom up, then joined for the knitted-in-one raglan yoke. Also knitted-in-one are the front borders and neckband, folded double for extra wear. Directions for childrens' cardigans, on opposite page.

Boys' and girls' raglan cardigan

MATERIALS: 5 [6, 6, 7, 7, 8] oz. PATONS BEEHIVE 3-ply, Patonised, or PATONS NYLOX 3-ply, Patonised. Two No. 13 and two No. 11 BEEHIVE or QUEEN BEE needles. Seven [Seven, Seven, Seven, Eight, Eight] buttons.

MEASUREMENTS: To fit 26 [27, 29, 31, 33, 35] ins. at underarm. Length, 15½ [17, 18½, 20, 21½, 23] ins. Sleeve seam, 11 [12, 13½, 15, 16, 17] ins.
SIZES: The figures in square brackets [ ] refer to the 27, 29, 31, 33 and 35 inch sizes respectively.
TENSION: 8 sts. and 10 rows to one square inch on No. 11 needles, measured over stocking stitch.

BACK: Using No. 13 needles, cast on 104 [108, 116, 124 132, 140] sts.
Work in K.1, P.1 rib for 1½ [1½, 1½, 2, 2, 2] ins.
Change to No. 11 needles and proceed in stocking stitch until work measures 9 [10, 11, 12, 13, 14] ins. from beg., finishing with a K. row.
Shape raglan as follows:
** Next row — Cast off 3 [2, 3, 4, 5, 6] sts., P. to last 3 [2, 3, 4, 5, 6] sts., cast off these sts. Break off wool.
Rejoin wool and continue as follows:
1st row — K.1, K.2 tog., K. to last 3 sts., K.2 tog.t.b.l., K.1.
2nd row — P. **
Rep. these 2 rows until 32 [34, 36, 38, 40, 42] sts. remain, finishing with a 1st row.
Change to No. 13 needles and work 2 [2, 3, 3, 4, 4] rows. Cast off.

LEFT FRONT: Using No. 13 needles, cast on 50 [52, 56, 60, 64, 68] sts.
Work as Back to cast-off row at armhole shaping, finishing with a K. row.
Next row — P. to last 3 [2, 3, 4, 5, 6] sts., cast off these sts. Break off wool.
Rejoin wool and continue as follows:
1st row — K.1, K.2 tog., K. to end.
2nd row — P.
Continue as on these 2 rows until 24 [25, 28, 29, 32, 33] sts. remain, finishing with a 1st row.
Still dec. at armhole edge on every alt. row as before, **at the same time shape neck** by casting off 7 [8, 9, 10, 11, 12] sts. at beg. of next row, then dec. 1 st. at neck edge on every alt. row until 6 dec. have been worked at neck edge for **all sizes**.
Continue dec. at armhole edge **only** until all sts. are worked off.

RIGHT FRONT: Work as Left Front until cast-off row at armhole is reached, finishing with a K. row.
Next row — Cast off 3 [2, 3, 4, 5, 6] sts., P. to end.
1st row — K. to last 3 sts., K.2 tog. t.b.l., K.1.
2nd row — P.
Complete to match Left Front reversing shapings.

SLEEVES: Using No. 13 needles, cast on 46 [48, 50, 52, 54, 56] sts.
Work in K.1, P.1 rib for 2 [2, 2, 2½, 2½, 2½] ins.
Change to No. 11 needles and proceed in stocking stitch inc. 1 st. at both ends of every following 5th row until there are 76 [78, 86 92, 100, 106[sts.
Continue on these sts. until work measures 11 [12, 13½, 15, 16, 17] ins. from beg., finishing with a K. row.
Work as Back from ** to ** then rep. 1st and 2nd rows until 4 [4, 6, 6, 8, 8] sts. remain, finishing with a 1st row. Cast off.

TO MAKE UP: Omitting ribbing, with wrong side of work facing block and press each piece using a warm iron and damp cloth. Using a flat seam for ribbing and a fine back-stitch seam for remainder, join side and sleeve seams and stitch Sleeves into position matching shapings, stitching 2 [2, 3, 3, 4, 4] rows at top of Back to centre of cast-on sts. at top of sleeve.

NECKBAND: With right side facing using No. 13 needles, **knit up** 91 [95, 99, 103, 109, 115] sts round neck.
1st row — * K.1, P.1, rep. from * to last st., K.1.
2nd row — K.2, * P.1, K.1, rep. from * to last st., K.1.
Rep. these 2 rows until work measures 1½ [1½, 2, 2, 2½, 2½] ins. from beg. Cast off.
Fold Neckband at centre to inside and flat-stitch cast-off edge to knitted-up edge.

BUTTONHOLE BAND: (Right side for Girl, Left side for Boy) With right side facing using No. 13 needles, **knit up** 111 [123, 135, 147, 159, 171] sts. along front edge, knitting up through both edges along Neckband.

Rep. 1st and 2nd rows as on Neckband twice for Girl, rep. 1st and 2nd once then 1st row once for Boy.
Next row — Rib 3 [3, 3, 3, 3, 3], (cast off 3, one st. on needle after cast-off, rib 11 [13, 15, 17, 15, 17] sts.) 6 [6, 6, 6, 7, 7] times, cast off 3, rib to end.
Next row — Rib all across, casting on 3 sts. over cast-off sts. of previous row.
Work 10 more rows in rib.
Work 2 more buttonhole rows.
Work 4 more rows for Girl, 3 more rows for Boy in rib.

Cast off in rib. Fold Front Band to inside and flat-stitch cast-off edge to knitted-up edge. Using a flat seam join top and bottom edges of Band.
Work buttonhole stitch round buttonholes.

SECOND FRONT BAND: With right side facing using No. 13 needles, **knit up** 111 [123, 135, 147, 159, 171] sts. along Front edge knitting up through both edges of Neckband. Omitting buttonholes work to match Buttonhole Band. Attach buttons. Press seams.

Raglan pullover

MATERIALS: 24 [25, 26] hanks PATONS BIG BEN. Two No. 6 BEEHIVE needles or QUEEN BEE and two No. 3 BEEHIVE needles.

MEASUREMENTS: To fit 38 [40, 42] inch chest. Length 25 [25½, 26] ins. Sleeve seam, 18 [19, 20] ins.
SIZES: The figures in square brackets [ ] refer to the medium and large sizes respectively.
TENSION: 3½ sts. and 4½ rows to one square inch on

No. 3 needles, measured over stocking stitch.
PATTERN 1st and every row — * P.1, K.1 in row below, rep. from * to last 2 sts., P.2.
This row forms the patt.

FRONT AND BACK (Both alike) Using No. 6 needles, cast on 70 [74, 78] rib. sts.
Work in P.1, K.1 rib for 3 ins.
Change to No. 3 needles and proceed in **patt.** until work measures 14½ [15, 15½] ins. from cast-on edge.
Shape raglan armholes thus:
1st row — Patt.4, P.3, patt. to last 6 sts., P.3, K.1 in row below, P.2.
2nd row — P.1, K.1 in row below, P.1, sl.1, K.2 tog., p.s.s.o., patt to last 7 sts., sl.1, K.2 tog., p.s.s.o., P.1, K.1 in row below, P.2 (2 st. dec. at each end.)
** Work 6 rows in patt.
Rep. 1st and 2nd rows of armhole shaping. **
Rep. from ** to ** 8 [8, 9] times more (30 [34, 34] sts.).
Work 0 [3, 0] rows.
Change to No. 6 needles and work in K.1, P.1 rib for 2½ ins. Cast off loosely in rib.

SLEEVES Using No. 6 needles, cast on 34 [38, 42] sts.
Work in K.1, P.1 rib for 3 ins.
Change to No. 3 needles and **proceed in patt.**, inc. 1 st. at both ends of every 7th row until there are 50 [54, 58] sts. working extra sts. into patt.
Continue on these sts. until work measures 18 [19, 20] ins. from beg.
Shape raglan as on Back until 10 [14, 14] sts. remain. Work 0 [3, 0] rows.
Change to No. 6 needles and work in K.1, P.1 rib to match Back. Cast off loosely in rib.

TO MAKE UP: Omitting K.1, P.1 rib, block and press very lightly on wrong side using a warm iron and damp cloth. Using a flat seam for K.1, P.1 rib and a fine back-stitch seam for remainder, join side and sleeve seams and stitch Sleeves into position matching shapings. Flat-stitch edges of neckband together. Fold neckband to inside and loosely flat-stitch cast-off edge to knitted-up edge. Press seams.

Fisherman's rib is the stitch for this boatnecked pullover quickly made on big needles.

Outsize raglan cardigan

MATERIALS: 14 [15, 16, 17] oz. PATONS NYLOX 3-ply, Patonised, or PATONS BEEHIVE 3-ply, Patonised. Two No. 13 and two No. 11 BEEHIVE or QUEEN BEE needles. Nine buttons.

MEASUREMENTS: To fit 50 [52, 54, 56] inch bust. Length, 25½ [25¾, 26, 26½] ins. Sleeve seam, 18½ ins.
SIZES: The figures in square brackets [ ] refer to the 52, 54 and 56 inch sizes respectively.
TENSION: 8 sts. and 10 rows to one square inch on No. 11 needles, measured over stocking stitch.

BACK: Using No. 13 needles, cast on 212 [220, 228, 236] sts.
Work in K.1, P.1 rib for 3 ins.
Change to No. 11 needles and proceed in stocking stitch until work measures 15 ins. from beg. for all sizes, finishing with a K. row.
** Next row — Cast off 14 [15, 16, 17] sts., P. to last 14 [15, 16, 17], cast off these sts. Break off wool. Rejoin wool and complete raglan as follows:
1st row — K.1, K. 2 tog., K. to last 3 sts., K.2 tog.t.b.l., K.1.
2nd row — P.1, P.2 tog.t.b.l., P. to last 3 sts., P.2 tog., P.1.
3rd to 26th row — Rep. 1st and 2nd rows 12 times.
27th row — K.1, K.2 tog., K. to last 3 sts., K.2 tog.t.b.l., K.1.
28th row — P. **
Rep. 27th and 28th rows until 48 [50, 52, 54] sts. remain.
Change to No. 13 needles and work 4 rows on these sts. Cast off.

RIGHT FRONT: Using No. 13 needles, cast on 104 [108, 112, 116] sts.
Work as Back to cast-off row at armhole shaping, finishing with a K. row.
Next row — Cast off 14 [15, 16, 17] sts., P. to end.
1st row — K. to last 3 sts., K.2 tog.t.b.l., K.1.
2nd row — P.1, P.2 tog.t.b.l., P. to end.
3rd to 26th row — Rep. 1st and 2nd rows 12 times.
27th row — K. to last 3 sts., K.2 tog., K.1.
28th row — P.
Continue as on 27th and 28th rows until 38 [39, 40, 41] sts. remain, finishing at front edge.
Still dec. at armhole edge on every alt. row as before, shape neck by casting off 12 [13, 14, 15] sts. at beg. of next row, then dec. 1 st. at neck edge on every alt. row until 10 dec. have been worked at neck edge.
Continue dec. at armhole edge only on every alt. row as before until all sts. are worked off.

LEFT FRONT: Work as Right Front to cast-off row at armhole shaping, finishing with a P. row.
Next row — Cast off 14 [15, 16, 17], K. to end.
1st row — P. to last 3 sts., P.2 tog.t.b.l., P.1.
2nd row — K.1, K.2 tog.t.b.l., K. to end.
3rd to 26th row — Rep. 1st and 2nd rows 12 times.
27th row — P. to last 3 sts., P.2 tog.t.b.l., P.1.
28th row — K.
Complete to match Right Front reversing shapings.

SLEEVES: Using No. 13 needles, cast on 78 [80, 82, 84] sts.
Work in K.1, P.1 rib for 2½ ins.
Next row — Rib 4 [4, 5, 7] (inc. in next st., rib 6 [4, 3, 2]) 10 [14, 18, 22] times, inc. in next st., rib to end (89 [95, 101, 107] sts.).
Change to No. 11 needles and proceed in stocking stitch inc. 1 st. at both ends of every 4th row until there are 171 [177, 183, 189] sts.
Continue on these sts. until work measures 18½ ins. from beg., finishing with a K. row.
Work as Back from ** to ** then rep. 27th and 28th rows until 7 sts. remain. Cast off.

TO MAKE UP: Omitting ribbing, block and press on wrong side using a warm iron and damp cloth. Using a flat seam for ribbing and a fine back-stitch seam for remainder, join side and sleeve seams and stitch Sleeves into position matching shapings, stitching 4 rows at top of Back to centre of cast-off sts. at top of sleeve.

NECKBAND: Using No. 13 needles, **knit up** 167 [171, 175, 179] sts. round neck.
1st row — * K.1, P.1, rep. from * to last st., K.1.
2nd row — K.2, * P.1, K.1, rep. from * to last st., K.1.
Rep. these 2 rows until work measures 2¼ ins from beg. Cast off loosely.
Fold Neckband at centre and loosely flat-stitch cast-off edge to knitted-up edge.

RIGHT FRONT BAND: With right side facing using No. 13 needles commencing at lower edge, **knit up** 205 [209, 213, 217] sts., knitting up through both edges of Neckband.
Rep. 1st and 2nd rows of Neckband 3 times.
Next row — Rib 3 (cast off 3, rib 21) 8 times, cast off 3, rib to end.
Next row — Rib all across casting on 3 sts. to match cast-off sts. of previous row. Work 12 rows in rib.
Next row — Rib 3, (cast off 3, rib 21) 8 times, cast off 3 rib to end.
Next row — Rib all across, casting on 3 sts. to match cast-off st. of previous row. Work 6 rows in rib. Cast off.
Omitting buttonholes work Left Front Band to match.

TO COMPLETE MAKE UP: Fold Front Bands at centre to inside and flat-stitch to form Double Band. Stitch top and bottom edge of Front Bands together.
Buttonhole stitch round buttonholes. Attach buttons. Press seams.

Raised diamond slip-on

MATERIALS: 16 [17] oz. PATON DOUBLE KNIT-TING, or PATONS TOTEM Double Crepe. Two No. 8 and two No. 6 BEEHIVE or QUEEN BEE needles and set of 4 No. 9 QUEEN BEE needles with points at both ends. One stitch-holder.

MEASUREMENTS: To fit 34–35 [37–38] inch bust. Length, 23]23½] ins. Sleeve seam, 17½ ins. (adjustable). **SIZES:** The figures in square brackets [ ] refer to the large size.

TENSION: 5 sts. and 6½ rows to one square inch on No. 6 needles, measured over stocking stitch.

DIAMOND PATTERN
1st row — K.5, * P.5, K.5, rep. from * to end.
2nd row — P.5, * K.5, P.5, rep. from * to end.
3rd row — P.1, K.4, * P.4, K.1, P.1, K.4, rep. from * to end.
4th row — P.4, K.1, * P.1, K.4, P.4, K.1, rep. from * to end.
5th row — P.2, K.3, * P.3, K.2, P.2, K.3, rep. from * to end.
6th row — P.3, K.2, * P.2, K.3, P.3, K.2, rep. from * to end.
7th row — P.3, K.2, * P.2, K.3, P.3, K.2, rep. from * to end.
8th row — As 5th row.
9th row — As 4th row.
10th row — As 3rd row.
11th row — As 2nd row.
12th row — As 1st row.
13th row — K.1, P.4, * K.4, P.1, K.1, P.4, rep. from * to end.
14th row — K.4, P.1, * K.1, P.4, K.4, P.1, rep. from * to end.
15th row — K.2, P.3, * K.3, P.2, K.2, P.3, rep. from * to end.
16th and 17th rows — K.3, P.2, * K.2, P.3, K.3, P.2, rep. from * to end.
18th row — As 15th row.
19th row — As 14th row.
20th row — K.1, P.4, * K.4, P.1, K.1, P.4, rep. from * to end.
These 20 rows form the pattern.

BACK Using No. 8 needles, cast on 84 [94] sts.
Work in K.1, P.1 rib for 1½ ins., inc. 1 st. at end of last row (85 [95] sts.).
Change to No. 6 needles and proceed in patt., commencing with a 1st row until work measures 15 ins. from beg.
Shape armholes by casting off 4 [5] sts. at beg. of next

2 rows, then dec. 1st. at both ends of every alt. row until 71[75] sts. remain. Continue on these sts. until work measures 7½[8] ins. from beg. of armhole shaping.
Shape shoulders by casting off 5[5] sts. at beg. of next 8 rows, 3[5] sts. at beg. of next 2 rows.
Slip remaining 25 sts. on to stitch-holder.
FRONT Proceed as Back commencing patt. on 11th row in place of 1st row until work measures 14½ ins. from beg.
Divide for neck thus: —
Next row — Patt. 42[47], slip next st. on to safety-pin; join in 2nd ball of wool and patt. remaining 42[47] sts.
Proceed on **each group of sts. as follows:** —
Dec. 1 st. at neck edge on every 4th row 12 times, **at the, same time** when work matches Back to armhole shaping cast off 4[5] sts. at beg. of next row, then dec. 1 st. at armhole edge on every alt. row 3[5] times.
Continue until 12 neck dec. are completed (23[25] sts.). Continue on these sts. until work matches Back to shoulder shaping.
Shape shoulder by casting off 5 sts. on next and every alt. row 4[4] times; 3[5] sts. once.

SLEEVES Using No. 8 needles, cast on 38[40] sts.
Work in K.1, P.1 rib for 2½ ins.
Next row — Rib 3[4], (inc. in next st., rib 4[7]) 6[4] times, inc. in next st., rib to end (45[45] sts.).
Change to No. 6 needles and proceed in patt., inc. 1 st. at both ends of every 5th row 1[10] times; then every 6th row 11[5] times (69[75] sts.).
Continue on these sts. until work measures 17½ ins. from beg. (adjust length here).
Shape top by casting off 4[5] sts. at beg. of next 2 rows.
Dec. 1 st. at both ends of every alt. row 15[17] times. Cast off 3 sts. at beg. of next 6 rows.
Cast off.

NECKBAND Join shoulders of Back and Front.
With right side facing using set of No. 9 needles, **knit up** 142[146] sts. round neck including st. from safety-pin at Front and sts. from stitch-holder at Back.
Work 8 rounds in K.1, P.1 rib., dec. 1 st. at each side of st. knitted up from safety pin at centre V.
Work 2 rounds.
Work 8 more rounds, inc. 1 st. at each side of st. knitted up at centre V.
Using No. 8 needle, cast off.

TO MAKE UP Omitting ribbing, block and press on wrong side using a warm iron and damp cloth.
Join side and sleeve seams and stitch Sleeves into position. Fold Neckband at centre to inside. Loosely flat-stitch cast-off edge to knitted-up edge. Press seams.

Raised Diamond Slip-on, featured on this page, is illustrated on page 142

Woman's two tone sweater

MATERIALS: 8 [9, 10] oz. Light, 10 [11, 12] oz. Dark, PATONS TOTEM Double Knitting, or PATONS Double Knitting. Two No. 10 and two No. 8 needles, set of four No. 10 needles with points at both ends. Two stitch-holders.

MEASUREMENTS: To fit 34 [36, 38] inch bust. Length, 23¼ [23¾, 24¼] ins. Sleeve seam, 18 ins. (adjustable).

SIZES: The figures in square brackets [] refer to the medium and large sizes respectively.

ABBREVIATIONS: K. – knit; P. – purl; st. – stitch; tog. – together; inc. – increase by working into front and back of stitch; dec. – decrease by working 2 sts. together; beg. – beginning; alt. – alternate; rep. – repeat; patt. – pattern; ins. – inches; L – light; D. – Dark.

TENSION: 5½ sts. and 7½ rows to the square inch on No. 8 needles, measured over stocking stitch.

SPECIAL NOTE: As this garment is worked on rows up to armhole shaping it is essential for the tension to be correct if the final measurements are to be obtained.

BACK: Using No. 10 needles and Dark, cast on 96 [102, 108] sts.
Work in K.1, P.1 rib for 2 ins., inc. 1 st. at end of last row (97 [103, 109] sts.).
Change to No. 8 needles and proceed in patt. as folows:
Using Light
1st and 2nd rows — K.
Using Dark.
3rd and 4th rows — K.
Using Light.
5th row — K.
6th row — P.
7th to 10th row — Rep. 5th and 6th rows twice.
11th row — K. * 1D., 1L., rep. from * to last st., 1D.
12th row — P. * 1D., 1L., rep. from * to last st., 1D.
13th row — K. * 1L., 1D., rep. from * to last st., 1L.
14th row — P. * 1L, 1D., rep. from * to last st., 1L.
15th to 20th row — Rep. 5th and 6th rows 3 times.
21st and 22nd rows — As 3rd and 4th.
23rd and 24th rows — As 1st and 2nd.
Using Dark.
25th row — K.
26th row — P.
27th to 31st row — Rep. 25th and 26th rows twice, then 25th row once.
32nd row — P.
These 32 rows form the patt.
Continue in patt. until 30th row of 3rd patt. from beg. has been worked.
Keeping patt. correct throughout, **shape raglan armholes** by casting off 2 [3, 3] sts. at beg. of next 2 rows, then dec. 1 st. at both ends of next and every alt. row until 37 [37, 39] sts. remain.

Work 1 row.
Shape neck. Next row — Work 2 tog., patt. 26 [26, 28], slip the last 19 [19, 21] of these sts. on to a stitch-holder and leave, patt. 7 [7, 7], work 2 tog.
Proceed on **each group of sts.** as follows:
Dec. 1 st. at neck edge on every row until 4 dec. have been worked at neck edge **at the same time** continue dec. 1 st. at armhole edge on next and every alt. row as before until 1 st. remains.
Work 1 row.
Fasten off.

FRONT: Work as Back to armhole shaping.
Keeping patt. correct throughout, **shape raglan armholes** by casting off 2 [3, 3] sts. at beg. of next 2 rows, then dec. 1 st. at both ends of next and every alt. row until 47 [47, 49] sts. remain.
Work 1 row.
Shape neck. Next row — Work 2 tog., patt. 29 [29, 31], slip the last 15 [15, 17] of these sts. on to a stitch-holder and leave, patt. 14 [14, 14], work 2 tog.
Proceed on **each group of sts.** as follows:
Dec. 1 st. at neck edge on next and every alt. row until 6 dec. have been worked at neck edge, **at the same time** continue dec. 1 st. at armhole edge on every alt. row as before until 1 st. remains.
Work 1 row.
Fasten off.

SLEEVES: Using No. 10 needles and Dark, cast on 44 [46, 48] sts.
Work in K.1, P.1 rib for 2½ ins. (adjust length here).
Next row — Rib 3 [1, 2], (inc. in next st., rib 5 [6, 6] 6 times, inc. in next. st., rib to end (51 [53, 55] sts.).
Change to No. 8 needles and commencing with a 13th row, proceed in patt. as on Back, inc. 1 st. at both ends of 7th [3rd, 7th] and every following 9th [8th. 7th] row until there are 75 [81, 85] sts., working extra sts. in to patt.
Continue on these sts. until 30th row of 3rd complete patt. from beg. has been worked.
Keeping patt. correct throughout **shape raglan top** by casting off 2 [3, 3] sts. at beg. of next 2 rows, then dec. 1 st. at both ends of next and every alt. row until 7 sts. remain.
Work 1 row.
Cast off.

TO MAKE UP: Omitting ribbing, block and press on wrong side using a warm iron and damp cloth. Using a flat seam for ribbing and a fine back-stitch seam for remainder, join side and sleeve seams and stitch Sleeves into position. Using set of No. 10 needles and Dark, knit up 120 [122, 124] sts. round neck including sts. from stitch-holders.
Work in rounds of K.1, P.1 rib for 6 ins.
Cast off loosely in rib.
Press seams.

Knitting With Four Needles

Socks, mittens, gloves, hats, helmets, sleeves and necklines can all be knitted on four doublepointed needles in a tubular fashion. Stitches are cast on loosely and divided as evenly as possible on three needles; the fourth is used for the actual knitting. Stitch gauge is as important as in flat knitting; be sure the gauge agrees with that of the model for proper fit. As in flat knitting, shaping is accomplished by increasing or decreasing. Pattern stitches, including cables, are adaptable to four needle knitting. For twisting cables, an additional needle is required. Ribbing is worked by knitting over the knit stitches and purling over the purl stitches.

Working round and round in plain knit stitch produces a seamless stocking tube. Toes, fingers, etc. are finished by drawing the stitches together and sewing them securely or by weaving them in Kitchener stitch.

Socks are probably the most popular item made on four needles. A properly knitted sock fits well and wears well.

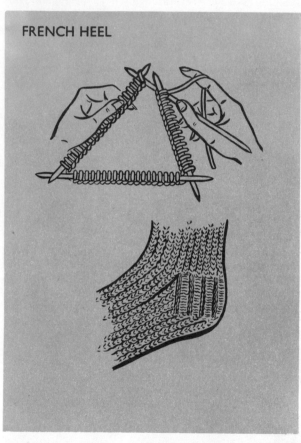

FRENCH HEEL

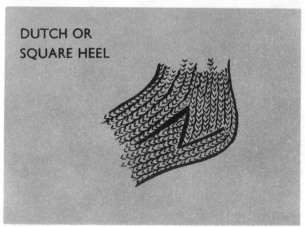

DUTCH OR SQUARE HEEL

CUFFS: Cast on cuff stitches loosely so they will not bind or be broken in putting on the sock. Leave an extra long end in casting on. Carry this end with yarn and knit with a double strand for first row of ribbing. To insure a snug fit, an elastic thread may also be carried along with yarn for the first few rows. Cuffs are always ribbed and are usually 1″ to 2″ deep for the shorter lengths of men's socks and 2½″ to 4″ deep for regulation length.

LEGS: Slack length socks for men are about 4½″ from top of sock to top of heel; regulation length are 8″ to 9″ from top of sock to top of heel. When making these lengths, no decreases are necessary from top to heel to insure a smooth fit. If longer socks are made, more stitches must be cast on to fit the calf. These extra stitches are decreased 2 at a time at even intervals down centre back of leg. The centre 2 stitches are marked and decreases are made either side of the marked stitches.

HEELS: Reinforce the heels by carrying a matching nylon thread along with yarn unless sock is knitted of nylon or nylon and wool yarn.

French Heel: This is the most popular heel for men's and women's socks because it wears well and provides "cushion comfort." The heel stitches are worked in alternate rows of k 1, sl 1, repeated across, and purl, producing a ribbed effect.

Dutch or Square Heel is similar to the French Heel, but without the ribbed effect.

Auto or Easy Heel is often suggested for children's socks. When the heel is reached, the yarn is dropped and the heel stitches are knitted across with a contrasting strand of yarn. These stitches are then slipped back on the left-hand needle and knitted again with the dropped yarn. The sock is continued until the toe is completed. The heel stitches are then slipped on two needles as the contrasting yarn is pulled out. One needle will have one stitch less then the other. This stitch is picked up on the first round. The heel is then completed in the same manner as a toe, weaving the remaining stitches together after the shaping is completed.

Foot Length: Sizes for socks are measured in inches from centre back of heel to tip of toe. A size 11 sock, for instance, is 11″ from front to back of foot. Tapering the toe section requires 2″ in length for men's and women's socks, 1½″ for children's socks; therefore, in making a size 11 sock, knit evenly around foot section until piece measures 9″ from back of heel straight forward to needles, then start toe decreases. When knitting a sock the same size as a ready-made one, mark off 2″ from toe. Measure back from this point to heel to determine how long foot should be before starting toe decreases.

TOES: Reinforce toes in same way as heels.

Round Toe: Stitches, evenly divided on three needles, are gradually decreased to a few stitches at the end which are drawn up and sewed together.

Pointed Toe: Instep and sole stitches are gradually decreased at sides. When sufficiently tapered, remaining stitches are woven together in Kitchener stitch.

Replacing Heels and Toes

If the heels or toes of hand-knitted socks wear out and the rest of the socks are still in good condition, replace as follows:

Toes: Run a line of basting thread through each stitch at the point where the toe shaping begins. Cut out worn area and ravel back the toe to the basting line, leaving a 2 to 3 inch yarn end. Using same size needles and weight of yarn as the original sock, pick up the stitches from the basting thread. Re-knit toe following any toe directions.

Heels: Run a line of basting around area to be replaced, carefully catching each stitch. Cut out the worn area and unravel the uneven edge up to the line of basting. Pick up the stitches along the back of the heel at the top and knit a new heel section, shaping the same as original heel. When the heel is long enough to join rest of sock, do not cast off stitches, but weave them together using Kitchener stitch. Weave together the sides of the instep and edges of the heel replacement, working from wrong side.

KITCHENER STITCH

Stitches are evenly divided on two needles and held parallel. To weave them together, proceed as follows: Break off yarn, leaving about 12″ end on work. Thread this into a tapestry needle. Working from right to left, * pass threaded needle through first st on front needle as if to knit and slip st off needle; pass yarn through 2nd st on front needle as if to purl but leave st on needle; pass yarn through first st. on back needle as if to purl and slip st off needle; pass yarn through 2nd st. on back needle as if to knit but leave st. on needle. Repeat from * until all sts. are woven together. Fasten off yarn.

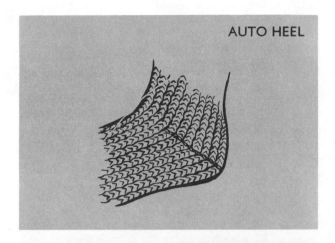

AUTO HEEL

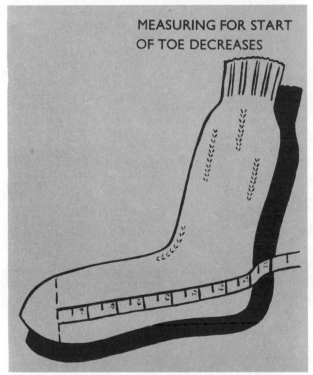

MEASURING FOR START OF TOE DECREASES

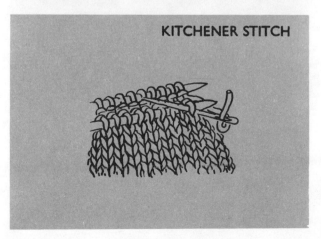

KITCHENER STITCH

Argyle socks

MATERIALS: 4 oz. Ground Shade, 1 oz. each of Scarlet, White and Black, PATONS PURPLE HEATHER 4-ply. Two No. 12 and two No. 11 needles with points at both ends and set of four No. 11 needles with points at both ends.

TENSION: 7½ sts. and 9½ rows to one square inch on No. 11 needles, measured over stocking stitch.

SPECIAL NOTE: Separate balls of wool are used for each White, Ground Shade and Scarlet diamond. Separate strands of Black are used for diamond outline sts. All wools must be twisted on the wrong side where they meet to avoid gaps in work.

TO MAKE: Using No. 12 needles and Ground Shade, cast on 64 sts.

Work in K.2, P.2 rib for 2½ ins.

Change to No. 11 needles and work in patt. from Chart, odd rows K., even rows P., commencing with K. row working K. rows from A to B, P. rows from B to A throughout.

On completing patt. from Chart, break off all wool except Ground Shade leaving end for running in at back of work.

Using Ground Shade, K. 1 row.

Break off wool.

Using set of No. 11 needles **divide sts. for Heel** as follows: —

Slip first and last 16 sts. on one needle, having seam at centre of heel, then divide remaining sts. on to two needles for instep.

HEEL: Rejoin Ground Shade, with right side facing proceed as follows: —

1st row — * K.1, sl. 1 purlwise, rep. from * to end.
2nd row — P.

Rep. these 2 rows 15 times more, then rep. 1st row.

Turn Heel thus: —

P.17, P.2 tog., P.1, turn: sl.1, K.3, K.2 tog. t.b.l., K.1, turn; sl.1, P.4, P.2 tog., P.1, turn; sl.1, K.5, K.2 tog. t.b.l., K.1, turn.

Continue in this manner working one st. more before decrease on each row until all sts. are worked off ending with K.18.

INSTEP: With heel needle pick up and K. 16 sts. on side of heel, using 2nd needle, K. across 32 instep sts; with 3rd needle pick up and K. 16 sts. on side of heel and K. 9 on same needle from heel sts.

25 sts. on 1st and 3rd needle; 32 sts. on second needle.

Shape gusset thus: —

1st round — K. to last 3 sts. on 1st needle, K.2 tog., K.1; K. sts. on 2nd needle; K.1, K.2 tog. t.b.l., K. to end of 3rd needle.

2nd round — K.

Rep. these 2 rounds until there are 16 sts. on 1st and 3rd needle; 32 sts. on 2nd needle.

Continue in rounds on these 64 sts. until foot measures 9 ins. (or desired length) from centre back of heel.

Shape toe thus: —

1st round — K. to last 3 sts., K.2 tog. K.1 on 1st needle; K.1, K.2 tog. t.b.l., K. to last 3 sts., K.2 tog., K.1 on 2nd needle; K.1, K.2 tog. t.b.l., K. to end on 3rd needle.

2nd round — K.

Rep. these 2 rounds until 20 sts. remain.

Knit 5 sts. from 1st needle on to 3rd needle (10 sts. on each of 2 needles). Graft sts. together.

Press on wrong side.

Flat-stitch seam together at centre back.

Argyle-patterned socks, unlike most socks, are worked back and forth on two needles until diamonds are completed; then socks are finished in four-needle knitting. Each colourful diamond is knitted from a separate ball of yarn as described in directions.

◤ BLACK   ⊡ SCARLET   □ GS   ⊠ WHITE

B

A

Heel-less sock for men or women

MATERIALS: 5 oz. Short length, 7 oz. Regulation length, PATONS MOORLAND Double Knitting. Set of four No. 11 QUEEN BEE needles with points at both ends.

MEASUREMENT: For Short or Regulation length.

TENSION: $6\frac{3}{4}$ sts. and 9 rows to one square inch on No. 11 needles, measured over stocking stitch.

Cast on 64 sts. on 3 needles, join for round.

Work in K.2, P.2, rib for 2 ins.

Proceed in **patt.** as follows: —

1st to 3rd round — * K.2, P.2, rep. from * to end of round.

4th to 6th round — P.1, * K.2, P.2, rep. from * to last 3 sts., K.2, P.1.

7th to 9th round — * P.2, K.2, rep. from * to end of round.

10th to 12th round — K.1, * P.2, K.2, rep. from * to last 3 sts., P.2, K.1.

These 12 rounds form the spiral pattern.

Continue in patt. until work measures for **short sock** $11\frac{1}{2}$ ins. (size 9), 12 ins. (size 10), $12\frac{1}{2}$ ins. (size 11), 13 ins. (size 12). For **regulation length** $18\frac{1}{2}$ ins. (size 9), 19 ins (size 10), $19\frac{1}{2}$ ins. (size 11), 20 ins. (size 12).

Divide sts. 16 on **first** needle, 32 on **second** needle, 16 on **3rd needle.**

1st round — On first needle, K. to last 3 sts., K.2 tog., K.1. On 2nd needle K.1, K.2 tog. t.b.l., K. to last 3 sts., K.2 tog., K.1. On 3rd needle K.1, K.2, tog. t.b.l., K. to end.

2nd round — K.

Rep. these 2 rounds until 12 sts. remain. Graft together 2 sets of 6 sts.

Men's socks with French heels

MATERIALS: 4 oz. PATONS PURPLE HEATHER 3-ply, or 4 oz. PATONS NYLOX 3-ply, Patonised for **lightweight** Socks. 4 oz. PATONS PURPLE HEATHER 4-ply or 4 oz. PATONS NYLOX 4-ply, Patonised for **medium weight** socks. One set of four No. 12 QUEEN BEE needles with points at both ends for **lightweight** socks and one set of four No. 11 QUEEN BEE needles with points at both ends for medium weight socks.

MEASUREMENT: Length of foot, 11 ins (adjustable).

SPECIAL NOTE: Figures in square brackets [] refer to medium weight size throughout.

TENSION: $8\frac{1}{2}$ sts. and $10\frac{1}{2}$ rows to one square inch on No. 12 needles in 3-ply wool (**lightweight**) measured over stocking stitch. $7\frac{1}{2}$ sts. and $9\frac{1}{2}$ rows to one square inch on No. 11 needles in 4-ply wool (**medium weight**) measured over stocking stitch.

Using No. 12 [11] needles, cast on 68 [64] sts. on 3 needles.

Work in rounds of K.2, P.2 rib for 4 ins.

Next round — (lightweight size) * K.16, inc. in next st., rep. from * to end (72 sts.).

Next round — (medium weight size) K. (64 sts.).

Proceed in rounds of stocking stitch, every round K. until work measures $9\frac{1}{2}$ ins. from cast-on edge (adjust length here), **noting** that 1st and last st. of round mark the 2 ins. at centre back.

Shape leg as follows: —

** **1st round** — K.1, K.2 tog., K. to last 3 sts., at end of round, K.2 tog. t.b.l., K.1.

Work 9 [8] rounds. **

Rep. from ** to ** once more (68 [60] sts.).

Continue in rounds until work measures 12 ins. from cast-on edge (adjust leg length here), finishing last round 18 [15] sts. from end of third needle.

Slip 18 [15] sts. from first needle on to end of third needle.

Divide remaining 32 [30] sts. on to two needles for instep leaving the 36 [30] sts. on one needle for heel.

Work heel as follows: —

1st row — * (Sl. 1 purlwise, K.1) 18 [15] times, turn.

2nd row — P.

Rep. these 2 rows 19 [15] times more (40 [32] rows in all)

Turn heel as follows: —

1st row — Sl. 1, K.20 [16], K.2 tog., K.1, turn.

2nd row — Sl.1, P.7 [5], P.2, tog. t.b.l., P.1, turn.

3rd row — Sl.1, K.8 [6], K.2 tog., K.1, turn.

4th row — Sl.1, P.9 [7], P.2 tog. t.b.l., P.1, turn.

Continue in this manner until there are 22 [18] sts. left, finishing with a K. row.

Gusset and Foot: Knit up 20 [16] sts. on side of heel, K.32 [30] instep sts. on to one needle, **knit up** 20 [16] sts. on second side of heel and 11 [9] sts. of heel on same needle.

Slip remaining 11 [9] heel sts. on to first needle (31 [25] sts. on 1st and 3rd needle, 32 [30] sts. on 2nd needle). K.1 round.

1st round — K. to last 3 sts. on 1st needle, K.2 tog., K.1; K. sts. on 2nd needle; K.1, K.2 tog. t.b.l., K. to end on 3rd needle.

2nd round — K.

Rep. these 2 rounds until 68 [56] sts. remain.

Continue in rounds of stocking stitch until foot measures 9 ins. (or length required).

Slip st. from end of 1st needle and beg. of 3rd needle on to 2nd needle, 17 [14] sts. on 1st needle; 34 [28] sts. on 2nd needle; 17 [14] sts. on 3rd needle.

1st round — K. to 3 sts. at end of 1st needle, K.2 tog., K.1; K.1, K.2 tog. t.b.l., K. to 3 sts., K.2 tog., K.1 on 2nd needle; K.1, K.2 tog. t.b.l., K. to end on 3rd needle.

2nd round — K.

Rep. these 2 rounds until 20 [16] sts. remain.

Knit 5 [4] sts. 1st needle on to 3rd needle and graft 2 sets of 10 [8] sts. together. Lightly press on wrong side.

Plain stocking stitch is used for these basic socks to make in any length, any size, in lightweight or medium-weight wools.

Cable gloves for men

MATERIALS: 3 oz. PATONS BEEHIVE 4-Ply Patonised or PATONS NYLOX 4-ply, Patonised. Set of four No. 12 QUEEN BEE needles with points at both ends. One cable needle.

MEASUREMENT: To fit average hand.

TENSION: 8 sts. and 10 rows to one square inch on No. 12 needles, measured over stocking stitch.

RIGHT GLOVE: Cast on 56 sts. on 3 needles.

Work in rounds of K.2, P.2 rib for 3 ins.

Proceed as follows: —

1st round — K.4 * P.1, K.6, P.1, K.4, P.1, K.6, P.1 *, K.6, K. into front, back and front of next st. (first inc. for Thumb), K. to end.

2nd and 3rd rounds — K.4, rep. from * to * of round 1, K. to end.

4th round — K.4, rep. from * to *, K.6, inc. in next st., K.1, inc. in next st., K. to end.

5th to 7th round — Rep. 2nd, 3rd and 2nd rounds.

8th round — K.4, P.1, C.3F., P.1, K.4, P.1, C.3F., P.1, K.6, inc. in next st., K.3, inc. in next st., K. to end of round.

These 8 rounds form the cable patt.

Continue in patt., inc. as before for **Thumb, noting** there will be 2 sts. more after each inc. between incs. on every 4th round from previous inc. until 9 inc. **in all** have been worked at each side of thumb (19 sts. for Thumb).

Next round — Work to 19 Thumb sts. slip 19 Thumb sts. on to a length of wool, cast on 5, work to end (60 sts.).

Keeping cable patt. correct, work 18 rounds.

Work 6 rounds in stocking stitch, finishing in st. before 5 cast-on sts.

1st Finger — Slip first 10 sts. on needle, K. next 5 sts. (over 5 cast–on sts.) K.2, slip remaining 43 sts. on a length of wool, cast-on 4 (21 sts.).

Work in rounds for 3 ins.

Next round — K.2 tog., K. to end.

K. 1 round.

1st round — * K.2 tog., K.3, rep. from * to end of round.

2nd round — K.

3rd round — * K.2 tog., K.2, rep. from * to end of round.

4th round — K.

5th round — (K. 2 tog.) 6 times.

Break off wool. Thread through 6 sts., draw up, fasten off on wrong side.

2nd Finger — Slip 7 sts. from thread on back of hand on to needle, **knit up** 4 sts. through 4 cast-on sts. of First Finger, K.7 from other end of thread, cast on 3 (21 sts.).

Work in rounds of stocking stitch for 3¼ ins.

Shape top as First Finger

3rd Finger — Slip 7 sts. from end of thread on back, K.3 sts. through 3 cast-on sts. of 2nd Finger, K.7 from other end of thread, cast on 3.

Work in rounds for 3 ins.

Shape top as First Finger.

4th Finger — Slip remaining 15 sts. from thread on to 3 needles, K.3 sts. through 3 cast-on sts. of 3rd Finger (18 sts.).

Work in rounds for 2¼ ins.

Next round — (K.2 tog., K.1) 5 times.

Next round — K.

Next round — (K.2 tog.) 6 times.

Break off wool and complete as First Finger.

Slip first 9 Thumb sts. on to first needle, next 10 thumb sts. on to second needle, M.1 by picking up loop between last st. and following st. and knitting into back of it, K.5 sts. across cast-on sts., M.1 as before—7 sts. on 3rd needle.

Slip 1st and 2nd sts. from 2nd needle on to 3rd needle, K. next 2 sts. on to 3rd needle: — 7 sts. on **1st needle**, 8 sts. on **2nd needle**, 11 sts. on **3rd needle**, K. 2 rounds.

Next round — K. to 11 sts. on 3rd needle, K.5, K.2 tog., K.4 on these sts.

Next round — K.

Next round — K. to 10 sts. on 3rd needle, K.4, K.2 tog., K.4.

Next round — K.

Next round — K. to 9 sts. on 3rd needle, K.3, K.2 tog., K. 4.

Next round — K.

Next round — K. to 8 sts. on 3rd needle, K.3, K.2 tog., K.3 (22 sts.).

Continue in rounds until Thumb measures 2½ ins. at, inside edge.

Of all four-needle projects, gloves are most fascinating to knit. Directions tell how to make thumb gusset, fingers; how to work left glove to correspond to right.

154

Next round — (K.2 tog., K.9) twice K.1.
Complete as First Finger commencing with first dec. round.
LEFT GLOVE: Work ribbing as on Right Glove.
Proceed as follows: —
1st round — K.25, K. into front, back and front of next st., K.6, * P.1, K.6, P.1, K.4, P.1, K.6, P.1 *, K.4.
Keeping cable patt. and inc. correct, work as Right

Glove to 1st Finger.
First Finger — Commence 2 sts. before 5 cast-on sts. over Thumb.
K. these 2 sts., K.5 through cast-off st. over thumb, K.10, cast on 4. Slip remaining sts. on to a length of wool.
Complete as for Right Glove. Press using a warm iron and damp cloth.

Reversible double thick mittens for men

MATERIALS: 3 oz. PATONS ARIEL. Two No. 3 BEEHIVE needles. Two stitch-holders.
MEASUREMENT: To fit average hand.
TENSION: 4 sts. and 5 rows to one square inch on No. 3 needles, measured over stocking stitch.
Cast on 48 sts.
Work in K. 2, P. 2 rib for 4 ins.
Next row— (inc. in each of next 2 sts., P. 2) 5 times, (inc. in each of next 4 sts.) twice, (inc. in each of next 2 sts., P. 2) 5 times. (76 sts.). Proceed in **double knitting patt.** as follows:-
1st to 10th row— * K.1, w.ft., sl.1P., w.b., rep. from * to end.
1st inc. for Thumb – Patt. 35, inc. in each of next 2 sts., patt.2, inc. in each of next 2 sts., patt. 35.
Patt. 3 rows.
2nd inc. for Thumb – Patt. 35, inc. in each of next 2 sts., patt. 6. inc. in each of next 2 sts., patt 35.
Work 3 rows.
Continue in this manner, inc. 2 sts. at each side of thumb as before on next and every following 4th row until there are 30 sts. on the thumb.
Thumb – Patt. 35, slip these sts. on to a stitch holder, inc. in first st. of thumb, patt. to last st. of thumb, inc. in last st (32 sts. for thumb), slip remaining 35 sts. on to a stitch-holder and leave: Work in patt. on 32 Thumb sts. for 2½ ins.

1st dec. row – * Patt. 4, (K. 2 tog.) twice, rep. from * to end. Work back in patt.
2nd dec. row – * Patt. 2, (K.2 tog.) twice, rep. from * to end. Work back in patt.
3rd dec. row – K.2 tog. all across. Break off wool.
Thread wool through sts. and draw up. Neatly flat-stitch thumb seam.
Hand – Slip sts. from first stitch-holder on to needle, join wool,
knit up 6 sts. under Thumb, slip second 35 sts. on to needle, patt. 35 (76 sts.).
Continue in patt. on these sts. for 4 inches.
1st dec. row – * Patt. 6, (K.2 tog.) twice, rep. from * to last 6 sts., patt. 6.
Work 3 rows in patt. (62 sts.)
2nd dec. row – * Patt. 5, (K.2 tog.) twice, rep. from * to last 8 sts., patt. 4, K.2 tog. twice.
Work 3 rows in patt. (48 sts.).
3rd dec. row – * Patt. 4, (K.2 tog.) twice, rep.from * to end. Work 3 rows in patt. (36 sts.).
4th dec. row – * Patt. 3, (K.2 tog.) twice, rep. from * slipping last st.
Work 1 row in patt. (26 sts.).
5th dec. row – * Patt.2, (K.2 tog.) twice, rep. from * to last 2 sts., K.1, sl.1.
Work 1 row in patt. (18 sts.).
6th dec. row — K.2 tog. all across row. Break off wool.
Thread through sts. and draw up. Flat-stitch side seam.

Snowflake pattern gloves for women

Coloured patterns can be worked in four-needle knitting, as in these authentic Norwegian gloves. Pattern colour forming large snowflakes on backs and smaller motifs on fingers and palms is carried around with background colour.

MATERIALS: 2 oz. Ground Shade (Blue) and 1 oz. Contrast (White), PATONS BEEHIVE 4-ply, Patonised. Two No. 11 BEEHIVE or QUEEN BEE needles, set of four No. 9 QUEEN BEE needles with points at both ends.

MEASUREMENTS: To fit average hand.

TENSION: 7½ sts. and 7½ rows to one square inch on No. 9 needles, measured over colour patt.

Special Note: When working patt. from Chart every round K., strand the colour not in use at back of work throughout.

RIGHT GLOVE: Using Ground Shade and No. 11 needles, cast on 45 sts.—15 on each of 3 needles.

Work 7 rounds in K.2, P.1, rib.

Continue in rib working in stripes as follows: —

Striped patt. rounds — (Work 1 round Contrast, 1 round in G.S.). 5 times.

Break off Contrast.

Using Ground Shade, work 6 rounds in K.2, P.1 rib.

Using Ground Shade, K.3 rounds.

Next round — (K.3, inc. in next st., K.2, inc. in next st.) 6 times, K. to end (57 sts.).

Change to No. 9 needles and proceed from Chart 1 as follows: —

Thumb gusset (1st round) — Reading Chart from right to left patt. 35, K.2C., using G.S., K. into front and back of next st., patt. 19

Round 2 — Following 2nd row Chart 1, keeping 2 sts. in G. S. for thumb gusset, work all round.

Round 3 — Patt. 35, K.2C., K.1, inc. in next st., K.2C., patt. to end.

Round 4 — Work from Chart 1, row 4, 3 sts. of thumb gusset being worked in Ground Shade.

Rounds 5 to 11
Continue in this manner, inc. 1 st. at each side of thumb gusset on next and every alt. row until there are 11 sts. on the thumb gusset (67 sts.).

Rounds 12-14 — Following Chart 1 work all round.

Round 15 — Patt. to 2 sts. in C. to side of thumb gusset, slip next 15 sts. on to a length of wool, using G.S. cast on 15 sts., work in patt. to end (67 sts.).

16th round — Following Chart patt. 33, using G.S. K.2 tog., K. to end (66 sts.).

Rounds 17-27 — Work in patt. from Chart 1.

Round 28 — Slip first 22 sts. on thread for back of hand, break off wool, join in G.S., patt. 19 as shown on Chart for first finger. using G.S. cast on 5 sts. Slip remaining 25 sts. on length of wool for palm.

First finger — Divide 24 sts. on 3 needles.

Join in wool, work as Chart 2 from right to left for Right Glove; (from left to right for Left Glove).

Continue on these 24 sts. until round 20 has been worked.

Shape top (Round 21) — Working as from Chart 2, after 1st C. stripe, K.2 tog. t.b.l., K. to last 4 sts. of round, K.2, tog., K.2C.

Rounds 22-24 — * K.2 tog. t.b.l., K. to 2 sts. from C. stripe, K.2 tog., K.2C., rep. from * once (10 sts.).

Round 25 — K.2 tog. t.b.l., G.S., K.2C., K.2 tog. t.b.l., K.2C. (6 sts.).

Break off G.S.

Round 26 — (K.2 tog.) 3 times.

Round 27 — Sl.1, K.2 tog., p.s.s.o. Draw wool through st. and fasten off securely.

Second Finger. Slip next 6 sts. from back of hand on to needle, join in G.S., K. sts. on needle, K.5 sts. through cast-on sts. of last finger, slip last 8 sts. of palm on to spare needle, (K. 3G.S., 1C). twice, with G.S. cast on 5 sts. (24 sts.).

Work as First Finger.

Third Finger — Work as Second Finger.

Fourth Finger — Slip last 10 sts. from back of hand on to needle, join C., K.2C., 8G.S., using G.S. **knit up** 5 sts. through cast-on sts. on last finger, slip 9 sts. of palm on spare needle, (K. 3G.S., 1C.) twice, K.1G.S.

Divide these 24 sts. on 3 needles.

Work to end of round 14 from Chart 2.

Keeping patt. correct (next row round 15), **shape top** as first finger.

Thumb. Slip 15 sts. from length of wool on to 2 needles,

join in G.S., **knit up** 15 sts. through cast-on sts.
Divide these 30 sts. on 3 needles. Join in C., K.2 C., follow Chart 3 from right to left to end of round 12.

Shape top — Rounds 13–14 — Following Chart 3, K. to after 1st C. stripe, K.2 tog. t.b.l., K. to last 4 sts., K.2 tog., K.2C. (26 sts.).

15th to 18th rounds — Work rounds 15–18 Chart 3, shaping top as on round 22 of directions for first finger (10 sts.).

19th to 21st round — Work as rounds 25–27 of first finger.

LEFT GLOVE. Reading rounds from left to right, work as Right Glove until 12th round has been completed.

Thumb gusset. Round 1 — Reading Chart 1 from left to right patt. 17, K.2C., using G.S. **knit up** front and back of next st., K.2C., patt. to end.

Rounds 2-27 — Reading Chart from left to right throughout, work as Left Glove.

Round 28 — Following Chart 1, slip first 25 sts. on thread for palm, break off wool, join C., patt. next 19 sts. from Chart for first finger, using G.S. cast on 5 sts., slip remaining 22 on length of wool.

Work fingers as Right Glove beg. fingers from palm side. Complete fingers as Right Glove.

TO MAKE UP. Omitting ribbing, block and press on wrong side using a warm iron and damp cloth.

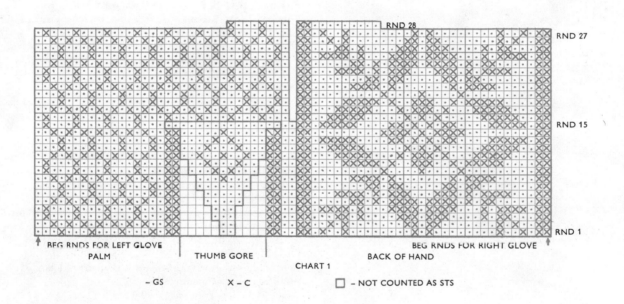

CHART 1

– GS   X – C   ☐ – NOT COUNTED AS STS

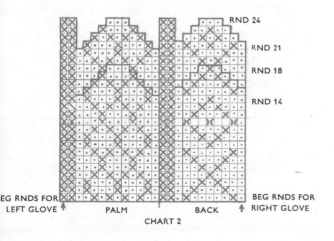

CHART 2

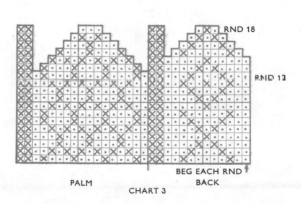

CHART 3

Tyrolean cardigan

Authentic Tyrolean cardigans combine lace patterns, raised patterns and touches of brightly coloured embroidery. Necklines and front edges are often crocheted in a contrasting colour.

MATERIALS: 10 [11, 12, 13] oz. Ground Shade, 1 [1, 1, 1] oz. Contrast for Neckband, PATONS BEEHIVE 4-ply, Patonised, or PATONS NYLOX 4-ply, Patonised. Oddments of three Contrasting Shades for embroidery. Two No. 12 and two No. 10 BEEHIVE or QUEEN BEE needles. Steel crochet hook. 1 yd. 1 inch wide grosgrain ribbon. Six buttons. Two press studs.

MEASUREMENTS: To fit 32 [34, 36, 38] inch bust. Length 20¾ [21½, 21¾, 22½] ins. Sleeve seam, 17 [17½, 17½, 18] ins.
SIZES: The figures in square brackets [ ] refer to the 34, 36 and 38 inch sizes respectively.
TENSION: 7 sts. and 9 rows to one square inch on No. 10 needles, measured over stocking stitch.
LACE PATTERN: 1st, 3rd, 5th and 7th rows — P.4, * w.o.n., sl.1, K.2 tog., p.s.s.o., w.r.n., P.5, rep. from * to last 7 sts., w.o.n., sl.1, K.2 tog., p.s.s.o., w.r.n., P.4.
2nd, 4th, 6th and 8th rows — K.
9th, 11th, 13th and 15th rows — P.1, K.2 tog., w.r.n., * P.5, w.o.n., sl.1, K.2 tog., p.s.s.o., w.r.n., rep. from * to last 8 sts., P.5, w.o.n., K.2 tog., P.1.
10th, 12th, 14th and 16th rows — K.
These 16 rows form the lace patt.

BACK: Using No. 12 needles, cast on 114 [122, 130, 138] sts.
Work in K.1, P.1 rib for 3½ ins., inc. 1 st. at end of last row (115 [123, 131, 139] sts.).
Change to No. 10 needles and proceed in lace patt. until work measures 13½ [14, 14, 14½] ins. from beg.
Shape armholes by casting off 4 sts. at beg. of next 2 rows, then dec. 1 st. at both ends of every 3rd row until 4 [5, 6, 7] sets of dec. have been completed (99 [105, 111, 117] sts.).
Continue on these sts. until work measures 7¼ [7½, 7¾, 8] ins. from beg. of armhole shaping.
Shape shoulders by casting off 11 [12, 12, 13] sts. at beg. of next 4 rows; 10 [10, 12, 12] sts. on next 2 rows.
Cast off remaining 35 [37, 39, 41] sts.

LEFT FRONT: Using No. 12 needles, cast on 67 [75, 75, 83] sts.

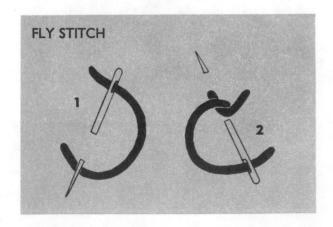

FLY STITCH

Fly Stitch is similar to lazy daisy stitch, but the ends of the loop stitch are widely separated. Make a small backstitch to anchor the centre in place, bringing needle up in position for next stitch.

Work in K.1, P.1 rib to match Back.

Change to No. 10 needles and proceed as follows: —

1st row — Work 1st row of lace patt. to last 8 sts., rib 8.

2nd row — Rib 8, lace patt. to end.

Continue in this manner (next row 3rd row of lace patt.) working 8 sts. at front edge in rib throughout until work matches Back to armhole shaping.

Shape armhole by casting off 4 [4, 4, 6] sts. at beg. of next row; then dec. 1 st. at armhole edge on every 3rd row 6 [8, 8, 8] times (57 [63, 63, 69] sts.).

Continue in patt. with ribbed border as before until work measures 4¾ [5, 5¼, 5½] ins. from beg. of armhole shaping, finishing at front edge.

Shape neck by casting off 9 [9, 9, 10] sts. at beg. of next row; 3 sts. at neck edge on every alt. row 5 [6, 6, 7] times, then dec. 1 st. at neck edge on alt. rows 1 [2, 0, 0] times (32 [34, 36, 38] sts.).

Continue on these sts. until work matches Back to shoulder shaping.

Shape shoulders by casting off 11 [12, 12, 13] sts. at beg. of next and following alt. row, then 10 [10, 12, 12] sts. on following alt. row. With pins mark position of 6 buttons on centre of Left Front Band, first one ½ inch from lower edge, last one ½ inch from neck edge. The buttonholes are worked on the Right Front Band to match buttons as follows: —

1st row of buttonhole — Rib 3, cast off 2, rib 2, patt. to end.

2nd row of buttonhole — Patt. to last 6 sts., rib 3, cast on 3. rib to end.

RIGHT FRONT: Using No. 12 needles, cast on 67 [75, 75, 83] sts.

Work ribbing as on Left Front, working buttonholes to correspond with pins on Left Front Band.

Change to No. 10 needles and proceed as follows: —

1st row — Rib. 8, patt. to end (1st row of patt.).

2nd row — Patt. to last 8 sts. (2nd row of patt), rib. 8.

Working buttonholes throughout Band as marked with pins, complete to match Left Front reversing shapings.

SLEEVES: Using No. 12 needles, cast on 52 [54, 60, 62] sts.

Work in K.1, P.1 rib for 4½ ins.

Next row — Rib 4 [7, 6, 7] (inc. in next st., rib 6 [9, 7, 11]) 6 [4, 6, 4] times, inc. in next st., rib to end (59 [59, 67, 67] sts.).

Change to No. 10 needles and proceed in patt., inc. 1 st. at both ends of 7th row following and every following 9th row until there are 85 [85, 93, 93] sts.

Continue on these sts. until work measures 14¾ [15½, 15½, 15¾] ins. from **top of ribbing.**

Shape top by casting off 4 [4, 4, 6] sts. at beg. of next 2 rows.

Dec. 1 st. at both ends of every 3rd row 6 [6, 8, 9] times, every row 22 [20, 23, 21] times.

Cast off.

TO MAKE UP: Omitting ribbing, block and press on wrong side using a warm iron and damp cloth. Join shoulder side and sleeve seams and stitch Sleeves into position.

NECKBAND: 1st row — Commencing in 6th st. of ribbed border, using crochet hook and Contrast, make loop through first stitch, 2 ch., * missing next st. work 1 single crochet in following st., rep. from * ending with 1 single crochet in 6th stitch of second Front Band, 1 ch., turn. **2nd row** — S.C. in first s.c., * 7 ch., s.c. in next space, rep. from * ending with s.c. in last s.c., 7 ch., turn. **3rd row** — S.C. in second s.c. * 7 ch., s.c. in next s.c. rep. from * to end.

Fasten off.

Face Front Bands on wrong side with ribbon, cutting buttonholes in ribbon to match buttonholes in band. Work in buttonhole stitch round buttonholes.

Attach buttons.

Stitch press studs at top of Front Bands.

TO EMBROIDER: Using single strand of Contrast, make 2 fly stitches 3 rows apart to form stem and leaves. Work vertical 7 st. buds of double strands of yellow, blue and red. Work vertical row of buds each side of centre band, alternating blue and yellow.

Scatter red, blue and yellow buds on Fronts and top of sleeves.

Satin Stitch is straight stitches worked side by side, usually slantwise, to fill small areas. For small circles, work centre long stitch first, then fill each side.

SATIN STITCH

Aran sweater

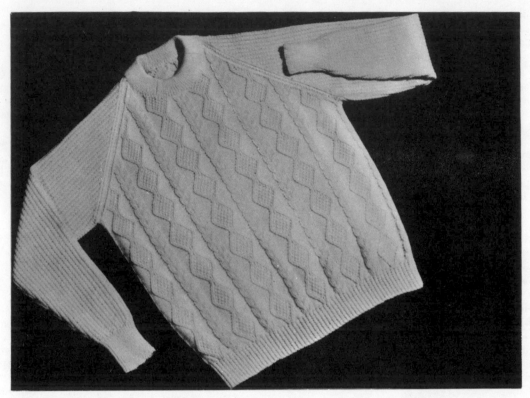

The Irish-knit sweater is distinguished for its variety of raised pattern stitches set side by side in vertical panels.

MATERIALS: 18 oz. PATONS BEEHIVE 4-ply, Patonised, or PATONS NYLOX 4-ply, Patonised, or 18 oz. PATONS PURPLE HEATHER 4-ply. Two No. 13 and two No. 11 BEEHIVE or QUEEN BEE needles, set of four No. 15 needles and set of four No. 13 QUEEN BEE needles with points at both ends. A BEEHIVE cable needle. Two stitch-holders.

MEASUREMENTS: To fit 34–36 inch bust. Length, 26 ins. Sleeve seam, 18 ins. (adjustable).

TENSION: 7½ sts. and 9½ rows to one square inch on No. 11 needles, measured over stocking stitch.

ARAN PATTERN: 1st row — K.1, * sl. 1 knitwise, K.B.4, P.8, K.B.5, P.8. K.B.4, rep. from * to last 2 sts., sl. 1, K. 1.

2nd row — P.1, * P.1, P.B.4, K.8, P.B.5, K.8, P.B.4., rep. from * to last 2 sts., P.2.

3rd row — K.1, * sl.1, K.B.4, P.7, Cr.1B, K.B.1, Cr.2F., P.7, C.2B., rep. from * to last 2 sts., sl. 1, K.1.

4th row — P.1, * P.1, P.B.4, K.7, P.B.2, K.1, P.B.1, K.1, P.B.2, K.7, P.B.4, rep. from * to last 2 sts., P.2.

5th row — K.1, * sl.1, K.B.4, P.6, Cr.1B, K.B.1, P.1, K.B.1, Cr.2F, P.6, K.B.4, rep. from * to last 2 sts., sl.1, K.1.

6th row — P.1, * P.1, P.B.4, K.6, P.B.2, (K.1, P.B.1), twice, K.1, P.B.2, K.6, P.B.4, rep. from * to last 2 sts. P.2.

7th row — K.1, * sl.1, C.2F, P.5, Cr.1B., (K.B.1, P.1) twice K.B.1, Cr.2F, P.5, K.B.4, rep. from * to last 2 sts., sl. 1, K.1.

8th row — P.1, * P.1, P.B.4, K.5, P.B.2, (K.1, P.B.1) 3 times, K.1, P.B.2, K.5, P.B.4, rep. from * to last 2 sts., P.2.

9th row — K.1, * sl.1, K.B.4, P.4, Cr.1B., (K.B.1, P.1) 3 times, K.B.1, Cr.2F, P.4, K.B.4, rep. from * to last 2 sts., sl.1, K.1,

10th row — P.1, * P.1, P.B.4, K.4, P.B.2, (K.1, P.B.1) 4 times, K.1, P.B.2, K.4, P.B.4, rep. from * to last 2 sts., P.2.

11th row — K.1, * sl.1, K.B.4, P.3, Cr.1B., (K.B.1, P.1) 4 times, K.B.1, Cr.2F., P.3, C.2B., rep. from * to last 2 sts., sl.1, K.1.

12th row — P.1, * P.1, P.B.4, K3, P.B.2, (K.1, P.B.1) 5 times, K.1, P.B.2, K.3, PB4., rep. from * to last 2 sts., P.2.

13th row — K.1.*sl.1. K.B.4, P.2, Cr.1B., (K.B.1, P.1) 5 times, K.B.1, Cr.2F., P.2, K.B.4, rep. from * to last 2 sts., sl.1, K.1,

14th row — P.1, * P.1, P.B.4, K.2, P.B.2, (K.1, P.B.1) 6 times, K. 1, P.B.2, K.2, P.B.4, rep. from * to last 2 sts., P.2.

15th row — K.1, * sl.1, C.2F., P.2, Cr.2F., (P.1, K.B.1). 5 times, P.1, Cr.1B., P.2, K.B.4, rep. from * to last 2 sts., sl.1, K.1.

16th row — As 12th row.

17th row — K.1, * sl.1, K.B.4, P.3, Cr.2F., (P.1, K.B.1) 4 times, P.1, Cr. 1B., P.3, K.B.4, rep. from * to last 2 sts., sl.1, K.1.

18th row — As 10th row.

19th row — K.1. * sl. 1, K.B.4, P.4, Cr.2F., (P.1, K.B.1) 3 times, P.1, Cr. 1B., P.4, C.2B., rep. from * to last

2 sts., sl.1, K.1,

20th row — As 8th row.

21st row — K.1, * sl.1, K.B.4, P.5, Cr.2F., (P.1, K.B.1) twice, P.1, Cr.1B., P.5, K.B.4, rep. from * to last 2 sts., sl.1, K.1.

22nd row — As 6th row.

23rd row — K.1, * sl.1, C.2F., P.6, Cr.2F., P.1, K.B.1, P.1, Cr.1B., P.6, K.B.4, rep. from * to last 2 sts., sl.1, K.1.

24th row — As 4th row.

25th row — K.1, * sl.1, K.B.4, P.7, Cr.2F., K.B.1, Cr.1B., P.7, K.B.4, rep. from * to last 2 sts., sl.1, K.1.

26th row – P.1, * P.1, P.B.4, K.8, P.B.5, K.8, P.B.4, rep. from * to last 2 sts., P.2.

These 26 rows form the Aran Diamond patt., the cables are worked on every 4th row alternating as on these 26 rows, the next cable falling on the next row.

BACK: Using No. 13 needles, cast on 184 sts.

Proceed in **twisted rib** as follows: —

1st row — * P.1, Tw.2, rep. from * to last st., P.1.

2nd row — * K.1, P.2, rep. from * to last st., K.1.

Rep. these 2 rows until work measures $2\frac{1}{4}$ ins. from beg., finishing at end of a 2nd row and dec. 1 st. at end of this row (183 sts.).

Change to No. 11 needles and proceed in cable and Aran patt. (repeats of rows 1 to 26 throughout) until work measures 16 ins. from beg., finishing with **wrong** side facing for next row.

Next row — Cast off 4, patt. to last 4 sts., cast off 4. Break off wool.

Rejoin wool and proceed as follows: —

1st row — K.1, K.2 tog. t.b.l., patt. to last 3 sts., K.2 tog., K.1.

2nd row — K.1, P.2, tog., patt. to last 3 sts., P.2 tog. t.b.l., K.1.

3rd row — K.2, patt. to last 2 sts., K.2.

4th row — As 2nd row.

5th row — As 1st row.

6th row — K.1, P.1, patt. to last 2 sts., P.1, K.1.

Continue as on these 6 rows until 63 sts. remain, thus finishing with **wrong** side facing for next row.

Next row — P.2, patt. 15, P. next 29 sts. on to a stitch-holder, patt. 15, P.2.

Proceed on first group of sts. as follows: —

1st row — K.1, K.2 tog. t.b.l., patt. 14.

2nd row — Cast off 3, patt. 9 (there now being 10 sts. on needle after cast-off), P.2 tog. t.b.l., K.1.

3rd row — K.2, patt. 10.

4th row — Cast off 3, patt. 5, P.2, tog. t.b.l., K.1.

5th row — K.1, K.2 tog. t.b.l., patt. 5.

6th row — Cast off 3, patt. 1, P.1, K.1.

7th row — K.1, K.2 tog. t.b.l., K.1.

8th row — P.2 tog. t.b.l., K.1.

9th row — K.2 tog.

Fasten off.

Rejoin wool to remaining group of sts. and complete to match First Half of Back, reversing shaping, **noting** that **2 tog.** in place of t.b.l. is worked at armhole edge throughout.

FRONT: Work as Back until 87 sts. remainn, finishig with

wrong side facing for next row.

Next row — K.1, P.1, patt. 32, P. next 19 sts. on to a stitch-holder, patt. 32, P.1, K.1.

Proceed on **each** group of sts. as follows: —

Still dec. at armhole edge as before, cast off 2 sts. at neck edge 5 times on every alt. row, and 1 st. at neck edge 4 times on every alt. row.

Continue dec. at armhole edge **only** as before until all sts. are worked off.

SLEEVES: Using No. 13 needles, cast on 64 sts.

Work in K.1, P.1 rib for 3 ins.

Next row — Rib 4 (inc. in next st., rib 3) 15 times (79 sts.).

Change to No. 11 needles and proceed in twisted rib as on Back, inc. 1 st. at both ends of 3rd and every following 4th row working extra sts. into twisted rib patt. until there are 139 sts.

Continue on these sts. until work measures 18 ins. from beg., finishing with right side facing for next row (adjust length at this point). Mark this point.

Work 6 rows.

Shape raglan top as follows: —

1st row — K.1, Tw.2, P.1, K.2 tog. t.b.l., patt. to last 6 sts., K.2 tog., P.1, Tw.2, K.1.

2nd row — K.1, P.2, K.1, P.2 tog., patt. to last 6 sts., P.2 tog. t.b.l., K.1, P.2, K.1.

3rd row — K.1, Tw.2, P.1, K.1, patt. to last 5 sts,. K.1, P.1, Tw.2, K.1.

4th row — As 2nd row.

5th row — As 1st row.

6th row — K.1, P.2, K.1, P.1, patt. to last 5 sts., P.1, K.1, P.2, K.1.

Continue as on these 6 rows until 15 sts. remain.

1st row — K.1, Tw.2, P.1, K.1, patt. to last 5 sts.,K.1, P.1, Tw.2, K.1.

2nd row — K.1, P.2, K.1, P.2 tog., P.3, P.2 tog. t.b.l., K.1, P.2, K.1.

3rd row — K.1, Tw.2, P.1, K.1, sl.1, K.2, tog., p.s.s.o., K.1, P.1, Tw.2, K.1.

4th row — K.1, P.2, K.1, P.3, K.1, P.2, K.1.

Cast off.

TO MAKE UP: Omitting ribbing block and press **very** lightly on wrong side using a warm iron and damp cloth. Using a flat seam for ribbing and a fine back-stitch seam for remainder, join side seams, join sleeve seams to marked point, stitching 6 rows at top of sleeve seam to 4 cast-off sts. at Back and Front. Using a flat seam stitch Sleeves into position matching raglan shapings.

NECKBAND: With right side facing using set of No 13 needles, **knit up** 174 sts. round neck, including sts. from stitch-holders.

Work in rounds of K.1, P.1 rib for 1 inch.

Change to set of No. 15 needles and continue in rounds until work measures 2 ins. from beg.

Change to set of No. 13 needles and continue in rounds until work measures 3 ins. from beg.

Using No. 11 needle, cast off loosely.

Fold Neckband at centre to inside of work and flat-stitch cast-off edge to knitted-up edge loosely in order to retain elasticity of neck. Press seams.

The lacy look

THE LACY LOOK
(Fuzzy Wuzzy Sweater with Blouse shape)

MATERIALS: 16 [17, 18] × ½ oz. balls PATONS FUZZY-WUZZY. Two No. 13 and two No. 11 BEE-HIVE or QUEEN BEE needles. Eight buttons. Sixteen press studs.

MEASUREMENTS: To fit 34 [38, 42] inch bust (loosely) Length, 23½ [24, 24½] ins. Sleeve seam, 12 ins.
SIZES: The figures in square brackets [ ] refer to the medium and large sizes respectively.

TENSION: 8 sts. and 10 rows to one square inch on No. 11 needles, measured over stocking stitch.

162

BACK: Using No. 13 needles, cast on 123 [137, 151] sts.
1st row — * P.1, K.1, rep. from * to last st., P.1.
2nd row — * K.1, P.1, rep. from * to last st., K.1.
Rep. these 2 rows until work measures 1¼ ins. from beg., finishing at end of a 2nd row.
Change to No. 11 needles and proceed in **striped lace patt.** as follows: —
1st row — * K.2, w.fwd., K.2 tog. t.b.l., M.1, sl. 1, K.2 tog., p.s.s.o., M.1, rep. from * to last 4 sts., K.2., w. fwd., K.2 tog. t.b.l.
2nd row — * P.2, w.r.n., P.2 tog., P.3, rep. from * to last 4 sts., P.2, w.r.n., P.2 tog.
3rd row — * K.2, w.fwd., K.2 tog. t.b.l., K.3, rep. from * to last 4 sts., K.2, w.fwd., K.2 tog. t.b.l.
4th row — * P.2, w.r.n., P.2 tog., P.3, rep. from * to

last 4 sts., P.2, w.r.n., P.2 tog.

These 4 rows form the patt.

Continue in patt. until work measures 16¼ ins. from beg.

Keeping patt. correct, **shape armholes** by casting off 6 [7, 8] sts. at beg. of next 2 rows, then dec. 1 st. at both ends of next and every alt. row until 95 [107, 119] sts. remain.

Continue on these sts. until work measures 7 [7½, 8] ins. from beg. of armhole shaping.

Change to No. 13 needles and shape shoulders as follows:-

1st and 2nd rows — Cast off 10 [11, 13], work to end.

3rd and 4th rows — Cast off 10 [12, 13], work to end.

5th and 6th rows — Cast off 11 [12, 13], work to end.

Cast off remaining 33 [37, 41] sts.

FRONT: Using No. 13 needles, cast on 127 [141, 155] sts.

Work in rib as on Back.

Change to No. 11 needles

Next row — Patt. 60 [67, 74] sts., cast off 7, patt. to end **noting** that after cast-off patt. will begin K.1 in place of K.2, there being one st. on needle after cast-off.

Proceed on **each group of sts. as follows:** —

Continue in patt., next row 2nd row, until work matches Back to armhole shaping, finishing at side edge.

Shape armhole by casting off 8 [9, 10] sts. at beg. of next row, then dec. 1 st. at armhole edge on next and every alt. row until 44 [50, 56] sts. remain.

Continue on these sts. until work measures 4½ [5, 5½] ins. from beg. of armhole shaping, finishing at front edge.

Shape neck by casting off 7 [8, 9] sts. at beg. of next row, then dec. 1 st. at neck edge on next and every alt. row until 31 [35, 39] sts. remain.

Continue on these sts. until work matches Back to shoulder shaping, finishing at armhole edge.

Change to No. 13 needles and shape shoulder as follows:-

1st row — Cast off 10 [11, 13], work to end.

2nd and 4th rows — Work all across.

3rd row — Cast off 10 [12, 13], work to end.

5th row — Cast off 11 [12, 13].

FRONT BANDS (2) Using No. 13 needles, cast on 9 sts.

1st row — K.2, (P.1, K.1), 3 times, K.1.

2nd row — (K.1, P.1) 4 times, K.1.

Rep. these 2 rows until Band measures sufficient to edge Front to cast-off sts. at neck edge when Band is slightly stretched. Cast off.

SLEEVES: Using No. 13 needles, cast on 67 [74, 81] sts.

Foundation row — P.

Proceed in patt. as on Back, inc. 1 st. at both ends of 7th row following and every following 8th row until work measures 2½ ins. from beg.

Change to No. 11 needles and continue in patt. still inc. 1 st. at both ends of every 8th row as before until there are 97 [104, 111] sts. Continue on these sts. until work measures 12 ins. from beg.

Shape top as follows. —

FIRST SLEEVE

1st row — Cast off 6 [7, 8], work to end.

2nd row — Cast off 8 [9, 10], work to end.

SECOND SLEEVE

1st row — Cast off 8 [9, 10], work to end.

2nd row — Cast off 6 [7, 8], work to end.

Continue for both Sleeves, dec. 1 st. at both ends of next and every alt. row until 67 [72, 77] sts. remain.

Cast off 8 [7, 6] sts. at beg. of next 6 [8, 10] rows.

Cast off.

COLLAR: Using No. 13 needles, cast on 155 [161, 167] sts.

Work in rib as on Back for 1½ ins.

Change to No. 11 needles and continue in rib until work measures 2½ ins. from beg.

Now dec. 1 st. at both ends of next and every alt. row until 149 [155, 161] sts. remain.

Cast off loosely in rib.

BELL FRILLING FOR SLEEVES: Using No. 13 needles, cast on 79 [84, 89] sts.

1st row — * P.4, K.B.1, rep. from * to last 4 sts., P.4.

2nd row — * K.4, P.B.1, rep. from * to last 4 sts., K.4.

3rd row — * P.4, w.o.n., K.B.1, w.r.n., rep. from * to last 4 sts., P.4.

4th row — * K.4, P.B.3, rep. from * to last 4 sts. K.4.

5th row — * P.4, w.o.n., K.B.3, w.r.n., rep. from * to last 4 sts., P.4.

6th row — * K.4, P.B.5, rep. from * to last 4 sts., K.4.

Continue in this manner, inc. as before on next and every alt. row until the row " * K.4, P.B.11, rep. from * to last 4 sts., K.4" has been worked.

Cast off in patt.

BELL FRILLING FOR COLLAR: Using No. 13 needles, cast on 159 [164, 169] sts.

Work as frilled edge for Sleeve.

TO MAKE UP: Omitting ribbing with right side of work facing block and steam press by holding a wet cloth one inch above surface of fabric and running a hot iron over surface of cloth. Using a fine back-stitch seam, join shoulder, side and sleeve seams and stitch Sleeves into position matching shapings. Flat-stitch Front Bands into position, stitching lower edges of Bands right over left to cast-off sts. at centre front. Stitch Collar into position from inside edge of Left Front Band to inside edge of Right Front Band. Using a flat seam stitch Frills to ends of Sleeves, join ends of frill together. Flat-stitch frilled edging round Collar stitching top edges of Frilled Edging to centre of Right and Left Front Bands. Attach press studs at each edge of Front Bands. Stitch buttons on centre of Right Front Band. Press seams.

Woman's Cardigan

Lace patterns are frequently used for evening sweaters. The "wool over" and decrease stitches present in all lace knitting can be combined in a wide variety of arrangements to produce exquisite openwork effects. In the women's cardigan shown here, a relatively simple lace pattern is used and accented with sewn-on beads and pearls.

MATERIALS: 8 [8, 9, 9, 10] oz. PATONS BEEHIVE 3-ply, Patonised, or PATONS NYLOX 3-ply, Patonised. Two No. 12 and two No. 10 BEEHIVE or QUEEN BEE needles. Two stitch-holders. Four Pearl buttons. Bugle heads and pearls for trimming (optional).

MEASUREMENTS: To fit 34 [36, 38, 40, 42] inch bust (loosely). Length, $20\frac{1}{2}$ [$20\frac{3}{4}$, $21\frac{1}{2}$, $21\frac{3}{4}$, $22\frac{1}{2}$] ins. Sleeve seam, 12 [12, $12\frac{1}{2}$, $12\frac{1}{2}$, 13] ins. (approx.).

SIZES: The figures in square brackets [] refer to the 36, 38, 40 and 42 inch sizes respectively.

TENSION: $7\frac{1}{2}$ sts. and $9\frac{1}{2}$ rows to one square inch on No. 10 needles, measured over stocking stitch.

LACE PATTERN (Multiple of 10+1) **1st row** — K.1, * w.fwd., K.2 tog. t.b.l., K.5, K.2 tog., w.fwd., K.1, rep. from * to end.

2nd and every alt. row — P.

3rd row — K.2, * w.fwd., K.2 tog. t.b.l., K.3, K.2 tog., w.fwd., K.3, rep. from * ending K.2.

5th row — K.3, * w.fwd., K.2 tog. t.b.l., K.1, K.2 tog., w.fwd., K.5, rep. from * ending K.3.

7th row — K.4, * w.fwd., sl.1, K.2 tog., p.s.s.o., w.fwd., K.7, rep. from * ending K.4.

8th row — P.

These 8 rows form the patt.

BACK: Using No. 12 needles, cast on 130 [130, 140, 140, 150] sts.

Work in K.1, P.1 rib for 20 rows, inc. 1 st. at end of last row (131 [131, 141, 141, 151] sts.).

Change to No. 10 needles and proceed in patt. until work measures 12 [12, $12\frac{1}{2}$, $12\frac{1}{2}$, 13] ins. from beg.

Shape armholes by casting off 10 sts. at beg. of next 2 rows, then dec. 1 st. at both ends of every alt. row until 101 [101, 109, 113, 117] sts. remain.

Continue in patt. until work measures $7\frac{1}{2}$ [$7\frac{3}{4}$, 8, $8\frac{1}{4}$, $8\frac{1}{2}$] ins. from beg. of armhole shaping.

Shape shoulders by casting off 5 [5, 4, 6, 3] sts. at beg. of next 2 rows. 10 sts. at beg of next 4 rows, 5 [5, 9, 8, 13] sts. at beg. of next 2 rows.

Cast off remaining 41 [41, 43, 45, 45] sts.

LEFT FRONT: Using No. 12 needles, cast on 85 [95, 95, 105, 105] sts.

1st row — * K.1, P.1, rep. from * to last 13 sts., K.6, sl. 1 purlwise. K.6.

2nd row — P.13, * K.1, P.1, rep. from * to end.

Rep. these 2 rows 9 times more.

Change to No. 10 needles.

Proceed as follows: —

1st row — Patt. 71 [81, 81, 91, 91], P.1, K.6, sl. 1, K.6.

2nd row — P.13, K.1, patt. to end.

Noting that next row will be 3rd row of patt., continue

until 8th row of 4th complete patt. has been worked. **Commence front slope** by dec. 1 st. inside P. st. of Front Band on next and every following 6th row 24 [5, 13, 2, 2] times, then on every 4th row 1 [30, 18, 37, 35] times, **at the same time** when work matches Back to armhole shaping, **shape armhole** by casting off 10 sts. at. beg. of next row, then dec. 1 st. at armhole edge on every alt. row 5 [5, 6, 7, 7] times.

On completion of armhole shaping, continue until front shapings are completed (44 [44, 47, 48, 50] sts.).

Continue on these sts. until work matches Back to shoulder shaping, **shape shoulder** by casting off 5 [5, 4, 3, 3] sts. on next row, 10 sts. for **all sizes** twice on following alt. rows, 5 [5, 9, 11, 13] sts. on following alt. row. Continue on remaining 14 sts. as before for 2½ [2½, 2¾, 3, 3] inches. Slip sts. on to a stitch-holder.

RIGHT FRONT: Using No. 12 needles, cast on 85 [95, 95, 105, 105] sts.

1st row — K.6, sl.1, K.6, * P.1, K.1, rep. from * to end.
2nd row — Rib to last 13 sts., P.13.
3rd and 4th rows — As 1st and 2nd.
5th row — (Buttonhole row) K.2, cast off 2, K.1 (2 sts. on needle after cast-off), sl.1, K.2, cast off 2, K.1, rib to end.
6th row — Rib to last 9 sts., P.2, cast on 2, P. to last 2 sts., cast-on 2, P.2.

Continue to match Left Front working buttonholes on every 13th and 14th rows from previous buttonholes until 4 sets of buttonholes in **all** have been worked. Work 4 rows more after last buttonhole.

Commencing front shaping on next row complete to match Left Front, reversing all shapings.

SLEEVES: Using No. 12 needles, cast on 65 [70, 75, 80, 85] sts.

Work in K.1, P.1 rib for 2 ins.

Next row — Rib 3 [5, 8, 5, 4], (inc. in next st., rib 3 [5, 3, 6, 4]) 15 [10, 15, 10, 15] times, inc. in next st., rib to end (81 [81, 91, 91, 101] sts.).

Change to No. 10 needles and proceed in patt., inc. 1 st. at both ends of 7th row following and every following 8th row until there are 101 [101, 111, 111, 121] sts. Continue on these sts. until work measures 12 [12, 12½, 12½, 13] ins. (approx.) from cast-on edge, finishing on same row of patt. as on Back.

Shape top by casting off 10 sts. at beg. of next 2 rows, then dec. 1 st. at both ends of every alt. row 14 [16, 16, 18, 18] times, then every row 8 [6, 10, 8, 12] times. Cast off remaining sts.

TO MAKE UP: Omitting ribbing, block and press on wrong side using a warm iron and damp cloth. Using a fine back-stitch seam, join shoulder, side and sleeve seams and stitch Sleeves into position. Fold Front Bands at centre (sl. st.), flat-stitch on wrong side.

Flat-stitch lower edge of Bands. Graft sts. at centre back.

Stitch Band into position along back of neck. Catch buttonholes together. Attach Luttons. Press seams. If desired, trim every other row of 'eyelets' on fronts and sleeves with bugle beads and pearls.

Sleeveless Blouse

MATERIALS: 9 [10, 11] oz. Dark, 3 [4, 4] oz. Light, PATONS TOTEM Double Crepe. Two No. 10 and two No. 8 needles. One No. 8 crochet hook. Three buttons. Four press studs.

MEASUREMENTS: To fit 34 [36, 38] ins. bust. Length, 21 [21¼, 21½] ins.

SIZES: The figures in square brackets [ ] refer to the medium and large sizes respectively.

ABBREVIATIONS: K. – knit; P. – purl; st. – stitch. tog-together; inc.-increase by working into front and back of stitch; dec.-decrease by working 2 sts. together; beg.-beginning; alt.-alternate; rep.-repeat; patt.-pattern; ins.-inches; d.c.-double crochet. (See page 186.)

TENSION: 5½ sts. and 7½ rows to the square inch on No. 8 needles, measured over stocking stitch.

BACK ** Using No. 10 needles and Dark, cast on 104 [112, 120] sts.

Work 6 rows in K.1, P.1 rib.

Next row – Rib 3[3, 4], (inc. in next st., rib 13 [14, 15]) 7 times, inc. in next st., rib to end (112[120, 128] sts.)

Change to No. 8 needles and proceed in blackberry stitch as follows: –

1st row – (Wrong side) K.2, * (K.1, P.1, K.1) in next st., P.3 tog., rep. from * to last 2 sts., K.2.
2nd row – P.
3rd – K. 2, * K.3 tog., (K.1, P.1, K.1) in next st., rep. from * to last 2 sts., K.2.
4th row – P.

These 4 rows form the patt.

Continue in patt. until work measures 14¼ ins. (approx) from inc. row, finishing at end of a 1st or 3rd row of patt. Break off Dark. **

Join in Light and K.1 row.

Keeping patt. correct (next row 1st or 3rd row of patt). continue until work measures 14¾ ins. from inc. row.

Shape armholes by casting off 4 sts. at beg. of next 6 rows.

Continue in patt. on these sts. until work measures 6 [6¼, 6½] ins. from beg. of armhole shaping.

Shape shoulders as follows: –

1st to 4th row – Cast off 9 [10, 11], work to end.

5th and 6th rows – Cast off 10 [11, 12], work to end.

Cast off.

FRONT Work from ** to ** as on Back.

Divide for front opening.

Next row – Join in Light and K.56 [60,64], turn and proceed for

Left Front as follows: –

Next row – Cast on 4 for under-flap, K. these 4 sts., patt to end. Knitting 4 sts. at front edge on every row, continue in patt. until work measures same as Back to armhole shaping, finishing at side edge.

Shape armhole by casting off 4 sts. at beg. of next and following 2 alt. rows.

Continue in patt. until work measures 3 ins. from beg. of armhole shaping, finishing at front edge.

Shape neck by casting off 8 sts. at beg. of next row, 4 sts. at beg. of every alt. row twice, then dec. 1 st. at beg. of every alt. row until 28 [31, 34] sts. remain.

Continue on these sts. until work measures same as Back to shoulder shaping, finishing at armhole edge.

Shape shoulder as follows: –

1st and 3rd rows – Cast off 9[10, 11], work to end.

2nd and 4th rows – Work all across.

5th row – Cast off 10[11, 12].

Join in Light to remaining 56[60, 64] sts. and continue in patt. on these sts. until work measures same as Back to armhole shaping, finishing at side edge.

Shape armhole by casting off 4 sts. at beg. of next and following 2 alt. rows.

Continue in patt. until work measures 3 ins. from beg. of armhole shaping, finishing at front edge.

Shape neck by casting off 4 sts. at beg. of next and following 2 alt. rows, then dec. 1 st. at. beg. of every alt. row until 28[31, 34] sts. remain.

Complete to match Left Front.

IN ORDER TO PRESERVE THE LOVELY CREPE APPEARANCE OF TOTEM FABRICS, THESE MUST BE PRESSED VERY LIGHTLY AS OVER PRESSING WILL SPOIL THE APPEARANCE OF THE FINISHED FABRIC.

TO MAKE UP AND EDGINGS Omitting ribbing with wrong side of work facing, block each piece by pinning out round edges. Omitting ribbing, press each piece **very lightly** using a warm iron and damp cloth for wool; a **cool** iron and **dry** cloth for yarn. Using a flat seam for ribbing and a fine back-stitch seam for remainder, join shoulder and side seams. Fold ribbing at lower edge to inside and flat-stitch to form hem. Commencing at lower edge of front opening, join in Dark and work 1 row of d. c. along Right Front opening and round neck to top of Left Front, turn and work a second row of d. c. to lower edge of Right Front opening. Fasten off.

Using Dark work 2 rows of d. c. round armholes. Fasten off. Stitch Under-flap and crochet edging into position. Stitch press studs on front opening. Trim Right Front with 3 buttons. as in photograph. Press seams.

Norwegian traditional sweaters

MATERIALS: 9 [10, 11] oz. Ground Shade, 3 [4, 4] oz. 1st Contrast, 7 [8, 9] oz. 2nd Contrast, 4 [5, 6] oz. 3rd Contrast, 1 [1, 1] oz. 4th Contrast, PATONS DOUBLE KNITTING. Two No. 11, two No. 10 and two No. 8 BEEHIVE or QUEEN BEE needles, set of four No. 10 and set of four No. 11 QUEEN BEE needles with points at both ends.

MEASUREMENTS: To fit 34 [38, 42] inch bust or chest (loosely). Length, 25¼ [26¼, 27¼] ins. Sleeve seam, 19 ins. (adjustable).

SIZES: The figures in square brackets [ ] refer to the medium and large sizes respectively.

TENSION: 5½ sts. and 7½ rows to one square inch on No. 8 needles, measured over stocking stitch. 6¼ sts. and 5½ rows to one square inch on No. 8 needles, measured over colour patt.

FRONT: Using No. 11 needles and Ground Shade, cast on 121 [133, 145] sts.
Work in K.1, P.1 rib for 1½ ins.
Change to No. 8 needles and proceed in patt. from Chart (odd rows K. reading from right to left, even rows P. reading from left to right), working odd st. at end of K. rows and beg. of P. rows as marked throughout until work measures 17½ ins. from beg. for **all sizes**, finishing with right side facing for next row.
Keeping patt. correct throughout, **shape armholes** by casting off 3 [4, 5] sts. at beg. of next 2 rows, then dec. 1 st. at both ends of next and every following alt. row until 103 [111, 119] sts. remain.
Continue on these sts. until work measures 5 [5¾, 6½] ins. from beg. of armhole shaping.
Shape neck as follows: —
Next row — Patt. across 45 [49, 53] sts., cast off 13, patt. to end. Proceed on **each group of sts.** as follows: —
Dec. 1 st. at neck edge on every row until 36 [38, 40] sts. remain.
Continue on these sts. until work measures 7½ [8½, 9½] ins. from beg. of armhole shaping, finishing at armhole edge.
Change to No. 10 needles and using Ground Shade only, **shape shoulder** as follows: —
1st row — Cast off 12 [12, 13], work to end.
2nd and 4th rows — Work all across.
3rd row — Cast off 12 [13, 13], work to end.
5th row — Cast off 12 [13, 14].

BACK: Work as Front until neck shaping is reached (103 [111, 119] sts.).
Continue on these sts. until work measures same as Front to shoulder shaping.
Change to No. 10 needles and using Ground Shade only, **shape shoulders** as follows: —
1st and 2nd rows — Cast off 12 [12, 13], work to end.
3rd and 4th rows — Cast off 12 [13, 13], work to end.
5th and 6th rows — Cast off 12 [13, 14], work to end.
Cast off.

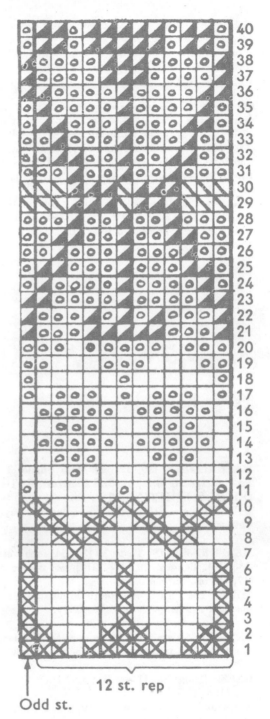

12 st. rep

Odd st.

☐ Ground Shade

☒ 1st Contrast

◉ 2nd Contrast

◤ 3rd Contrast

◺ 4th Contrast

SLEEVES: Using No. 11 needles and Ground Shade, cast on 56 [60, 64] sts.

Work in K.1, P.1 rib for 3 ins. (adjust length here).

Next row — Rib 4 [6, 4], (inc. in next st., rib 2 [3, 6]) 16 [12, 8] times, inc. in next st., rib to end (73 [73, 73] sts.).

Change to No. 8 needles and proceed in patt. from Chart and working extra sts. into patt., inc. 1 st. at both ends of 7th [7th, 3rd] row following and every following 9th [5th, 4th] row until there are 91 [103, 115] sts.

Continue on these sts. until work matches Back and Front to armhole shaping (approx. 19 ins. unless adjusted).

Change to No. 10 needles and using Ground Shade **only**, **shape top** by casting off 6 sts. at beg. of next 2 rows, 12 sts. at beg. of next 2 rows, 18 sts. at beg. of next 2 rows.   Cast off.

TO MAKE UP AND NECKBAND: Omitting ribbing, block and press each piece using a hot iron and wet cloth.

Using a fine back-stitch seam, join shoulders of Back and Front.

With right side facing using set of No. 10 needles and Ground Shade, **knit up** 100 [110, 122] sts. round neck. Work 6 rounds in K.1, P.1 rib.

Change to set of No. 11 needles and work 6 rounds more in K.1, P.1 rib.

Change to set of No. 10 needles and work 6 rounds more in K.1, P.1 rib. Cast off loosely.

Fold Neckband at centre to inside and flat-stitch to form Double Band. Using a flat seam for ribbing and a fine back-stitch seam for remainder, join side and sleeve seams and stitch Sleeves into position. Press seams.

Norwegian traditional cardigan for children

MATERIALS: 9 [10, 12] oz. Main Shade, 3 [4, 4] oz. 1st Contrast, 6 [6, 6] oz. 2nd Contrast, PATONS DOUBLE KNITTING. Two No. 11 and two No. 9 BEEHIVE or QUEEN BEE needles. Six [seven, seven] buttons.

MEASUREMENTS: To fit 30 [32, 34] inch bust or chest (loosely). Length, 20 [21¼, 21½] ins. Sleeve seam, 15½ [17, 18] ins. (adjustable).

SIZES: The figures in square brackets [ ] refer to the medium and large sizes respectively.

TENSION: 5¾ sts. and 7¾ rows to one square inch on No. 9 needles, measured over stocking stitch.

BACK: Using No. 11 needles and Main Shade, cast on 102 [108, 114] sts.

Work in K.1, P.1 rib for 1 inch, inc. 1 st. at end of last row (103 [109, 115] sts.).

Change to No. 9 needles and proceed in stocking stitch working rows 1 to 23 incl. from Chart A throughout, reading Chart from right to left on K. rows and left to right on P. rows, placing the first 2 rows as follows: —

1st row — Work first 3 [6, 1] sts. as marked on Chart, then work 16 st. repeat to last 4 [7, 2] sts., work last 4 [7, 2] sts. as marked on Chart.

2nd row — Work first 4 [7, 2] sts. as marked on Chart, then work 16 st. repeat to last 3 [6, 1] sts., work last 3 [6, 1] sts. as marked on Chart.

Continue until work measures 19¾ [21, 22¼] ins. from beg., marking point 12¾ [13½, 14¼] ins. from beg.

Shape shoulders by casting off 13 [14, 14] sts. at beg. of next 4 rows, 13 [13, 15] sts. at beg. of next 2 rows. Cast off.

RIGHT FRONT: Using No. 11 needles and Main Shade, cast on 52 [54, 58] sts.

Work in K.1, P.1 rib for 1 inch. inc. 1 st. at end of last row on **32 inch size only** (52 [55, 58] sts.).

Change to No. 9 needles and work rows 1 to 23 from Chart B, reading Chart from right to left on K. rows, and left to right on P. rows placing the first 2 rows as follows: —

1st row — Work first 0 [0, 8] sts. as marked on Chart, then work 16 sts. repeat to last 4 [7, 2] sts., work last 4 [7, 2] sts. as marked on Chart.

2nd row — Work first 4 [7, 2] sts. as marked on Chart, then work 16 st. repeat to last 0 [0, 8] sts., work last 0 [0, 8] sts. as marked on Chart. Continue until work measures same as Back to marked point, finishing with right side facing for next row. (Mark this point).

Keeping Chart correct, dec. 1 st. at front edge (beg.) of next and at same edge on every following 3rd row until 39 [41, 43] sts. remain.

Continue on these sts. until work measures same as Back to shoulder shaping, finishing at armhole edge.

Shape shoulder by casting off 13 [14, 14] sts. at beg. of next and following alt. row.

Instructions for making these Traditional Norwegian
Sweaters commence on page 167

See pages 168 and 169 for instructions to make these colourful Norwegian traditional cardigans for children, shown on the left

Woman's sweater with traditional Norwegian design neckline, shown below, is featured on page 170

Big enough to hold everything you need and decorative at the same time is this sequin-crochet evening bag made with I ch. loops. It measures 10½″ × 7″. Instructions for making both bag and spectacle case are on page 207.

Work 1 row.
Cast off.

LEFT FRONT: Work to match Right Front, reversing Chart and all shapings, **noting** that Chart will be read from left to right, then right to left placing the first 2 rows as follows: —

1st row — Work first 4 [7, 2] sts. as marked on Chart, then work 16 st. repeat to last 0 [0, 8] sts., work last 0 [0, 8] sts. as marked on Chart.

2nd row — Work first 0 [0, 8] sts. as marked on Chart, then work 16 st. repeat to last 4 [7, 2] sts., work last 4 [7, 2] sts. as marked on Chart.

SLEEVES: Using No. 11 needles and Main Shade, cast on 44 [46, 48] sts.
Work in K.1, P.1 rib for 2½ ins.
Next row — Rib 1 [3, 5], (inc. in next st., rib 3 [4, 2]) 10 [8, 12] times, inc. in next st., rib to end (55 [55, 61] sts.).
Change to No. 9 needles and working rows 1 to 23 from Chart A throughout as worked for Back on 30 [30, 32] inch sizes, inc. 1 st. at both ends of 11th and every following 5th row until there are 77 [77, 89] sts., every 3rd row until there are 85 [91, 97] sts., working extra sts. into patt.
Continue on these sts. until work measures 15½ [17, 18] ins. from beg. (adjust length at this point).
Cast off loosely.

FRONT BAND: Using No. 11 needles and Main Shade, cast on 11 sts.
1st row — K.2, (P.1, K.1) 4 times, K.1.
2nd row — (K.1, P.1) 5 times, K.1.
34 inch size only. Rep. 1st and 2nd rows once.
All sizes. Next row — Rib 4, cast off 3, rib to end.
Next row — Rib 4, cast on 3, rib to end.
Continue in rib working a buttonhole as on last 2 rows on every following 21st and 22nd [19th and 20th, 19th and 20th] row from previous buttonhole until 6 [7, 7] buttonholes in all have been worked.
Continue in rib without further buttonholes until work measures 44 [46¾, 49½] ins. from beg.
Cast off in rib.

TO MAKE UP: Omitting ribbing, block and press on wrong side using a hot iron and wet cloth. Using a flat seam for ribbing and a fine back-stitch seam for remainder, join shoulder and sleeve seams, join side seams to marked points. Stitch Sleeves into position. Stitch on Front Band placing buttonholes on right side for Girl, left side for Boy. Attach buttons. Press seams.

up

CHART A

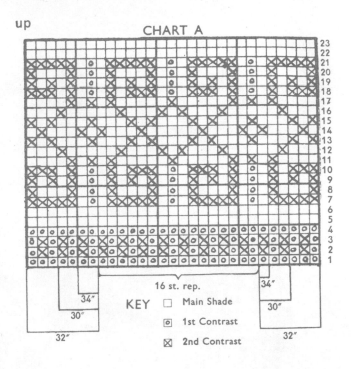

KEY ☐ Main Shade
⊙ 1st Contrast
⊠ 2nd Contrast

CHART B

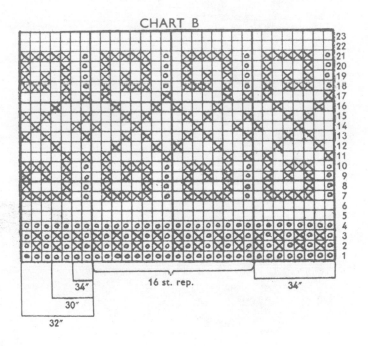

Norwegian traditional sweater

MATERIALS: 15 [16, 17] oz. Main Shade, 2 [2, 2] oz. 1st Contrast, 3 [3, 3] oz. 2nd Contrast, 1 [1, 1] oz. 3rd Contrast, PATONS DOUBLE KNITTING. Two No. 11 and two No. 9 BEEHIVE or QUEEN BEE needles, set of four No. 9 and set of four No. 11 QUEEN BEE needles with points at both ends. Two spare No. 9 needles with points at both ends.

MEASUREMENTS: To fit 34 [36, 38] inch bust (loosely). Length, 24 [24½, 25] ins. Sleeve seam, 18 ins. (adjustable).

SIZES: The figures in square brackets [ ] refer to the medium and large sizes respectively.

TENSION: 5¾ sts. and 7¾ rows to one square inch on No. 9 needles, measured over stocking stitch.

FRONT AND BACK (Both alike): Using No. 11 needles and Main Shade, cast on 106 [112, 118] sts.
Work in K.1, P.1 rib for 2½ ins.
Change to No. 9 needles and proceed in stocking stitch until work measures 16½ [17, 17½] ins. from beg., finishing at end of a P. row.
Cast off 6 sts. at beg. of next 2 rows (94 [100, 106] sts.). Slip these sts. on to a length of wool.

SLEEVES: Using No. 11 needles and Main Shade, cast on 48 [50, 52] sts.
Work in K.1, P.1 rib for 2½ ins.
Next row — Rib 2 [3, 4.] (inc. in next st., rib 5) 7 times, inc. in next st., rib to end (56 [58, 60] sts.).
Change to No. 9 needles and proceed in stocking stitch, inc. 1 st. at both ends of next and every following 9th row until there are 82 [84, 86] sts.
Continue on these sts. until work measures 18 ins. from beg., finishing at end of a P. row (adjust length at this point).
Cast off 6 sts. at beg. of next 2 rows (70 [72, 74] sts.). Slip these sts. on to a length of wool.

YOKE: Using No. 9 needles with points at both ends and Main Shade, with right side of work facing knit across sts. on lengths of wool in following order: — 94 [100, 106] sts. of Front; 70 [72, 74] sts. of 1st Sleeve; 94 [100, 106] sts. of Back and finally 70 [72, 74] sts. of 2nd Sleeve (328 [344, 360] sts.).
34 inch size only: Next round — K.40 (K.2 tog., K.30) 3 times, K.2 tog., K. to end of round (324 sts.).
36 inch size only: Next round — K.20 (K.2 tog., K.41) 7 times, K.2 tog., K. to end of round (336 sts.).
38 inch size only: Next round — K.14 (K.2 tog., K.28) 11 times, K.2 tog., K. to end of round (348 sts.).
All sizes: Work rounds 1 to 46 incl. as on Chart, every round K. reading from right to left, working repeat 27 [28, 29] times on every round.
Proceed for **Neckband** as follows: —
Change to set of No. 11 needles and using Main Shade, work 18 rounds in K.1, P.1 rib.
Cast off loosely in rib.

TO MAKE UP: Omitting ribbing, block and press on wrong side using a hot iron and wet cloth for Yoke and a warm iron and damp cloth for remainder. Using a flat seam for ribbing and a fine back-stitch seam for remainder, join side and sleeve seams matching cast-off sts. at top of sleeve seam to cast-off sts. at under-arm. Fold Neckband at centre to wrong side of work and flat-stitch to form Double Band. Press seams.

108/112, 116/sts.

135/140, 145/sts.

189/196, 203/sts.

243/252, 261/sts.

270/280, 290/sts.

☐ Main Shade

⊠ 1st Contrast

⊡ 2nd Contrast

◪ 3rd Contrast

◹ K.2 tog.

12 st. rep.

Lady's sweater

MATERIALS: 12 [13, 14] oz. PATONS CAMEO Crepe Patonised. Two No. 13 and two No. 11 BEEHIVE or QUEEN BEE needles.

MEASUREMENTS: To fit 34 [36, 38] inch bust. Length, 23¼ [23½, 23¾] ins. Sleeve seam, 12½ ins.
SIZES: The figures in square brackets [ ] refer to the medium and large sizes respectively.

TENSION: 7¾ sts. and 9¾ rows to one square inch on No. 11 needles, measured over stocking stitch.

BACK: Using No. 13 needles, cast on 139 [147, 155] sts. Work 8 rows in moss stitch (every row * K.1, P.1, rep. from * to last st., K.1).
Change to No. 11 needles and proceed in **patt.** as follows:—
1st and 5th rows — K.2 tog., * w.fwd., K.6, K.2 tog., rep. from * to last st., w.fwd., K.1.
2nd and 6th rows — P.1, * P.1, w.r.n., P.2 tog., P.3, P.2 tog., t.b.l., w.r.n., rep. from * to last 2 sts., P.2.
3rd and 7th rows — K.1, * K.2, w.fwd., sl.1, K.1, p.s.s.o., K.1, K.2 tog., w.fwd., K.1, rep. from * to last 2 sts., K.2.
4th and 8th rows — P.1, * P.3, w.r.n., P.3 tog., w.r.n., P.2, rep. from * to last 2 sts., P.2.
9th and 13th rows — K.1, * K.4, w.fwd., sl.1, K.1, p.s.s.o., K.2, rep. from * to last 2 sts., K.2.
10th and 14th rows — P.1, * P.2, P.2 tog. t.b.l., w.r.n., P.1, w.r.n., P.2 tog., P.1, rep. from * to last 2 sts., P.2.
11th and 15th rows — K.1, * K.1, K.2 tog., w.fwd., K.3, w.fwd., sl.1, K.1, p.s.s.o., rep. from * to last 2 sts., K.2.

12th and 16th rows — P.1, P.2 tog. t.b.l., *w.r.n., P.5, w.r.n., P.3 tog., rep. from * to last 8 sts., w.r.n., P.5, w.r.n., P.2 tog., P.1.
These 16 rows form the patt.
Continue in patt. until work measures 16 ins. from beg., finishing with right side facing for next row.
Next row — Cast off 8, K.8 (9 sts. on needle after cast-off), patt. to last 17 sts., K.17.
2nd row — Cast off 8, P. 8, patt. to last 9 sts., P.9.
3rd row — K.2 tog., K.7, patt. to last 9 sts., K.7, K.2 tog.
4th row — P.8, patt. to last 8 sts., P.8.
5th row — K.2 tog., K.6, patt. to last 8 sts., K.6, K.2og.
6th row — P.7, patt. to last 7 sts., P.7.
Continue dec. in this manner on next and every alt. row until 107 [115, 123] sts. remain.
Keeping patt. correct, continue on these sts. until work measures 7 [7½, 7½] ins. from beg. of armhole shaping.
Shape shoulders by casting off 12 [13, 14] sts. at beg. of next 6 rows. Cast off.

FRONT: Proceed as Back until armhole shaping is completed (107 [115, 123] sts.).
Next row — Patt. 44 [47, 50], cast off 19 [21, 23], patt. to end.
Proceed on each group of sts. as follows: —
Dec. 1 st. at neck edge on every alt. row 4 times, every following 3rd row 4 times (36 [39, 42] sts.).
Continue on these sts. until work matches Back to shoulder shaping, finishing at armhole edge.
Shape shoulder by casting off 12 [13, 14] sts. at beg. of

next and following alt. rows until all sts. are cast off.

SLEEVES: Using No. 13 needles, cast on 65 sts. for all sizes.
Work 7 rows in moss stitch.
Next row — P.5 (M.1P.), P.6) 9 times, M.1P., P. to end (75 sts.).
Change to No. 11 needles and proceed in patt. as on Back, inc. 1 st. at both ends of 5th [9th, 3rd] row following and every following 7th [7th, 6th] row until there are 109 [113, 117] sts.
Continue on these sts. until work measures 12½ ins. from beg.
Shape top by casting off 8 sts. at beg. of next 2 rows, then dec. 1 st. at both ends of next and every alt. row until 77 [81, 85] sts. remain.
Cast off 10 [8, 6] sts. at beg. of next 6 [8, 10] rows. Cast off.

NECKBAND: Using No. 11 needles, cast on 175 [181, 187] sts.
1st row — K.2, * P.1, K.1, rep. from * to last st., K.1.
2nd row — * K.1, P.1, rep. from * to last st., K.1.
3rd and 4th rows — As 1st and 2nd.
Change to No. 13 needles and rep. 1st and 2nd rows twice, then 1st row once.
Work 5 rows in moss stitch.
Change to No. 11 needles and work 4 rows in moss stitch. Cast off.

TO MAKE UP: Omitting Neckband, block and press on wrong side using a warm iron and damp cloth. Using a flat seam for moss stitch and a fine back-stitch seam for remainder, join side and sleeve seams and stitch Sleeves into position matching shapings. Commencing at centre back of neck, flat-stitch cast-off edge of Neckband to neck edge. Flat-stitch ends of Neckband together at centre back. Fold Neckband at centre to inside and loosely flat-stitch ribbed edge to edge of Neckband to form Double Band. Press seams.

Lady's casual coat in flair

MATERIALS: 25 [27, 29] oz. PATONS FLAIR with Courtelle. Two No. 9 and two No. 7 needles. Two stitch-holders. Five buttons.

MEASUREMENTS: To fit 34 [36, 38] inch bust. Length, 25 [25¼, 25½] ins. Sleeve seam, 18 ins. (adjustable).
SIZES: The figures in square brackets [ ] refer to the medium and large sizes respectively.

ABBREVIATIONS: K. – knit; P. – purl; K.B. – knit into back of stitch; P.B. – purl into back of stitch; st. – stitch; w. fwd. – wool forward; tog. – together; inc. – increase by working into front and back of stitch; dec. – decrease by working 2 sts. together; beg. – beginning; alt. – alternate; rep. – repeat; patt. – pattern; ins. – inches.

TENSION: 5 sts. and 6¼ rows to the square inch on No. 7 needles, measured over stocking stitch.

BACK: Using No. 9 needles, cast on 92 [98, 104] sts. Work in K.1, P.1 rib for 1½ ins., dec. 1 st. at end of last row (91 [97, 103] sts.).
Change to No. 7 needles and proceed in **pyramid rib patt.** as follows: —
1st row — * P.3, K.B.1, P.2, rep. from * to last st., P.1.
2nd row — * K.2, P.1, P.B.1, P.1, K.1, rep. from * to last st., K.1.
3rd row — * P.1, K.2, K.B.1, K.2, rep. from * to last st., P.1.
4th row — * K.3, P.B.1, K.2, rep. from * to last st., K.1.
5th row — * P.2, K.1, K.B.1, K.1, P.1, rep. from * to last st., P.1.
6th row — * K.1. P.2, P.B.1, P.2, rep. from * to last st., K.1.
These 6 rows form the patt.
Continue in patt. until work measures 17½ ins. from beg. for **all sizes.**
Shape armholes by casting off 5 [5, 5] sts. at beg. of next 2 rows, then dec. 1 st. at both ends of next and every alt. row until 71 [75, 79] sts. remain.
Continue on these sts. until work measures 7¼ [7½, 7¾] ins. from beg. of armhole shaping.
Shape shoulders as follows: —
1st and 2nd rows — Cast off 12 [12, 13], work to end.
3rd and 4th rows — Cast off 12 [13, 13], work to end.
Cast off remaining 23 [25, 27] sts.

POCKET: Using No. 9 needles, cast on 25 sts.
Work in stocking stitch for 4½ ins., finishing at end of a K. row. Slip sts. on to a stitch-holder and leave.

RIGHT FRONT: Using No. 9 needles, cast on 50 [56, 62] sts.

Work in K.1, P.1 rib for 1½ ins., dec. 1 st. at end of last row (49 [55, 61] sts.).
Change to No. 7 needles and proceed in patt. as on Back as follows: —
Rep. 1st to 6th row of patt. 6 times.
Place Pocket as follows: —
Next row — Patt. 12 [15, 18]. K.25, slip these 25 sts. on to a stitch-holder and leave, patt. 12 [15, 18].
Next row — Patt. 12 [15, 18], slip sts. from top of pocket on to left-hand needle, patt. across these sts., patt. to end. Continue in patt. until work measures 15 ins. from beg., finishing at front edge.
Commence front slope by dec. 1 st. at front edge on next and every following 5th [4th, 4th] row until work matches Back to armhole shaping, finishing at side edge.
Still dec. at front edge on every 5th [4th, 4th] row as before, **at the same time shape armhole** by casting off 7 sts. at beg. of next row for **all sizes**, then dec. 1 st. at armhole edge on next and every alt. row until 5 [6, 7] dec. have been worked at armhole edge.
Continue dec. 1 st. at front edge **only** on every 5th [4th, 3rd] row from previous dec. until 24 [25, 26] sts. remain.
Continue on these sts. until work matches Back to shoulder shaping, finishing at armhole edge.
Shape shoulder as follows: —
1st row — Cast off 12 [12, 13], work to end.
2nd row — Work all across.
3rd row — Cast off 12 [13, 13].

POCKET TOP: With right side facing slip 25 sts. from stitch-holder on to No. 9 needle.
1st row — K.2, * P.1, K.1, rep. from * to last st., K.1.
2nd row — * K.1, P.1, rep. from * to last st., K.1.
Rep. these 2 rows once more.
Cast off in rib.

POCKET, LEFT FRONT AND POCKET TOP: Work to match Right Front, reversing all shapings.

SLEEVES: Using No. 9 needles, cast on 48 [50, 52] sts. Work in K.1, P.1 rib for 3 ins.
Next row — Rib 5 [5, 8], (inc. in next st., rib 5 [9, 16]) 6 [4, 2] times, inc. in next st., rib to end (55 sts. for all sizes).
Change to No. 7 needles and proceed in patt. as on Back, inc. 1 st. at both ends of 9th [7th, 3rd] row following and every following 11th [9th, 8th] row until there are 73 [77, 81] sts.
Continue on these sts. until work measures 10 ins. from beg., finishing with right side facing for First Sleeve, wrong side facing for Second Sleeve. (adjust length here).
Shape top as follows: —
1st row — Cast off 5 [5, 5], work to end.
2nd row — Cast off 7 [7, 7], work to end.
Now dec. 1 st. at both ends of next and every alt. row until 51 [53, 55] sts. remain.
Cast off 6 sts. at beg. of next 6 rows.
Cast off.

FRONT BAND: Using No. 9 needles, cast on 9 sts.
1st row — K.2, (P.1, K.1) 3 times, K.1.
2nd row — (K.1, P.1) 4 times, K.1.
3rd and 4th rows — As 1st and 2nd.
5th row — K.2, P.1, K.1, w.fwd., K.2 tog., P.1, K.2.
6th row — (K.1, P.1) 4 times, K.1.
Continue in this manner working buttonholes as on 5th and 6th rows on every 25th and 26th rows from previous buttonhole until 5 buttonholes in all have been worked.
Continue in rib until Band measures 57 [57¾, 58½] ins. from beg. (slightly stretched.)
Cast off.

TO MAKE UP: Omitting ribbing, block and **very lightly** press on wrong side using a warm iron and damp cloth. Flat-stitch Pockets into position on wrong side, Pocket Tops on right side. Using a flat seam for ribbing and a fine back-stitch seam for remainder, join shoulder, side and sleeve seams and stitch Sleeves into position matching shapings. Flat-stitch Front Band into position. Attach buttons. Press seams.

Boatneck pullover

MATERIALS: 14 [15, 16] oz. Ground Shade, 2 [2, 3] oz. Contrast, PATONS DOUBLE KNITTING, or PATONS TOTEM Double Crepe. Two No. 6 and two No. 8 BEEHIVE or QUEEN BEE needles.

MEASUREMENTS: To fit 34 [38, 42] inch bust or chest. Length, 22 [24, 25½] ins. Sleeve seam, 17 [19, 20] ins.

SIZES: The figures in square brackets [ ] refer to the medium and large sizes respectively.

TENSION: 5 sts. and 6½ rows to one square inch on No. 6 needles, measured over stocking stitch.

PATTERN STRIPE (Multiple of 5+2)
Special Note: In working the patt. stripe the Ground Shade is used for the knitting the Contrast being used for the woven effect throughout.
1st row — K.1G.S., * bring Contrast to front, K.3G.S., take Contrast to back, K.2, rep. from * to last st., K.1.
2nd row — P.1G.S., * take Contrast to back, P.3G.S., bring Contrast to front, P.2G.S., rep. from * ending last rep. P.3G.S.
3rd row — K.4G.S., * bring Contrast to front, K.3G.S., take Contrast to back:, K.2G.S., rep. from * to last 3 sts., K.3G.S.
4th row — P.4G.S., * take Contrast to back, P.3G.S., bring Contrast to front, P.2G.S., rep. from * to last 3 sts., P.3G.S.
5th row — K.1G.S., * bring Contrast to front, K.3G.S., take Contrast to back, K.2G.S., rep. from * to last st., K.1G.S.
6th row — P.2G.S. ,* take Contrast to back, P.3G.S., bring Contrast to front, P.2G.S., rep. from * to end.
7th to 11th row — Rep. rows 5, 4, 3, 2, 1.
It is important to have the Contrast stranded loosely throughout the weaving in order not to tighten up the knitted fabric.

BACK: Using Ground Shade and No. 8 needles, cast on 90 [100, 110] sts.
Work 5 rows in P.1, K.1 rib.
Change to No. 6 needles and using Contrast, K.4 rows.
Using Ground Shade work 3 rows in stocking stitch (1 row K., 1 row P.).
Next row — Using Ground Shade inc. in next st., P. to last st., inc. in last st. (92 [102, 112] sts.).
Work 1st to 11th row of pattern stripe.
Next row — Using Ground Shade, P.2 tog., P. to last 2 sts., P.2 tog. (90 [100, 110] sts.).
Using Ground Shade, work 3 rows in stocking stitch.
Using Contrast, P.4 rows. Break off Contrast.
Using Ground Shade proceed in stocking stitch until work measures 14 [15, 16] ins. from top of ribbing, finishing with a P. row.
Shape armholes by casting off 5 [6, 7] sts. at beg. of next 2 rows.
Dec. 1 st. at both ends of every alt. row 4 [5, 7] times (72 [78, 82] sts.), finishing with a dec. row (P. row).
Using Contrast, K. 4 rows.
Using Ground Shade, work 4 rows in stocking stitch, dec. 1 st. at end of last row for **38 inch size only** (72 [77, 82] sts.).
Work 1st to 11th row of stripe patt.
Using Ground Shade, work 4 rows in stocking stitch.
Using Contrast, P.4 rows.
Using Ground Shade, continue in stocking stitch until work measures 8 [9, 9½] ins. from beg. of armhole shaping, finishing with a P. row.
Shape shoulders by casting off 10 [11, 12] sts. at beg. of next 4 rows (32 [33, 34] sts.).
K. 2 rows.
Neck and shoulder facing. Continue in stocking stitch casting on 10 [11, 12] sts., at beg. of next 4 rows (72 [77, 82] sts.).
Work 4 rows in stocking stitch.
Cast off.

FRONT: Work as Back.

SLEEVES: Using No. 8 needles and Ground Shade, cast on 40 [46, 50] sts.
Work in K.1, P.1 rib for 2 ins.
Next row — Rib 3 [3, 2], (inc. in next st., rib 2 [4, 4]) 11 [8, 9] times, inc. in next st., rib to end (52 [55, 60] sts.).
Change to No. 6 needles and proceed in stocking stitch, inc. 1 st. at both ends of 9th row following and every following 10th row until there are 70 [75, 80] sts.
Continue on these sts. until work measures 17 [19, 20] ins. from cast-on edge.
Shape top by casting off 5 [5, 6] sts. at beg. of next 2 rows.
Dec. 1 st. at both ends of next and every alt. row until 15 [18, 21] sets of dec. have been worked.
Cast off 3 [3, 2] sts. at beg. of next 4 rows.
Cast off 18 [17, 18] sts.

TO MAKE UP: Omitting ribbing, block and press on wrong side using a warm iron and damp cloth. Fold at ridge at neck edge and flat-stitch two sets of shoulder sts. together. Flat-stitch lower edge of facing into position on wrong side and open ends at sides. Using a flat seam for ribbing and a fine back-stitch seam for remainder, join shoulder, side and sleeve seams and stitch Sleeves into position. Press seams.

Boatneck pullover, featured on this page, and Novelty stitch pullover on page 175 are illustrated opposite pages 112 and 113.

Novelty stitch pullover

MATERIALS: 6 [7, 8] oz. Ground Shade, 5 [5, 6] oz. Contrast, PATONS DOUBLE KNITTING, or PATONS TOTEM Double Crepe. Two No. 8 and two No. 6 BEEHIVE or QUEEN BEE needles, set of four No. 9 QUEEN BEE needles, with points at both ends. Two stitch-holders.

MEASUREMENTS: To fit 24 [28, 32] inch chest. Length, 14 [16, 18¼] ins. Sleeve seam, 12 [14½, 16½] ins.

SIZES: The figures in square brackets [ ] refer to the medium and large sizes respectively.

TENSION: 5 sts. and 6½ rows to one square inch on No. 6 needles, measured over stocking stitch.

CHART FOR COLOUR PATTERN
BACK: Using No. 8 needles and Ground Shade, cast on 65 [73, 81] sts.
Work in K.1, P.1 rib for 2 ins.
Change to No. 6 needles and proceed in patt. from Chart, odd rows K., even rows P., working odd st. at end of K. rows and beg. of P. rows until work measures 9 [10, 11½] ins. from cast-on edge.
Shape armhole by casting off 3 sts. at beg. of next 2 rows, then dec. 1 st. at both ends of every alt. row until 53 [61, 69] sts. remain.
Continue on these sts. until work measures 5 [6, 6¾] ins. from beg. of armhole shaping.
Shape shoulders by casting off 5 [6,7] sts. at beg. of next 6 rows. Slip remaining 23 [25, 27] sts. on to a stitch-holder and leave.

FRONT: Proceed as Back until work measures 3 [3½, 4] ins. from beg. of armhole shaping.
Shape neck as follows: —
Next row — Patt. 21 [24, 27], patt. next 11]13, 15] sts. on to stitch-holder, patt. 21 [24, 27].
Proceed on **each** group of sts. as follows: —
Dec 1 st. at neck edge on every row until 15 [18, 21] sts. remain. Continue on these sts. until work matches Back to shoulder shaping.
Shape shoulder by casting off 5 [6, 7] sts. at beg. of next and every alt. row until all sts. are worked off.

SLEEVES: Using No. 8 needles and Ground Shade, cast on 32 [40, 40] sts.
Work in K.1, P.1 rib for 2 ins., inc. 1 st. at end of last row (33 [41, 41] sts.).
Change to No. 6 needles and proceed in patt. from Chart, inc. 1 st. at both ends of 7th row following and every following 8th row until there are 49 [57, 61] sts.
Continue on these sts. until work measures 12 [14½, 16½] ins. from beg.
Shape top by casting off 5 sts. at beg. of next 2 rows, then dec. 1 st. at both ends of every alt. row until 23 [25, 27] sts. remain. Cast off.

NECKBAND: Join shoulders of Back and Front.
With right side facing, using set of No. 9 needles and Ground Shade, **knit up** 66 [72, 78] sts. round neck including sts. from stitch-holder.
Work in rounds of K.1, P.1 rib for 3¼ [3½, 4½] ins.
Using No. 8 needles, cast off.

TO MAKE UP: Omitting ribbing, block and press on wrong side using a warm iron and damp cloth. Join side and sleeve seams. Stitch Sleeves into position. Press seams.

CAP: Using Ground Shade and No. 8 needles, cast on 82 [82, 90] sts.
Work in K.1, P.1 rib for 3 ins., dec. 1 st. at end of last row (81 [81, 89] sts.).
Change to No. 6 needles and proceed in patt. from Chart until work measures approximately 7½ [8½, 9½] ins. from cast-on edge, finishing with 4th or 8th row of patt.
Break off Contrast.
1st dec. row — K.4 (K.2 tog., K.6), 9 [9, 10] times, K.2 tog., K.3.
2nd row — P.3 (P.2 tog., P.5), 9 [9, 10] times, P.2 tog., P.3.
3rd row — K.2, * K.2 tog., K.4, rep. from * to last 5 sts., K.2 tog., K.3.
4th row — P.3 (P.2 tog., P.3), 9 [9, 10] times, P.2 tog., P.1.
5th row — K.2 tog. all across row.
Break off wool. Draw through sts. on needle.
Omitting ribbing press on wrong side.
Draw up sts. at top and fasten off.
Join sides.
Using Ground Shade make pompon see page 253 and attach to centre top of Cap.

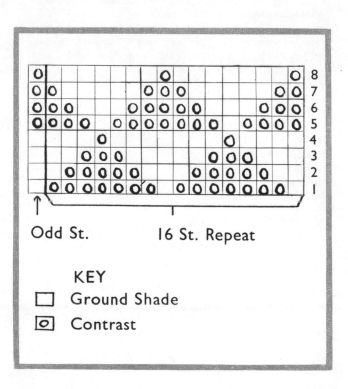

Odd St.   16 St. Repeat

KEY
☐ Ground Shade
◉ Contrast

Jack and Jill cardigan

MATERIALS: 5 [6, 7] oz. Ground Shade, 2 [2, 2] oz. Light, 1 [1,1] oz. Medium, PATONS DOUBLE KNITTING, or PATONS TOTEM Double Crepe. Two No. 8 and two No. 6 BEEHIVE or QUEEN BEE needles. Five buttons. A crochet hook.

MEASUREMENTS: To fit 20 [21, 22] inch chest. Length, 12 [12½, 13¾] ins. Sleeve seam, 8 [9, 10] ins.
SIZES: The figures in square brackets [ ] refer to the medium and large sizes respectively.

TENSION: 5 sts. and 6½ rows to one square inch on No. 6 needles, measured over stocking stitch.

BACK: Using No. 6 needles and Ground Shade, cast on 59 [61, 65] sts.
1st row — P.1, * K.1, P. I, rep. from * to end.
2nd row — K.1, * P.1, K.1, rep. from * to end.
These 2 rows form the rib patt.
Continue in patt. until work measures 7½ [8, 9] ins. from beg.
Shape armholes by casting off 3 sts. at beg. of next 2 rows, then dec. 1 st. at both ends of every alt. row until 49 [51, 55] sts. remain.
Continue on these sts. until work measures 4½ [4½, 4¾] ins. from cast-off row at armhole edge.
Shape shoulders by casting off 5 sts. at beg. of next 4 rows; 4 [5, 6] sts. at beg. of next 2 rows. Cast off remaining 21 [21, 23] sts.
Buttonhole Note: For **Girl's Cardigan** — Work Left Front first, for **Boy's Cardigan**—work Right Front first. When this front is completed mark position of 5 buttonholes with a pin, first one, 1 inch above hem line, last one ¼ inch below neck edge.
When working second front, work double buttonholes to match markings as follows: —
1st row — Patt. 2, cast off 2, patt. 4 (there now being 5 sts. on needle after cast-off), cast off 2, patt. to end.
2nd row — Patt. all across casting on 2 sts. over 2 sets of cast-off sts. of previous row.
Special Note: All sts. are slipped purlwise with wool on **wrong** side, carry unused colour up side of work.

LEFT FRONT: Using No. 6 needles and Light, cast on 24 [28, 28] sts.
Work 5 rows in stocking stitch.
Next row — Cast on 13 sts. for **Front Band** at beg. of row and K. across this row (**wrong** side) for hemline (37 [41, 41] sts.).
K.1 row; P.1 row.
Pattern (multiple of 4+1)
1st row — Using Ground Shade, K.1, * sl.1, K.1, rep. from * to end.
2nd row — Using Ground Shade, P.
3rd row — Using Medium, as 1st row.
4th row — Using Medium, P.1, * sl.1, P.1, rep. from * to end.
5th and 6th rows — Using Ground Shade. K.1, row; P.1

row.
7th row — Using Light, as 1st row.
8th to 10th row — Using Light, P.1, row, K.1 row, P.1 row.
11th row — Using Ground Shade, K.1, * sl.3, K.1, rep. from * to end.
12th row — Using Ground Shade, P.2, * sl.1, P.3, rep. from * to last 3 sts., sl.1, P.2.
13th row — Using Light, sl.1, * K.3, sl.1, rep. from * to end.
14th row — Using Light, P.
15th row — Using Medium, sl.2, * K.1, sl.3, rep. from * to last 3 sts., sl.1, K.2.
16th row — Using Medium, sl.1, * P.3, sl.1, rep. from * to end.
17th row — Using Light, K.2, * sl.1, K.3, rep. from * to last 3 sts., sl.1, K.2.
18th row — Using Light, P.
19th to 22nd row — Rep. 11th to 14th row.
23rd and 24th row — Using Light, K.1 row, P.1 row. These 24 rows form the patt.
Proceed in patt. as on these 24 rows until work measures same as Back to cast-off row at armhole shaping from ridge at lower edge of Front, finishing at side edge.
Shape armhole by casting off 3 sts. at beg. of next row, then dec. 1 st. at armhole edge on every alt. row until 32 [35, 36] sts. remain. Continue on these sts. until work measures 3 [3½, 3½] ins. from cast-off row at armhole shaping, finishing at front edge.
Shape neck by casting off 14 [14, 15] sts. at beg. of next row, then dec. 1 st. at neck edge on every row until 14 [15, 16] sts. remain. Continue on these sts. until work measures same as Back to shoulder shaping.
Shape shoulders by casting off 5 sts. at beg. of next and following alt. row, then 4 [5, 6] sts. on next alt. row.

RIGHT FRONT: Casting on 13 sts. for Front Band at opposite end to Left Front, work to match Right Front, reversing all shapings.

SLEEVES: Using No. 8 needles and Ground Shade, cast on 35 [37, 39] sts.
Work in rib as on Back for 1 inch.
Change to No. 6 needles and continue in rib., inc. 1 st. at both ends of next and every following 5th row until there are 49 [51, 53] sts.
Continue on these sts. until work measures 8 [9, 10] ins. from beg.
Shape top by casting off 3 sts. at beg. of next 2 rows. Dec. 1 st. at both ends of every alt. row until 29 sts. remain for **all sizes**. Cast off 2 sts. at beg. of next 4 rows. Cast off.

COLLAR: Using No. 6 needles and Ground Shade, cast on 77 sts.
Work in rib as on Back for 3 ins. for Girl's Cardigan, 2½ ins. for Boy's Cardigan.
Cast off.

TO MAKE UP: Omitting ribbing, block and press on wrong side using a warm iron and damp cloth. Join shoulder, side and sleeve seams and stitch Sleeves into position. Fold hem to inside at ridge to lower end of Front and flat-stitch. Fold centre band of Right Front in half to inside matching buttonholes, flat-stitch in place. Join top and bottom edge of centre band, catch buttonholes together. Fold centre band of Left Front in half, flat-stitch in place, complete as Right Front omitting buttonholes. Using Ground Shade, work 1 row of double crochet up front edge and across top edge of centre bands.

Stitch Collar into position from centre of Right Front Band to centre of Left Front Band. Attach buttons. Press seams.

No charts are needed for this unusual cardigan for the very young. Patterned fronts are combined with ribbed sleeves and backs of a single colour.

Bunny with a Twinkle

MATERIALS: PATONS ARIEL. 3 (2 oz.) balls each Blue, Red and White. A pair No. 8 QUEEN BEE needles. Scraps of Black wool for features. Kapok for stuffing (approx. 27 oz.).

MEASUREMENT: Height, 31 ins. to top of Head. N.B.—Rabbit is knitted in garter stitch, i.e. every row knit, unless otherwise stated. Join all seams neatly on right side when making up. B.—Blue; R—Red; W—White.

LEGS AND BODY: With B. wool cast on 27 sts.
Knit 88 rows, then leave sts. on a spare needle.
Make another piece the same.
Place both sets of sts. on to one needle and continue over all sts. as follows: —
Knit 5 rows:
Next row — K.2 tog., K. to last 2 sts., K.2 tog.
Knit 3 rows.
Next row — (K.2 tog., K.10) twice, (K.2 tog.,) twice, (K.10, K.2 tog.) twice: 46 sts.
Next 2 rows—Knit.
Break B.
Join in R. and knit 1 row.
Change to K.1, P.1 rib and work 8 rows.
Change back to garter-stitch and knit 54 rows.
Shape shoulders by casting off 7 sts. at beg. of next 4 rows.
Cast off remaining sts.
Make another piece the same.
Join halves together leaving neck open for stuffing.
Stuff Legs and Body firmly, then gather up opening.

HEAD: With W. wool, cast on 19 sts.
Knit 6 rows.
Next row — K. twice in first st., K. to end.
Next row — K. to last st., K. twice in last st.
Next row — K. twice in 1st st., K. to end.
Next row — Knit, increasing 1 st. at each end.
Rep. the last 4 rows twice more: 34 sts.
Knit 12 rows.
Next row — K.2 tog., K. to end.
Next row — K. to last 2 sts., K.2 tog.
Rep. the last 2 rows, 5 times more: 22 sts.
Next row — K.2 tog., K. to last 2 sts., K.2 tog.: 20 sts.
Next row — K. to last 2 sts., K.2 tog.
Next row — Knit.
Rep. the last 2 rows 3 times more: 16 sts.
Now decrease 1 st. at each end of next 2 rows.
Cast off.
Make another piece the same.
Join halves together, leaving cast-on edges open for stuffing.

NOTE: Seam comes over centre of Head.
Stuff firmly, pushing head out to a good shape.
Features: Eyes filled satin-stitch, half blue and half black; outlined black straight-stitches. Eyebrows, black slanting straight-stitch.
Nose, black satin-stitch. Mouth, curved lines black stem-stitch.
Whiskers, long black straight-stitches.

NECK: With W. wool, cast on 34 sts.
Knit 3 rows.
Break W.
Join in R. and knit 1 row, then work 6 rows K.1, P.1 rib. Cast off. Join short ends and stuff. Sew edge in R. round top of body, then sew edge in W. to head adding as much stuffing as possible so that neck will support head firmly.

EARS: With W. wool, cast on 3 sts. and knit 1 row.
Next row — Knit, increasing 1 st. at each end.
Next 3 rows — Knit.
Rep. the last 4 rows until there are 25 sts.
Knit 15 rows straight.
Next row — K.2 tog., K. to last 2 sts., K.2 tog.
Next row — Knit.
Next row — Rep. the last 2 rows twice more.
Next row — (K.2 tog.) 4 times, K.3 tog., (K.2 tog.) 4 times.
Knit 1 row.
Cast off.
Make 3 more pieces the same.
Sew each pair together.
Fold cast-off edge of each ear in half and sew to head as illustrated.

FEET: With W. wool, cast on 11 sts. and knit 1 row, then increase 1 st. at each end of following 3 rows.
Knit 40 rows straight.
Now decrease 1 st. at each end of next 3 rows.
Cast off.
Make 3 more pieces the same. Sew each pair together, leaving an opening for stuffing.
Stuff and sew up opening.
Sew feet to legs.

TAIL: With W. wool, cast on 12 sts. and knit 1 row, then increase 1 st. at each end of next 3 rows.
Knit 20 rows straight.
Now decrease 1 st. at each end of next 3 rows.
Cast off.
Make another piece the same.
Sew halves together leaving cast-off edges open for stuffing.
Stuff and sew up opening. Sew tail to body.

PAWS AND ARMS: With W. wool, cast on 17 sts.
** Knit 1 row, then increase 1 st. at each end of next 3 rows.
Knit 6 rows straight.
Next row — K.11, K. twice in next st., K.11.
K.12 rows straight.
Now decrease 1 st. at each end of next 3 rows. **
Break W. Push sts. to end of needle and leave for the time being, then on to same needle cast on 17 sts. in W. and work from ** to **. Now working over all 36 sts., knit 2 rows.

177

Break W.

Join in R. and knit 1 row, then work 9 rows K.1, P.1 rib.

Change back to garter-stitch and continue as follows: —

Next row — Knit, increasing 1 st. at each end.

Next 9 rows — Knit.

Rep. the last 10 rows once more: 40 sts.

Next row — Knit, increasing 1 st. at each end.

Knit 15 rows.

Next row — K. twice in 1st st., K.19, K. twice in each of next 2 sts., K.19, K. twice in last st.: 46 sts.

Next row — Knit.

Next row — K.23, turn and leave remaining 23 sts. on a spare needle.

* Next row — Knit.

Now decrease 1 st. at each end of next and every alternate row until 11 sts. remain.

Cast off. *

Rejoin wool to last 23 sts. at centre and K. to end.

Rep. from * to * as for first half.

Make another the same. Fold in half lengthways leaving an opening for stuffing. Stuff firmly and sew up opening. Sew arms to shoulders.

If required knit a strip from oddments of wool available for his scarf.

Quick-Knit Afghan

MATERIALS: 26 hanks Ground Shade, 8 hanks, Contrast, PATONS BIG BEN. Three pairs No. 1 QUEEN BEE needles. One plastic crochet hook, No. 4.

TENSION: 3 sts. and 4 rows to one square inch on No. 1 needles, measured over stocking stitch.

PATTERN (Multiple of 2 sts.)

1st row — Using Contrast, * K.1, keeping wool at back, sl.1 purlwise, rep. from * to end.

2nd row — Using Contrast, * wool to front, sl.1, wool to back, K.1, rep. from * to end.

3rd and 4th rows — Using Ground Shade, K.

5th row — Using Contrast, keeping wool at back, * sl.1, K.1, rep. from * to end.

6th row — Using Contrast, * K.1, wool to front, sl.1, wool to back, rep. from * to end.

7th and 8th rows — Using Ground Shade, K.

These 8 rows form the patt.

AFGHAN: Using Ground Shade cast on 48 sts. on each of 3 No. 1 needles.

Using these 3 needles as though they were one needle and working across 3 needles with the 3 remaining needles, proceed as follows: —

K.24 rows, dec. 1 st. at both ends of 2nd and every alt. row (120 sts.).

Proceed in patt. until work measures approximately 56 ins. from cast-on edge, ending with 2nd row of patt. Using Ground Shade, work 24 rows in garter stitch, inc. 1 st. at both ends of next and every alt. row (144 sts.).

Cast off.

SIDE BORDERS: Using 3 needles and Ground Shade as before, cast on 156 sts., 52 on each needle.

K.24 rows, inc. 1 st. at both ends of every alt. row (180 sts.).

Cast off.

Work Second Border to match.

TO COMPLETE: Flat-stitch Border along side, flat-stitch mitred corners together. Fringe each end of Afghan, making fringe by winding the Ground Shade round a 10 inch strip of cardboard using 3 strands for each tassel on the fringe.

An easy two-colour pattern is knitted of bulky yarns on big needles. Except for garter stitch borders at sides, afghan is worked entirely in one piece. Directions, page 178, suggest what to do when needles are crowded.

Knitted Aster Doily

SIZE 20″ diameter

MATERIALS: Six Cord Mercerized Crochet Cotton, size 30, 3 220-yd. balls. Five No. 12 needles. Steel Crochet Hook No. 13.

NOTE: Circular needles may be substituted for No. 12 needles after Rnd 21 as follows: Rnd 22 (11″ needle), Rnd 28 (16″ needle), Rnd 38 (24″ needle).

Stitches and additional abbreviations

C.2.—Cross 2 stitches: Sk.1 st., K. in front lp of next st., K. in front lp of skipped st., sl. both sts. from left-hand needle.

T 1-Turn 1 Stitch: K. in back lp of st.

D 1-Butterfly Drop Stitch: with crochet hook, sl. st. off left-hand needle and unravel it for 5 or 3 rows as specified, place this st. back on left-hand needle; with hook in back of work, pick up the 5 or 3 strands and place them on left-hand needle, then K. the st. and 5 or 3 strands off tog.

R 2 decs — Reverse 2 Decreases: Sl.1, K.1 p.s.s.o. (1 dec), sl. remaining K. st. to left-hand needle and pass next st. on left-hand needle over this slipped st. (1 dec), then sl. the slipped st. back to right-hand needle.

DOILY: Beg. at centre, cast on 12 sts. Divide on 3 needles (4 sts. on each needle) and work with 4th needle.

Round 1 — Join, K. around. Sl. and keep a marker on needle between last and first st. of rnd.

Round 2 — Knit.

Round 3 and all odd rounds: — Knit.

Round 4 — (Y. fwd., K.1) 12 times—24 sts.

Round 6 — (Y. fwd., C 2) 12 times—36 sts.

Round 8 — (Y. fwd., K.1, C 2) 12 times—48 sts.

Round 10 — (Y. fwd., K.2, C 2) 12 times—60 sts.

Round 12 — (Y. fwd., K.3, C 2) 12 times—72 sts.

Round 14 — (Y. fwd., K.1, C 2, K.1, C 2) 12 times—84 sts.

Round 16 — (Y. fwd., K.1, C 2, K.2, C 2) 12 times—96 sts.

Round 18 — (Y. fwd., K.1, C 2, K.3, C 2) 12 times—108 sts.

Round 20 — (Y. fwd., K.1, C 2, K.4, C 2) 12 times—120 sts.

Round 22 — (Y. fwd., K.1, C 2, K.5, C 2) 12 times—132 sts.

Round 24 — (Y. fwd., sl.1, K.1, p.s.s.o., C 2, K.5, C 2) 12 times—132 sts.

Round 26 — (Y. fwd., K. in back and front of next st., y. fwd., sl.1, K.1, p.s.s.o., C 2, K.4, C 2) 12 times—156 sts.

Round 28 — (Y. fwd., K.4, y fwd., sl.1, K.1, p.s.s.o., C 2, K.3, C 2) 12 times—168 sts.

Round 30 — * (Yrn, P.3, pass the first P. st. over 2 remaining P. sts.) twice, y. fwd., sl.1, K.1, p.s.s.o., C 2, K.2, C 2, repeat from * 11 times more—168 sts.

Round 32 — * Y. fwd., K.2, yrn, P.3, pass first P. st. over 2 remaining P. sts., y. fwd., K.2, y. fwd., sl.1, K.1, p.s.s.o., C 2, K.1, C 2, repeat from * 11 times more—192 sts.

Round 34 — * Y. fwd., K.2, (yrn., P.3, pass first P. st. over remaining 2 P. sts.) twice, y. fwd., K.2, y. fwd., sl.1, K.1, p.s.s.o., C 2 twice, repeat from * 11 times more —216 sts.

Round 36 — * Y. fwd., K.2, (yrn, P.3, pass first P. st. over 2 remaining P. sts.) 3 times, y. fwd., K.2, y.fwd., sl.1, K.1 p.s.s.o., K.1, C 2, repeat from * 11 times more²—240 sts.

Round 38 — * Y. fwd., C 2, (yrn, P.3, pass first P. st. over 2 remaining P. sts.,) 4 times, y. fwd., C 2, y. fwd., sl.1, K.1, p.s.s.o., C 2, repeat from * 11 times more—264 sts. Divide sts. on 4 needles and work with 5th needle.

Round 40 — * (Y. fwd., K.2 tog.,) 4 times, y. fwd., sl.2, K.1, pass 2 sl. sts. over K. st., y. fwd., (sl.1, K.1, p.s.s.o., y. fwd.,) 4 times, sl.1, K.1, p.s.s.o., K.1, repeat from * 11 times more—252 sts.

Round 42 — * (Y. fwd., K.2 tog.,) 4 times, y. fwd., sl.2, K.1, pass 2 sl. sts. over K. st., y. fwd., (sl.1, K.1, p.s.s.o., y. fwd.,) 4 times, C.2, repeat from * 11 times more—252 sts.

Round 44 — * K.2 tog., (y. fwd., K.2 tog.,) 3 times, y. fwd., K.3, y. fwd., (sl.1, K.1, p.s.s.o., y. fwd.,) 3 times, sl.1, K.1, p.s.s.o., C 2, rep. from * 11 times more—252 sts.

Round 46 — Remove marker, sl.1, st., insert marker, * K.2 tog., (y. fwd., K.2 tog.,) twice, y. fwd., K.5, y. fwd., (sl.1, K.1, p.s.s.o., y. fwd.,) twice, sl.1, K.1, p.s.s.o., C 2 twice, rep. from * 11 times more—252 sts.

Round 48 — Remove marker, sl.1 insert marker, * (y. fwd., K.2 tog.,) twice, y. fwd., K.3, y. fwd., D 1 for 5 rows, y. fwd., K.3, y. fwd., (sl.1, K.1, p.s.s.o., y. fwd.,) twice, sl.1, K.1, p.s.s.o., C 2, K.2 tog., repeat from * 11 times more—276 sts.

Round 50 — * K.2 tog. twice, y. fwd., K.5, y. fwd., K.1, y. fwd., K.5, y. fwd., (sl.1, K.1, p.s.s.o.,) 3 times, K.2 tog., repeat from * 11 times more—252 sts.

Round 52 — Remove marker, sl.2 sts., insert marker, * y. fwd., K.3, y. fwd. D 1 for 5 rows, y. fwd., K.3, y. fwd., T 1, y. fwd., K.3, y. fwd., D 1 for 5 rows. y. fwd., K.3, y. fwd., sl.1, K.1, p.s.s.o., K.2, K.2 tog., repeat from * 11 times more—324 sts.

Round 54 — * Y. fwd., K.5, y. fwd., K.1, y. fwd., K.5, y. fwd., T 1, y fwd., K.5, y. fwd., K.1, y. fwd., K.5, y. fwd., sl.1, K.1, p.s.s.o., K.2 tog., repeat from * 11 times more—396 sts.

Round 56 — * Sl.1, K.1, p.s.s.o., K.11, K.2 tog., y. fwd., T 1, y. fwd., sl.1, K.1, p.s.s.o., K.11, K.2 tog., C 2, repeat from * 11 times more—372 sts.

Round 58 — * Sl.1, K.1, p.s.s.o., K.9, K.2 tog., y. fwd., K.1, y. fwd., T 1, y. fwd., K.1, y. fwd., sl.1, K.1, p.s.s.o., K.9, K.2 tog., y. fwd., C 2, y. fwd., rep. from * 11 times more—396 sts.

Round 60 — * Sl.1, K.1, p.s.s.o., K.7, K.2 tog., y. fwd., K.3, y. fwd., T 1, y. fwd., K.3, y. fwd., sl.1, K.1, p.s.s.o., K.7, K.2 tog., y. fwd., sl.1, K.1, p.s.s.o., K.2 tog., y. fwd., repeat from * 11 times more—396 sts.

Round 62 — * Sl.1, K.1, p.s.s.o., K.5, K.2 tog., y. fwd., K.2, y. fwd., D 1, for 3 rows, y. fwd., K.2, y. fwd., T 1,

No beginner's project, the knitted doily with its intricate lace patterns in circular knitting is a challenge even to the experienced knitter. Directions for Aster Doily, page 180, include helpful hints for making doily.

y. fwd., K.2, y. fwd., D 1 for 3 rows, y. fwd., K.2, y. fwd., sl.1, K.1, p s.s.o., K.5, K.2 tog., y. fwd., sl.1, K.1, p.s.s.o. K.2 tog., y. fwd., repeat from * 11 times more—444 sts.

Round 64 — * Sl.1, K.1, p.s.s.o., K.3, K.2 tog., y. fwd., K.9, y. fwd., T 1, y. fwd., K.9, y. fwd., sl.1, K.1, p.s.s.o., K.3, K.2 tog., y. fwd., sl.1, K.1, p.s.s.o., K.2 tog., y. fwd., repeat from * 11 times more—444 sts.

Round 66 — * Sl.1, K.1, p.s.s.o., K.1, K.2 tog., y. fwd., sl.1, K.1, p.s.s.o., K.7, K.2 tog., y. fwd., K.1, y. fwd., sl.1, K.1, p.s.s.o., K.7, K.2 tog., y. fwd., sl.1, K.1, p.s.s.o., K.1, K.2 tog., y. fwd., K.2 tog., y. fwd., sl.1, K.1, p.s.s.o., y. fwd., repeat from * 11 times more—408 sts.

Round 68 — * Sl.1, K.2 tog., p.s.s.o., y. fwd., K.1, y. fwd., sl.1, K.1, p.s.s.o., K.5, K.2 tog., y. fwd., K.3, y. fwd., sl.1, K.1, p.s.s.o., K.5, K.2 tog., y. fwd., K.1, y. fwd., R 2 decs., y. fwd., K.2 tog., y. fwd., K.1, y. fwd., sl.1, K.1, p.s.s.o., y. fwd., repeat from * 11 times more—408 sts.

Round 70 — Remove marker, sl.1, insert marker, * y. fwd., K.2, tog., y. fwd., K.1, y. fwd., sl.1, K.1, p.s.s.o., K.3, K.2 tog., y. fwd., K.2 tog., y. fwd., K.1, (y. fwd., sl.1, K.1, p.s.s.o.,) twice, K.3, K.2 tog., y. fwd., K.1, y. fwd., (sl.1, K.1, p.s.s.o., y. fwd.,) 3 times, K.1, (y. fwd., K.2 tog.,) twice, repeat from * 11 times more—432 sts.

Round 72 — * (Y. fwd., K.2 tog.,) twice, y. fwd., K.1, y. fwd., sl.1, K.1, p.s.s.o., K.1, K.2 tog., y. fwd., K.2 tog., (y. fwd., K.1.,) 3 times, y. fwd., sl.1, K.1, p.s.s.o., y. fwd., sl.1, K.1, p.s.s.o., K.1, K.2 tog., y. fwd., K.1, y. fwd., (sl.1, K.1, p.s.s.o., y. fwd.,) 4 times, K.1, (y. fwd., K.2 tog.,) twice, repeat from * 11 times more—480 sts.

Round 74 — * (K.2 tog., y. fwd.,) 3 times, K.1, y. fwd., sl.1, K.2 tog., p.s.s.o., (y. fwd., K.2 tog.,) twice, y. fwd., K.3, y. fwd., (sl.1, K.1, p.s.s.o., y. fwd.,) twice, R 2 decs., y. fwd., K.1, (y. fwd., sl.1, K.1, p.s.s.o.,) 5 times, y. fwd., K.1, y. fwd., (K.2 tog., y. fwd.,) twice, repeat from * 11 times more—504 sts.

Round 76 — * (Sl.1, K.1, p.s.s.o., y. fwd.,) 7 times, sl.2, K.1, pass 2 sl. sts. over K. st., (y. fwd. K.2 tog.,) 9 times, y. fwd., K.3, y. fwd., (sl.1, K.1, p.s.s.o., y. fwd.,) twice, repeat from * 11 times more—504 sts.

Round 78 — * (Sl.1, K.1, p.s.s.o., y. fwd.,) 5 times, (sl.1, K.1, p.s.s.o.,) twice, K.1, (K.2 tog.,) twice, (y. fwd., K.2 tog.,) 7 times, y. fwd., K.5, y. fwd., (sl. 1, K.1, p.s.s.o., y. fwd.,) twice, repeat from * 11 times more—480 sts.

Round 80 — * (Sl.1, K.1, p.s.s.o., y. fwd.,) 4 times, (sl.1, K.1, p.s.s.o.,) twice K.1 (K.2 tog.,) twice, (y. fwd., K.2 tog.,) 6 times, y. fwd., K.3, y. fwd., D 1 for 5 rows, y. fwd., K.3, y. fwd., (sl.1, K.1, p.s.s.o., y. fwd.,) twice, repeat from * 11 times more—480 sts.

Round 82 — Remove markers, sl.1, insert marker, * (K.2 tog., y fwd.,) 3 times, K.1, y. fwd., sl.1, K.1, p.s.s.o., K.1, K.2 tog., K.1, (y. fwd., sl.1, K.1, p.s.s.o.,) 7 times, K.5, (K.2 tog., y. fwd.,) 4 times, repeat from * 11 times

more—480 sts.

Round 84 — Remove marker, sl.1, insert marker, * (K.2 tog., y. fwd.,) twice ,K.3, y. fwd.,sl.2, K.1, pass 2 sl. sts. over K. st., y. fwd., K.3, (y. fwd., sl.1, K.1, p.s.s.o.,) 7 times, K.3, (K.2 tog., y. fwd.,) 5 times, repeat from * 11 times—480 sts.

Round 86 — Remove marker, sl.1, insert marker, * K.3, y. fwd., sl.1, K.2 tog., p.s.s.o., y. fwd., (K.1, y. fwd.,) 3 times, sl.1, K.2 tog., p.s.s.o., y. fwd., K.3, (y. fwd., sl.1, K.1, p.s.s.o.,) 6 times, K.1, (K.2 tog., y. fwd.,) 6 times, repeat from * 11 times more—504 sts.

Round 88 — Remove marker, sl.1, insert marker, * K.1, K.2 tog., (y. fwd., K.1, y. fwd., K.3.,) twice, y. fwd., K.1, y. fwd., sl.1, K.1, p.s.s.o., K.1, K.2 tog., (y. fwd., sl.1, K.1, p.s.s.o.,) 5 times, y. fwd., sl.2, K.1, pass 2 sl. sts. over K. st., y. fwd., (K.2 tog., y. fwd.,) 5 times, sl.1, K.1, p.s.s.o., repeat from * 11 times more—528 sts.

Round 90 — Remove marker, sl.1, insert marker, * (K.3, y. fwd., sl.1, K.2 tog., p.s.s.o., y. fwd.,) 3 times, K.1, y. fwd., (sl.1, K.1, p.s.s.o., y fwd.,) 4 times, sl.1, K.1, p.s.s.o., K.1, K.2 tog., (y. fwd., K.2 tog.,) 4 times, y. fwd., K.1, y. fwd., sl.1, K.2 tog., p.s.s.o., y. fwd., repeat from * 11 times more —528 sts.

Round 92 — * (Y. fwd., sl.1, K.2 tog., p.s.s.o., y. fwd., K.3.,) 3 times, (y. fwd., K.1.,) twice, y. fwd., (sl.1, K.1, p.s.s.o., y. fwd.,) 4 times, sl.2, K.1, pass 2 sl. sts. over K. st., (y. fwd., K.2 tog.,) 4 times, y. fwd., (K.1, y. fwd.,) twice, K.3, repeat from * 11 times more —576 sts.

Round 94 — * K.3, y. fwd., sl.1, K.2 tog., p.s.s.o., y. fwd., (K.1, y. fwd.,) 3 times, (sl. 1, K.2 tog., p.s.s.o., y. fwd., K.3, y. fwd.,) twice, (K.1, y. fwd.,) twice, (sl.1, K.1, p.s.s.o., y. fwd.), twice, (sl.1, K.1, p.s.s.o.,) twice, K.1 (K.2 tog.,) twice, (y. fwd., K.2 tog.,) twice, y. fwd., (K.1, y. fwd.) twice, K.3, y. fwd., sl.1, K.2 tog., p.s.s.o., y. fwd., repeat from * 11 times more—624 sts.

Round 96 — * Y. fwd., sl.1, K.2 tog., p.s.s.o., y. fwd., K.3, (y. fwd., K.1, y. fwd., K.3.,) twice, (y. fwd. sl.1, K.2 tog., p.s.s.o., y. fwd., K.3.,) twice, (y. fwd., K.1.,) twice, y. fwd., (sl.1, K.1,p.s.s.o.,) 3 times, K.1, (K.2 tog.,) 3 times, y. fwd., (K.1.,y. fwd.,) twice, K.3, y. fwd., sl.1, K.2 tog., p.s.s.o., y. fwd., K.3, repeat from * 11 times more—672 sts.

Round 98 — Sl. last st. of rnd. on crochet hook, * sl. first 3 sts. from left-hand needle on crochet hook, y. fwd. and through 3 lps. on hook, y. fwd. and through 2 lps. on hook (sc. on 3 sts. tog.,) ch 8, sc. next 3 sts tog. as before, ch 9, sc. next 3 tog., (ch 10, sc. next 3 tog.,) twice, ch 9, sc. next 3 tog., ch 8, sc next 3 tog., ch 7, sc next 3 tog., ch 6, sc next 3 tog., ch 5, sc next 3 tog., ch 4, sc next 3 tog., ch 3, sc next 2 tog., ch 3, (sc 1 st. off at a time, no ch between.,) 7 times, ch 3, sc 2 tog., ch 3, sc 3 tog., ch 4, sc 3 tog., ch 5, sc 3 tog., ch 6, sc 3 tog., ch 7, repeat from * around, end last repeat sc 2 tog., ch 7, sl. st. in first sc. End off. If desired, draw cast-on sts tog at centre. Wash, starch and pin out to size, let dry.

5 Crochet

The origins of crochet are obscure but we know that fine crochet was worked by nuns in Europe in the 16th century. In the early 1800's Ireland adopted the art and gave its name to the now universally popular Irish crochet. It spread to England as a fad, lasted for some twenty years. and kept ladies high born and low born busy turning out copies of rose point and Venetian lace. Though there is really only one stitch in crochet—interlocking loops produced with a single thread and hook—there are endless variations of the basic stitch. The most popular of these are illustrated here.

Just as some of the hooks used for crochet have changed from tortoiseshell and bone to plastic and aluminium, so the uses to which crochet has been put have kept pace with changing times. Today crochet has proved its worth for making high-style garments and everything from the lowly pot holder to tea cloths of delicacy and distinction. Boys race off to school in the morning wearing crocheted pullovers, and after dark their mothers appear at first nights carrying sequin-crocheted evening bags. You will find crochet one of the most functional of all the needle arts.

Crochet

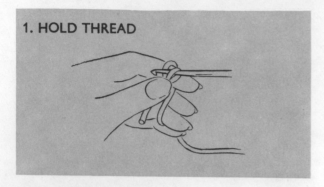

1. HOLD THREAD

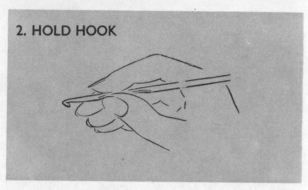

2. HOLD HOOK

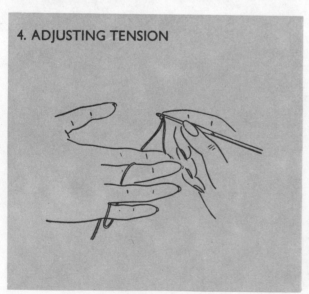

3. MAKE LOOP

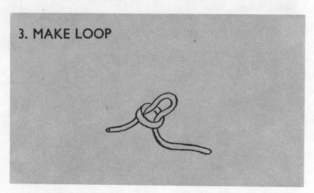

4. ADJUSTING TENSION

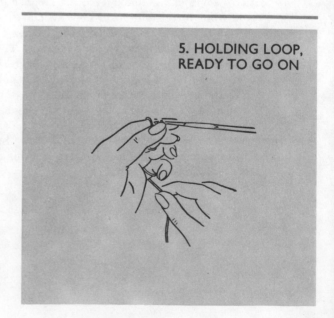

**5. HOLDING LOOP,
READY TO GO ON**

Crochet, which originated as a method for making fine laces, has developed into a versatile technique for making many things—high-style garments and accessories, lovely table mats and cloths, bedspreads and afghans.

Edges or trimmings of crochet combine well with fabric for a smart finishing touch. Crochet is also used for finishing knitted garments.

All crochet stitches are based on a loop pulled through another loop by a hook. For a practice piece, work simple stitches until you are familiar with them, and always make a practice sample of each new stitch before proceeding with an article.

To start, make a loop at the end of the thread by lapping long thread over short end. Hold in place between thumb and forefinger of left hand. See Figure 1. With the right hand grasp the bar of the hook as you would a pencil (Figure 2). Insert the hook through the loop and under the long thread. Pull this thread through loop with hook. This forms a loop or first stitch (Figure 3).

Now adjust the long thread around the left hand for proper tension. Have it pass under and around the little finger and over ring finger, under middle finger and over forefinger towards the thumb (Figure 4). Grasp the thread firmly enough to hold the tension but not so tightly as to make it difficult to pull loops through (Figure 5.)

CROCHET ABBREVIATIONS

ch	—chain stitch	dc	—double crochet
st	—stitch	sl st	—slip stitch
sts	—stitches	tr	—treble
lp	—loop	hlf tr	—half treble
inc	—increase	dbl tr	—double treble
dec	—decrease	trip tr	—triple treble
rnd	—round	quad tr	—quadruple treble
beg	—beginning	bl	—block
sp	—space	cl	—cluster
pat	—pattern	yo	—yarn over hook
tog	—together	sk	—skip
		p	—picot

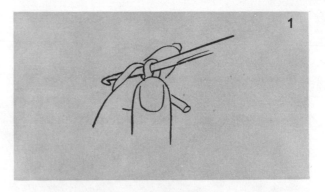

CHAIN STITCH (CH)

Chain stitch is the foundation of all crochet. The photograph and detail diagrams show how each loop is drawn through the preceding loop. Pass hook through loop under thread to catch thread with hook. Draw thread through first loop to make 1 chain (I ch). Repeat to make the required number of chains according to the instructions. By holding thumb and forefinger near the stitch in work you can control the tension. Keep 1 loop always on hook until end of chain (Figures 1, 2,). When you begin a piece of crochet, work your starting row of chain stitches more loosely than the following rows.

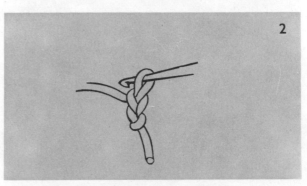

SLIP STITCH (SL. ST.)

After forming chain of desired sts, turn, insert hook in 2nd ch from hook, put thread over hook, and pull through stitch and loop.

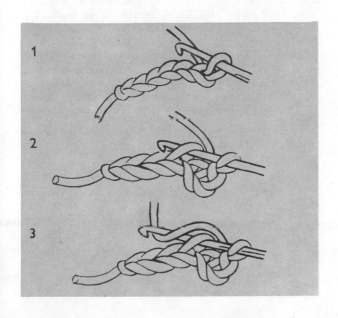

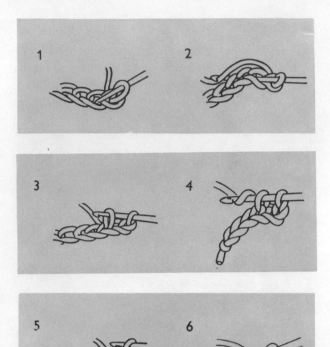

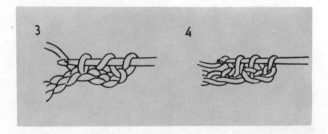

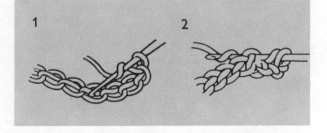

DOUBLE CROCHET (DC)

This uses the chain as a foundation. Ch 20 sts for practice. Insert hook in top 2 threads of 2nd ch from hook (Figure 1). Draw thread through loop making 2 loops on hook (Figures 2 and 3). Thread over and draw through 2 loops leaving 1 loop on hook (Figures 4 and 5). This completes 1 dc. For the next dc insert hook under top strands of next ch and repeat. See Figure 6.

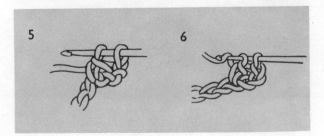

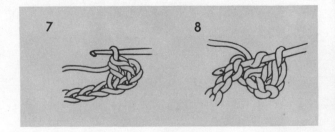

TREBLE (TR)

After making the starting chain (20 ch for practice sample) pass thread over hook, insert hook from front under top 2 strands of 4th ch from hook (Figure 1). Thread over, draw through stitch (Figure 2). There are now 3 loops on hook (Figure 3). Thread over (Figure 4) and draw through 2 loops, with 2 loops left on hook (Figure 5). Thread over again (Figure 6) and draw through remaining 2 loops with 1 loop remaining on hook (Figure 7). 1 tr is now completed. For next tr, thread over, insert hook from front under top 2 threads of next chain (Figure 8). Repeat these steps until there is a tr in each ch. At the end of the row ch 3, turn and repeat. This turning ch 3 is always counted as the first tr of next row. Therefore first tr of each row is always missed.

HALF TREBLE (HLF. TR)

With 1 loop on hook put thread over hook, insert hook in stitch, put thread over hook, draw through st, thread over hook and draw through all 3 loops. See photograph.

HALF TREBLE CROCHET

DOUBLE TREBLE (DBL. TR)

With loop on hook put thread over hook twice, insert in 5th st from hook, pull loop through. Thread over and draw through 2 loops at a time 3 times. Repeat. At end of row, ch 4 and turn. See photograph.

TO INCREASE

When instructions call for an increase make 2 sts in 1 st. This forms an extra st in the row.

DOUBLE TREBLE

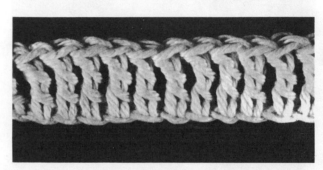

TO DECREASE DOUBLE CROCHET

Complete 1 dc to point where 2 loops are on hook. Begin another dc until 3 loops are on hook (Figure 1). Bring thread through 3 loops at once to work 2 dc together and form the decrease (Figure 2).

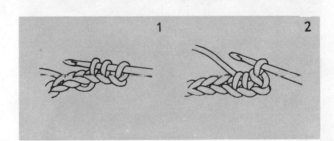

TO DECREASE TREBLE CROCHET

Complete 1 tr to point where 2 loops are on hook. Begin another tr until 4 loops are on hook (Figure 1). Thread over, draw through 2 loops (Figure 2), thread over again, draw through 3 loops. 1 loop remains on needle ready to resume work. (Figure 3).

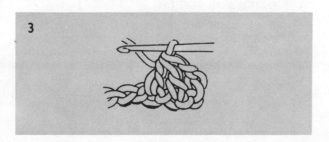

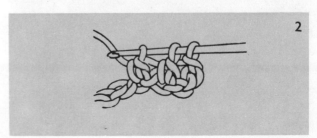

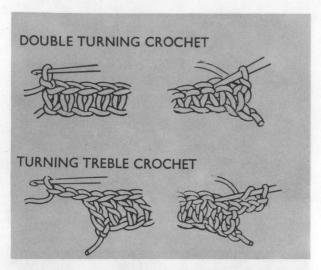

DOUBLE TURNING CROCHET

TURNING TREBLE CROCHET

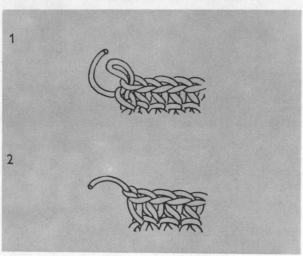

1

2

HOW TO TURN YOUR WORK

In crochet a certain number of ch sts are needed at the end of each row to bring work into position for the next row. Then work is turned so reverse side is facing the crocheter. Follow the stitch table below for the number of ch sts required to make a turn.

Double Crochet (dc)	Ch 1 to turn
Half treble (hlf tr)	Ch 2 to turn
Treble (tr)	Ch 3 to turn
Double treble (dbl tr)	Ch 4 to turn
Triple treble (trp tr)	Ch 5 to turn
Quadruple treble (quad tr)	Ch 6 to turn

HOW TO END WORK

Do not make a turning chain at end of last row. Cut working strand about 3 inches from work (Figure 1). Bring loose end through the final loop remaining on hook and pull through. This fastens the end of the work. (Figure 2). Do not cut this strand but pass end through eye of yarn needle or darning needle and weave back into body of work so it is hidden.

HOW TO FOLLOW CROCHET INSTRUCTIONS

An asterisk (*) is often used in crochet instructions to indicate repetition. For example, when instructions read " * 2 dc in next st, 1 dc in next st, repeat from * 4 times" this means to work instructions after first * until second * is reached, then go back to first * 4 times more. Work 5 times in all.

When () (parentheses) are used to show repetition, work instructions within parentheses as many times as specified. For example, "(dc, ch 1) 3 times" means to do what is within () 3 times altogether.

"Work even" in instructions means to work in same stitch without increasing or decreasing.

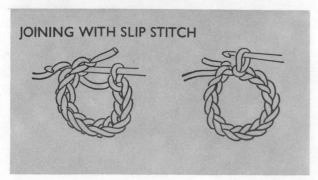

JOINING WITH SLIP STITCH

SLIP STITCH FOR JOINING

When directions say **join** always use a sl st. Insert hook from front under 2 top threads of stitch. Thread over and with one motion draw thread through stitch and loop on hook. One loop still remains on hook for continuing work.

PICOT (P)

With loop on hook, turn and ch 7, sl st in 4th ch from hook to form a picot, ch 3, skip 3 sts of foundation crochet, dc in next st and repeat across. See Photograph. There are variations in size for the picot and these are given with the crochet directions.

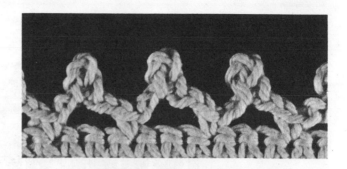

The importance of gauge in crochet

Before crocheting a garment, make a sample to check your gauge using the thread and hook called for in the instructions.

Start with a chain about four inches long and work the sample in the pattern stitch of the garment until piece is about three inches deep. Block sample by smoothing it out, pinning it down along edges and steam-pressing it. Measure across two inches, counting the number of stitches to the inch. If you have more stitches to the inch than instructions call for, you are working too tightly; try a new sample with a larger hook or work more loosely. If you have fewer stitches to the inch, you are working too loosely; try a smaller hook or work more tightly.

If you wish to substitute one thread for another, be sure the substitute thread produces the proper gauge. By crocheting a sample you will be able to check your gauge and determine the texture of the substitute thread in the pattern stitch.

In crocheting household designs, you may wish to alter the appearance of the design by choosing a different thread from the one recommended. In this case be sure to work a small sample first, then check the appearance and gauge to be sure you will obtain the result you wish.

The three examples illustrated here show a single motif worked in six cord mercerized crochet thread of three different sizes: the smallest motif in size 80, the middle motif in size 60, largest motif in size 30.

Crochet hooks – their sizes and uses

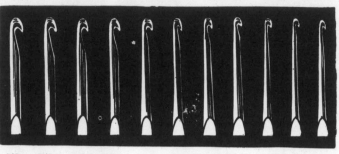

English Size	4/0	3/0	2/0	1/0	1	1½	2	—	2½	—	3
American Size	—	2/	1/0	1	2	3	4 (5)6		7	8	9
French Size (Redditch standard)	10	11	12	13	14	15	16		17	—	18
French Size (Studley standard)	6	7	8	10	12	14	16	17	18	19	20

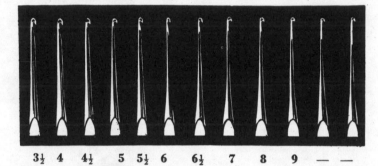

English Size	3½	4	4½	5	5½	6	6½	7	8	9	—	—
American Size	—	10	11	12	13	14	15	16	—	—	—	—
French Size (Redditch standard)	19	20	21	22	23	24	25	26	27	28	29	30
French Size (Studley standard)	21	22	23	24	25	26	27	28	29	30	—	—

Crochet hooks come in a large range of sizes, from the very fine No. 9 steel hook for fine crochet cotton to larger hooks of aluminium or plastic for coarser cotton, wool or other yarns.

CROCHET HOOKS

These are the correct numbers to use with Coats Mercer-Crochet:—

Mercer Crochet	Milwards Crochet Hook	Mercer Crochet	Milwards Crochet Hook
No. 3	No. 1½	No. 40	No. 4
No. 5	No. 2	No. 50	No. 4½
No. 10	No. 2½	No. 60	No. 5
No. 15	No. 2½	No. 70	No. 5½
No. 20	No. 3	No. 80	No. 6
No. 30	No. 3½	No. 100 and 150	No. 6½

Useful Crochet Pattern Stitches

FILET CROCHET

Make a ch of desired length.

Row 1: Tr in 8th ch from hook (1 sp), * ch 2, sk 2 ch, tr in next ch, repeat from * across ch. Ch 5, turn.

Row 2: Tr in next tr, * ch 2, tr in next tr, repeat from * across to last tr, ch 2, sk 2 ch of turning-ch, tr in next ch. Ch 5, turn.

Repeat row 2 for pattern.

CLUSTER STITCH

A cluster stitch is a group of 3 or more stitches gathered together at the top to form one pattern stitch. For a practice piece, make a ch of 20 sts.

Row 1: Thread over hook 3 times (for 1 trip tr), insert hook in 6th ch from hook and draw loop through (5 loops on hook); thread over and draw through 2 loops at a time 3 times (2 loops remain on hook); work another trip tr in next ch until 3 loops remain on hook; work another trip tr in next ch until 4 loops remain on hook; yarn over and through all 4 loops on hook—1 cluster made. * Ch 4, work trip tr cluster in next 4 ch, repeat from * across.

PUFF STITCH PATTERN

This pattern uses the cluster stitch. Make a ch of desired length.

Row 1: (wrong side): Holding back on hook last loop of each tr work 4 tr in 4th ch from hook, thread over and through 5 loops on hook, ch 1 loosely (puff st made); * sk next ch, puff st of 4 tr in next ch (include the ch 1); repeat from * across row. Ch 1, turn.

Row 2: (right side): Dc in top 2 loops of first puff st, * dc in each of ch 1 sp and top 2 loops of next puff st; repeat from * across row. Ch 1, turn.

Row 3: Pull up loop on hook to height of puff st, puff st in next dc, * sk 1 dc (this is over sp between 2 puff sts), puff st in next dc; repeat from * across row. Ch 1 more, turn. Repeat rows 2 and 3 for pattern. In illustration, pattern is decorated with sewn-on sequins and seed beads.

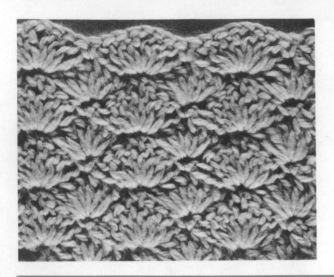

FAN SHELL STITCH

Multiple of 6 ch.

Row 1: Work 2 tr in 3rd ch from hook, ch 1, 3 tr in same ch, sk 2 ch, 1 dc in next ch, * sk 2 ch, 3 tr in next ch, ch 1, 3 tr in same ch, sk 2 ch, 1 dc in next ch; repeat from * across row, ch 3, turn.

Row 2: 2 tr in first dc, * sk 3 tr, 1 dc in ch 1 sp, sk 3 tr, 3 tr in dc between 2 shells, ch 1, 3 tr in same st, repeat from * across row, end with sk 3 tr, 1 dc in ch 1 sp, sk 2 tr, 3 tr in last st, ch 1, turn.

Row 3: * 3 tr in next dc (between shells), ch 1, 3 tr in same st, sk 3 tr, dc in next ch 1 sp, sk 3 tr; repeat from * across row, end with shell in last dc, sk 2 tr, 1 dc in last st (top of turning ch), ch 3, turn.

Repeat rows 2 and 3 for pattern.

BOX STITCH

Multiple of 6 ch.

Row 1: Tr in 3rd ch from hook, tr in each of next 2 ch, sk 2 ch, sl st in next ch, * ch 2, tr in each of next 3 ch, sk 2 ch, sl st in next ch; repeat from * across, ending last shell with tr in last 4 ch. Turn.

Row 2: Sl st across top of 4 tr, sl st under ch 2 loop of shell, * ch 2, 3 tr under same ch-2 loop, sl st under ch 2 loop of next shell; repeat from * across to last shell, make shell in ch-2 loop of last shell. Turn.

Repeat row 2 for pattern, having same number of shells in each row.

SOLOMON'S KNOT STITCH

Multiple of 6 ch. Make ch desired length.

Row 1: * Pull up loop on hook to ½″ length, draw thread through this loop and hold single strand at back of loop between thumb and middle finger: insert hook under this single strand and work dc; repeat from * once (double knot st made), sk 3 ch, 1 dc in each of next 3 ch; repeat from first * across, ending with 1 dc into each of last 3 ch.

Row 2: Work double knot st to turn. * Work 1 dc in loop on one side of knot st of previous row, work 1 dc in loop on other side of same knot st, work double knot st; repeat from * across row.

Repeat row 2 for pattern.

Instructions for making this elegant tea cloth are on page 216

AN ATTRACTIVE TROLLEY CLOTH IN WHEAT EAR DESIGN FROM COATS
SEWING GROUP BOOK No 773.

Crocheted table mat

MATERIALS: 2 balls Coats Mercer-Crochet No. 40 (20 grm.). This model is worked in shade 439 (Rose Madder), but any other shade may be used. Milward's steel crochet hook No. 4.

SIZE OF MOTIF: 2½ in. from point to point.

MEASUREMENTS: 15 in. by 16¾ in. approx.

FIRST MOTIF: Commence with 8 ch, join with a ss to form a ring.

Row 1: 3 ch, into ring work 17 tr, 1 ss into 3rd of 3 ch.

Row 2: 1 dc into same place as last ss, * 8 ch, 1 ss into 5th ch from hook (picot made), 3 ch, miss 2 tr, 1 dc into next tr; repeat from * omitting 1 dc at end of last repeat, 1 ss into first dc.

Row 3: 1 ss into each of next 3 ch and into picot, 3 ch, 8 tr into same picot, 9 tr into each of next 5 picots, 1 ss into 3rd of 3 ch.

Row 4: 1 ss into each of next 2 tr, * 1 dc into each of next 3 tr, 9 ch, miss 6 tr; repeat from * ending with 9 ch, 1 ss into first dc.

Row 5: 1 dc into next dc, * 7 ch, 1 dc into 5th of next 9 ch, 7 ch, 1 dc into 2nd of next 3 dc; repeat from * omitting 1 dc at end of last repeat, 1 ss into first dc.

Row 6: * 11 dc into next 7 ch loop, 6 dc into next 7 ch loop, 7 ch, turn, miss 11 dc, 1 ss into next dc, turn, 6 dc into 7 ch loop just made, 4 ch, 1 ss into top of last dc, 5 dc into same 7 ch loop, 5 dc into next uncompleted loop; repeat from * ending with 1 ss into first dc.

SECOND MOTIF: Work same as for first motif for 5 rows.

Row 6: (11 dc into next 7 ch loop, 6 dc into next 7 ch loop, 7 ch, turn, miss 11 dc, 1 ss into next dc, turn, 6 dc into 7 ch loop just made, 2 ch, 1 ss into corresponding picot of first motif, 2 ch, 1 ss into top of last dc of second motif, 5 dc into same 7 ch loop, 5 dc into next uncompleted loop) twice and complete as for first motif. Make 35 more motifs, joining adjacent sides as second was joined to first (see diagram for placing).
Damp and press.

Crocheted Pullovers

CROCHETED PULLOVERS

Easy to make pullovers for the men in the family, feature pattern stripes worked in long double crochet. The yarn is double knitting Orlon; the main colour is blue, the bands navy and red. Shawl collars are crocheted in one with the fronts. Directions are given for boys sizes 24"–28", men's sizes 38"–44".

SIZES: Directions for boy's size 24". Changes for boys' sizes 26", 28" and men's sizes 38", 40", 42" and 44" in parentheses.

BODY CHEST SIZE: 24" (26"–28"–38"–40"–42"–44").
BLOCKED CHEST SIZE: 27" (29"–31"–41"–43"–45"–47").

MATERIALS: 12 (14–16–24–26–28–30) ozs. Coats' SPINELLE double knitting orlon in main colour (MC).
1 (1–1–2–2–2–2) oz. Coats' SPINELLE double knitting orlon in navy (N).
1 oz. Coats' SPINELLE double knitting orlon in scarlet (S). Milwards Phantom crochet hooks No. 5 and 7.

GAUGE: 3 dc = 1"; 4 dc row = 1" (size 5 hook).

Note: Before making garment, circle sts and measurements in size you plan to make. This will facilitate reading directions.

To cast off: At beg of row, sl st loosely across specified dc, ch 1, work dc across; **at end of row,** leave specified dc unworked. Ch 1, turn.

To dec 1 dc: Pull up a lp in each of 2 dc, yo and through 3 lps on hook.

To inc 1 dc: Work 2 dc in same dc.

Pullovers: Back: Beg at lower edge, with MC and size 5 hook, ch loosely 41 (45–47–63–65–69–71). Dc in 2nd ch from hook and in each ch across—40 (44–46–62–64–68–70) dc. Ch 1, turn.

Pattern Stripe: Row 1 (wrong side): With MC, dc in both lps of each of first 1 (1–2–2–1–1–2) dc, * dc in front lp of each of next 2 dc, dc in both lps of each of next 2 dc, repeat from * across, end last repeat dc in both lps of last 1 (1–2–2–1–1–2) dc. Drop MC. Tie in N yarn, ch 1, turn.

Note: Conceal yarn ends by working over them on the following rows.

Row 2: (right side): With N, dc in back lp of first 1 (1–2–2–1–1–2) dc, * insert hook in back lp of next dc as before on 2nd row below and pull up a long lp to reach top of last row, yo and through 2 lps on hook (long dc made), make a 2nd long dc in back lp of next dc as before on 2nd row below, dc in back lp of each of next 2 dc on last row, repeat from * across, end last repeat dc in back lp of last 1 (1–2–2–1–1–2) dc. Ch 1, turn.

Row 3: With N, dc in both lps of each of first 3 (3–4–4–3–3–4) dc, * dc in front lp of each of next 2 dc, dc in both lps of each of next 2 dc, repeat from * across, end last repeat dc in both lps of each of last 3 (3–4–4–3–3–4) dc. Cut N. With MC, ch 1, turn.

Row 4: With MC, dc in back lp of each of first 3 (3–4–4–3–3–4) dc, * long dc in back lp of each of next 2 dc as before on 2nd row below, dc in back lp of each of next 2 dc on last row, repeat from * across, end last repeat dc in back lp of each of last 3 (3–4–4–3–3–4) dc. Ch 1, turn.

Row 5: With MC, repeat row 1. Drop MC. Tie in S, ch 1, turn.

Rows 6 and 7: With S, repeat rows 2 and 3. Cut S. With MC, ch 1, turn.

Rows 8 and 9: With MC, repeat rows 4 and 1. Drop MC. Tie in N, ch 1, turn.

Rows 10 and 11: With N, repeat rows 2 and 3. Cut N. With MC, ch 1, turn.

Row 12: With MC, repeat row 4. Pattern stripe completed. With MC, ch 1, turn.

Working in both lps of each dc, work MC dc until piece measures 7" (7½"–8"–12"–12"–13"–13") from start or 2¾" less than desired length to underarm, end on right side. Ch 1, turn. Check gauge. Piece should be 13½" (14½"–15½"–20½"–21½"–22½"–23½") wide. Work 12 rows of pattern stripe as before. With MC, ch 1, turn. Work

even in MC dc until piece measures 10½" (11"–11½–15½"–15½"–16½"–16½") from start, end on wrong side. Ch 1, turn.

Shape Armholes: Cast off. (See To Cast Off). 2 (3–3–4–4–4–4) dc each side of next row. Dec 1 dc each side every other row 2 (2–2–3–3–5–5) times—32 (34–36–48–50–50–52) dc. Work even in dc until armholes measure 6" (6½"–7"–9½"–9½"–10 "–10") above first cast off sts.

Shape Shoulders: Cast off 4 dc each side of next 2 (2–2–3–3–3–3) rows, then 2 (2–3–4–4–4–4) dc each side of next row. End off. Leave 12 (14–14–16–18–18–20) dc remaining for back of neck.

Front: Work as for back until armhole decs are completed, end on wrong side. Ch 1, turn.

Front Opening and Shawl Collar: Left half: Dc in each of first 16 (17–18–24–25–25–26) dc. Ch 1, turn.

Working on left half only, work even in dc for 1", end at centre edge. Ch 1, turn. Continue in dc, inc 1 dc (see To Inc) in 2nd dc from centre edge on next row, then every 1" 3 (3–3–5–5–5–5) times—20 (21–22–30–31–31–32) dc. Work even until armhole measures same as back, end at arm side.

Shape Shoulder: Cast off 4 dc at arm side of next 2 (2–2–3–3–3–3) rows, then 2 (2–3–4–4–4–4) dc at arm side of next row—10 (11–11–14–15–15–16) dc remain. Work even on remaining dc for 2" (2¼"–2¼"–2½"–3"–3"–3¼"). End off.

Right Half: From right side, join MC at neck edge, work as for left half.

Sleeves: Begin at lower edge, with MC and size 7 hook, ch loosely 25 (25–27–35–37–37–39). Dc into 2nd ch from hook and in each ch across—24 (24–26–34–36–36–38) dc. Ch 1, turn. Work the 12 rows of pattern stripe as for back. With MC, ch 1, turn. Change to size 5 hook. Work in MC dc, inc 1 dc each side of next row, then every 1½" (1"–1"–2"–2"–2"–2") 4 (6–6–6–6–6–6) times—34 (38–40–48–50–50–52) dc. Check gauge: piece above last inc row should be 11½" (12½"–13½"–16"–16½"–16½"–17½") wide. Work even in dc until piece measures 11½" (13"–14½"–18½"–18½"–19"–19") from start, or desired length to underarm. Ch 1, turn.

Shape Top: Cast off 2 (3–3–4–4–4–4) dc each side of next row. Dec 1 dc each side every other row 5 (6–7–11–11–12–12) times. Cast off 2 dc each side of next 3 (3–3–2–2–2–2) rows. End off.

Finishing: Run in all yarn ends on wrong side. Block pieces to measurements. Sew seams with MC, overcasting seams tog on wrong side as follows: Sew shoulder seams. Sew in sleeves. Matching pattern stripes, sew side and sleeve seams. Press seams flat on wrong side using a cool iron. Turn pullover to right side. Turn collar down to right side. From right side, weave short ends of collar tog. Sew neck edge of collar to neck with seam at centre back of neck. Beg at centre back of collar, from right side, with MC and size 7 hook, work 1 row dc evenly around entire outer edge of collar. Join in first dc. Ch 1, turn. Sl st loosely in each dc around edge of collar. End off.

Crochet bonnet and jacket edged with loop stitch

The delicate loop-stitch edging adds appeal to these cuddly garments for your favourite baby. Use white baby 'Orlon' yarn for the jacket and bonnet. Use the same yarn in traditional baby pink or blue for the loop-stitch trimming. Satin ribbons, to match or to contrast with the trimming, add the final touch of elegance.

SIZE: Infants' size—16 inch chest

MATERIALS: 3 oz. Coats 'Orlon' Baby Knitting, White. 1 oz. Coats 'Orlon' Baby Knitting. Blue. Milwards 'Phantom' Crochet Hook No. 10. 2 yds blue satin ribbon.

GAUGE: 3 pats = 1″; 5 pat rows = 1″.

PATTERN STITCH: Row 1.: Dc in 2nd ch from hook, draw up a lp in same ch (2 lps on hook), * sk 1 ch, draw up a lp in next ch (3 lps on hook), yo and through 3 lps on hook, ch 1 (1 pat made), draw up a lp in same ch as last st; repeat from * across, end ch 1, dc in last ch (with last st of last pat). Ch 1, turn.
Row 2: Dc in first dc, draw up a lp between first dc and first pat of last row (2 lps on hook), * draw up a lp between next 2 pats (3 lps on hook), yo and through all 3 lps on hook, ch 1, draw up a lp in same sp as last st, repeat from * across to last pat, work pat over last pat, ch 1, dc in dc of previous row. Ch 1, turn. Repeat row 2 for pattern st.
LOOP STITCH TRIMMING: Row 1 (right side): With B, dc across work. Ch 1, turn.
Row 2 (wrong side): With yarn over left index finger, insert hook in first dc, * draw 2 strands (strand on top of index finger and strand under index finger) through st forming 1″ loop on index finger; remove finger from loop, hold loop in back, yo and through 3 lps on hook (1 loop st made on right side of work). Insert hook in next dc; repeat from * in each dc. Ch 1, turn.
Row 3: Dc in each loop st. Ch 1, turn.
Row 4: Repeat row 2. End off.

JACKET. Back: Beg at lower edge, with W, ch 56. Work in pat (27 pats) until piece measures 5½″. Make dc at end of row, ch 33 for sleeve. Drop lp off hook. With another strand of W, make lp on hook, sl st in dc at opposite end of last row, ch 31 for sleeve. End off. Pick up dropped lp, turn.
Work row 1 of pat st on ch 33 until there are 15 pats, draw up a lp in same ch as last st, sk last ch and dc, draw up a lp between dc and first pat, yo and through 3 lps on hook, ch 1, work in pat across back, draw up a lp in same sp as last st, sk dc, draw up a lp in first ch of ch 31, yo and through all 3 lps on hook, ch 1, work 15 pats across ch; end ch 1, dc in last ch (with last st of last pat)—59 pats. Ch 1, turn. Work even in pat until sleeves measure 3½″ straight up from sleeve ch. Ch 1, turn.
Right Shoulder and Front: Work 24 pats, dc in same sp as last st. Ch 1, turn. Work 2 more rows of 24 pats for shoulder. Ch 9 for front, turn. Work 4 pats and ch 9, 1 pat over dc at neck edge, continue across in pat—29 pats. Work even on 29 pats until sleeve is 3½″ from top of shoulder; end centre front edge. Ch 1, turn. Work across 14 pats for front, dc in same sp as last st. Ch 1, turn. Work even on 14 pats until front measures same as back to sleeve. End off.
Left Shoulder and Front: Sk 11 pats for back of neck on

last row of 59 pats. With lp on hook, join W with sl st in sp before next pat, dc in sp. Work in pat on next 24 pats to end of row. Work 2 more rows of 24 pats, end at sleeve edge. Drop lp off hook. Attach a separate strand of W at neck edge (beg of last row), ch 8. Break off. Pick up lp at sleeve edge, ch 1, turn. Work across 24 pats, work 1 pat over dc at neck edge, work 4 pats on ch 8—29 pats. Complete left front as for right front. Sew side and sleeve seams.
Trimming: Row 1: With B, from right side of work, beg at left front neck edge, work 1 row of dc along front and bottom edges, making 1 dc in end of each row on front edges, 2 dc in each pat on bottom edge and 3 dc in each corner; end at right front neck edge. Ch 1, turn. Work rows 2–4 of Loop-Stitch Trimming.
From right side, join B to right front neck edge in end st of trimming. Ch 1, work dc around neck edge, skipping every 5th st to hold in neck edge slightly. Ch 1, turn. Work row 2 of Loop-Stitch Trimming around neck edge. End off.
From right side, join B to cuff edge of sleeve at underarm seam, work 30 dc around cuff edge. Sl st in first dc. Ch 1, turn. Work rows 2–4 of Loop-Stitch Trimming, joining each rnd with sl st before turning.
Do not press Orlon. Cut two 12″ lengths of ribbon. Sew at neck edge for ties.

BONNET: Crown: With W, ch 4, sl st in first ch to form ring.
Rnd 1: 6 dc in ring. Do not join rnds; mark ends of rnds.
Rnd 2: 2 dc in each dc—12 dc.
Rnd 3: * Dc in next dc, 2 dc in next dc, repeat from * around—18 dc.
Rnd 4: * Dc in each of next 2 dc, 2 dc in next dc, repeat from * around—24 dc. Continue to inc 6 dc each rnd, having 1 more dc between incs each rnd, until there are 11 dc between incs—78 dc. Work even in dc for 3 rnds. Ch 1. turn.
Front: Row 1: Dc in first dc, draw up a lp in same st, * sk 1 dc, draw up a lp in next st, yo and through 3 lps on hook, ch 1 (1 pat made); draw up a lp in same dc as last st, repeat from * until there are 32 pats, end ch 1, dc in next dc. Ch 1, turn. Work in pat for 11 more rows—12 rows of 32 pats. Do not ch 1 at end of last row; end off W; turn.
Cuff: Join B in first st, dc in first st, * 2 dc in each of 3 pats, 1 dc in next pat, repeat from * across —58 dc. Ch 1, turn. Work rows 2–4 of Loop-Stitch Trimming. End off. Turn back cuff to right side.
Neck Edge: From right side, attach W to left front cuff edge. Working along side edge of front, catching in side edge of cuff, make 11 dc along side edge; continue across back edge of crown, making 10 dc on back edge; make 11 dc along other side edge, catching in side edge of cuff—32 dc. Ch 1, turn. Work 2 more rows of dc. End off.
Cut 24″ lengths of ribbon for ties. Fold one end of each piece into 3 graduated loops; sew looped end to side of bonnet.

Girl's Afghan-square sweater

SIZES: Directions for size 2. Changes for sizes 4, 6, 8, 10 are in parenthesis.
BODY CHEST SIZE: 21″ (23″–24″–26″–28″).
BLOCKED CHEST SIZE: 24″ (26″–28″–30″–32″).

MATERIALS: 8 (9–10–12–13) ozs. Coats 'SPINELLE' Double Knitting Orlon in blue (B). 4 (4–5–5–6) oz. Coats 'SPINELLE'. Double Knitting Orlon in white (W). Milwards 'Phantom' Crochet Hook No. 8. Snap fastener. Small button for sizes 6, 8 and 10.
GAUGE: Small motif—2″ square. Medium motif—2⅛″ square. Large motif—2¼″ square. 7 dc—2″ (Waistband, cuffs, collar).

Small Motif (see gauge): Beg at centre with W, ch 4. Join with sl st to form ring.
Rnd 1 (right side): With W, in ring make (dc, ch 2, tr, ch 2) 4 times. Join with tight sl st in ring. End off.
Rnd 2: From right side, join B in back lp of any dc, ch 3, in same st as ch-3 make tr and hlf tr; working in back lp of each st, dc in next tr, * in next dc make hlf tr, 3 tr and hlf tr, dc in next tr, repeat from * around, end hlf tr and tr in same dc worked in at beg of rnd—24 sts. Join in back lp at top of ch-3. End off. Weave all ends in on wrong side.
Medium Motif (see gauge): Beg and work rnds 1 and 2 as for small motif. Do not end off.
Rnd 3: Working in back lp of each st, from right side, * sl st loosely in each of 5 sts, sl st twice in corner st; repeat from * around—28 sts. End off.
Large Motif (see gauge): Beg and work rnds 1 and 2 as for small motif. Do not end off.
Rnd 3: Working in back lp of each st, from right side, 2 dc in same place as sl st, * dc in each of 5 sts, 3 dc in next st; repeat from * around, end last repeat with 1 dc in same st worked in at beg of rnd—32 sts. Join in first dc. End off.
Half Small Motif: Beg at centre with W, ch 4. Join with sl st to form ring.
Row 1 (right side): In ring make dc, (ch 2, tr, ch 2, dc) twice. End off.
Row 2: From right side, join B in back lp of first dc on last row, ch 3, in same st as ch-3, make tr and hlf tr; working in back lp of each st, dc in next tr; in next dc make hlf tr, 3 tr and hlf tr, dc in next tr; in last dc make hlf tr and 2 tr—13 sts. End.

Half Medium Motif: Beg and work rows 1 and 2 as for half small motif.
Row 3: From right side, join B in back lp at top of ch-3, sl st loosely in same st as ch-3; working in back lps (sl st in each of 5 sts, 2 sl sts in corner st) twice—16 sts. End off.

Crocheted afghan squares, each with a flower centre, are sewn together to make an unusual sweater of double knitting 'Orlon' The pompon ties give extra interest.

Half Large Motif: Beg and work rows 1 and 2 as for half small motif.
Row 3: From right side, join B in back lp at top of ch-3, 2 dc in same st as ch-3; working in back lps, dc in each of 5 sts, 3 dc in corner st, dc in each of 5 sts, 2 dc in last st—17 dc. End off.

BLOUSE: For size 2: Make 92 small motifs and 2 half small motifs.
For size 4: Make 112 medium motifs and 2 half medium motifs.
For size 6: Make 161 small motifs and 2 half small motifs.
For size 8: Make 175 medium motifs and 2 half medium motifs.
For size 10: Make 185 large motifs and 2 half large motifs.

Joining: Beg at lower edge of front, following chart page 200 with B, sew motifs tog catching tog back lps st by st from one corner st to the other until 3 (4–5–6–6) motif rows are joined, omitting the half motifs at underarms shown by dotted lines. Check gauge; piece should measure 6″ (8½″–10″–12¾″–13½″) in length, 12″ (13″–14″–15″16″) in width. Leaving an opening at front of neck, continue to join motifs as shown on chart to lower edge of back, filling in corners at front of neck with half motifs.

Finishing: Fold work across shoulders, with lower edges of back and front meeting. Sew side and sleeve seams in same way to within 1 motif of underarm. Sew one motif to each underarm, forming gussets as shown on chart by dotted lines; one corner will meet side seam and opposite corner will meet underarm sleeve seam.
Waistband: Rnd 1: From right side, join B at lower right side seam; working in back lp of sts around lower edge, ch 1, work 42 (46–49–52–56) dc across front and 42 (45–49–52–56) dc across back—84 (91–98–104–112) dc. Join in ch-1. Do not turn.
Rnd 2: Working in back lps, * dc in each of 4 (5–5–6–6) dc, pull up a lp in each of next 2 dc, yo and through 3 lps on hook (1 dec made), repeat from * 13 (12–13–12–13) times—70 (78–84–91–98) sts. Join in ch-1. Do not turn.
Rnd 3: Ch 1, dc in back lp of each dc around. Join in ch-1. Repeat rnd 3 until waistband measures 1½″ (1½″–1½″–1–1). End off.
Cuffs: From right side, join B at lower side seam of sleeve; working in back lp of sts, ch 1 work 28 (30–36–36–40) dc on sleeve edge. Join in ch-1.
Rnd 2: Working in back lps, ch 1, * dc in each of 2 (3–2–2–2) dc, dec 1 dc, repeat from * 6 (5–8–8–9) times—21 (24–27–27–30) dc. Join in ch-1. Beg with rnd 3 of waistband, complete cuffs as for waistband or desired sleeve length.
Collar: Beg at neck edge with B, ch 36 (39–41–44–49) to measure 10″ (10½″–11½″–12″–13¼″).
Row 1: Dc in 2nd ch from hook and in each ch across—35 (37–40–43–48) dc. Ch 1, turn each row.

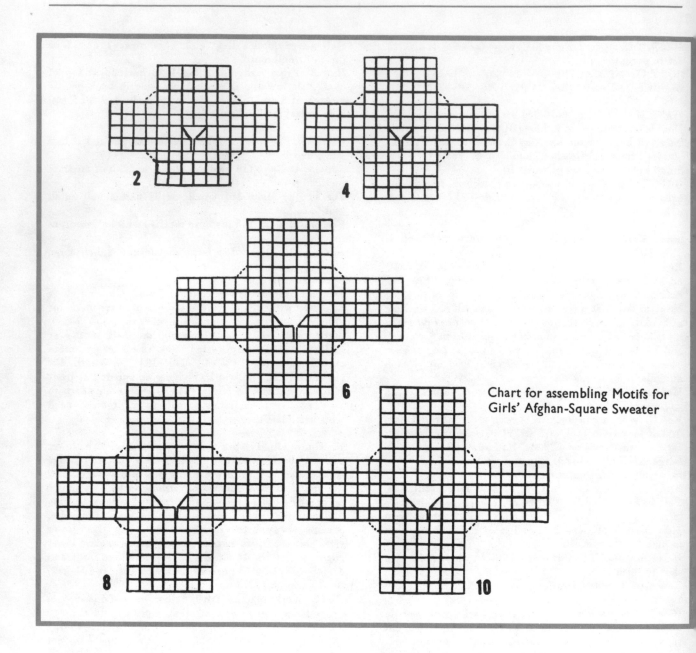

Chart for assembling Motifs for Girls' Afghan-Square Sweater

Row 2: Dc in back lp each dc across.

Row 3: Dc in front lp of each dc. Repeat last 2 rows 1 (2–2–3–3) times more. Repeating rows 2 and 3 alternately, dec 1 dc at each side of next 3 rows—29 (31–34–37–42) dc. End off. Work 1 row dc around outer edge of collar.

Beg at opening edge of front neck, from right side, with B, work 35 (37–40–43–48) dc evenly around neck edge. Ch 1, turn. Work 1 (1–2–2–2) rows more of dc around neck edge. End off.

On Sizes 2 and 4: Sew neck edge of collar to neck with ends at centre front. Close neck with snap fastener.

On Sizes 6, 8 and 10: Beg 1″ from right front neck opening, sew collar to neck edge, ending at front opening and to within 1″ of end of collar (collar overlap). Close side opening with button and buttonloop. Close corner of collar overlap with snap fastener inside edge of collar of right front (bringing ends of collar to centre front).

TIES: Make 2 chains desired length. Sew ties under front edges of collar. Trim ends of ties with W pompons. (See Index for directions, "How to Make a Pompon".)

Picture pot holders

Making any or all of these 6" square picture pot holders is an easy matter with heavy cotton rug yarn. Directions for each, instructions for changing from one colour to another, and how to work reverse double crochet are on pages 202–203. The pot holders make useful gifts, and are a practical way of using up odd balls of yarn.

GENERAL DIRECTIONS: Design Note: When a row has more than one colour, start extra colour or colours at beginning of row. Work over colour not being used. When changing colours, work last dc or reverse dc of one colour until there are 2 lps on hook, drop strand to wrong side of work. Pick up new colour and finish dc.

GAUGE: 4 sts = 1"; 7 rows = 2".

PATTERN: Row 1 (right side): Dc in 2nd ch from hook and in each ch across —23 dc: ch 1, turn.

Row 2: Work in reverse dc as follows: * Holding yarn in front of work, insert hook under yarn from back to front in next dc, pull lp through and complete dc; repeat from * across, ch 1, turn.

Row 3: Dc in each dc. Ch 1, turn. Repeat rows 2 and 3 for pat.

BORDER: Rnd 1: From right side, work dc around entire edge of pot holder, making 3 dc in each corner. Join with sl st in first dc.

Rnd 2: Working in back lp of sts, work sl st in each dc around. Join in first sl st. End off.

RING: Ch 8, join with sl st in first ch. Cut yarn, leaving an end for sewing. Sew ring to top of pot holder.

PINE TREE POT HOLDER: Materials: Heavy cotton rug yarn, 1 skein each of white, evergreen and dark green. Aluminium crochet hook size 7 or 8.
Design Section: With white, ch 24. Following General Directions and Pine Tree Chart, work in pat for 20 rows. End.
Border and Ring (see General Directions): Work with dark green.

STAR FLOWER POT HOLDER: Materials: Heavy cotton rug yarn, 1 skein each of medium blue, white, yellow and evergreen. Aluminium crochet hook size 7 or 8.
Design Section: With medium blue, ch 24. Following General Directions and Star Flower Chart, work design in pat for 20 rows. End off.
Border and Ring (see General Directions): Work border with white, ring with medium blue.

SAIL BOAT POT HOLDER: Materials: Heavy cotton rug yarn, 1 skein each of white, red, royal blue, medium blue; small amount of black. Aluminium crochet hook size 7 or 8.
Design Section: With royal blue, ch 24. Following General Directions and Sail Boat Chart, work design in pat for 20 rows. End off.
Mast: Untwist a piece of black yarn and with 2 strands embroider mast in stem stitch.
Border and Ring (see General Directions): Work border with white, ring with red.

TULIP POT HOLDER: Materials: Heavy cotton rug yarn, 1 skein each of white, dark green and cerise. Aluminium crochet hook size 7 or 8.
Design Section: With white, ch 24. Following General Directions and Tulip Chart, work pat for 20 rows. End off.
Border and Ring (see General Directions): Work cerise border, white ring.

BUTTERFLY POT HOLDER: Materials: Heavy cotton rug yarn, 1 skein each of light yellow, yellow, turquoise and black. Aluminium crochet hook size 7 or 8.
Design Section: With light yellow, ch 24. Following General Directions and Butterfly Chart, work design in pat for 20 rows. End off.
Antennae: Untwist a piece of black yarn and with 2 strands, embroider antennae in outline st.
Border and Ring (see General Directions): Work border with yellow, ring with turquoise.

COUNTRY COTTAGE POT HOLDER: Materials: Heavy cotton rug yarn, 1 skein each of white, black, dark green, medium blue and royal blue; small amount of red. Aluminum crochet hook size 7 or 8.
Design Section: With dark green, ch 24. Following General Directions and Country Cottage Chart, work design in pat for 19 rows. End off.
Tree Trunk: Untwist a piece of black yarn and with 2 strands, embroider tree trunk in outline st.
Border and Ring (see General Directions): Work border with white, ring with medium blue.

To follow any of these charts: Begin at lower right-hand corner of chart and work back and forth until chart is completed.

CHARTS FOR MAKING PICTURE POT HOLDERS

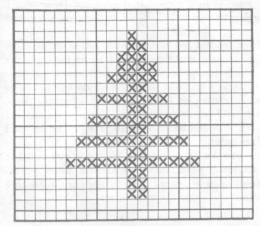

WHITE ☐ EVERGREEN ☒

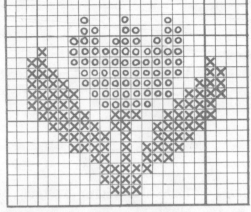

WHITE ☐ CERISE ◉ DK. GREEN ☒

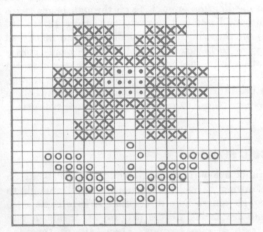

MED. BLUE ☐ EVERGREEN ◉
YELLOW ⊡ WHITE ☒

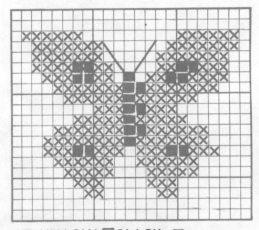

LT. YELLOW ☐ BLACK ■
TURQUOISE ☒

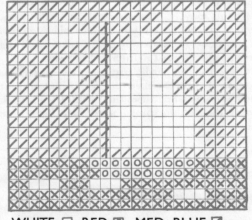

WHITE ☐ RED ⊡ MED. BLUE ◪
ROYAL BLUE ☒

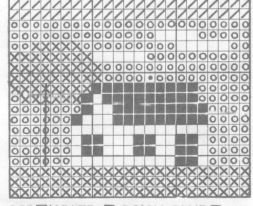

RED ⊡ WHITE ☐ ROYAL BLUE ◪
MED. BLUE ◉ DK. GREEN ☒ BLACK ■

Crochet with Beads or Sequins

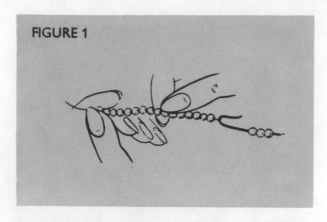

FIGURE 1

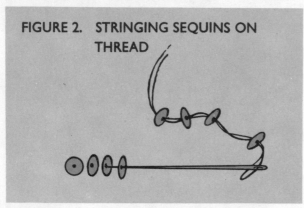

FIGURE 2. STRINGING SEQUINS ON THREAD

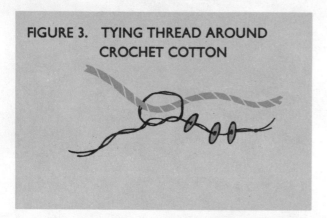

FIGURE 3. TYING THREAD AROUND CROCHET COTTON

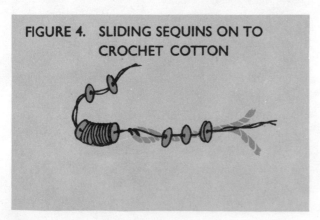

FIGURE 4. SLIDING SEQUINS ON TO CROCHET COTTON

Many attractive accessories can be made of bead or sequin crochet. It is possible, too, to work a design of beads or sequins into a crocheted garment. Or separate collars and cuffs can be crocheted to decorate a knitted garment.

The threads used for crochet with beads or sequins should be smooth, and fine enough to fit through the holes of the beads or sequins. For seed beads, use fine crochet cotton or metallic thread. Medium-size beads or pearls can be strung on to heavier crochet cottons, wool yarns such as 3-ply fingering yarn, metallic yarns and fine mohair. Wooden beads with large holes can be used with bulky yarns.

Sequins can be strung on to knitting and crochet cotton, fingering yarn, and fine smooth dress yarns. Large bangles can be threaded on to any yarn, including bulky yarns.

STRINGING BEADS

If the beads are not already strung on a fine thread, thread a needle, fine enough to go through beads, with nylon thread. Knot end securely and string 12″ to 18″ of beads on thread. Remove needle. Tie end of thread around yarn to be used in crochet. Slide beads gently over knot on to crochet cotton (Figure 1), taking care not to break the finer thread on which beads are strung. Remove bead thread. Thread as many beads on to cotton as you expect to use in crocheting that amount of cotton.

STRINGING SEQUINS

If sequins are not already strung, thread them on doubled sewing thread, using needle small enough to pass through centre hole of sequin. Be sure right sides of sequins are facing needle (Figure 2). Inside of cup is right side of cup sequins. About 10″ of threaded sequins pushed tightly together is equivalent to one strand (about 120 flat sequins or 105 cup sequins per inch).

If crochet cotton is to be used for working sequin crochet, sequins may be strung directly on to the yarn. Thread end of crochet cotton into an embroidery needle the right size to accommodate both the sequin and the yarn. Have needle 12″ to 15″ from end of yarn.

Pick up sequins with needle with right side of sequins facing you as they are picked up. Use a flat tray or dish to hold sequins while threading them. Do not push sequins past the double thread until they have been measured.

THREADING SEQUINS ON CROCHET COTTON

Holding string of sequins with right side of sequins facing cotton, tie end of thread around cotton (Figure 3). Do not tie cotton around thread.

Slide all sequins carefully over knot on to cotton. (Short

1. Position of sequin when hook picks up thread. Push sequin firmly against hook. With taut thread pass thread and sequin over hook for a tr.

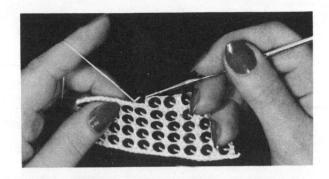

2. Start of tr with sequin position. Insert hook in top of dc below. For flat work hold sequin towards you right side up.

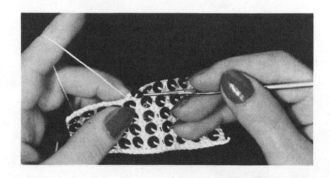

3. Completed tr position of sequin. Take lps off hook, 2 at once, behind sequin to complete tr Make 1 tr without sequin in each of next 2 dc.

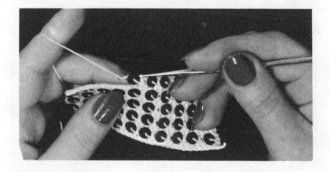

cotton end doubles back as sequins are slipped on; Figure 4). Thread one strand of sequins on to one skein of cotton. Cut off empty thread.

When last sequin on cotton has been worked and additional sequins are needed, cut cotton 3″ from last stitch made, repeat threading procedure.

BEAD CROCHET

Beads are crocheted into the work from the wrong side. String required number of beads on to yarn and push beads down on yarn, out of the way, until ready for use. Work background of dc with yarn, ending on right side of work.

Bead Row (wrong side): Dc in each dc to place where bead pattern should begin, * pull up a loop in next dc, slip a bead up close to last loop made, hold bead in back of work, yarn over hook and through 2 loops on hook (beaded dc made), dc in next dc; repeat from * for bead pattern.

Work all right side rows in plain dc.

SEQUIN TREBLE STITCH

In this stitch, the sequins are crocheted on to the right side of the work. Each sequin requires 3 sts (1 sequin st and 2 plain sts). Thus, for a row of 30 sequins, you will need 90 sts, plus 1 for the end st. Two rows complete the pattern, the tr row with sequins and a plain dc row. Thread required number of sequins on to yarn with right side of sequins going on first. Slide sequins out of the way on yarn and make a ch the required length.

Row 1: Dc into 3rd ch from hook, 1 dc in each remaining ch, ch 3, turn.

Row 2: Push a sequin firmly against hook, throw thread and sequin over hook, as for a tr, insert hook in top of 2nd dc (making certain sequin is towards you and right side up); take loops off hook 2 at a time **behind** the sequin, thus completing a sequin tr; 1 tr (without sequin) in each of next 2 dc. * Push a sequin firmly against hook and make a sequin tr, 1 tr (without sequin) in each of next 2 dc; repeat from * across row; ending with 2 tr (without sequins). Ch 1, turn.

Row 3: Dc in top of 2nd tr of sequin row, 1 dc in each of remaining tr of row, ending with dc in turning ch 3 of sequin row. Ch 3, turn. Repeat rows 2 and 3 alternately for pattern.

Sequin crochet with chain loops

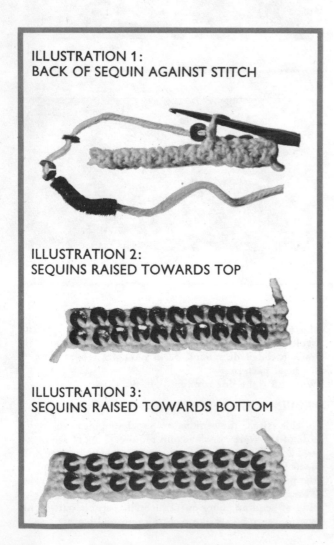

ILLUSTRATION 1:
BACK OF SEQUIN AGAINST STITCH

ILLUSTRATION 2:
SEQUINS RAISED TOWARDS TOP

ILLUSTRATION 3:
SEQUINS RAISED TOWARDS BOTTOM

This method for working sequin crochet is the one used most often for jackets, blouses and dresses. The sequin row is worked from the wrong side, using a simple chain loop and double crochet. If sequins are small, a ch-1 1p (chain one loop) is used for a closely-worked surface of sequins. The evening bag and spectacle case shown on opposite page are made with ch-1 1ps. Larger sequins can be worked with ch-2 or ch-3 1ps.

Thread sequins on yarn as directed, page 204.

SEQUIN CROCHET WITH CH-1 LPS

To work sequin row, slide one sequin close to st on hook. Back of sequin will be against hook; Illustration 1. Holding sequin firmly at back of work and with yarn taut so that sequin will lie flat, make 1 dc in ch-1 lp of row below. * Ch 1, slide one sequin close to ch 1 on hook, dc in next ch-1 sp, repeat from * across row.

Sequins placed after the ch 1 and before the dc as in directions above, will be raised towards top of work; Illustration 2. When article is worked from top down, this method is generally preferred.

Sequins placed after the dc and before the ch 1 will be raised towards bottom of work ;Illustration 3. When article is worked from bottom up, this method is generally preferred.

Sequin crochet bag

Illustrated opposite page 169

SIZE: 10½" wide × 7" deep.

MATERIALS: 2 Balls Coats 'Chain' Mercer-Crochet No. 10 (20 grm); Milwards steel-crochet hook No. 2½; Sequins; 8" metal sew-in bag frame; ½ yard satin for lining; Piece of Vilene, 14" × 18"; Cardboard; 2½ × 10".
GAUGE: 5 sequins = 1"; 5 sequin rows (10 rows) = 1".

Note: Follow directions for threading sequins on to yarn, page 204.

BAG (make 2 pieces): Starting at top of bag, with sequin threaded yarn, ch 113.
Row 1 (right side): Dc in 3rd ch from hook, * ch 1, sk 1 ch, dc in next ch; repeat from * across—56 sps. Ch 2, turn.
Row 2 (sequin row): * Slide sequin close to hook, dc in ch—1 sp, ch 1, repeat from * across, making last dc in turning ch—sp—56 sequins. Ch 2, turn.
Row 3: Dc in first ch—1 sp, * ch 1, dc in next ch—1 sp, repeat from * across —52 sps. Ch 2, turn. Repeat row 2 and 3 until piece measures 6¾" from start, end row 3–35 sequin rows. Ch 2, turn.
Base: Next row (sequin row): Dc in first sp, (ch 1, dc in next sp) 4 times, ch 1, work in sequin crochet until there are 46 sequins, (ch 1, dc in next sp) 5 times. Ch 1, turn.

Next row: Sl st in each sp and dc to sp before first sequin; ch 2, dc in next ch—1 sp, * ch 1, dc in next ch—1 sp; repeat from * across to sp in back of last sequin—46 sps. Ch 2, turn. Work in sequin—crochet until there are 5 rows of 46 sequins. Work 1 row of ch—1 sp. End off.

FINISHING: Cut two pieces of Vilene same size and shape as crochet pieces. Whip Vilene pieces together along side edges down to indentations at base of bag. Whip bottom edges together. Close openings formed by indentations each side. Place cardboard piece inside Vilene interlining to fit snugly at base.
From wrong side, with yarn, sew crochet pieces together. Cut lining satin 13½" wide × 18" long. If pocket for mirror is desired, cut piece 5½" × 8"; fold in half crosswise, wrong side out; stitch side seams taking ½" seams, turn to right side; press. Insert piece of Vilene, 4½" × 3½", inside pocket; close bottom edges. Stitch pocket to lining. Fold lining in half crosswise, wrong side out; stitch side seams. Place lining inside interlining. Fold excess at bottom corners of lining neatly under cardboard; tack. Tack lining to interlining at seams. Place lining inside bag; turn under raw edges around top and hem to bag. Sew bag to bag frame along top edges of frame only with buttonhole twist.

Sequin spectacle case

Illustrated opposite page 169

SIZE: 6" × 3¼".

MATERIALS: 1 Ball Coats Mercer-Crochet No 10 (20 grm); Milwards steel crochet hook No 2½; Sequins; ¼ yd satin for lining; Cardboard, two pieces 3" × 6".

GAUGE: 5 sequins = 1"; 5 sequin row (10 rows) = 1".
Note: Follow directions for threading sequins on to yarn, page 204.

SPECTACLE CASE: (make 2 pieces): Starting at closed end of case, with sequin-threaded yarn, ch 31.
Row 1 (right side): Dc in 3rd ch from hook, * ch 1, sk 1 ch, dc in next ch, repeat from * across —15 sps. Ch 2, turn.
Row 2 (sequin row): Dc in first sp, * slide sequin close to hook, ch 1, dc in next sp, repeat from * across—14 sequins. Ch 2, turn.
Row 3: Dc in first sp (behind sequin), * ch 1, dc in next sp, repeat from * across—15 sps. Ch 2, turn. Repeat row 2 and 3 until there are 29 rows of sequins, end row 3. End off.

FINISHING: Cover both sides of two pieces of cardboard, 3" × 6", with satin. Sew one to wrong side of each crochet piece. From right side, whip crochet pieces together, leaving one end open and 1" each side of end, make twisted cord from 3 strands of yarn, cut 2½ yds long. Twist strands together very tightly until cord buckles. Place finger at centre, double strands and allow to twist together. Knot ends. Sew cord around case and around open edge.

Filet Crochet

Filet crochet is the technique of forming designs with little solid and openwork squares called blocks and spaces. Usually the background is worked in the openwork mesh with the design formed by the blocks. In this section, we show some simple variations of filet crochet, together with useful charts of the designs given. Filet crochet makes attractive wide edgings for cloths and place mats, as well as appliqué motifs for linen and clothing.

It is a medium for the crochet enthusiast who can work out an original design on a piece of graph paper, the charts given show the method for doing this, and crochet a set of mats or a border on a cloth that is truly her own work.

Here, one large motif worked in blocks, forms a table-protecting place mat, 17″ x 18″. Mat is worked in white crochet cotton, glistening with silver. Crocheted rose leaf is appliquéd to napkin. Directions and chart for this filet rose place mat and leaf motif are on pages 210–211.

Leaf-and-scroll design of filet crochet borders a linen place mat. Flowers are worked separately and sewn to the background for a three-dimensional effect. Lacet stitch, a variation of filet crochet, adds interest to the border 5″ deep; mat measures 23″ by 16½″ overall. Chart and directions for the Embossed Daisy Mat are on pages 212–213.

Filet rose mat and leaf motif

SIZES: Mat 17″ × 18″. Napkin 16″ square.

MATERIALS: Coats 'Chain' Mercer Crochet No. 40 (20 grm). 12 balls. Milwards Steel Crochet Hook No. 4. Reel Metallic Thread. Piece of linen 17″ × 17″ for each napkin.
GAUGE: 12 tr = 1″: 4 rows = 1″. (Approx.)

GENERAL DIRECTIONS: Each square on chart represents 3 tr; each × represents 1 mesh.
To Inc One or More Tr Squares on Chart: At beg of row, ch 6 for a tr square inc, ch 3 more for each additional square: tr in 5th ch from hook, tr in next ch (1 square), tr in each of 3 ch for each additional square. **At end of row,** yo, draw up a lp in top of turning ch into which last tr was worked; holding last lp close to work, yo, draw through one lp on hook (this st is base st), yo and through 2 lps on hook twice for 1 tr, * yo, draw up a lp in base st, yo and through 1 lp on hook for next base st, yo and through 2 lps on hook twice for 1 tr, repeat from * once (a tr square inc made); work from first * to 2nd * 3 times for each additional square inc.
To Inc One Mesh: At beg of row, ch 7, tr in first tr. At end of row, ch 2, yo hook 3 times, draw up a' lp in turning ch into which last tr was worked, yo and through 2 lps 4 times (quad tr made for mesh).
To Dec One Tr Square or One Mesh: At beg of row, ch 1, sl st across 3 sts of each tr square or mesh, then sl st in next tr, ch 5, sk next 2 tr, tr into next tr if row starts with a mesh (ch 3, tr in next tr if row starts with tr squares), finish row. **At end of row,** leave 3 sts of each tr square or mesh unworked.

MAT: Ch 54.
Row 1 (wrong side): Tr in 5th ch from hook and in each ch across—51 tr, counting turning ch. Turn each row.
Rows 2-4: Work in tr, inc tr square (see General Directions) as shown in chart—81 tr.
Row 5: Ch 5, tr in 4th tr (mesh made at beg of row), tr in each st across, inc 1 mesh at end of row.
Row 6: Inc 1 mesh at beg of row, 2 tr in next mesh, tr in each tr to last mesh, 2 tr in mesh, tr in 3rd ch of ch 5, inc 1 mesh at end of row, ch 5. End off. Put work aside.
Row A on Chart: Ch 33. Tr in 5th ch from hook and in each ch across—30 tr, counting turning ch. Turn.
Joining Row: Ch 9, drop lp off hook, insert hook in 5th ch at end of row 6 on first piece worked and draw dropped lp through; working back on 2nd piece, tr in 5th ch from hook and in each of 4 ch, tr in each st across, inc 2 tr squares at end of row—42 tr on 2nd piece. Turn, do not twist pieces.
Row 7: Ch 3, tr in 2nd tr (always beg even tr edge this

way), tr in each of next 40 tr, ch 2, sk next 2 ch of first piece, tr in next ch, ch 2, sk 2 ch, tr in top of quad tr of mesh, ch 2, sk next 2 ch of same mesh, tr in next tr (3 meshes made), tr in each tr across to last mesh, ch 2, sk 2 ch of turning ch, tr in next ch (mesh made over mesh at end of row).
Row 8: Ch 5, sk 2 ch, tr in next tr (mesh over mesh at beg of row), tr in each tr to next mesh, (ch 2, tr in next tr) twice, 2 tr in next mesh, tr in tr (tr square worked over mesh), tr in each st across, inc 1 tr square at end of row.
Row 9-63: Follow chart for pat and shaping.
Shape Top of Petals: First Petal: Row 64: Dec 2 tr squares, work tr to within 3 tr of next mesh, ch 2, sk 2 tr, tr in next tr. Turn.
Row 65: Dec each side as on chart—18 tr. End off.
Second Petal: Row 64: Make lp on hook, sk next 2 meshes on row 63 from first petal, tr in last tr of 2nd mesh, tr in each st across—93 tr. Work to top of chart on 2nd petal. End off.
Steam press mat, using steam iron or dry iron and damp cloth.

THREE LEAF CLUSTER MOTIF: Centre Leaf: Ch 19, dc in 2nd ch from hook and in each of 17 ch—18 dc. Mark beg of following rnds.
Rnd 1: Ch 1; working on other side of starting ch, * sl st in each of 2 sts, dc in each of 2 sts, hlf tr in next st, ch 1, sk 1 st, tr in next st, ch 1, sk next st, dbl tr in next st, ch 1, (dbl tr, ch 1) in each of 4 sts, sk 1 st, tr in next st, ch 1, sk 1 st, hlf tr in next st, dc in next st *, 3 dc in turning ch at point; working on other side, work from 2nd * back to first *, sl st in first ch 1.
Rnd 2: Ch 1, * work 2 sl st, 2 dc, 1 hlf tr, (tr in next sp, tr in next st) twice, 2 tr in next sp, tr in next st, 2 dbl tr in next sp, dbl tr in next st, 2 dbl tr in next sp, tr in next st, 2 tr in next sp, tr in next st, tr in next sp, hlf tr in next st, hlf tr in next sp, hlf tr in next hlf tr, dc in each of next 2 dc *, 2 dc in next dc (tip), ch 4, sl st in last dc made, dc in same dc last worked in; working on other side work from 2nd * back to first *, sl st in first ch 1.
Rnd 3: Ch 1, sl st in back lp of each st around, join. Do not end off.
Stem: Make 1¼″ ch, sl st in 2nd ch from hook and in each ch, sl st at base of leaf. End off.
Outer Leaves (make 2): Work as for centre leaf for 3 rnds. Do not end off, join with sl st to centre of stem.
FINISHING: Holding leaves closely tog, place cluster motif at one corner of linen with tip of centre leaf ½″ in from corner. Sew cluster motif in place. Make ¼″ hem around napkin, following outline of cluster at corner.

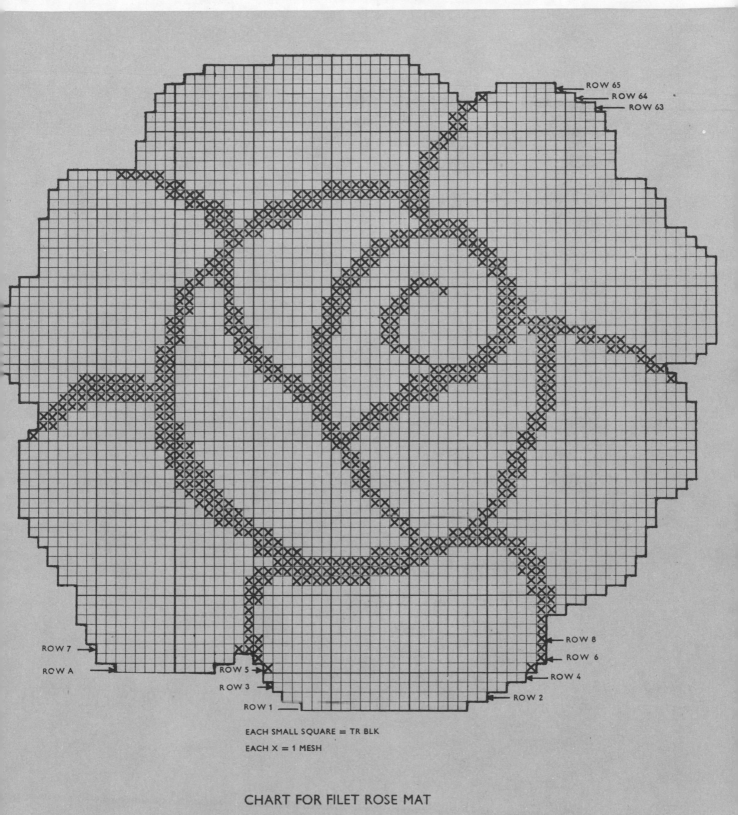

ROW 65
ROW 64
ROW 63

ROW 7
ROW A
ROW 5
ROW 3
ROW 1

ROW 8
ROW 6
ROW 4
ROW 2

EACH SMALL SQUARE = TR BLK

EACH X = 1 MESH

CHART FOR FILET ROSE MAT

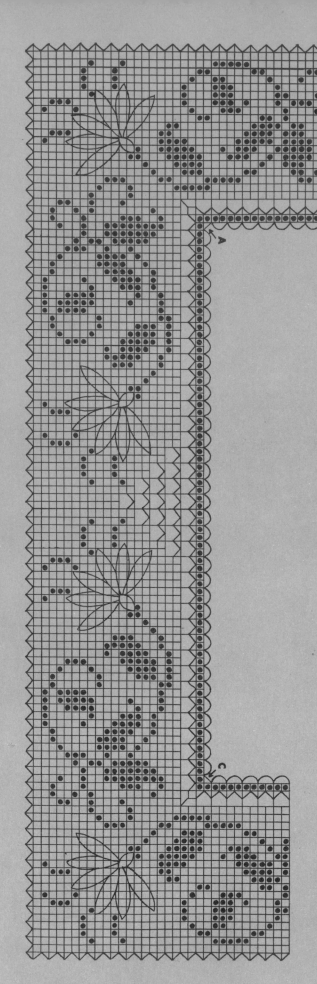

Actual-size detail

CHART FOR EMBOSSED DAISY MAT

BL	CH-2 SP
LACET ST	CH-5 SP

Embossed daisy mat

SIZE: 23″ × 16½″ approx.

MATERIALS: Coats 'Chain'. Mercer-Crochet No. 20 (20 grm). Milwards Steel Crochet Hook No. 3. Piece of linen 15½″ × 9½″.
GAUGE: 5 sps = 1″; 5 rows = 1″.
Note: Daisies are made separately.

LACE EDGING: Rnd 1: Beg at inner edge, * (ch 8, dbl tr in 8th ch from hook) 19 times across one end, ch 4, dbl tr in 4th ch from hook (corner), (ch 8, dbl tr in 8th ch from hook) 35 times, ch 4, dbl tr in 4th ch from hook (corner); repeat from * once, join with sl st (with work untwisted) in base of first dbl tr at A on chart. Keep lps on inner edge. Turn.

Rnd 2 (right side): Ch 3, 2 tr over dbl tr bar of last corner, * 7 tr through 2 threads in centre of same bar, 2 tr over balance of same bar, tr between bars, make (5 tr over next dbl tr bar, tr between bars) across to next corner, 2 tr over bar of corner; repeat from * 3 times, end 5 tr over last dbl tr bar, join in top of ch 3. Sl st in next 6 tr (corner). Turn.

Rnd 3: Ch 6, sk next 2 tr, dc in next tr, ch 3, sk 2 tr, tr in next tr (lacet st), * make (ch 3, sk 2 tr, dc in next tr, ch 3, sk 2 tr, tr in tr between bars) across to centre tr at corner (21 lacet sts), ch 5, tr in same corner tr, make 37 lacet sts to next corner *, ch 5, tr in same corner tr; repeat from first * to 2nd * once, ch 2, join with tr in 3rd ch of ch 6, ending at exact corner. Turn.

Rnd 4: Ch 9, sk first sp, tr in next tr, * (ch 5, tr in next tr) across to first tr at corner, ch 5, tr in corner sp, ch 5, tr in next tr; repeat from * around, end ch 5, ss in 4th ch of ch 9. Turn.

Rnd 5: Ch 5, tr in centre of first sp, ch 2, tr in next tr, * (ch 2, tr in next sp, ch 2, tr in next tr) 8 times, (ch 3, dc in next sp, ch 3, tr in next tr for lacet st) 5 times, (ch 2, tr in next sp, ch 2, tr in next tr) 9 times to corner tr, ch 5, tr in same tr, following chart across wide end, make 32 sps, 7 lacet sts, 32 sps to next corner tr *, ch 5, tr in same tr, ch 2, tr in centre of next sp, ch 2, tr in next tr; repeat from first * to 2nd * once, end ch 2, tr in 3rd ch of ch 5 (exact corner). Turn.

Rnd 6: Ch 5, sk first sp, tr in next tr, * following chart from C to B, make 15 ch—2 sps (2 tr in next sp, tr in next tr for 1 bl) 5 times, make 12 sps, 7 ch—5 sps, 12 sps, 5 bls, 16 ch—2 sps to corner sp, ch 5, 3 tr in balance of corner sp, tr in next tr, 4 bls, 14 ch—2 sps, 5 ch—5 sps, 14 ch—2 sps, 5 bls *, ch 5, tr in corner sp, ch 2, tr in next tr; repeat from first * to 2nd * once, end ch 2, tr in 3rd ch of ch 5 (corner). Turn.

Rnd 7: Ch 4, 3 tr in top of corner tr (½ corner shell), * following chart from B across narrow end, 2 tr in corner sp, tr in next tr, 4 sps, continue across, make 2 tr in next corner sp, 7 tr in 3rd ch of same sp, 4 sps, continue across wide end *, make 6 more tr in same corner ch, repeat from first * to 2nd * once, end ch 2, 3 tr in same st with first half shell, join with ss in top of ch 4. Turn.

Rnds 8 and 10: Ch 4, 3 tr in corner tr, * following chart from C to B, work across wide end to next corner, make 6 more tr in corner tr (7 in all), continue across narrow end *, make 6 more tr in corner tr (7 in all); repeat from first * to 2nd * once, end ch 2, 3 tr in same st with first half shell, join in top of ch 4. Turn.

Rnd 9: (wrong side): Following chart from B to C, begin, work corners, and end as for rnd 8. Turn.

Rnd 11: Ch 3, tr in each of next 3 tr (1 bl), * following chart from B to C, work across narrow end to next corner (ending 2 sps), tr in each of next 3 corner tr, ch 5, tr in tr last worked in, tr in each of next 3 corner tr (1 bl), continue across wide end (ending 3 sps) *, work corner as before; repeat from first * to 2nd * once, end 1 bl, ch 2, join with tr in top of ch 3 (exact corner). Turn.

Rnd 12: Ch 5, sk first sp, tr in next tr, * following chart from C to B, work across wide end to 3rd ch of corner sp, ch 5, tr in same ch, continue across narrow end to 3rd ch of next corner sp *, ch 5, tr in same ch; repeat from first * to 2nd * once, end ch 2, join with tr in 3rd ch of ch 5 (exact corner). Turn.

Rnd 13 (wrong side): Following chart from B to C, begin, work corners, and end as for rnd 12. Turn.

Rnds 14-23: Repeat rnds 12 and 13 alternately.

Rnd 24: Ch 6, sk first sp, dc in next tr, ch 3, tr in next tr, * continue in lacet st to centre ch of next corner sp, ch 3, tr in same ch; repeat from * around, end ch 3, join with ss in 3rd ch of ch 6. Do not turn.

Rnd 25: * Ch 7, dc in next tr, repeat from * around, end ch 7, ss in first lp. Do not turn.

Rnd 26: In each lp around, make (4 dc, ch 4, ss in last dc for P, 4dc); join end of rnd and end off.

DAISY (make 8): * Ch 20, sk 2 ch, dc in next 2 ch, hlf tr in next ch, tr in next 2 ch, (dbl tr in next 2 ch; holding back last lp of each of the following dbl tr, make dbl tr in next 2 ch, yo and through 3 lps on hook) twice, tr in next 3 ch, hlf tr in next ch, ss in end ch; repeat from * 5 times more—6 petals. Ch 1, make dc in base of each of 6 petals. Ch 5, turn. Holding back last lp of each dbl tr, make dbl tr in each of 5 dc, 2 dbl tr in last dc, yo and through 8 lps on hook. End off.

FINISHING: Turn daisies right side up, sew in place on edging as shown on chart. Stretch and pin edging, right side down, in true shape, pinning out each lp on inner and outer edges. Steam and press dry through a damp cloth.

Place edging, right side up, over linen. Baste inner edge of edging to linen. Hem down inner edge of rnd 2 (tr row) and lps of rnd 1. Cut linen ¼″ outside stitching, turn under edge next to edging and hem.

Small doily

Of European origin, this small doily with its pattern of leaves on miniature squares can be crocheted very quickly, using the chart method detailed on the opposite page.

SMALL DOILY
SIZE: 9½″ in diameter.
MATERIALS: Coats 'Chain' Mercer Crochet No. 60 (20 grm.). 1 ball. Milwards Steel Crochet Hook No. 5.
Ch 8, join with a ss to form a ring.
Rnd 1: Ch 4 (counts as 1 dbl tr), 3 dbl tr in ring leaving last lp of each dbl tr on hook, thread over and through all lps on hook, * ch 4, 4 dbl cluster in ring; repeat from * 4 times, ch 4, join. Complete doily from chart, following General Directions.
GENERAL DIRECTIONS: This doily is worked from a chart of stitch symbols rather than from row by row directions. The symbols are given with the chart. Doily has six equal sections or repeats. The chart gives one complete section.
At right of chart are numbers marking beginning of each rnd. Start at number for each rnd, work sts for that rnd to the left-hand edge of chart and repeat sts 5 times. This completes rnd. Rnd 1 is shown in its entirety.
Ch 4 at beg of each rnd to count as 1 dbl tr.
Join all rnds with sl st in top of ch 4.

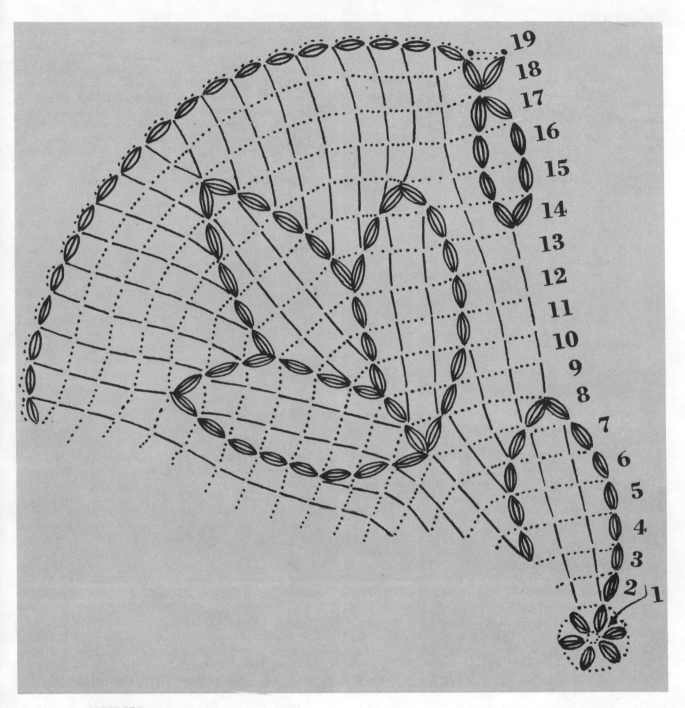

SYMBOLS

· —1 ch (chain)

● —1 dc (double crochet)

/ —1 dbl tr (double treble)

/ —4 dbl tr cluster (4 dbl tr in same sp leaving last loop of each dbl tr on hook, thread over and through all loops on hook).

—Rice st (ch 4, 3 dbl tr into 4 ch from hook leaving last loop of each dbl tr on hook, thread over and through all loops on hook).

Tea cloth

SIZE: 41″ × 41″.

MATERIALS: Coats 'Chain' Mercer Crochet No. 20 (20 grm). Milwards Steel Crochet Hook No. 3. 1 yd Coloured linen.

GAUGE: Block = 6″ Square.
Note: Work tightly for best results.

CENTRE MOTIF: Beg at centre, ch 8, join with ss to form ring.
Rnd 1: Ch 1, 12 dc in ring. Join with sl st in first dc.
Rnd 2: Ch 8, dbl tr in same dc as sl st, * ch 10, sk 2 dc, (dbl tr, ch 3, dbl tr), in next dc; repeat from * twice, ch 5 join with dbl tr in 5th ch of ch-8—4 ch—3 sps and 4 ch—10 lps.
Rnd 3: * 3 dbl tr in next ch-3 sp, ch 4, sl st in last dbl tr (p made); in ch-3 sp last worked in make (4 dbl tr, p) twice and 3 dbl tr, dc in next ch-10 lp; repeat from * twice, join with sl st in first dbl tr of rnd—4 petals.
Rnd 4: * Ch 7, (dbl tr, ch 5, trip tr) in 3rd dbl tr after next p, ch 7, (trip tr, ch 5, dbl tr) in 2nd dbl tr after next p, ch 7, dc in dc between petals; repeat from * 3 times, end rnd with sl st.
Rnd 5: Ch 3; holding back on hook last lp of each tr, make 2 tr in next sp, yo and draw tightly through 3 lps on hook (½ cl made), * 4 tr in balance of sp, tr in next dbl tr, 5 tr in next sp, tr in next trip tr, 3 tr in next sp, (2 tr, p, 2 tr), in centre ch of same sp, (corner), 3 tr in balance of same sp, tr in next trip tr, 5 tr in next sp, tr in next dbl tr, 4 tr in next sp; holding back on hook last lp of each tr, make tight cl of (2 tr in same sp, tr in dc between petals and 2 tr in next sp, yo and draw tightly through 6 lps on hook); repeat from * 3 times, ending last repeat with first 2 tr of cl, insert hook in first ½ cl of rnd, yo and draw tightly through cl and 3 lps on hook. End off.

BLOCK: Border: Beg with inner 4 sides of block, (ch 6, tr in 6th ch from hook) 48 times. Join with sl st in starting st of border, forming a ring with ch-lps on inside edge and straight tr-sps on outside edge of border.
First Corner Section: Ch 3, 2 tr in same place as sl st, ** (3 tr in next tr-sp, tr in st between tr-sps) 6 times, 2 tr in next tr-sp, ch 7, turn. Sk 4 tr, sl st in next tr, ch 1, turn.
9 dc in lp just made, sl st in top side of last tr, tr in balance of sp on border, tr between tr-sps, 3 tr in next tr-sp, tr between tr-sps, 2 tr in next tr-sp, ch 5, turn.
Dbl tr in 2nd dc over lp, ch 5, sk 2 dc, (3 dbl tr, ch 5, 3 dbl tr) in next (centre) dc, ch 5, sk 2 dc, dbl tr in next dc, ch 5, sk 7 tr over border, sl st in next tr, ch 1, turn.
(3 dc, p, 3 dc) in first sp, dc in next dbl tr, (3 dc, p, 3 dc) in next sp, dc in each of 3 dbl tr, 5 dc in next sp, dc in each of 3 dbl tr, (3 dc, p, 3 dc), in next sp, dc in next dbl tr, (3 dc, p, 3 dc) in end sp, sl st in top side of last tr, tr in balance of tr-sp on border, tr between tr-sps, 3 tr in next tr-sp, tr between tr-sps, 2 tr in next tr-sp, ch 5, turn.

Sk 7 tr, trip tr in next tr, (ch 5, dbl tr in dc over next dbl tr) twice, ch 5, (3 dbl tr, ch 5, 3 dbl tr) in dc over next sp between 3-dbl tr groups (centre sp), ch 5, sk 4 dc, dbl tr in next dc, ch 5, dbl tr in dc over next dbl tr, ch 5, trip tr in same tr at base of last row, ch 5, sk 7 tr on border, sl st in next tr, ch 1, turn.
(3 dc, p, 3 dc) in each of next 4 sps, dc in each of next 3 dbl tr, 5 dc in next sp (centre sp), dc in each of next 3 dbl tr, (3 dc, p, 3 dc) in each of last 4 sps, sl st in top side of last tr on border, tr in balance of tr-sp, tr in st between tr-sps, 3 tr in next tr-sp, 3 tr in st between tr-sps (first half-corner made), ch 5, turn.
Sk 7 tr, dbl tr in next tr, (ch 5, tr in centre dc between next 2 p) 3 times, ch 5, dbl tr in dc over next dbl tr, ch 5, (3 trip tr, ch 7, 3 trip tr) in centre dc over next sp, ch 5, sk 4 dc, dbl tr in next dc, (ch 5, tr in centre dc between next 2 p) 3 times, ch 5, dbl tr in same tr at base of last row, ch 5, sk 7 tr over border, sl st in top of ch 3, ch 1, turn.
(3 dc, p, 3 dc in next sp, dc in next st) 6 times, dc in each of 3 trip tr, in next sp (centre sp) make (dc, a ch-4 p, 4 dc, a ch-7 p, 4 dc, a ch-4 p, dc), dc in each of 3 trip tr, (3 dc, p, 3 dc in next sp, dc in next st) 6 times, ss in top side of last tr of corner 3-tr group made over border, make 3 more tr at base of same corner 3-tr group (2nd half-corner made) **. Make 3 more corner sections, working from first ** to 2nd **, omitting 2nd half corner at end of last repeat, join with sl st to top of ch 3 at beg of first section. End off.
Stretch the 4 inner sides of tr border of block to form a true square. Cut a square of linen $\frac{1}{16}$″ larger all around than outside edge of tr border that forms inner square of block. Pin or baste tr border around edge of linen. Hem down inner edge of tr border and tack down centre of each ch-5 lp. Working on back of work, turn edge of linen under, against back of tr border and hem down. Stretch and pin centre motif right side down on ironing board. Steam through a doubled wet cloth, then press dry through a doubled dry cloth. Pin motif in centre of linen and hem down around outside edge. On back of work, cut out linen $\frac{1}{4}$″ inside stitching; turn this $\frac{1}{4}$″ edge under, against tr border and hem down.
Make 49 blocks. Join blocks 7 × 7 as follows.
Joining-Edge, First Block: Join thread with dc in 3rd dc to right of a corner p on first bl (block), * (4 tr, ch 7, 4 tr) in corner p, sk 2 dc, dc in next dc, (ch 10, dc midway between next 2 p) 13 times, ch 10, dc in 2nd dc to left of next p, repeat from * around, joining final ch-10 with sl st to first dc. End off.
Joining — Edge, 2nd Block: Join thread with dc in 3rd dc to right of a corner p on 2nd bl, 4 tr in corner p, ch 3, join with sl st in 1 lp of centre st of a corner ch-7 lp on first bl, ch 3, 4 tr back in same corner p on 2nd bl, sk 2 dc, dc in next dc, (ch 5, join with sl st under next ch 10 of first bl, ch 5, dc back midway between next 2 p on 2nd bl) 13 times, ch 5, sl st in next ch 10 lp on first bl, ch 5, dc back in 2nd dc to left of next p on 2nd bl, 4 tr in next corner p, ch 3, join with sl st in 1 lp of centre ch of next corner lp on first bl, ch 3, 4 tr back in same p on 2nd bl, sk 2 dc, dc in next dc. Complete edge as for first

bl. Forming square, join 3rd bl to 2nd bl, then join a 4th bl to first and 3rd bls in same way.

Note: Where 4 corners meet, always join to same st where first 2 corners were joined. Continue in this way until all bls are joined.

EDGE: Rnd 1: Join thread with dc in right-hand end of ch-7 lp at one corner of cloth, ** ch 13, dc in left end of same lp, (ch 10, dc in next ch-10 lp) 14 times, * ch 10, sk 4 tr, dc in right end of next joined corner sp, ch 10, dc in left end of next joined corner sp, (ch 10, dc in next ch-10 lp) 14 times *; repeat from first * to 2nd * across side, ch 10, dc in right end of corner ch-7 lp; repeat from ** around. Omit last ch-10 lp, make ch 5 and join with dbl tr in first dc.

Rnd 2: ** Ch 4, 3 trip tr in 5th ch of corner ch-13 lp, (ch 5, sk next ch of same lp, 3 trip tr in next ch) twice, ch 4, dc in next ch-10 lp, * (ch 4, 3 trip tr in 5th ch of next ch-10 lp, ch 5, 3 trip tr in next ch of same lp, ch 4, dc in next lp) *; repeat from first * to 2nd * across side; repeat from ** around, end with sl st instead of dc.

Rnd 3: Sl st in each of 4 sts of next ch, sl st in next 3 trip tr, sl st in next sp, ch 7, (2 trip tr, ch 5, 3 trip tr) in same sp, ** ch 5, sk next trip tr, 3 trip tr in next trip tr, (ch 5, 3 trip tr) twice in next sp, * in centre sp of next shell make (3 trip tr, ch 5, 3 trip tr, ch 5, 3 trip tr) *; repeat from first * to 2nd * across side, sk first 3 trip tr at corner, (3 trip tr, ch 5, 3 trip tr) in next sp; repeat from ** to end of rnd, end rnd at 2nd *, join with sl st in top of ch 7.

Rnd 4: Dc in each of next 2 trip tr, 5 dc in next sp, * dc in each of next 2 trip tr, make ch-4 p, dc in next trip tr, 2 dc in next sp, ch 10 lp, turn, sk p, sl st in 2nd dc over next sp, ch 1, turn, (6 dc, p, 6 dc, 1 sl st) in ch-10 lp just made, ch 1, 3 dc in balance of ch-5 sp; repeat from * twice, dc in each of next 2 trip tr, sk 2 trip tr (1 each side of angle), ** dc in each of next 2 trip tr, 5 dc in next sp, dc in each of next 2 trip tr, make p, dc in next trip tr, 2 dc in next sp, ch 10 lp, turn, sk p, ss in 2nd dc over next sp, ch 1, turn, (6 dc, p, 6 dc, sl st) in ch-10 lp just made, ch 1, 3 dc in balance of ch-5 sp, dc in each of next 2 trip tr, sk next 2 trip tr (1 each side of angle), repeat from ** across side; repeat from beg of rnd, join with ss in first dc.

Placing a rustproof pin in each scallop, pin cloth right side down on padded board, stretching to 41″×41″. Steam through a wet cloth, press dry.

Illustration for this design is opposite page 192

Crochet lace cloth

SIZE. 34″×34″

MATERIALS: Coats 'CHAIN' Mercer Crochet No 10 (20 grm). 29 balls Milwards Steel Crochet Hook No 2½.
GAUGE: 1 Motif = 2″.

FIRST MOTIF: Ch 8, sl st in first ch to form a ring.
Rnd 1: Ch 3, 15 tr in ring—16 tr counting ch 3 as 1 tr. Join with sl st to top of ch 3.
Rnd 2: Ch 4, tr between first and next tr, * ch 1, tr between next 2 tr; repeat from * around, ch 1, join to 3rd ch of ch 4—16 tr with ch 1 between.
Rnd 3: Ch 5, * tr in next ch—1 sp, ch 2; repeat from * around, join to 3rd ch of ch 5.
Rnd 4: Sl st in first sp, ch 4; holding back last 2 lps of each dbl tr, make 3 dbl tr in same sp, thread over hook and through all 4 lps on hook (4-dbl tr cluster made); * ch 5, 4-dbl tr cluster in next sp, ch 5, 4-dbl tr cluster in next sp, ch 14, 4-dbl tr cluster in next sp, turn work around, 7 dc over half of ch 14, ch 7, turn work around, 4-dbl tr cluster in next sp, repeat from * around, end ch 7, sl st in top of first cluster. End off.

2nd MOTIF: Work as for first motif through rnd 3.

Rnd 4: Sl st in first sp, ch 4, make dbl tr-cluster in first sp, ch 2, sl st in corresponding (2nd) ch — 5 lp on one side of first motif, ch 2, dbl tr-cluster in next sp of 2nd motif, ch 2, sl st in next ch — 5 lp (to left) of first motif, ch 2, dbl tr-cluster in next sp of 2nd motif, ch 7, sl st in 7th ch at corner of first motif, ch 7, dbl tr-cluster in next sp of 2nd motif, turn work around, 7 dc over ch — 7 just made, ch 7, turn work around, 4-dbl tr cluster in next sp; repeat from * of rnd 4 of first motif twice, ch 5, 4-dbl tr cluster in next sp, ch 5, 4-dbl tr cluster in next sp, ch 14, 4-dbl tr cluster in last sp, turn work around, 7 dc over half of ch 14, turn work around, sl st in 7th ch at corner of first motif, ch 7, sl st in top of first cluster of 2nd motif. End off.

Join 3rd and succeeding motifs in same way, always joining motifs at ch — 5 lps and at sides of corners. Make cloth 26 by 26 motifs, or desired size.

BORDER: Rnd 1: Join thread at corner of cloth, sl st to ch — 7 lp, ch 6, 4-trip tr cluster (ch 6 counts as 1 trip tr) in ch — 7 lp, †* ch 5, 4-trip tr cluster in same lp, ch 5, (4-trip tr cluster in next sp, ch 5) twice, 4-trip tr cluster in next ch — 7 lp, ch 5, 4-trip tr cluster in same ch — 7 lp, ch 5, 4-trip tr cluster in next ch — 7 lp; repeat from *

Illustration for this design is on the next page

across one side, ending 2 clusters with ch — 5 between in end ch — 7 lp, ch 7 for corner, 4-trip tr cluster in next ch — 7 lp on next side; repeat from† around, end ch 7 for

---

This delicately webbed crocheted lace can be made in any size from a bridge table cover to a banquet cloth by combining 1¼" motifs and edging them with a cluster stitch border. Make the size of your choice with crochet cotton. Directions are on page 217.

last corner, join to top of first cluster.

Rnd 2: Sl st to first sp, work 4-trip tr cluster in each ch — 5 sp on side with ch 5 between clusters; work 2 clusters with ch 7 between in ch — 7 lps at corners. Join to top of first cluster.

Rnd 3: Repeat rnd 2.

Rnd 4: * 5 dc in each of next 2 sps, ch 4, sl st in 4th ch from hook for picot, repeat from * around. Join in first dc.

Pin out cloth to square shape. Steam press.

Crocheted and Woven Mats

Place mats which simulate weaving so closely that even experts are deceived can be made easily by threading coloured and metallic yarns through filet mesh. Crochet your mesh first, then "weave," using a tapestry needle.

The sturdy yarns woven through give sufficient body to the mats to keep warm plates from marring the finish of a table, and yarn ends make the fringes pictured here.

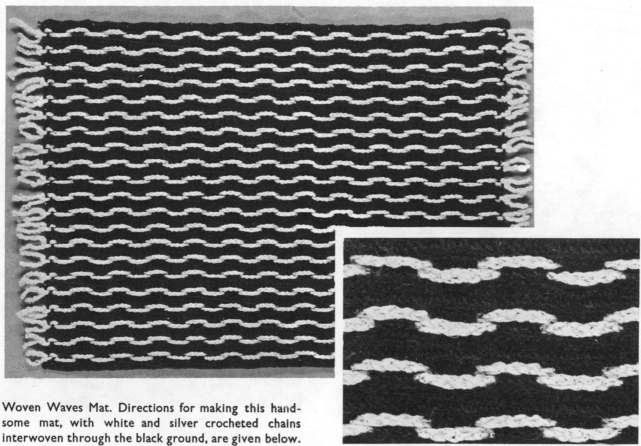

Woven Waves Mat. Directions for making this handsome mat, with white and silver crocheted chains interwoven through the black ground, are given below.

SIZE: 18″ × 12″ approx (without fringe).
MATERIALS: Coats 'CHAIN' Mercer-Crochet No. 20 (20 grm.) in black, 4 balls; in white, 2 balls. Silver metallic thread. Milwards steel crochet hook No. 1.
GAUGE: 8 tr = 1″, 7 rows = 2″.

PLACE MAT BACKGROUND: Using double thread throughout, beg at wide side with black, ch 152.
Row 1: Tr in 4th ch from hook and in each ch across— 150 tr, counting turning ch. Turn each row.
Row 2: Ch 3 (counts as 1 tr), tr in 2nd tr, * ch 2, sk 2, tr (sp), tr in each of 4 tr (bl); repeat from * across, end ch 2, sk 2 tr, tr in each of 2 tr—25 sps.
Row 3: Ch 3, tr in 2nd tr, * 2 tr in next sp, tr in each of 4 tr; repeat from * across, end last repeat with 2 tr— 150 tr. Repeat rows 2 and 3 for pat until piece measures 12″ from start, end row 2 of pat. End off.

WEAVING: Work from right to left edge each time.
Woven Stripe: Step 1: Using white and metallic thread together, make a 21″ ch. Conceal loose ends of ch by drawing them back through ch. With ch and tapestry needle, weave under first st of first sp row, over next tr, * under next bl, over next bl; repeat from * across, end under 2nd tr from end, over last tr. Pull row out flat, leaving 1¼″ fringe each side.
Step 2: Using white and metallic thread together, make a 21″ ch. Making fringe as before, weave ch over first st of same sp row, under next tr, * over next bl, under next bl; repeat from * across, end over 2nd tr from end, under last tr. Pull row out flat. Tie ends of fringe together in a single knot. Stitch knot securely on each edge. Work woven stripe in each sp row to top edge.
Steam-press to measurements, using steam iron or dry iron and damp cloth.

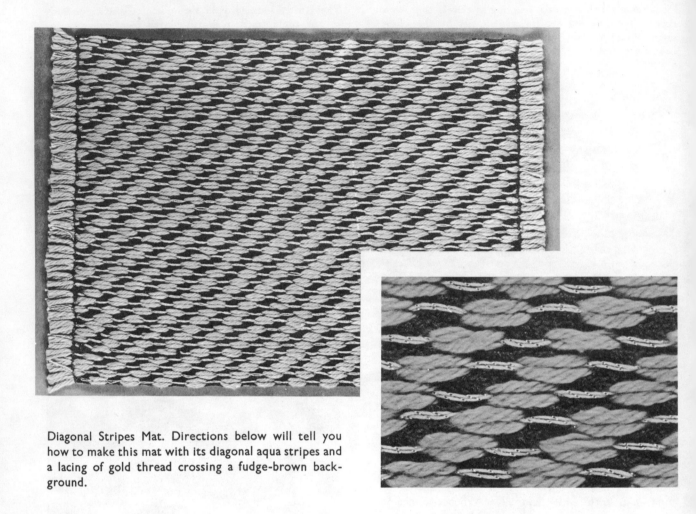

Diagonal Stripes Mat. Directions below will tell you how to make this mat with its diagonal aqua stripes and a lacing of gold thread crossing a fudge-brown background.

SIZE: 18″×12″ approx (without fringe).
MATERIALS: Coats 'CHAIN' Mercer Crochet No. 20 (20 grm) in brown, 4 balls; in jade, 1 ball, for weaving; Gold metallic thread. Cotton rug yarn in jade. Milwards steel crochet hook No. 1.
GAUGE: 2 bls and 1 sp = 1″; 7 rows = 2″.

PLACE MAT: BACKGROUND: Using double thread throughout, beg at wide side, with brown, ch 170.
Row 1: Tr in 4th ch from hook and in each of 3 ch, * ch 2, sk 2 ch (sp), tr in each of 4 ch (bl); repeat from * across, end last repeat tr in each of 5 ch—28 tr bls, 27 sps. Turn each row.
Row 2: Ch 3 (counts as 1 tr), tr in 2nd tr, * ch 2, sk 2 tr, tr in next tr, 2 tr in next sp, tr in next tr; repeat from * across, end tr in top of turning ch—27 bls, 28sps.
Row 3: Ch 3, tr in 2nd tr, * 2 tr in next sp, tr in next tr, ch 2, sk 2 tr, tr in next tr; repeat from * across, end tr in top of ch 3. Repeat rows 2 and 3 for pat until piece measures 12″ from start.

WEAVING: Work from right to left edge each time.
First Woven Stripe: Step 1: Cut length of rug yarn 44″ long. Using strand doubled in tapestry needle, weave under first st of first row, * over next bl, under next bl; repeat from * across, end under last 4 tr, over last tr. Pull row out flat, cut yarn, leaving 1″ fringe each side.
Step 2: Using metallic thread and jade mercer crochet together, cut a strand 44″ long, double it, and working across same row, weave over the rug yarn sts worked under and under the sts worked over, previously.
Second Woven Stripe: Step 1: With 44″ length of rug yarn doubled, weave over first st of next row, under next tr, * over next bl, under next bl; repeat from * across, end under 2nd tr from end, over last tr.
Step 2: Work as for step 2 of first woven stripe.
Third Woven Stripe: Step 1: With 44″ length of rug yarn doubled, weave over first st of next row, * under next bl, over next bl; repeat from * across, end over last 4 tr, under last tr.
Step 2: Work as for step 2 of first woven stripe.

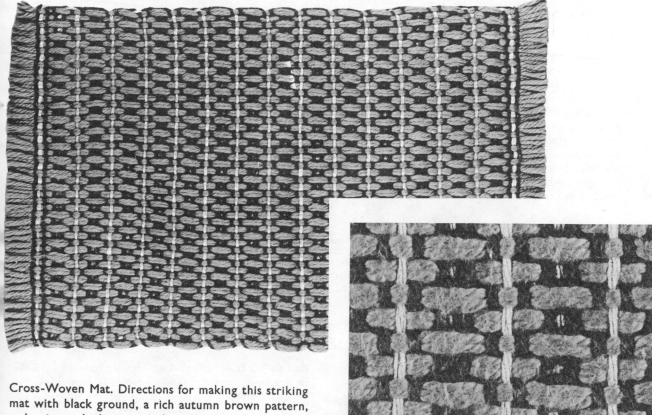

Cross-Woven Mat. Directions for making this striking mat with black ground, a rich autumn brown pattern, and spice-and-silver vertical stripes are given below.

Fourth Woven Stripe: Step 1: With 44″ length of rug yarn doubled, weave under first st of next row, over next tr, * under next bl, over next bl; repeat from * across, end over 2nd tr from end, under last tr.
Step 2: Work as for step 2 of first woven stripe.

Repeat these 4 stripes alternately, forming diagonal stripes, to top edge.

FINISHING: Sew fringe securely to mat. Trim fringe evenly. Steam-press to measurements.

SIZE: 18″ × 12″ approx. (without fringe).

MATERIALS: Coats 'CHAIN' Mercer-Crochet No 20 (20 grm) in black (A), 4 balls; light brown (B), ball (for weaving). Silver metallic thread; Cotton rug yarn in brown (C); Milwards steel crochet hook No. 1.

GAUGE: 2 bls and 1 sp = 1″, 4 rows = 1″.

PLACE MAT: BACKGROUND: Beg at wide side, with A, ch 174.
Row 1: Tr in 4th ch from hook and in each of 2 ch, * ch 2, sk 2 ch (sp), tr in each of 4 ch (bl); repeat from *

across —29 bls, 28 sps. Turn each row.
Row 2: Ch 3 (counts as 1 tr) sk 1 tr, tr in each of 3 tr, 2 tr in sp, * tr in next tr, ch 2, sk 2 tr, tr in next tr, 2 tr in next sp; repeat from * across, end tr in each of last 3 tr, tr in top of turning ch.
Row 3: Ch 3, sk 1 tr, tr in each of 3 tr, * ch 2, sk 2 tr, tr in next tr, 2 tr in next sp, tr in next tr; repeat from * across, end ch 2, sk 2 tr, tr in each of 4 tr.
Repeat rows 2 and 3 for pat until 49 rows are completed. End off.

WEAVING: Work from right to left edge.
First Woven stripe (right side): Cut C strand 44″ long.

Using strand doubled, work across first row, weave under first st, over 2 tr, under 1 tr, * over 4 tr, under 1 tr, over 2 tr, under 1 tr; repeat from * across row—15 short C sps, 14 long C sps. Pull row out flat, cut C, leaving 1″ fringe each side.

Second Woven Stripe (right side): With 44″ C strand doubled and working across next row, weave (under 1 tr, over 2 tr) twice, (under 2 tr, over 6 tr) 13 times, under 2 tr, (over 2 tr, under 1 tr) twice—13 long C sps; make fringe as before. Repeat these 2 stripes alternately to top edge. Sew fringe securely to mat. Trim fringe evenly.

First Vertical Stripe (edge): Using light brown (B) mercer crochet and metallic thread tog, cut 4 strands about 3½ yards long. Start on right side of mat at lower right-hand corner. Leaving 1″ end (weave this end in on wrong side later), work as follows: Weave under first 2 C strands of first short C sp, * over next 2 C strands above, under next 2 C strands above; repeat from * to top edge. Pull row out flat. Pass B through centre of next bl to the left, thus bringing B to wrong side.

Second Vertical Stripe: From wrong side, weave under next line of long C strands to lower edge. Pull row out flat. Turn to right side. This stripe is visible throughout the background sps.

Third Vertical Stripe: From right side with B, * weave under short C sp, over next long C sp above; repeat from * to top edge. Pull row out flat. Pass B through centre of next bl to the left, thus bringing B to wrong side. Repeat last 2 vertical stripes alternately across mat, ending with 2nd vertical stripe. Turn to right side, work edge as for first stripe. Cut B, leaving 1″ end. Weave in ends on wrong side.

Flower and fern mat

SIZE: 16″ in diameter.
MATERIALS: Coats 'CHAIN' Mercer Crochet No 20 (20 grm). 2 balls. Milwards Steel Crochet Hook No 3.

CLUSTERS: 3-Tr Clusters (cls): At beg of a rnd, ch 3 (counts as first tr), holding back on hook last lp of each tr, make 2 tr in same sp, yo and through 3 lps on hook; **on rnd,** holding back on hook last lp of each tr, make 3 tr in same sp, yo and through 4 lps on hook.
3-Dbl Tr Cls: At beg of a rnd, ch 4 (counts as first dbl tr), holding back no hook last lp of each dbl tr, make 2 dbl trs in same sp, yo and through 3 lps on hook; **on rnd,** holding back on hook last lp of each dbl tr, make 3 dbl tr in same sp, yo and through 4 lps on hook.

MAT.: Beg at centre, ch 9, join with sl st to form ring.
Rnd 1: In ring, make eight 3-tr cls with ch-4 sp between each cl, ch 4, join in top of first cl.
Rnd 2: Sl st in first sp, make two 3-tr cls with ch-3 sp between in same sp; * ch 3, two 3-tr cls with ch-3 sp between in next sp, repeat from * around, end ch 3, join in top of first cl — 16 cls.
Rnd 3: 3-tr cl in first cl, * ch 3, 3-tr cl in next sp, ch 3, 3-tr cl with ch-3 sp between in each of next 2 cls; repeat from * around, end last repeat with 1 cl, ch 3, join in first cl—24 cls.
Rnd 4: 3-tr cl in first cl, * ch 3, two 3-tr cls with ch-3 sp between in next cl, ch 3, 3-tr cl with ch-3 sp between in each of next 2 cls; repeat from * around, end last repeat with 1 cl, ch 3, join in first cl—32 cls.
Rnd 5: 3-tr cl in first cl, ch 3, 3-tr cl in next cl, * ch 3, 3-tr cl in next sp, ch 3, 3-tr cl with ch-3 sp between in each of next 4 cls; repeat from * around, end last repeat with 2 cls, ch 3, join—40 cls.

Rnd 6: * 3-tr cl with ch-3 sp between in each of 5 cls, ch 5, repeat from * around, join ch 5 in first cl—40 cls.
Rnd 7: * 3-tr cl with ch-3 sp between in each of 5 cls, ch 9; repeat from * around, join ch 9 in first cl—40 cls.
Rnd 8: 3-tr cl in first cl, * ch 3, 3-tr cl with ch 1 sp between in each of next 3 cls, ch 3, 3-tr cl in next cl, ch 6, tr in 5th ch of ch 9, ch 6, 3-tr cl in next cl; repeat from * around, omit last cl, join ch 6 in first cl—40 cls.
Rnd 9: 3-tr cl in first cl, * ch 3, 3-tr cl in next cl, ch 1, sk next cl, cl in next cl, ch 3, cl in next cl, ch 6, (tr, ch 7, tr) in next tr, ch 6, cl in next cl; repeat from * around, omit last cl, join ch 6 in first cl—32 cls.
Rnd 10: 3-tr cl in first cl, * ch 1, sk next cl, cl in next ch-1 sp, ch 1, cl in next cl, ch 7, tr in next tr, ch 7, tr in 4th ch of next ch 7, ch 7, tr in next tr, ch 7, cl in next cl, repeat from * around, omit last cl, join ch 7 in first cl—24 cls.
Rnd 11: 3-tr cl in first cl, * ch 1, sk next cl, 3-tr cl in next cl, ch 7, tr in next tr, ch 7, (tr, ch 5, tr) in next tr, ch 7, tr in next tr, ch 7, 3 tr-cl in next cl, repeat from * around, omit last cl, join ch 7 in first cl—16 cls.
Rnd 12: Sl st in first ch 1 sp, 3-tr cl in first sp * ch 12, dc in next tr, ch 12, sk next sp, dc in next ch-5 sp, ch 12, sk next tr, dc in next tr, ch 12, 3-tr cl in next ch-1 sp between cls; repeat from * around, omit last cl, join ch 12 in first cl—8 cls.
Rnd 13: Sl st to 5th ch of first ch-12 sp, 3-dbl tr cl in next ch of same sp, * ch 11, 2 dbl tr in 6th ch of next ch-12 sp, ch 11, 3-dbl tr cl in 6th ch of next ch — 12 sp; repeat from * around, omit last cl, join ch 11 in first cl—16 cls and 16 groups of dbl tr.
Rnd 14: 3-dbl tr cl in first cl, * ch 5, 5 dbl tr in next dbl tr, ch 2, dbl tr in same dbl tr, dbl tr in next dbl tr, ch 2, 5 dbl tr in same dbl tr (shell made), ch 5, 3 dbl tr cl in next

cl, repeat from * around, omit last cl, join ch 5 in first cl—16 shells, 16 cls.

Rnd 15: 3-dbl tr cl in first cl, * ch 1, 3-dbl tr cl in same cl, ch 4; holding back on hook last lp of each dbl tr, make 1 dbl tr in each of first 5 dbl tr of shell, yo and through 6 lps on hook (5-dbl tr cl st made); ch 5, 3 dbl tr in next dbl tr, 2 dbl tr in next dbl tr, ch 5, 5-dbl tr cl st over last 5 dbl tr of same shell, ch 4, 3-dbl tr cl in next cl; repeat from * around, omit last cl, join ch 4 in first cl.

Rnd 16: 3-dbl tr cl in first cl, * ch 4, dbl tr in next ch-1 sp, ch 4, 3-dbl tr cl in next cl, ch 7, sk first 5-dbl tr cl st of shell, dc in each of next 5 dbl tr, ch 7, sk last 5-dbl tr cl st of same shell, 3-dbl tr cl in next 3-dbl tr cl; repeat from * around, omit last 3-dbl tr cl, join ch 7 in first cl.

Rnd 17: 3-dbl tr cl in first cl, * ch 6, dbl tr in next dbl tr, ch 6, 3-dbl tr cl in next cl, ch 7, 5-dbl tr cl st over next 5 dc, ch 7, 3-dbl tr cl in next cl; repeat from * around, omit last 3-dbl tr cl, join ch 7 in first cl.

Rnd 18: 3-dbl tr cl in first cl, * ch 8, (dbl tr, ch 3, dbl tr) in next dbl tr, ch 8, 3-dbl tr cl in next cl, ch 6, dc in next 5-dbl tr cl st, ch 6, 3-dbl tr cl in next cl; repeat from * around, omit last cl, join ch 6 in first cl.

Rnd 19: 3-dbl tr cl in first cl, * ch 8, 5 dbl tr in next dbl tr, ch 2, 2 dbl tr in next ch-3 sp, ch 2, 5 dbl tr in next dbl tr (shell); ch 8, 3-dbl tr cl in next cl, ch 6, dc in next dc, ch 6, 3-dbl tr cl in next cl, repeat from * around, omit last cl, join ch 6 in first cl.

Rnd 20: 3-dbl tr cl in first cl, ch 8, sl st in top of cl just made (p), * ch 8, 5-dbl tr cl st over first 5 dbl tr of shell, ch 5, 5 dbl tr in next dbl tr, ch 2, dbl tr in same dbl tr, dbl tr in next dbl tr, ch 2, 5 dbl tr in same dbl tr, ch 5, 5-dbl tr cl st over last 5 dbl tr of same shell, ch 8, 3-dbl tr cl in next cl, ch 8, sl st in top of last cl made (p), 3-dbl tr cl in next cl; repeat from * around, omit last ch-8 p and 3-dbl tr cl, join in first cl.

Rnd 21: Sl st in first p, (3-dbl tr cl, ch 7, 3-dbl tr cl) in first p, * ch 8, sk first 5-dbl tr cl st of shell, 5-dbl tr cl st over next 5 dbl tr, ch 5, 5 dbl tr in next dbl tr, ch 2, dbl tr in same dbl tr, dbl tr in next dbl tr, ch 2, 5 dbl tr in same dbl tr, ch 5, 5-dbl tr cl st over next 5 dbl tr, ch 8, sk last 5-dbl tr cl st of same shell, (3-dbl tr cl, ch 7, 3-dbl tr cl) in next p; repeat from * around, omit last 2 cls, join ch 8 in first cl.

Rnd 22: 3-dbl tr cl in first cl, * ch 5, 3-dbl tr cl in next sp, ch 5, 3-dbl tr cl in next cl, ch 7, sk first 5-dbl tr cl st of shell, 5-dbl tr cl st over next 5 dbl tr, ch 7, 3 dbl tr in next dbl tr, 2 dbl tr in next dbl tr, ch 7, 5-dbl tr cl st over next 5 dbl tr, ch 7, sk last 5-dbl tr cl st of same shell, 3-dbl tr cl in next cl; repeat from * around, omit last 3-dbl tr cl, join ch 7 in first cl.

Rnd 23: Two 3-dbl tr cls with ch 3 between in first cl, * (ch 4, two 3-dbl tr cls with ch 3 between in next cl) twice, ch 10, sk first 5-dbl tr cl st of shell, dc into each of next 5 dbl tr, ch 10, sk last 5-dbl tr cl st of same shell, two 3-dbl tr cls with ch 3 between in next cl; repeat from * around, omit last 2 cls, join ch 10 in first cl.

Rnd 24: 3-dbl tr cl in first cl, * (ch 3, 3-dbl tr cl in next sp, ch 3, 3-dbl tr cl in next cl, ch 4, 3-dbl tr cl in next cl) twice, ch 3, 3-dbl tr cl in next sp, ch 3, 3-dbl tr cl in next cl, ch 9, 5-dbl tr cl over next 5 dc, ch 9, 3-dbl tr cl

Clusters and chain loops arranged in a variety of leaf and petal forms give this circular mat its charm.

in next cl; repeat from * around, omit last 3-dbl tr cl, join ch 9 in first cl.

Rnd 25: 3-dbl tr cl in first cl, * (ch 3, 3-dbl tr cl in next cl) twice, (ch 4, 3-dbl tr cl with ch 3 between in each of next 3 cls) twice, ch 8, dc in next 5-dbl tr cl st, ch 8, 3-dbl tr cl in next cl; repeat from * around, omit last cl, join ch 8 in first cl.

Rnd 26: 3-dbl tr cl in first cl, * (ch 2, 3-dbl tr cl in next cl) twice, (ch 4, dbl tr in next sp, ch 3, dbl tr in same sp, ch 4, 3-dbl tr cl in next cl, ch 2, 3-dbl tr cl in next cl, ch 2, 3-dbl tr cl in next cl) twice, ch 8, dc in next dc, ch 8, 3-dbl tr cl in next cl; repeat from * around, omit last cl, join ch 8 in first cl.

Rnd 27: 3-dbl tr cl in first cl, * (sk next cl, 3-dbl tr cl in next cl, ch 4, dbl tr in next dbl tr, ch 4, dbl tr in next sp, ch 4, dbl tr in next dbl tr, ch 4, 3-dbl tr cl in next cl) twice, sk next cl, 3-dbl tr cl in next cl, ch 4, dbl tr in cl last worked in, dbl tr in next cl, ch 4, 3-dbl tr cl in cl last worked in; repeat from * around, ending with last dbl tr in same place as first cl, ch 4, join in first cl.

Rnd 28: Sl st between first 2 cls, ch 11, sl st in 6th ch from hook (p), ch 7, sl st in same ch as before (2nd p), ch 6, sl st in same ch as before (3rd p), dbl tr between first 2 cls, * (ch 6, dc in next dbl tr, ch 6, dbl tr in next dbl tr; make 3-p group: ch 6, sl st in top of last dbl tr worked for first p, ch 7, sl st in same place for 2nd p, ch 6, sl st in same place for 3rd p; dbl tr in same dbl tr as last dbl tr was worked in, ch 6, dc in next dbl tr, ch 6, dbl tr between next 2 cls, make 3-p group, dbl tr in same sp as last dbl tr was worked in) twice, ch 6, dc between next 2 single dbl tr, ch 6, dbl tr between next 2 cls, make 3-p group, dbl tr in same sp as last dbl tr was worked in; repeat from * around, ending last repeat with ch 6, dc between next 2 single dbl tr, ch 6, join in first dbl tr of rnd. End off. Block mat.

Irish Crochet Motif

Raised petals and picot loops are characteristic of Irish crochet. In the square motif shown here, ridged leaves are crocheted separately and appliquéd to the corners.

Irish crochet with its raised petals and picot loops lends itself to a variety of decorative purposes. In cotton or wool yarns it can be used for bedspreads; the crochet mounted on the same colour or a contrasting coloured material background. Crochet in cotton can be used as insertions for linens etc. Delightful cot covers and shawls can be made in lightweight wool yarns.

MATERIALS: In Coats 'CHAIN' Mercer Crochet No 10, with Milwards steel crochet hook No 2½, motif should measure 4″ approx.
In Coats Mercer Crochet No 20, with Milwards steel crochet hook No 3, motif should measure 3″ approx.

DIRECTIONS: Beg at centre of rose, ch 7, sl st in first ch to form ring.
Rnd 1: Ch 1, 16 dc in ring. Join in first dc of rnd.
Rnd 2: * Ch 5, sk 1 dc, sl st in next dc; repeat from * around—8 lps.
Rnd 3: (1 dc, 5 tr, 1 dc) in each lp around. Sl st in joining—st of last lp.
Rnd 4: * Ch 6, sl st in back of work between next 2 petals; repeat from * around, ending with sl st between last and first petals.
Rnd 5: (1 dc, 6 tr, 1 dc) in each lp around. Sl st in joining—st of last lp.
Rnd 6: Repeat rnd 4.
Rnd 7: (1 dc, 7 tr, 1 dc) in each lp around. Sl st in joining—st of last lp.
Rnd 8: * (Ch 9, sl st in 6th ch from hook for picot) twice, ch 3, dc in sp between next 2 petals, (ch 13, sl st in 6th ch from hook for picot) twice, ch 7, sl st in same sp between petals (corner), (ch 9, sl st in 6th ch from hook) twice, ch 3, dc in sp between next 2 petals; repeat from * 3 times, ending with sl st in joining st of rnd 7.
Rnd 9: Sl st to centre of next lp, keeping picot to front, * (ch 3, ch-6 picot) twice, ch 3 (picot—lp made), dc in next lp between picots; repeat from * around, sl st in last sl st at beg of rnd.
Rnd 10: Sl st to centre of next lp keeping picot to front, * make picot—lp, dc in next dc at corner, (picot—lp, dc in next lp between picots) 3 times; repeat from * around, ending with sl st in last sl st at beg of rnd.
Rnd 11: Sl st to centre of next lp keeping picot to front, * make picot-lp, dc in next lp between picots; repeat from * around, sl st in last sl st at beg of rnd. End off motif.
To Join Motifs: Mark two adjacent corners of first motif with safety pins (corners are at centre of picot—lps). Join 2nd motif to first motif through 8 picots on one side as follows.
2nd Motif: Work as for first motif through rnd 10.
Rnd 11: Sl st to centre of next lp, keeping picot to front, ch 3, picot, ch 6, join to corresponding picot of first motif, ch 2, sl st in 4th ch of ch-6, * ch 3, dc between picots in next lp of 2nd motif, (ch 6, join to next picot of first motif, ch 2, sl st in 4th ch of ch-6) twice; repeat from * twice, ch 3, dc between picots in next lp of 2nd motif, ch 6, join to next picot of first motif, ch 2, sl st in

4th ch of ch-6 (8 picots joined), ch 3, picot, ch 3, dc between picots in next lp, complete motif as for first motif.

Leaf (Make 4 for each motif): Ch 10, dc in 2nd ch from hook and in each of next 7 ch, 3 dc in last ch; working on opposite side of ch, make dc in each of next 6 ch, * ch 3, turn; working in back lp of sts, make dc in each of next 6 dc, 3 dc in next dc, dc in each of next 6 dc; repeat from * 4 times. End off. Appliqué leaves to corners of motifs, joining tips of leaves of each motif to tips of leaves of adjacent motifs.

IRISH CROCHET EDGING:

Row 1: Ch 9, dbl tr in 9th ch from hook, * ch 9, dbl tr in dbl tr; repeat from * for desired length. End off.
Row 2: With right side of ch-9 lps towards you, attach thread in centre of first ch-9 lp, dc in same place, * ch 4, sl st in dc for picot, sl st in same ch-9 lp, ch-7, sl st in 4th ch from hook for picot, ch 3, dc in next ch-9 lp; repeat from * across. End off.

SIZE: Twin size bedspread with 9″ ruffle. 9″ square pillow with 2″ ruffle.

MATERIALS: For bedspread and pillow: 6 yards yellow fabric, 45″ wide. Seven yards yellow bias cording. Seven yards yellow bias binding. Mercerized sewing thread: yellow and white. Kapok or other stuffing for pillow. For crochet: Coats 'CHAIN' Mercer Crochet No. 10, 24 balls white for bedspread used with bolster (29 balls for longer bedspread), pillow and edging. Milwards Steel Crochet Hook No. 2½.

CUTTING AND SEWING DIRECTIONS: If bolster is to be used with bedspread, cut piece for top of bedspread, 75″ long and 42″ wide. If no bolster is to be used, cut piece for top, 96″ long and 42″ wide. Cover bolster, if any, with yellow fabric, inserting bias cording in seams at ends of bolster. Cut remaining fabric lengthwise into 11″ wide strips. From end of one strip, cut two pieces for pillow, each 10″ square. Use 3″ wide strip left over from bedspread top to make pillow ruffle.

Make 1″ hem at top of bedspread. From right side, baste and stitch bias cording to sides and bottom of bedspread top, 1″ in from edges, raw edges out. Join 11″ wide strips in one continuous strip to measure twice the distance around three sides of bedspread top. Make narrow hem at each end and along one long edge. Gather in remaining edge to fit around sides and bottom of bedspread. With right sides together and raw edges even, baste and stitch gathered edge of ruffle to bedspread top, stitching close to cording. Trim seams; cover with bias binding.

Cut 3″ wide strip, 2 yards long, for pillow ruffle. Join ends. Make a narrow hem around one edge. Gather other edge to measure one yard. Baste and stitch gathered edge around pillow top, right sides together, raw edges even, taking ½″ seam. Stitch remaining 9″ square to pillow top and ruffle, ruffle inside, raw edges even, leaving opening for turning and stuffing pillow. Turn pillow to right side, stuff, close opening.

Make two strips of Irish crochet 18 motifs long for sides of bedspread (23 motifs long for longer bedspread), one strip 8 motifs long to fit across bottom between long strips. Block strips, pinning each picot at sides and ends of strips so that each motif is 4″ square.

Sew strips to bedspread with white sewing thread, catching down each picot.

Make Irish-crochet edging for edges of bedspread. Sew to hemmed edges of ruffle with yellow thread.

Pillow: Work one motif. Work 2nd motif, joining to first motif in last rnd as for bedspread. Join 3rd motif to side of 2nd motif. Join 4th motif to first and 3rd motifs. Appliqué leaves to motifs, four leaves touching at centre. Sew piece to pillow top with white thread, catching down each picot around edge.

Make Irish-crochet edging for edge of pillow ruffle. Sew to hemmed edge with yellow thread.

How to Make Hairpin Lace

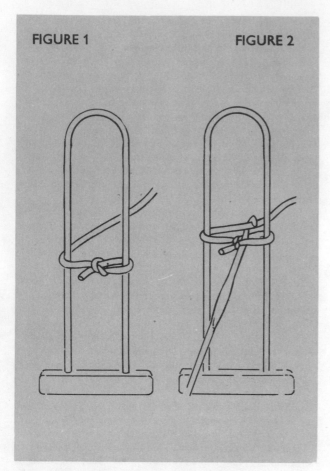

FIGURE 1   **FIGURE 2**

Use a crochet hook and a hairpin lace staple. Width of hairpin lace depends on the size of hairpin staple used. This staple is sometimes called a fork.

With crochet hook, make a loose chain stitch, Take hook out of stitch and insert left-hand prong of staple through chain stitch.

Draw out ch (loop) until knot is halfway between prongs.

Then bring thread to front and around right-hand prong to back (Fig. 1).

Insert crochet hook up through loop on left-hand prong, draw thread through and make a chain (Figs. 2 and 3).

* To get crochet hook in position for next step, without drawing out loop on hook, turn handle of crochet hook upwards parallel with prongs, then pass it through the prongs to back of staple (Fig. 4).

Now turn staple towards you from right to left once (a loop over right prong).

With a loop on hook, insert crochet hook up through loop on left-hand prong, in back of front thread, draw thread through (Fig. 5) and complete double crochet. Repeat f om *

Note: Some prefer to withdraw crochet hook from loop, turn staple over as directed and reinsert hook, instead of method illustrated in Fig. 4.

When staple gets crowded, remove base, slide most of loops off, leaving last few on and replace base.

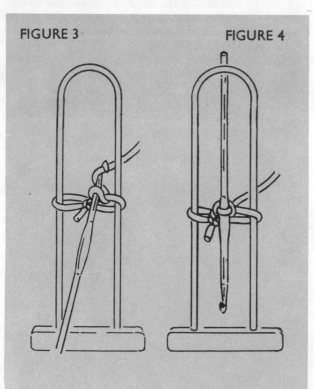

FIGURE 3   **FIGURE 4**

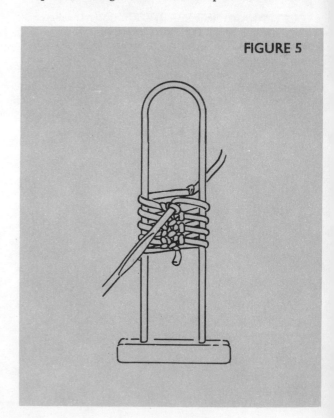

FIGURE 5

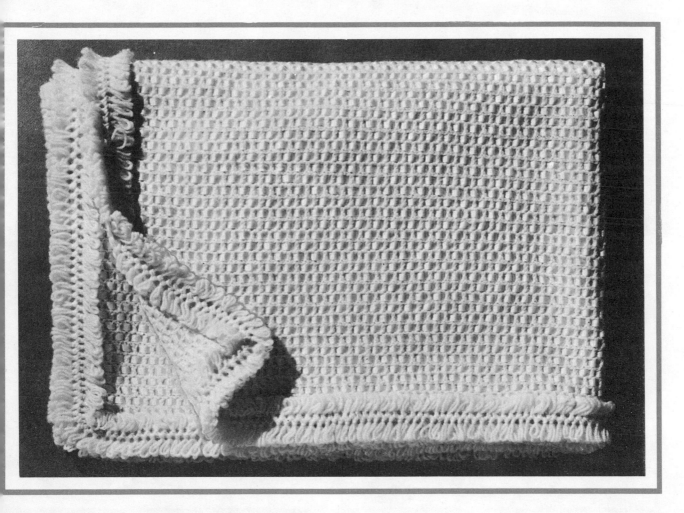

This lightweight, and reversible carriage blanket is crocheted of Bri-Nylon in a mesh pattern, then woven with taffeta knitting ribbon and trimmed with hairpin lace. A generous 30'' x 36'' size. Instructions below.

MATERIALS: Coats Carefree Bri-Nylon 3 ply.
9, 1 oz balls selected colour.
100 yds baby ribbon $\frac{3}{16}''$ wide.
Hairpin Lace Staple $1\frac{1}{2}''$ wide.
Use bodkin or safety pin for weaving. Sewing thread.
Mesh Pattern:
Row 1: Tr in 6th ch from hook, * ch 1, sk 1 ch, tr in next ch; repeat from * across, turn.

Row 2: Ch 5, tr in 2nd tr, * ch 1, tr in next tr; repeat from * a cross, end ch 1, tr in 4th ch of turning ch, turn. Repeat row 2 for mesh pat.
BLANKET: Ch 244 loosely. Work in mesh pat (120 mesh) for 116 rows, turn.
Edge: Ch 1, work 1 row dc around edge of shawl, making 1 dc in each ch 1 and tr across top and bottom, 3 dc in each corner, 2 dc in end st of each row on sides.

Wool cover of hairpin lace

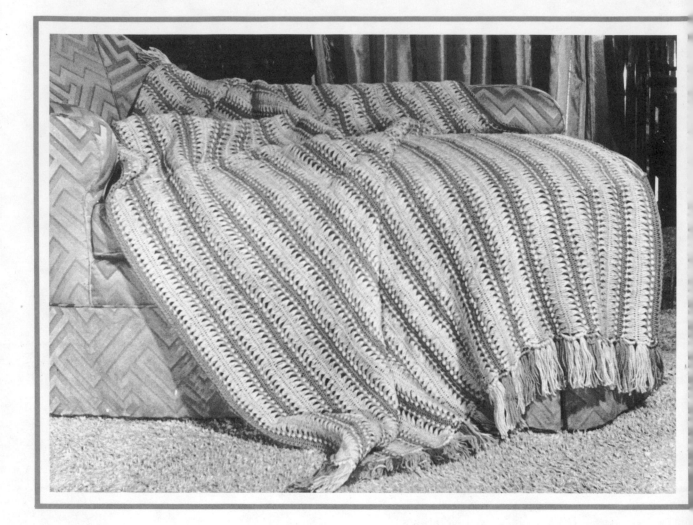

Striped wool coverlet of hairpin lace alternates wide and narrow strips of lace in contrasting colours. Make it of Bri-Nylon in afghan size, 44″ × 66″, and add a two–colour fringe at the top and bottom.

SIZE: Approximately 44″ × 66″.

MATERIALS: 17 balls Coats CAREFREE Bri-Nylon Double Knitting, main colour (MC). 11 balls Coats CAREFREE Bri-Nylon Double Knitting, constrasting colour (CC). Hairpin Lace Staple 1½″ wide. Hairpin Lace Staple 3″ wide. Milwards 'Phantom' (aluminium) Crochet Hooks No. 6 and No. 8.

WIDE STRIP (make 15): Use MC, 3″ staple and No. 6 hook.· Following directions for hairpin lace, make strip until there are 459 lps on each side. Finish off.

NARROW STRIP (make 16): Using CC, 1½″ staple and No. 8 hook, work same as wide strips.

JOINING STRIPS: Use No. 6 hook. Insert hook through first 3 lps on narrow strip, pick up first 3 lps on wide strip and pull them through lps on hook, * pick up next 3 lps on narrow strip and pull them through, pick up next 3 lps on wide strip and pull them through. Repeat from * to top. Place safety pin through last 3 lps to hold. Always starting at same end with first 3 lps of narrow strips, join another narrow strip to other side of wide strip and continue joining wide and narrow strips alternately.

FINISHING: Finish side edges by drawing 2 lps through 2 lps. Using a double strand of MC and No. 6 hook, attach yarn at top right corner. Working across top of afghan, ch 3 loosely, dc in joining between strips (through 3 lps held by pin), * ch 3, dc in centre of MC strip, ch 3, dc in next joining, ch 3, dc in next joining. Repeat from * across. Repeat edging at bottom.

FRINGE: Cut 4 strands CC 10″ long. Always working from same side of afghan, insert hook through first ch-3 lp, catch centre of these strands and pull them part way through, forming a lp, then draw cut ends through lp and pull tight. Make 2 pieces of fringe in each ch-3 lp in this manner, using colours to correspond with colours of strips.

PLACE MAT MOTIF

MATERIALS: Coats 'CHAIN' Mercer Crochet No. 20 (20 grm). Ball selected colour. Hairpin Lace Staple ¾″ wide. Milwards Steel Crochet Hook No. 3.

MOTIF: Make 28 lps of hairpin lace on each prong. Remove from staple, and join last dc made to first dc neatly to form a circle. Cut thread and fasten off.
To Make Centre: Join thread in one lp at centre (keeping the lps straight). Dc in two lps at centre, dc in next 2 lps; repeat around. Tie threads and cut.
Outer Edge: Fasten thread in one lp. * Ch 7, dc in next lp; repeat from * around. Fasten off.
2nd AND OTHER MOTIFS: Join with 4 side lps, (ch 3, sl st in ch-7 of corresponding motif, ch 3) 4 times.

FILL-IN MOTIF: Ch 7, sl st in a free lp between group of 4 motifs, ch 7, sl st in first ch made, * ch 7, sl st in next loop, ch 7, sl st in centre; repeat from * around. End with a sl st in first ch made (12 lps in all). Tie ends and fasten off.

Wheels of hairpin lace are edged with crochet and joined together with fill-in motifs to make a square or rectangular tablecloth or place mat. Actual-size detail of hairpin lace and fill-in motifs, worked of crochet cotton No. 20, shown on the right; directions above.

TOWEL INSERTION AND EDGING

MATERIALS: Coats 'CHAIN' Mercer Crochet No. 20 (20 grm). Milwards Steel Crochet Hook No. 3. Coats 'CHAIN' Mercer Crochet No. 60, constrasting colour (CC). Milwards Steel Crochet Hook No. 5. Hairpin Lace Staple ¾″ wide.

INSERTION: With Mercer Crochet No. 20 and No. 3 hook, make 2 strips of hairpin lace in length desired (for a 17″ wide towel, 168 lps). Fasten off. Insert hook in 3 lps of first strip, * pick up 3 lps of 2nd strip, draw through lps of first strip, draw through lps on hook; repeat from * to end. With CC and hook No. 5, insert hook in first 3 outside lps of strip, make 1 dc, * 5, 1 dc through next 3 lps; repeat from * across. Ch 8, make half turn; working along end, * 1 dc in dc, ch 8; repeat from * twice more, work along opposite side to correspond. Fasten off.

EDGING: Work hairpin lace as for insertion. With CC finish one side as for insertion. On opposite side, work edging as follows:
Row 1: * 1 dc in next 3 lps, ch 6; repeat from * across.
Row 2: Ch 6, turn, * 1 dc in next lp, ch 6, 1 dc in 3rd ch from hook (picot), ch 3; repeat from * across. Fasten off.

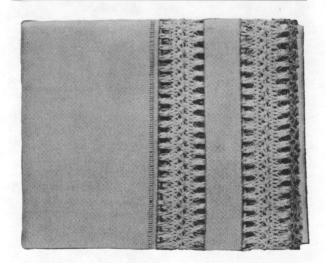

Hairpin lace turns a plain towel into a pretty guest towel. Edging and insertion are done in two colours, they can match your own colour scheme. Made of No. 20 crochet cotton. Towel insertion and edging directions are given on the left.

Hairpin lace trimmings

FIGURE 1.   UNEDGED HAIRPIN LACE

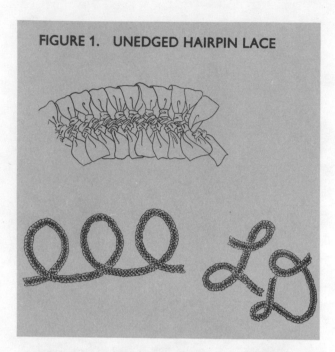

FIGURE 2.   EDGED HAIRPIN LACE

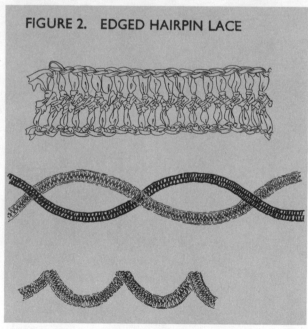

FIGURE 3.   FRINGED TRIMMING

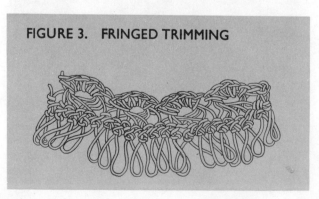

Hairpin lace can be used for smart and decorative trimmings on suits, coats and dresses. Many yarns are suitable for making the braids and edgings: wool yarns from fingering weight to bulky types; novelty yarns, such as knitting ribbon in taffetta or silk organdie, metallic yarns, and cordé.

Ribbon hairpin lace, $\frac{1}{2}''$ or $\frac{3}{4}''$ wide, makes a trimming braid which can be formed into scallops, loops, frogs, initials or other designs. If design curves a great deal, as in forming loops or initials, do not edge the hairpin lace with crochet; Figure 1. Unedged hairpin lace is elastic and can be easily curved and stretched.

For crisper, sharper trimming, edge the lace with double crochet; Figure 2. Edged hairpin lace can be curved somewhat as in the intertwined design of two braids illustrated. The two braids may be made in two different colours for variety, or the hairpin lace may be worked in one colour and the crocheted edges in another. For a scalloped edge, fold braid over at each inner point, as illustrated.

Before sewing ribbon braid to garment, steam-press, then pin in place in desired design. Sew it in place from wrong side of garment along centre of trimming.

Fringed hairpin lace trimming has one edge finished in crochet, the other edge left in free-hanging loops. If a wool yarn is used, loops can be cut to form fringe. To make fringed hairpin lace trimming, Figure 3, use a 2″ hairpin staple and make lace in usual way with a multiple of 5 loops. On one edge, place 5 twisted loops together, one over the other and work 5 double crochet in each cluster of loops across. Be sure all loops twist in same direction.

A smart scalloped braid can be made by working scallops of crochet on both edges of the hairpin lace. Make $1\frac{1}{2}''$ lace a little longer than desired length having multiple of 4 loops each side..With matching or contrasting yarn, crochet groups of loops together on both sides of lace as follows:

Make lp on hook; place first 4 loops tog, sl st these loops tog, make 5 dc in same place as sl st (spread loops apart as you work; scallop should measure $\frac{1}{2}''$), * sl st next 4 loops tog, make 5 dc in same place as sl st; repeat from * across. Repeat scallops on other edge of hairpin lace directly opposite scallops of first side, or alternate scallops by working first 2 loops together, then repeating from * across and working last 2 loops together.

Crocheted trimmings

CROCHETED TUBULAR CORD

May be used for a tie belt or, pressed flat, for a trimming braid. Use yarn single or double and suitable steel crochet hook.

Rnd 1: Ch 2, 6 dc in 2nd ch from hook. Do not join rnds.
Rnd 2: Dc in front lp of each dc around. Repeat rnd 2 for desired length. Dc in every other dc around. Cut yarn leaving 8" end. Thread end in yarn needle, draw end through remaining sts, fasten off securely.

CROCHET-COVERED BUTTONS

Rnd 1: Ch 2, 12 dc in 2nd ch from hook. Do not join rnds.
Rnd 2: * Dc in next dc, 2 dc in next dc; repeat from * around. Continue around in dc, inc as necessary to keep work flat, until piece is same size as button mould.
Next Rnd: * Pull up a lp in each of next 2 sts, yo and through 3 lps on hook (dec made), dc in next dc; repeat from * around. Insert button mould. Continue to dec as necessary to cover back of button mould.

CROCHETED SOUTACHE

Makes a beautiful braid for a suit or dress. Make a chain with soutache a little longer than you need for edge to be trimmed. Double crochet in each chain for desired length. Use wrong side of crochet for right side of braid.

CROCHETED BUTTONS

Buttons can be made without moulds, following directions above and stuffing with cotton.

RING BUTTONS

Lightweight buttons can be made by using plastic rings as a base. With same yarn used in garment, work dc closely around ring. Join with a sl st in first dc. Turn crochet to inside of ring to fill centre and sew centre stitches together, leaving end for sewing to garment. For larger rings, 1 or 3 rnds of dc may be required to fill centre with decreases on each rnd. A small shank type button, beads or rhinestones may be sewn to centre of ring button for decoration. Rings may be covered with soutache, too.

CROCHET-COVERED BUCKLES

A self-belt made for a knitted or crocheted dress should always have a buckle to give the belt a professional look. Buy a buckle in proper size for belt, dc closely over buckle with same yarn as belt, keeping top of stitches at outer edge of buckle.

RING BUCKLE

One, two, three or more plastic rings can be used to make a buckle. With same yarn used in belt, work dc closely around ring. Join with sl st in first dc. Sew rings together as shown. Lap one end of belt through ring at one side: sew end to wrong side. Lap other end of belt through ring at other side; finish with snap fastener.

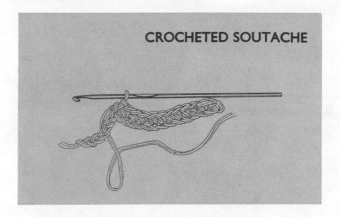

CROCHETED SOUTACHE

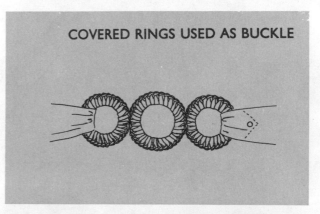

COVERED RINGS USED AS BUCKLE

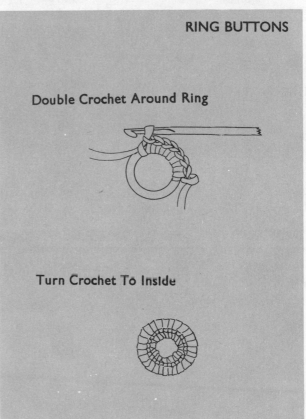

RING BUTTONS

Double Crochet Around Ring

Turn Crochet To Inside

6 Tatting

Stitches and picots which produce rings and half-rings are the essentials of tatting. Varying arrangements of these produce different designs. The French call tatting "frivolité," the Italians call it "occhi," which means "eyes," and in the Orient the work is referred to as "makouk" which describes the shuttles on which tatting is done, rather than the needlecraft itself.

Tatting, which is simply another method of lace-making, looks very delicate, but is actually quite strong because every stitch is a unit all by itself which does not lean on its neighbours for strength. The two stitches which are the basis of the craft are reversals of each other, and once learned, can be done easily and in large part without even watching the work in progress.

Edgings are perhaps the most popular use for tatting today, with round or square table mats close seconds.

The technique is somewhat difficult to describe. If you do not know how to tat and would like to learn, try to augment the information in this chapter with a lesson or two from a friend who knows the art.

How to Tat

Tatting is the technique for forming lace designs of loops, rings and picots by means of a shuttle and thread. The tool used is called a tatting shuttle and may be of plastic, bone or tortoise shell. Some are made with a hook at one end but these are harder for the beginner to use. For practise work, use Coats 'CHAIN' Mercer Crochet cotton size 10, 20, 40, or 60. No. 10 is the easiest to use because of its thickness.

TO WIND THE SHUTTLE BOBBIN: If there is a hole in the bobbin centre, insert thread through hole, tie a knot and wind bobbin. If bobbin is removable, wind it and replace it in shuttle. Only wind enough thread to fill shuttle without projecting at the sides.

TO HOLD THREAD AND SHUTTLE: Hold end of thread between thumb and forefinger of left hand. Bring thread around back of left hand, spreading fingers, and grasp thread again between thumb and forefinger for a ring of thread; Fig. 1. Unwind shuttle so thread is about 12″ long. Hold shuttle between thumb and forefinger of right hand with pointed end facing left hand and thread coming from back of bobbin.

TO MAKE DOUBLE STITCH: First Half: With shuttle in right hand, pass shuttle thread under fingers of right hand, then over back of hand; Fig. 2. Bring shuttle forward and slide flat top of shuttle under ring thread on left hand; Fig. 2. (Do not let go of shuttle; the ring thread will pass between shuttle and fingers.) Then slide shuttle back over ring thread; Fig. 3. Pull shuttle thread taut and at the same time, drop middle finger of left hand so that ring of thread lies loose. This will cause loop to turn over; Fig. 4. Keep shuttle thread taut (this is very important) while you raise middle finger of left hand again. Loop will pull close to left thumb as you pull ring thread taut; Fig. 5. Hold loop firmly between thumb and forefinger.

Second Half: The second half of double stitch is made in reverse. Allow shuttle thread to fall slack without puttig it over right hand. Slide shuttle over ring thread, Fig. 6, back under ring thread and over shuttle thread. Pull shuttle thread taut and hold it taut as you slacken ring thread and tighten it again. Second half of stitch slips into place beside first half; Fig. 7.

By pulling the shuttle thread, stitch should slip back and forth. If it does not, the stitch has been locked by a wrong motion and must be made over again. Practise double stitch, the basic stitch of tatting, until you can make it without looking at instructions. When loop around hand becomes too small to work in, pull shuttle thread at left of stitches to enlarge loop.

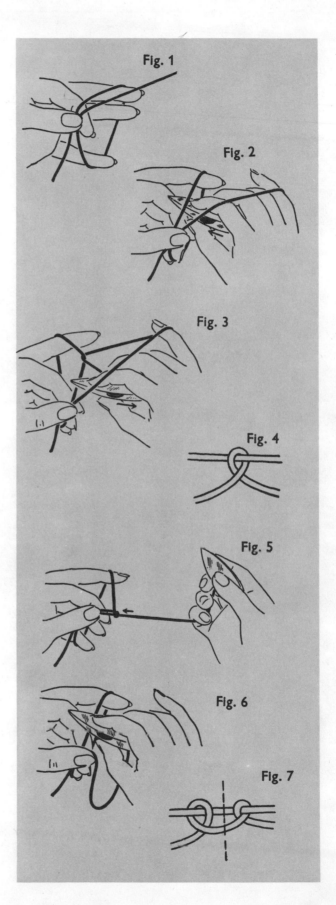

Fig. 1

Fig. 2

Fig. 3

Fig. 4

Fig. 5

Fig. 6

Fig. 7

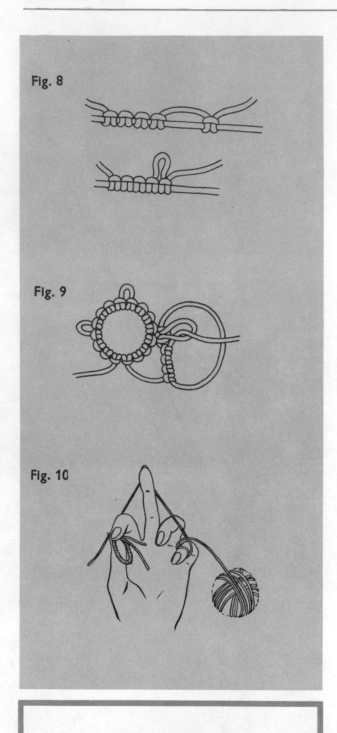

Fig. 8

Fig. 9

Fig. 10

TO MAKE RINGS AND PICOTS: Rings and picots are characteristic of all tatting. To make first ring, work 4 double stitches (4 d), then make first half of another double stitch; slide it on thread, stopping about ¼" from last stitch. Complete double stitch and draw entire stitch in position next to 4 d, forming picot (p); Fig. 8. Work 3 more d, work another picot, 3 more d, work another picot and 3 more d. Hold stitches firmly in left hand, draw shuttle thread until first and last stitches meet, forming a ring.

TO JOIN RINGS: Wind thread around left hand as for first ring and work first double stitch of next ring about ¼" from ring just made. Work 3 more d. If you are using a shuttle with one pointed end, or a hook at one end, insert this end through the last picot of previous ring (or use a crochet hook) and pull ring thread through. Pull up a loop large enough to insert shuttle. Draw shuttle through this loop, Fig. 9, and draw shuttle thread tight. This joins the rings and counts as the first half of a double stitch. Complete double stitch, work 3 more d, a picot, 4 d, a picot, 4 d, close ring same as first ring.

TO REVERSE WORK: Turn work so that base of ring just made is at the top and work next ring as usual.

TO JOIN THREADS: Make a flat knot close to the base of the last ring or chain, but do not cut off the ends, as the strain during working may loosen the knot. With a single strand of Mercer-Crochet cotton over-sew the ends on the wrong side. If a knot occurs on the thread cut it off and tie the new thread close to the last ring. Knots prevent the ring from being drawn up, as they will not pass through the double stitches.

TO WORK WITH TWO THREADS: By using two threads, a wider range of patterns can be made. One method of working with two threads is to use the ball of thread for making chains and the shuttle thread for making rings. Tie ball and shuttle threads together. Use shuttle thread to form a ring. When ring is completed turn it so base is held between thumb and forefinger. Stretch thread from ball over back of fingers and loop it twice around little finger; Fig. 10. Work over ball thread with the shuttle in the usual way to form a chain, pull stitches together when chain is finished and resume work with the shuttle thread only for next ring.

When two colours are used in making rings, two shuttles must be used. These colours may be alternated, or the second colour may be worked over the first as described in making a chain with a shuttle and a ball.

TO MAKE A JOSEPHINE KNOT: Work a small ring consisting of only the first half of double stitches.

TATTING ABBREVIATIONS

r—ring	d—double stitch
ch—chain	rw—reverse work
rnd—round	sep—separated by
j—join	lr—large ring
p—picot	sm—small
cl—close	sp—space
beg—beginning	

Tatted Edgings

WILD ROSE EDGING

MATERIALS: Coats 'CHAIN' Mercer-Crochet No. 60 (20 grm). 1 ball selected colour. 1 handkerchief. Milwards Tatting Shuttle. Milwards Steel Crochet Hook No. 5.

Use ball and shuttle.

Rnd 1: J thread in edge of handkerchief ⅛" before one corner. * Ch (4 d, p) 3 times, 4 d, j in edge of handkerchief on other side of same corner ⅛" past corner. ** Ch (4 d, p) 3 times, 4 d, j in edge of handkerchief ¼" from last joining. Repeat from ** across to within ⅛" of next corner. Repeat from * around. Tie and cut.

Rnd 2: J in centre p of corner ch. * Ch (4 d, p) 3 times, 4 d, j in centre p of next ch. Repeat from * around. Tie and cut.

Rnd 3: R 3 d, j in first p of first ch after corner ch, 3 d, cl r. * Leave ¼" thread, r 3 d, j in next p of same ch, 3 d, cl r. Leave ¼" thread, r 3 d, j in same p, 3 d, cl r. Leave ¼" thread, r 3 d, j in last p of same ch, 3 d, cl r. Leave ¼" thread, j in centre p of next ch. Leave ¼" thread, r 3 d, j in first op f next ch, 3 d, cl r. Repeat from * around. Tie and cut.

STAR FLOWER EDGING

MATERIALS: Coats 'CHAIN' Mercer-Crochet No. 60 (20 grm). 1 ball selected colour. 1 handkerchief. Milwards Tatting Shuttle. Milwards Steel Crochet Hook No. 5.

Use ball and shuttle.

Rnd 1: J thread in edge of handkerchief at one corner. * Ch 6 d, p, 6 d, rw. R 3 d, p, (4 d, p) twice, 3 d, cl r, rw. Ch 6 d, p, 6 d, j in edge of handkerchief ⅜" from last joining †. Ch 4 d, j in edge ⅛" from last joining, repeat from * across to next corner ending at †. Repeat from * around edge of handkerchief. Tie and cut.

Rnd 2: J thread in edge at same corner between first and last motif. * Ch (3 d, p) 3 times, 3 d, j in first p of r, ch 3 d, p, (4 d, p) twice, 3 d, j in same p. Ch 3 d, j in next p of same r, ch 3 d, p, (4 d, p) twice, 3 d, j in same p. Ch 3 d, j in last p of r, ch 3 d, p, (4 d, p) twice, 3 d, j in same p. Ch (3 d, p) 3 times, 3 d, j over ch in edge between motifs. Repeat from * around, joining centre p of first round ch to centre p of last round ch of last motif. Tie and cut.

Tatting makes a rich and delicate lace for edging handkerchiefs. Wild Rose and Star Flower Edgings, are joined to the hemstitched handkerchiefs during the first round of tatting.

Tatted Doily

Tatted doily design suggests a medieval rose window framed in smaller flowers and petals. In size 10 cotton, an easy size for the beginner to work.

SIZE: 10″ in diameter.

MATERIALS: Coats 'CHAIN' Mercer-Crochet No. 10 (20 grm). 2 balls selected colour. Milwards Tatting Shuttle. Milwards Steel Crochet Hook No. 2½.

Centre Motif: Rnd 1: Make r of (3 d, p) 11 times, cl r, rw.

Rnd 2: Draw thread in last p, (ch 3 d, j in next p, make sm p) 11 times.

Rnd 3: J in p, * ch 6 d, p (9 d, p) twice, 6 d, j in same p (ch-lp made), ch 2 d, j in next p last rnd, repeat from * around, joining first p of new ch-lp to last p of last ch-lp. At the end of rnd, j last p of ch-lp to first p of first ch-lp. Tie and cut. There are 11 ch-lps with ch 2 d between. Centre motif completed.

Rnd 4: * Make r of 4 d, j in p at point of ch-lp, 4 d, cl r, rw. Ch 5 d, p, (10 d, p) twice, 5 d, rw. Repeat from * around, j in first r. Tie and cut.

Rnd 5: * Make r of 5 d, j in p at point of ch, 5 d, cl r, rw. (Ch 5 d, p) 7 times, 5 d, rw. Repeat from * around, j in

first r. Tie and cut.

Rnd 6:First Motif: Work rnds 1 and 2 as for centre motif. **Next Rnd:** J in p, (4 d, j in next p) twice, work from first * to 2nd * of rnd 3 until there are 7 ch-lps, (4 d, j in next p) twice, tie to centre p of ch on rnd 5, cut thread. Make 10 more motifs in same way, joining centre p of first ch-lp new motif to centre p of last ch-lp last motif. At end of rnd, j centre p of last ch-lp to centre p of first ch-lp first motif.

Rnd 7: * Make r of 4 d, j in centre p of 2nd ch-lp on a motif, 4 d, cl r. rw. (Ch 5 d, p, 10 d, p, 10 d, p, 5 d, rw. R 4 d, j in centre p of next ch-lp same motif, 4 d, cl r, rw) 4 times. Repeat from * around, j in first r. Tie and cut.

Rnd 8: * Make r of 4 d, j in centre p of ch to right of double r last rnd, 4 d, cl r, rw. (Ch 5 d, 7 p sep by 5 d, 5 d, j in centre p of next ch) twice, ch 5 d, 7 p sep by 5 d, 5 d, rw. R of 4 d, j in centre p of next ch, 4 d, cl r, rw. Repeat from * around, j in first r. Tie and cut.

Tatted Squares

Two motifs combine to form a square medallion for place mats, tablecloths. Illustration shows one complete at lower right, and four corner motifs joined at left.

MATERIALS: Coats 'CHAIN' Mercer-Crochet No. 20 (20 grm). Milward Tatting Shuttle. Milwards Steel Crochet Hook No. 3.

FOUR-LOOP SQUARE: R 5 d, 7 p sep by 2 d, 5 d, cl r. * R 5 d, j in last p of last r, 2 d, 6 p sep by 2 d, 5 d, cl r*. Repeat from * to * twice more joining last p of 4th r first p of first r.

Second Four-Loop Square: Work as for first square, joining to first square by 5th p of first r and 3rd p of 2nd r. Make 9 squares in all, joining to form a cross 5 squares high by 5 squares wide.

CORNER MOTIF: R 2 d, 3 p sep by 2 d, 2 d, j in 4th free p of r at end of cross, 2 d, 3 p sep by 2 d, 2 d, cl r. * Rw, ch 2 d, 5 p sep by 1 d, 2 d. Rw, ** r 2 d, p, 2 d, j in next to last p of last r, 2 d, p, 2 d, j in middle p of next r of square, 2 d, 3 p sep by 2 d, 2 d, cl r *. Repeat from * to *, ch 3 d, p, 3 d.

Rw, r 2 d, p, 2 d, j in next to last p of last r, 2 d, p, 2 d, j in middle p of next r of square, 2 d, p, 2 d, j in middle p of next r of square, 2 d, 3 p sep by 2 d, 2 d, cl r.

Rw, ch 3 d, j in p of last ch, 3 d. Repeat from ** to *. Repeat from * to * twice, ch 7 d, p, 7 d, p, 5 d.

Rw, r 3 d, p, 3 d, j in middle p of 2nd from last ch, 3 d, p, 3 d, cl r.

Rw, ch 3 d, r 3 d, 11 p sep by 2 d, 3 d, cl r. Ch 3 d, rw, r 3 d, j in last p of last r, 3 d, j in middle p of next ch, 3 d, p, 3 d, cl r.

Rw, ch 5 d, p, 7 d, p, 7 d. Cut and tie in first r. Fill in other 3 corners in same way.

Join medallions by middle picots of adjacent rings and chains. Where four corner motifs meet, join 3 large rings in middle picot of large ring of first medallion.

Tatted Daisy Doily

MATERIALS: Coats 'CHAIN' Mercer-Crochet No. 20 (20 grm). 1 ball white and 1 ball 582 (straw yellow). This model is worked in these two shades but any other shade of mercer-crochet may be used. Milwards Tatting Shuttle. Milwards Steel Crochet Hook No. 3.

CENTRE MEDALLION: Row 1: With yellow, r 1 d, 10 p sep 1 d, cl.

Row 2: * Ch 2 d, small p, j to next p. Repeat from * making 10 p.

Row 3: * Ch 3 d, small p, j p. Repeat from * around.

Row 4: * Ch 2 d, small p, 2 d, small p, j p. Repeat from * around. Tie and cut.

With white, tie to a p, ch 10 d, p, 8 d, p, 2 d, p, 8 d, p, 10 d, j next yellow p, 10 d, j last p previous. Ch 8 d, p, 2 d, p, 8 d, p, 10 d, j next yellow p. Repeat around. (10 petals made). Tie and cut.

Tie thread at j of petals. Ch 10 d, p, 10 d, j next petal j. Continue around. Tie and cut. Ch as previous round, making 11 d.

SIDE MEDALLIONS: With yellow, 2 rows same as centre medallion.

Row 3: Ch 2 d, p, 2 d, j p, 2 d, p, 2 d, j p. Continue around 10 times. Tie and cut.

Make 7 white petals same as centre medallion. For second rnd, j p centre medallion at same time to end p of new medallion. Ch 10 d, j at joining, 10 d, p, 10 d, etc., j next free centre medallion. Tie and cut. Make 5 side medallions joining last one to first one.

EDGE: Row 1: With yellow, r 3 d, p, 6 d, j to p of sixth petal, 6 d, p, 3 d, cl. R 3 d, j last p last r, 6 d, 2 p sep 6 d, 3 d, cl. R 3 d, j p last r, 6 d, j second petal next medallion, 6 d, p, 3 d, cl, rw. With white ch 9 d, 3 p sep 9 d, rw. With yellow * r 9 d, j next petal, 9 d, cl, rw. With white ch 9 d, 3 p sep 9 d, 9 d, rw. Yellow r 9 d, j same petal, 9 d, cl, rw. White ch 9 d, p, 9 d, rw. Repeat from * twice, then ch 9 d, 3 p sep 9 d, 9 d, rw. Repeat from beginning with 3 r group. Join to correspond. Tie and cut.

Row 2: White thread, j to p of long ch, ch 9 d, 3 p sep 9 d, 9 d, rw. Yellow r 3 d, p, 6 d, j end p same loop, 6 d, p, 3 d, cl. R 3 d, j p last r, 6 d, j p next ch, 6 d, p, 3 d, cl. R 3 d, j p last r, 6 d, j p next long ch, 6 d, p, 3 d, cl, rw. White ch 9 d, 3 p sep 9 d, 9 d, j next p same loop. Repeat once from beginning of row, ch 9 d, 3 p sep 9 d, 9 d, rw. Yellow r 9 d, j second p next loop, 9 d, cl. R 9 d, j first p next loop, 9 d, cl, rw. White ch 9 d, 3 p sep 9 d, 9 d. Repeat around. Tie and cut.

Row 3: With white, r 3 d, p, 3 d, cl, rw. Ch 13 d, j centre p on ch previous row, 13 d, rw. R 3 d, p, 3 d, cl. Repeat around. Tie and cut.

Row 4: With white, r 3 d, j r previous row, 3 d, cl, rw. Ch 13 d, p, 13 d, rw. R 3 d, j next r, 3 d, cl, rw. Ch 13 d, p, 13 d, rw. R 3 d, j same p, 3 d, cl. Continue around.

Outside medallions are made same as side ones, except that they are completed with 10 petals, joining to previous row with a petal to long loop, next two to next ch's, and fourth to next long loop.

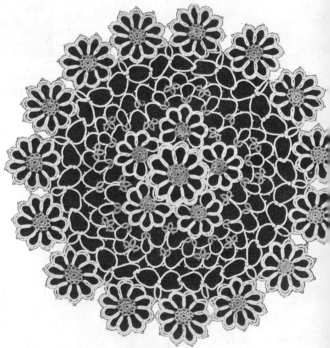

Tat a field of daisies for your table. Tatted doily, makes a pretty place mat in yellow and white. Motif of daisy is shown actual size. In two-colour tatting, two shuttles are used.

Padded Tatting Motif

MATERIALS: Coats 'CHAIN' Mercer-Crochet No. 10 (20 grm). 1 ball selected colour. Milwards Tatting Shuttle. Milwards Steel Crochet Hook No. 2½.

NOTE: In padded tatting, all joinings are made with ball thread, as it would be difficult to draw 4 strands through a picot.

FLORAL MOTIF: Centre (make 2): Make r of (1 d, p) 6 times; cl r, j in last p. **Rnd 1:** Ch (2 d, j in next p, make smp) 6 times.

Rnd 2: Ch (3 d, j in smp, make smp) 6 times.

Rnd 3: Ch (4 d, j in smp, make smp) 6 times.

Rnd 4: Ch (5 d, j in smp, make smp) 6 times.

Rnd 5: Ch (6 d, j in smp, make smp) 6 times. Tie and cut thread.

Petals: For padding, measure about 6 yards of crochet cotton size 10, fold into 4 equal lengths; tie the 4 strands to shuttle and wind on. Tie the 4 strands to ball thread. Draw through picot of one flower centre and ch (3 d, p, 20 d, p, 3 d, j in next p) 6 times, joining first p of every ch to last p of previous ch; do not join last petal to first petal. Rw and ch back, 3 d, j in last p, ch (22 d, j where chains are joined) 6 times, joining last ch in first petal.

Stem and Leaves: Rw, ch 60 d for stem, p, ch 25 d, p,

25 d, j in p of stem, 30 d, j in p at point of leaf. Tie and cut. Join in smp of 2nd flower centre, ch 30 d, j in bottom p of stem, ch 30 d, j in same p of tatted centre. Tie and cut.

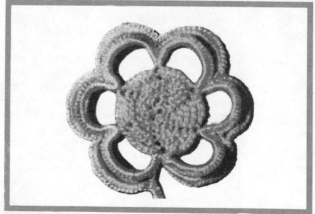

Floral motifs in padded tatting ring a circular cloth of pastel linen. Flower petals shown in detail, stems and leaves, are formed over "padding" of four strands of cotton.

7 Technical Aids

The current professional approach to designing, making, and finishing handwork has taken needlework of all kinds away from the home-made look and out of the amateur field. Today's needlework has been developed to a very high degree of perfection and the hand made item is the prestige item. This doubtless is one of the reasons why handknitted and crocheted garments have become high fashion, and unusual hand-made accessories for the home are sought by leading decorators. In this section we give you much of the technical know-how for obtaining these professional results.

The choice of equipment is of utmost importance. The good workman also knows and understands the materials with which he is creating an object, so he chooses the material which is best suited to the purpose.

While this is a learn-and-make book, it is our hope that readers will not only learn the basic techniques of needlework but will develop to the point where they can create their own designs. In this section we have given you many helpful aids for designing, working and finishing needlework. Here is one more important suggestion. Be sure that you know how to do the stitch or stitches with which you plan to execute the designs, and have tried out the stitches with the type of yarns you plan to use on a sample of the background material. Then design within the limitations of your materials and take full advantage of them.

Embroidery Equipment

Once you decide to make an embroidered piece, it is important to collect the proper equipment. Not many items are needed, so choose the best you can afford. Good tools produce good work. Learn to use your embroidery accessories properly and you will find your work to be neater.

Different embroidery techniques require different needles. For embroidery on fabric, be sure your needles are smooth and sharp. Embroidery needles are rather short and have a long, slender eye. They are made in sizes 1 to 10; the higher numbers are the finest. Blunt needles are used for needlepoint, huck weaving and embroidery on net. Keep a good selection of needles on hand and protect them by storing them in a needle case. It is also advisable to run your needles through an emery strawberry occasionally to clean and sharpen them. To thread stranded cotton through the needle eye, double it over the end of the needle and slip it off, holding it tightly as close as possible to the fold. Push the flattened, folded end through the needle eye and pull yarn through.

You will need proper scissors. Embroidery scissors should be small, with narrow, pointed blades and must be sharp. Protect the blade points by keeping them in a sheath.

You may or may not find it convenient to embroider with a thimble. But you will find that in some instances a thimble is necessary. Generally, metal thimbles are better than plastic or bone. Be sure that the closed end and sides are deeply indented to prevent the needle end from slipping off when in use. Thimbles come in different sizes. Try on a few for correct fit before you buy one.

Embroidery is usually worked in a frame. With the material held tautly and evenly, your stitches are more likely to be neat and accurate than if the fabric were held in the hand while working. Many embroidery hoops and frames are equipped with stands or clamps to hold the embroidery piece and leave both your hands free.

There are two main types of frames, round and rectangular. The round frame or hoop consists of two pieces, a smaller hoop which fits into the larger one. There is usually a spring or screw adjustment to keep them fitting snugly. The fabric for embroidery is placed over the smaller hoop and the larger hoop is pressed over the fabric on to the smaller hoop. These frames may be of either wood or metal. When embroidering on very delicate fabric, it is advisable to place tissue paper over the inner hoop first, or wrap the inner hoop with a thin material to prevent marking the fabric.

The rectangular frame consists of four pieces: two roller pieces at top and bottom and either two screw-type ends for tightening, or flat ends with holes for adjusting. The embroidery piece or tapestry is tacked on to the strips of fabric on the roller pieces and laced on to the ends to hold it taut. Specific instructions for mounting the embroidery fabric will come with each frame.

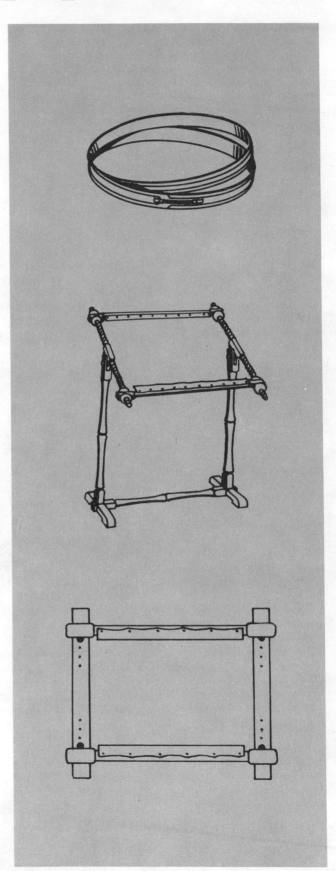

Threads for embroidery

The appearance of your work is greatly influenced by the material that you choose. You can make a delicate piece of work with fragile fabric and a fine thread, or translate the identical design on to coarser fabric, using a heavier thread. In needlepoint, for instance, the yarn required for each canvas is chosen for its covering quality. Crewel wool used single would not cover the mesh of gros point canvas; a heavier yarn is required, or two or more strands of fine wool. The needle to use with each thread should have an eye large enough to accommodate the yarn, but not larger than needed. Some types of embroidery traditionally use a certain thread while others technically require a specific kind. Chart relates threads and needles to type of work.

Materials or Type of Work	Threads	Needle*
Fine Fabrics or thin material	Clark's '*Anchor*' Stranded Cotton (1, 2 or 3 strands). Clark's '*Anchor*' Pearl Cotton No. 8. Clark's '*Anchor*' Coton a Broder No. 18 Rayon floss or cord	Crewel No. 6–8 (for free style embroidery). Tapestry No. 23–25 (for counted thread or canvas work)
Medium Textures such as linen, pique (or other cottons); or light-weight sweaters of wool, nylon, or angora	Clark's '*Anchor*' Stranded Cotton (2, 3 or 4 strands). Clark's '*Anchor*' Pearl Cotton No. 8. Clark's '*Anchor*' Coton a Broder No. 18 Fine wool yarns	Crewel No. 6–7 (for free style embroidery). Tapestry No. 23–24 (for counted thread or canvas work). Darning No. 4 to 8
Heavyweight or coarse fabrics such as Monk's cloth, burlap, felt, wool suiting, or heavy sweaters	Clark's '*Anchor*' Stranded Cotton (6 strands). Clark's '*Anchor*' Pearl Cotton No. 5. Coats '*Anchor*' Tapisserie Wool. Sock and Sweater Yarn, Nylon, Angora, Chenille, Germantown	Crewel No. 5. Tapestry 19–21 Chenille needle No. 19. Darning No. 1 to 3
Cutwork	Clark's '*Anchor*' Stranded Cotton (2–3 strands). Clark's '*Anchor*' Pearl Cotton No. 8. Clark's '*Anchor*' Coton a Broder No. 18	Crewel No. 6
Huck Weaving	Clark's '*Anchor*' Sranded Cotton (6 strands). Clark's '*Anchor*' Pearl Cotton No. 5. Fine wool yarn	Tapestry No. 21
Quilting or **Appliqué**	Clark's '*Anchor*' Stranded Cotton (2–6 strands). Coats Satinised No. 40	Crewel No. 5–7. Sharps No. 8
Beading, Sewing on Sequins	Coats Cotton No. 60	Beading No. 10–13
Machine Embroidery	Clark's '*Anchor*' Machine Embroidery Thread No. 30 & 50	Machine No. 11
Candlewick Embroidery or for heavy yarns worked through sweaters or fabrics	Candlewick Yarn Rug yarn of cotton, wool, or rayon lustre	Candlewick needle
Petit Point **Needlepoint** **Gros Point** **Quick Point**	Clark's '*Anchor*' Stranded Cotton (3–6 strands). Coats '*Anchor*' Tapisserie Wool Tapestry Wool (Double) Rug Yarn	Tapestry No. 21–23 Tapestry No. 19 Tapestry No. 18 Large-eyed rug needles

*In embroidery and sewing needles the largest number is the finest needle.

How to transfer designs

If you are spending your own precious time to create an heirloom for tomorrow you will want to be sure the design is as attractive as possible.

If you have a fine museum in your neighbourhood study the lovely embroidery designs they show. Sometimes you can choose an embroidery motif from a bed hanging and apply it around the border of a luncheon cloth. Sometimes you may choose to translate a painting into needlepoint.

Even if you do not copy exactly what you see, some old tapestry or hanging might give you inspiration for an original design of your own. Fabric designs both old and new are also a worthwhile study. Do not think that an original design must be complicated to be good; some of the most successful and lasting have been the simplest. Look at the many delightful samplers, that are simplicity itself, and are now collector's pieces!

If you have a reference library with fine books on art or design, on rare old china, or beautiful linens, then you can use these as possible sources of ideas.

If you plan to copy a museum design, or a print from some other source, place tracing paper over the photograph of the design and carefully copy the complete design; to protect the print, place a piece of glass between the design and the tracing paper. Mark the correct colours and shades, using coloured crayon or pencils. The design, if it is to be used in the same size, is now ready to be used on your fabric; there are a number of ways of transferring a design.

CARBON PAPER: Typewriter carbon may be used between your fabric and the tracing. However, this is apt to be smudgy and can soil the fabric. Dressmakers' carbon is better to use for this purpose and comes in light and dark colours. Anchor the fabric to a smooth surface with masking tape; place carbon face down on fabric with tracing on top in correct position; tape in place. With an instrument such as a dry ball point pen, carefully mark all lines of design, using enough pressure to transfer clearly.

BACK TRACING: A design may also be transferred to a smooth fabric by going over all lines on back of tracing with a soft pencil. Then tape tracing on to your fabric, right side up, and trace all lines again, using a hard pencil.

DIRECT TRACING: If the fabric and tracing are not too large and unwieldy, the design can be transferred by means of a light box, or ordinary glass window. With this method, the fabric must be of a light colour and not very heavy. Place tracing (which must be marked with heavy, dark lines) right side up on a light box, or tape to window in bright daylight. Tape fabric on top of tracing. With the light coming from the back, the traced design will show clearly through the fabric and can be traced directly on the fabric, using a sharp pencil.

PERFORATED PATTERN: There is another method, which makes a good permanent pattern, called perforating. To make your own perforated pattern, mark design accurately on heavy quality tracing paper. Then the traced design is perforated on all outlines.

With tracing on a lightly padded surface, use a pin or unthreaded sewing machine to make the holes in the tracing paper, about $\frac{1}{16}''$ apart.

Hold the pin straight up and push through paper enough to make clear holes. When the perforating is finished, place it over your fabric, smooth side up and weight it down around edges to hold it in place while transferring.

The design may be transferred by means of a perforating powder called pounce, and a pouncer.

To make a pouncer, roll up a strip of flannel or felt tightly, sewing it so it remains rolled. Dip the end of the pouncer in powder, tap off excess; then dab and rub it over the perforated outlines. Carefully lift up corner of perforated pattern to see if design has been transferred clearly.

If not, go over it again with pounce. When the transferring is completed, carefully lift off pattern. Perforating paste may be used instead of powder. Directions for its use will come with the paste.

TRANSFER PATTERN: If you do not wish to create your own design, you can use one of the lovely designs already prepared for you, ready to be transferred to your fabric by means of a hot iron. The McCall's Transfer Patterns which are printed in blue will transfer on both light and dark fabrics. These transfers are available at pattern departments.

To use the transfer pattern always cut away the pattern name or number or any other parts that you do not wish to use. Shake the paper to remove any loose particles. Lay the fabric on an ironing board or lightly padded surface and pin in position so it will not slide. Pin transfer design in place, design side down on fabric.

Experiment first with a small piece of transfer on a sample of material. Before stamping test heat of the iron with the number or trial sample on a sample of the material, selecting a low heat or rayon heat for all materials. Transfer design with a downward stamp of the iron (never press slowly and heavily as in ironing). If your test sample is not clear, the heat of iron is not correct.

When the iron is the correct temperature, stamp the design. Before removing the transfer lift a corner to see if the design has been transferred satisfactorily. When completely stamped, remove the transfer by running the warm iron lightly over it. This prevents the transfer ink from sticking to the paper as it is pulled away from the material.

How to enlarge or reduce designs

There are various ways of enlarging or reducing a design so that all parts of the design will be enlarged or reduced in proportion. Two methods are given here. The most commonly used is the "square" method. No. 1. Which roughly explained is a method in which graph paper has its uses. By dividing up the original design into squares, you can use the same number of squares on the graph paper, either larger or smaller than those drawn on the design, depending on the size you want

your design. Then you can carefully copy the origina design, helped by the squared paper. Another simpl procedure is the "diagonal" method, No. 2. This i similar to the preceding method, but is more suitabl for certain designs than others.

If you wish to keep the original design unmarked trace outlines of design on to tracing paper, as explaine on opposite page, "How to Transfer Designs."

Method No. 1: Mark off squares over the design to be enlarged if they are not already there. Use $\frac{1}{8}$" squares for small designs and $\frac{1}{4}$", $\frac{1}{2}$" or 1 "squares for proportionately larger designs. Make the same number of squares, similarly placed, in the space to be occupied by the enlarged design. Copy outline of design from smaller squares to corresponding larger squares. Reverse procedure for reducing designs.

A "trick of the trade" is to place a fine wire screen over the original design for "squaring off". Another short cut is to transfer original design to graph paper.

Method No. 2: Make a rectangle to fit around desig to be enlarged. Draw a diagonal line from corner t corner and extend line far enough to form diagonal a rectangle to fit desired size.

Subdivide large and small rectangles by first makin opposite diagonals to find centre. Then draw lines t quarter the space. Make diagonal of quarter sections t find centres. Draw lines to quarter the space. Cop outlines of design from smaller areas to larger areas o vice versa. An easy way to divide the rectangles int spaces described above is to fold the paper into halves quarters and eighths, then draw diagonal lines int folds.

Method No. 1. Small "m" enlarged by squares to place-mat size.

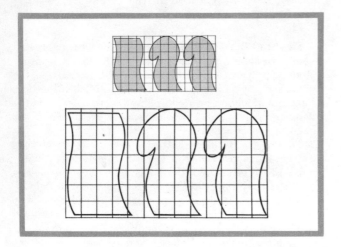

Method No. 2. By drawing diagonals, small "e" becomes place-mat size.

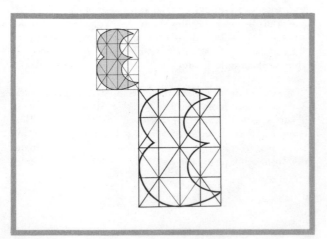

Aids in designing

HOW TO DRAW AN OVAL

Here is the simple geometrical method of making ovals large or small to fit any desired space.

Fig. 1: Draw a straight line length of, or longer than, desired length of oval. At centre of line establish point A. With compass (or pencil tied to string) swing arcs to establish B and C, the length of oval.

Fig. 2: From B and C swing arcs above and below line BC. Connect their intersections with line DE. On this line mark points F and G equal distances from A, to establish width of oval.

Fig. 3: Mark points 1 and 2 to match A and C on a straight, firm strip of paper.

Fig. 4: Turn this measuring paper vertically along line FG so that point 1 is at F. Mark point 3 at A.

Fig. 5: Rotate the measuring paper clockwise, moving point 3 along line AC and point 2 along AG. Make dots opposite point 1. Connect these dots with a line which completes the first quarter of the oval. Repeat this procedure in the other three parts or make a tracing and transfer curve to complete oval.

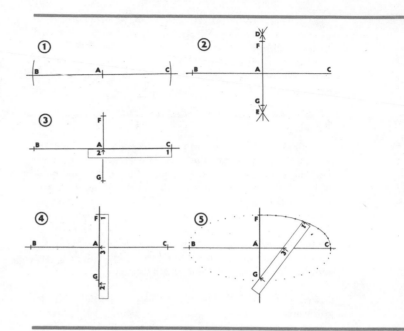

HOW TO DIVIDE ANY LINE INTO EQUAL PARTS

Fig. 1: The line to be divided will be called line X. Rule off line AB shorter than line X by marking off AB into the desired number of equal parts, using simple divisions on ruler such as $\frac{1}{2}''$, $\frac{1}{4}''$, etc.

Fig. 2: With a draftsman's triangle, or holding an ordinary ruler at right angles to line AB, raise perpendicular lines at each division.

Fig. 3: Measure line X and mark off length on ruler. Place ruler so that line X extends from A to line BC; where it touches is point D. Line X is now divided into equal parts.

HOW TO MAKE A STAR

1. Draw a circle desired size of star. With compass or dividers, find five equidistant points A on circumference of circle. Draw lines to connect points to form a pentagon.

2. Using same centre of circle, draw another circle inside larger circle as illustrated (distance of inner circle from outer circle controls depth of star points). Find centres of five sides of pentagon (points B). From these centres, draw lines through centre of circle to opposite points A.

3. Draw lines from points A of pentagon to where dividing lines intersect inner circle (points C).

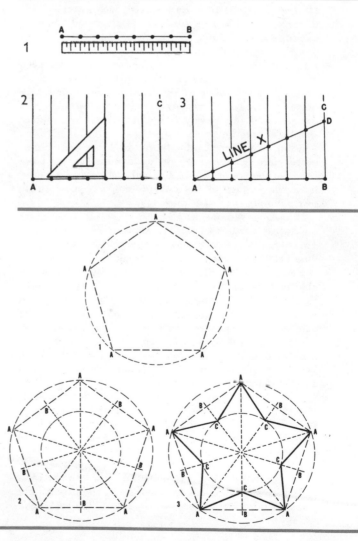

Care of embroidery

When your needlework is completed, it often needs to be pressed or blocked into shape. Sometimes it is soiled from working and must be laundered. This should always be done with care to preserve as much of the freshness of the fabric and thread as possible. Treat embroidery gently.

Wash it in mild frothy soap or detergent suds. Do no rub embroidery. Rinse it thoroughly, but do not wrin or squeeze it out. Always iron on the wrong side, th prevents the design being flattened and helps preserv the colours of the silks or wools used.

To help keep your work neat and clean, keep it in a plastic bag when not embroidering. When your embroidered piece is completed, finish off the back neatly by running ends into the back of the work and clipping off any excess strands. If wool embroidery or needlepoint is not really soiled but needs just a little freshening, simply brushing over the surface with a clean cloth dipped in carbon tetrachloride or other good cleaning fluid may be satisfactory. This will brighten and return colours to their original look.

FABRIC EMBROIDERY: Better results will be obtained by blocking (directions below) rather than pressing an embroidered piece for a picture or hanging. However, articles that are hemmed, such as tablecloths or runners, should be pressed as blocking would damage the edge of the fabric. To press your embroidered piece use a well-padded surface and steam iron, or regular iron and damp cloth. Embroideries that have been worked in a frame will need very little pressing. If the embroidery was done in the hand it will no doubt be quite wrinkled and may need dampening. Sprinkle it to dampen and roll loosely in a clean towel. Embroidery should always be pressed lightly so that the stitching will not be flattened into the fabric. Place the embroidered piece face down on the padded surface and press from the centre outwards. For embroidery that is raised from the surface of the background, use extra thick, soft padding, such as a thick blanket.

If beads or sequins are added to embroidery, take care not to use too hot an iron, as some of these may melt. These should also be pressed wrong side down. The padding below protects them from breaking.

Embroideries made of colourfast threads and washable fabrics can be laundered without fear of harming them. Wash with mild soap or detergent and warm water, swishing it through the water gently—do not rub. Rinse in clear water without wringing or squeezing. When completely rinsed, lift from the water and lay on a clean towel: lay another towel on top and roll up loosely. When the embroidery is sufficiently dry, press as described above.

After blocking or pressing, an embroidered picture should be mounted right away to prevent creasing. To store other embroidery, place blue tissue paper on front and roll smoothly, face in, on to a cardboard tube. Then wrap outside in tissue.

TO REMOVE STAMPING FROM THE MATERIAL: It is almost impossible to remove transfers from light coloured fabrics that cannot be washed. Try soaking in cleaning fluid for about ten minutes. Rub carefully an rinse in clean fluid, until material is clean; let dry, an press. For woollens, place material right side up wit a blotter under the fabric. Rub gently with a clean clot saturated in cleaning fluid. As the cloth absorbs th colour use a fresh cloth.

Washable fabrics may have the blue transfer patter removed by washing them with a good laundry soap an warm water, rubbing by hand until the marks disappea To wash silks or rayons, soak the fabric in cleanin fluid for about five minutes, rubbing lightly. This wi loosen and spread the transfer. Then wash in lukewar water with a mild soap rubbing carefully until th marks disappear. After rinsing thoroughly, place fabr wrong side up. Cover with a damp cloth and press wit medium hot iron.

TO BLOCK NEEDLEPOINT: If a small piece of needl point is pulled slightly askew through working, spong the surface on the wrong side. Lay it face down on damp towel, pull into shape and pin all round the edge Cover with another damp towel and steam press wit a regular iron.

For larger pieces that become badly out of shape, th needlepoint should be blocked as follows: Cover a sof wood surface with brown paper. Mark the canvas siz on this, being sure corners are square. Place needlepoin right side down over guide and fasten with drawing pin about $\frac{1}{2}''$ apart all along edges of canvas. Wet with co water thoroughly and let dry. Repeat as many times s necessary.

TO BLOCK EMBROIDERED PICTURE: With need and colourfast thread, following the thread of the line and taking $\frac{1}{4}''$ stitches, mark guide lines around th entire picture to designate the exact area where th picture will fit into the rabbet of the frame. The bord of plain linen extending beyond the embroidery in framed picture is approximately $1\frac{1}{4}''$ at sides and to and $1\frac{1}{2}''$ at bottom. In order to have sufficient line around the embroidered design for blocking and moun ing, $3''$ or $4''$ of linen should be left around the embroid red section. Now, matching corners, obtain the exa centres of the four sides and mark these centres wit a few stitches.

If the picture is soiled, it should be washed, but should be blocked immediately after washing. In prep ration, cover a drawing board or soft-wood bread boar with a piece of brown paper held in place with drawin pins, and draw the exact original size of the linen the brown paper. Be sure linen is not pulled beyond original size when the measurements are taken. (Embroidery sometimes pulls linen slightly out of shape.) Check drawn rectangle to make sure corners are square.

Wash embroidery in mild soap with plenty of suds; squeeze suds through material; do not rub embroidery. Rinse thoroughly, but do not wring or squeeze. Let drip for a few moments. Place embroidery right side up on the brown paper inside the guide lines and tack down the four corners. Pin centres of four sides. Continue to stretch the linen to its original size by pinning all around the sides, dividing and sub-dividing the spaces between the tacks already placed. This procedure is followed until there is a solid border of drawing pins around the entire edge. In cross-stitch pictures, if stiches were not stamped exactly even on the thread of the linen, it may be necessary to remove some of the pins and pull part of embroidery into a straight line. Use a ruler as a guide for straightening the lines of stitches. Hammer in the pins or they will pop out as the linen dries. Allow embroidery to dry thoroughly.

TO MOUNT EMBROIDERED PICTURE: Cut a piece of heavy white cardboard about $\frac{1}{8}''$ smaller all around than the rabbet size of the frame to be used. Stretch the embroidery over the cardboard using the same general procedure as for blocking the piece. Following the thread guide lines, use pins to attach the four corners of the embroidery to the mounting board. Pins are placed at the centres of sides, and embroidery is then gradually stretched into position until there is a border of pins completely around picture, about $\frac{1}{4}''$ apart. When satisfied that the design is even, drive pins into the cardboard edge with a hammer. If a pin does not go in straight, it should be removed and reinserted. The edges of the linen may be pasted down on the wrong side of the cardboard or the edges may be caught with long zigzag stitches. Embroidered pictures can be framed with glass over them, if desired.

TO MOUNT NEEDLEPOINT PICTURE: After canvas has been blocked, stretch it over heavy cardboard or plywood cut same size as worked portion of canvas. Use heavy cardboard for small pictures (12″ or less); for larger pictures and panels, use $\frac{1}{4}''$ plywood. If cardboard is used, hold canvas in place with pins pushed through canvas into edge of cardboard. If canvas is mounted on plywood, use carpet tacks. Push pins or tacks only part way into edge; check needlepoint to make sure rows of stitches are straight. Carefully hammer in pins or tacks the rest of the way. Using a large-eyed needle and heavy thread, lace loose edges of canvas over back of cardboard or plywood to hold taut; lace across width then length of picture.

Frame mounted picture as desired, without glass.

TO REFINISH OLD FRAMES: Here are a few hints for redoing frames, which you may find useful.

There are a number of easy ways to modernize or

Illustration shows how basting was used to outline the exact area of linen where it fits frame. Pins show how needlework has been stretched over cardboard following basting thread.

change the colour of frames. In oversize gold frames you will find that most of the very wide and elaborate ones are actually two or three frames, one inside the other. Place frame face down on a rug and remove the outer frame by pulling out with pliers the few small nails that hold it.

To glaze gold frames: You have seen gold frames coated with an off-white, cream or other soft tint. The gold shows through only at the high spots, giving a very modern and pleasing effect. It is the simplest thing in the world to give your own gold frames this "new look". Materials needed are: Small can of flat white paint. One or two tiny tubes of artists' oil colours. A small inexpensive varnish brush. A half pint of turpentine or paint thinner. A soft rag.

To tint with oil colours: Raw sienna will make a cream colour; raw umber makes a nice off-white; burnt sienna gives a dull pinkish cast. To paint, pour a little turpentine into a dish. Dip the varnish brush in the turpentine and brush lightly on a sheet of clean paper to remove dust and grease. Wipe lightly with a soft cloth. Stir flat white paint well and pour into dish. In a separate cup squeeze a small amount of oil colour and add a few drops of turpentine. Stir the colour with a knife until there are no lumps. Now add some colour to the white and stir it. Add the colour a little at a time until you get the depth of tint desired. With varnish brush apply a coat quickly to entire frame. Immediately start wiping the colour off the high spots with a cloth until the right amount of gold shows through. Do not rub hard. If colour does not come off easily, moisten the cloth with turpentine. If you wipe off too much on any spot, apply more paint with brush and wipe again. On flat surfaces wipe with long even strokes. Allow to dry overnight.

How to Design Needlepoint

Today, more and more women are interested in finding a medium of self-expression. Needlepoint is one way to fill this need. Once the basic stitches are mastered, the competent needlewoman is ready to take the further step of creating her own designs. Therefore, we offer some how-to suggestions on creating individual needlepoint designs. It is really quite a simple matter to design a piece of needlepoint to fit your personal requirements and taste. The satisfaction of "making your own" rather than executing a ready-made design is well worth the effort and time required.

WHERE TO FIND A DESIGN

Those who are talented in drawing will have no trouble creating an entirely original needlepoint design. Others may wish to obtain the aid of an artist friend, or the art teacher in a local school. However, even those who have no creative talent and wish to "do it themselves" may still obtain distinctive results by using the following suggestions.

1. Take your inspiration from something purely personal—a favourite picture in your home, your pet, a pictorial representation of your hobby, a sampler of daily activities, your coat of arms.

2. Work out a design inspired by your decor—repeat a motif taken from your wallpaper, or drapery fabric. Change the size or proportion to suit your needs and to fit the item you plan to make. You can enlarge a small design for a bold, contemporary effect, reduce a large one to repeat for all over pattern. Use the colours of your decor.

3. Research designs—look up and copy old designs from books on needlepoint in your library, or study actual pieces in museums. Use them as shown, or vary designs to suit your own taste. Usually illustrations have been reduced from the size of the original; perhaps your library or museum has a photostating service, so that you can get the design you wish to use blown up to full size. If not, for "How to Enlarge by Squares," see Index. Trace the design carefully and do the enlarging at home. (Note: When making a copy, remember not to use someone else's design for an item to be sold unless the design is in public domain.)

4. Adapt designs from other needlework. Cross-stitch designs are worked on squares, for example, and can be adapted easily to needlepoint.

CHOOSING YOUR MATERIALS

For delicate, traditional designs, small stitches are most suitable: simple, bold, contemporary designs should be worked in large stitches.

Petit point employs the smallest stitches, and is suited to small designs, detailed traditional designs and delicate effects, such as are used on evening bags and French boudoir chairs. Choose a fine canvas and fine yarn such as crewel wool.

Needlepoint is suited to upholstery, pictures, etc. Use a medium single or double thread canvas, and two strands of crewel wool, or one of tapestry yarn.

Gros point is suited to upholstery, as well as to pictures and pillows. Use medium large double thread canvas, one or two strands of tapestry yarn.

Quick point is especially suited to bold designs. Use a large mesh canvas and rug wool, or two or more strands of tapestry yarn. In using this for upholstery, care should be taken that when mounted on a chair or stool seat, it is not too bulky for inserting into the frame.

Note: Knitting worsted is not considered desirable for needlepoint, as it does not have enough twist, and may wear thin in working. However, it may be used in pictures, where there will be no wear.

PUTTING A DESIGN ON CANVAS

There are three ways of getting your design on the canvas. One is to make the design into a chart or graph, each square of which represents one stitch, with symbols to indicate the colours; you follow this chart in working the canvas. Another way is to work from a design with outlines filled in with colour. You draw the design outlines on your canvas and fill in the colours with embroidery. The easiest method for the needleworker to follow is to have the design painted on canvas, with various areas coloured to correspond exactly to the wools to be used.

1. How to Make a Chart or Graph

Draw the design on a piece of graph paper with the count the same as your canvas (i.e., 10-squares-to-the-inch paper represents 10-mesh-to-the-inch canvas); each square represents a stitch. On most graph papers you can fill in colour areas with water colours. If paper buckles, use coloured pencils.

Another method is to rule lines representing canvas threads over the design, scaled to exact size of finished piece. If necessary, enlarge or reduce design before ruling lines.

2. How to Mark Outline on Canvas

Place design, heavily outlined, under canvas; trace lines that show through; complete outline with India ink and a very fine brush, or with a felt-tipped marker. In using this method (particularly good for coarse canvas), paint curved lines as curves; do not attempt to indicate where individual stitches fall. Planning placement of stitches while working is interesting.

Outlines of design may also be perforated (see Index) at close intervals, placed over your canvas and stamped with a felt pad and stamping paste.

With small meshed canvas, you can transfer your design directly to the canvas. Pin canvas to a flat surface; establish a vertical and a horizontal centre as placement guides. Cover canvas with carbon paper; centre pattern over carbon, and trace around outline of design with a blunt point such as tip of a knitting needle. After transferring is completed, paper towels should be placed over outline and pressed with a hot iron to remove any excess carbon that might discolour yarn. Go over outlines with India ink.

HOW TO PAINT IN THE DESIGN

1. For a simple design with few colours, colour areas can be filled in with wax crayons. Fix colours by pressing canvas under paper towels with warm iron.

2. For complex designs, painting design on canvas with oil paints is not difficult. Use decorator oils (they are less expensive). Buy the following colours: white, lemon yellow, cadmium light, yellow ochre, vermilion, alizarin crimson, ultramarine blue, cobalt blue, cerulean blue, emerald green, veridian, Vandyke brown, burnt sienna, black. With these colours, desired shade can be mixed to match yarns.

Canvas to be painted is stretched tightly on a board over a piece of brown paper to absorb oil. Colours are mixed and then thinned to consistency of light cream with cleaning fluid (naphtha). This cuts oil and keeps colours from spreading; it makes paint dry quickly. Skill is required to learn how to mix exact consistency of paint so that it is not so thin it changes colour when applied and not so thick it clogs canvas.

Some colours, black, for instance, have a tendency to take a long time to dry. In this case, add a tiny bit of Japan drier to naphtha. Usually, oil paint thinned with naphtha alone will dry overnight.

Use soft, pointed brushes for painting. Japanese water-colour brushes are very good for this purpose; they hold quite a bit of paint, and have a good point. You need turpentine for washing brushes frequently.

CHOICE OF STITCHES

The stitch used has a great deal to do with the wearing quality of the embroidery. There are three familiar methods of working needlepoint: half cross-stitch, continental stitch and the diagonal method.

1. Half cross-stitch, practical for pictures or areas that receive little wear, works up quickly and saves yarn. This method barely covers canvas, and must be done carefully for good coverage on front; there is practically no yarn on back.

2. Continental stitch uses more yarn, covers canvas front and back. The work is more attractive, wearing quality is increased by slight padding on back.

3. The diagonal method is best for needlepoint that will receive the most wear, particularly chair seats or rugs. It uses the same amount of yarn as the continental stitch, covers the front of the canvas well, and also forms a durable web which reinforces the back of the canvas.

PROFESSIONAL TIPS

For a professionally finished piece, plan to leave a margin of bare canvas around work; embroidering more needlepoint than will show on the surface of the finished piece is a waste of yarn and time. The bare edge of the canvas is turned back on a sampler, turned under in upholstery, or covered with a frame for a picture. In deciding what size of canvas to buy, allow a 3″ margin to leave bare for blocking finished piece.

Wetting needlepoint for blocking softens glue sizing of the canvas. When piece dries, canvas resets and holds its shape unless it is unmounted, as in rugs, or subject to handling, as with handbags. For such pieces, it is advisable to stiffen the back of the work with glue while it is wet and fastened face down. Dry glue can be obtained at a hardware store. Mix one-half cup of dry glue with one-half cup of boiling water, then thin with three cups of cold water; mixture should be brushed on back of embroidery.

In making a bag or other item made of more than one piece, do not sew pieces together on a sewing machine. Trim unworked canvas margin to $\frac{1}{2}″$ or $1″$; turn margin to back and whip to embroidery; finish each piece as a separate section. Join pieces at the edges with a connecting row of needlepoint; or sew together by hand with a slipstitch and cover the joining with a twisted cord. When joining two pieces, match design stitch by stitch.

FINAL FINISH FOR WOOL EMBROIDERY

Pieces embroidered in wool yarns and needlepoint pieces often become quite fuzzy from working and handling. It is advisable to remove this fuzz to bring design outlines back into clear focus and give a clean, professional look to the embroidery. For this process, a long thin wax lighting taper (waxed wick) is used. Light the taper, and holding it just above the surface of the embroidery, move it rapidly back and forth, singeing the fuzz off the embroidery. Blow away the singed fuzz, or brush it lightly with a soft brush. This process may be repeated if necessary.

Aids to upholstering with needlepoint

French period chair, ideally upholstered with petit point.

Medium-weight chair, suitable for gros point.

Stool top fits into framework, not recommended for quick point.

Designs become bolder and simpler with large stitches and finer and more detailed with small stitches. The character of the design is thus in keeping with the stitch count of the needlepoint which in turn should harmonize with the character of the furniture it is to cover.

Petit point is ideal for very delicate furniture such as French chairs. Needlepoint and gros point are well suited to average weight chairs such as Chippendale and Queen Anne. Quick point goes well with bulky, unembellished contemporary furniture and some Provincial styles.

Technically, almost any chair can be upholstered with petit point and gros point. However, the bulkiness of quick point limits its uses slightly. It should not be recommended for upholstering chair seats or stool tops which fit down into a frame unless the stool or chair has been specially built to allow for the extra bulk. If a piece of needlepoint too bulky for such a chair is forced into its frame, the frame may split when sat upon. Examples of such chairs and stools are given below, and comment as to which weight of needlepoint should be used.

HOW TO MAKE A PATTERN OF AREA TO BE EMBROIDERED

The second bit of advice is to work only that area of the canvas which will show after the piece has been upholstered. It is a mistake to fill in the background to the edge of the canvas.

Important are the money and time saved by working only the necessary area; important to the upholsterer is ease in upholstering without extra bulk of worked canvas at mitreings and tucking-in places.

One must also remember when choosing a suitably-sized piece of needlepoint canvas that a 3″ margin for blocking and upholstering must extend around the embroidery.

You must be able to place the centre of the embroidered design motif ½″ in front of centre line of seat

Contemporary chair, with a removable seat, boxing, suitable for quick point.

Contemporary chair, loose cushions, best for quick point.

pattern to adjust visual balance of background area in perspective on chair.

In order to determine the exact area to be embroidered, a muslin pattern is made as follows:

On a square piece of muslin, a little larger than enough to cover the seat, mark a vertical and horizontal line at the centre with a soft pencil, using the thread of the muslin as a guide.

On the seat of the chair or stool, draw corresponding centre lines. Place muslin on chair seat along these lines. Beginning at centre of the seat and working towards edges on all four sides, place pins 3″ apart (Fig. 1). Continue pinning muslin at either side of pins at edges of seat, alternating from side to side to keep muslin from pulling out of shape. Slash muslin to fit around back legs and tuck it down in. Pin the corners to make mitres wherever necessary.

Using a soft pencil, mark all around the lower edge of the chair seat; mark around the legs, reaching down into tucked-in area; mark on both sides of all mitred corners; make a line to indicate top area of chair seat to be used later in placing design correctly on chair seat pattern.

With a tape measure, verify the muslin pattern against the length and width of the chair seat. The measurements of centre lines on the chair and the muslin should correspond exactly. Pin muslin down on a board, threads straight. You will find that despite great care, the shape of the muslin is slightly irregular. Being sure that all distances are the same, make a perfectly symmetrical version of pattern on brown paper, with horizontal and vertical lines corresponding to those on the muslin. Cut out on edge (Fig. 2).

Place paper pattern on the canvas on which a horizontal and vertical line has also been established through centre of needlepoint design. Horizontal line on paper should be placed ½″ behind horizontal line on canvas for proper placing of chair design as described above. Leave a 3″ margin all around for blocking (Fig. 3).

Pin the brown paper pattern to the canvas and mark the outline on the canvas with India ink or indelible marking pen. This will slightly enlarge the chair pattern and allow for possible work shrinkage. Save the brown paper pattern and use it later as a guide when blocking the embroidered needlepoint.

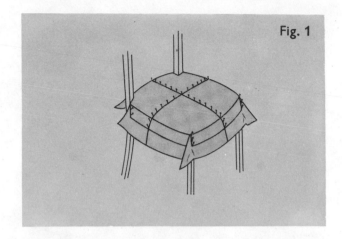

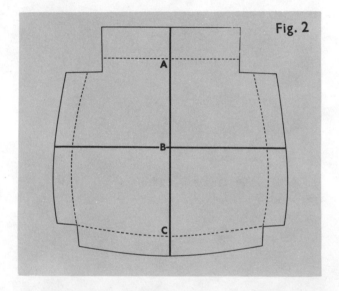

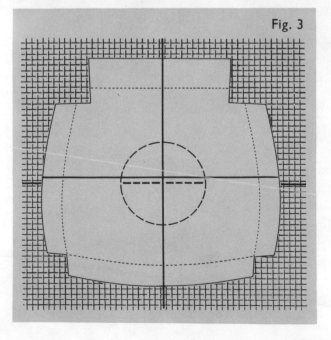

Illustration shows how to make muslin and brown paper patterns of area to be embroidered, and allowances for upholstering when outlining on canvas.

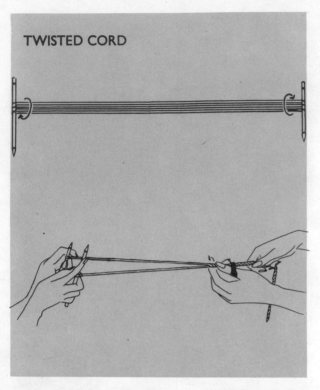

TWISTED CORD

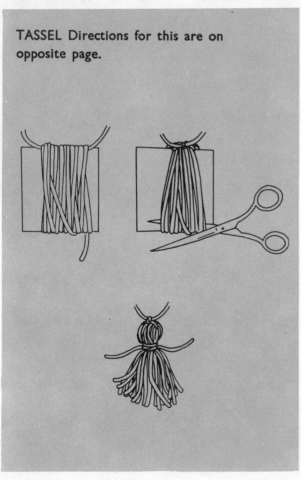

TASSEL Directions for this are on opposite page.

HOW TO MAKE A NEEDLEPOINT PILLOW

If a foam rubber form is used, the finished needlepoint should be exactly the size of the foam rubber. If a pillow form is used which is filled with kapok, feathers or similar material, the finished needlepoint should be about $\frac{1}{4}''$ smaller all around so that the pillow form will fit well into corners.

To make pillow with boxing strips, cut off canvas after blocking to within $\frac{3}{4}''$ of embroidery. Turn canvas back on edge of embroidery on pillow top and boxing strips and whip-stitch to hold in place. Join boxing pieces to top whipping them to top at right angles; whip corners together with matching wool. Prepare material for back of pillow in the same way as for top and whip to edge of three boxing strips. Insert pillow form. Whip fourth boxing strip to back of pillow. Cover joining at top and back with twisted cord. (To make, see below).

TO UPHOLSTER CUSHIONS FOR CHAIRS AND STOOLS

If unattached, use same method as for pillow.

TO UPHOLSTER CHAIRS WITH REMOVABLE SEATS

Remove seats. Using vertical and horizontal lines marked on canvas of embroidered needlepoint piece, place needlepoint in position on chair. Use the unworked canvas for tacking to the bottom of seat; tack centre front and centre back at edges, then tack centres of sides, working towards corners. Pull needlepoint in position, but not too tightly.

TO UPHOLSTER A CHAIR WHEN FABRIC IS ATTACHED TO FRAMEWORK OF CHAIR SEAT

Usually, when removing the old upholstery fabric of a chair or stool, it will be seen how upholstery was handled before, and the same method can be used. Needlepoint differs from fabric in that only the unworked canvas should be turned back in mitreing corners to avoid bulkiness.

Because a piece of needlepoint is too valuable for the average amateur upholsterer to handle, have this kind of furniture upholstered by a professional.

HOW TO MAKE A TWISTED CORD

(Method requires two people). Tie one end of yarn around a pencil. Loop yarn over centre of second pencil, then back to first, around first pencil and back to second, making as many strands between pencils as desired for thickness of cord. Length of yarn between pencils should be $2\frac{1}{2}$ times length of cord desired. Each person holds end of yarn just below pencil with one hand and twists pencil with other hand, keeping the yarn taut. When yarn begins to kink, catch it over a doorknob; keep yarn taut. One person now holds both pencils together while other grasps centre of yarn, sliding hand down yarn and releasing yarn at short intervals, letting it twist.

HOW TO MAKE TASSELS

See illustrations on opposite page. Wind yarn around a cardboard cut to size of tassel desired, winding it 25 to 40 times around, depending on thickness of yarn and plumpness of tassel required. Tie strands tightly together around top as shown, leaving at least 3″ ends on ties; clip other end of strands. Wrap a piece of yarn tightly around strands a few times about $\frac{1}{2}$″ or 1″ below top tie and knot. Trim ends.

HOW TO MAKE POMPONS

One method is to cut two cardboard disks the desired size of pompon; cut out $\frac{1}{4}$″ hole in centre of both disks. Thread needle with two strands of yarn. Place disks together; cover with yarn, working through holes. Slip scissors between disks; cut all strands at outside edge. Draw a strand of yarn down between disks and wind several times very tightly around yarn; knot, leaving ends for attaching pompon. Remove disks by cutting through to centre. Fluff out pompon and trim uneven ends.

HOW TO MAKE FRINGE

Cut strands of yarn double the length of fringe desired. Fold strands in half. Insert a crochet hook from front to back of edge where fringe is being made, pull through the folded end of yarn strand as shown in Fig. 1. Insert the two ends through loop as shown in Fig. 2 and pull ends to tighten fringe. Repeat across edge with each doubled strand, placing strands close together, or distance apart desired. For a fuller fringe, group a few strands together, and work as for one strand fringe.

The fringe may be knotted after all strands are in place along edge. To knot, separate the ends of two adjacent fringes (or divide grouped fringes in half); hold together the adjacent ends and knot 1″ or more below edge as shown in Fig. 3. Hold second end with one end of next fringe and knot together the same distance below edge as first knot. Continue across in this manner. A second row of knots may be made by separating the knotted ends again and knotting together ends from two adjacent fringes in same manner as for first row of knots.

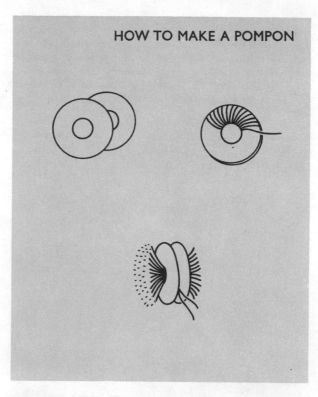

HOW TO MAKE A POMPON

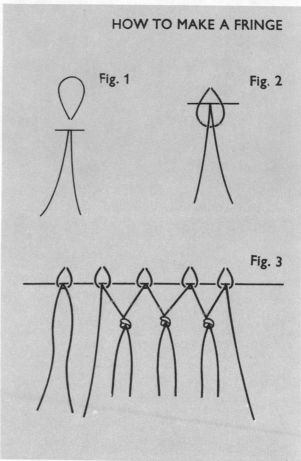

HOW TO MAKE A FRINGE

Fig. 1   Fig. 2

Fig. 3

Professional Blocking and Finishing for Knitted and Crocheted Fashions

Professional blocking and finishing often make the difference between a beautiful knitted or crocheted garment and a mediocre one. A perfectly knitted item can be ruined by slipshod finishing, while even an indifferently knitted one can be made smart by careful corrective blocking and finishing. Professional techniques are given here as a guide to the shop offering finishing service and to the individual knitter who has the proper equipment and wants to do her own blocking and finishing. The most important ingredients are time and patience, a knowledge of dressmaking techniques and a feel for the fabric. Do not hurry. Allow a day to block and finish a high-style sweater or jacket, two days or more for a suit or coat or dress which requires a lining.

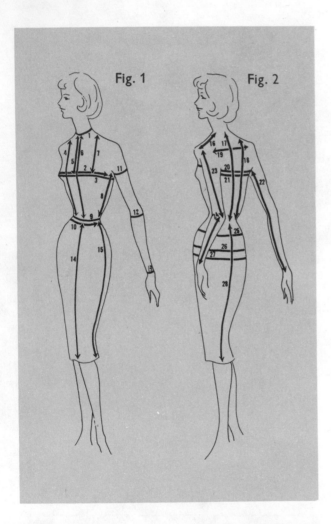

Fig. 1   Fig. 2

1 NECK 2 BUST FRONT	16 NECK TO END OF SHOULDER
3 BUST 4 SHOULDER TO WAIST	17 NECK TO WAIST
5 NECK TO BUSTLINE	18 SHOULDER TO WAIST
6 NECK TO WAIST	19 BACK—4″ BELOW NECK
7 SHOULDER TO BUSTLINE	20 CHEST 21 BUST BACK
8 UNDERARM TO WAIST	22 UNDERARM TO WRIST
9 WAIST	23 SHOULDER TO ELBOW
10 WAIST FRONT 11 UPPER ARM	24 ELBOW TO WRIST
12 LOWER ARM 13 WRIST	25 HIPS—3″ BELOW WAIST
13 WRIST 14 WAIST TO HEM—FRONT	26 HIPS—7″ BELOW WAIST
15 WAIST TO HEM—SIDE	27 HIPS—9″ BELOW WAIST
28 WAIST TO HEM—BACK	

BLOCKING

Blocking is the method used to set a knitted or crocheted piece to desired shape, size and texture. Cables, ribs and raised patterns can be blocked by steaming to shape but should not be pressed flat. Stocking stitch in most wools can be pressed flat. Every piece of a garment must be blocked individually before a seam or other joining is made.

Blocking Equipment:

1. Blocking table (40″ × 60″ or larger).
2. Heavy rug padding nailed to table and covered tightly with muslin sheet.
3. Rust-proof T pins or large bank pins.
4. Steam iron adjusted to maximum amount of steam.
5. Transparent pressing cloth.
6. Yardsticks and tape measures.
7. Tailors' chalk (white and coloured).
8. Pressing pads for bustline and darts.
9. Shaped sleeve pad.
10. Sleeve board for pressing seams and edges.
11. Heavy strings tied to large safety pins at each end to mark centre of garment, and as guide to a straight line between two points.

Determining Measurements for Blocking: As many actual body measurements as possible should be taken; see Figures 1 and 2 for complete body measurements. Any adjustment for the style and fit of the design can be taken into consideration in blocking. Check with the blocking measurements recommended in the instructions and with picture of the garment.

If blocking measurements for individual pieces are not given in the instructions, work them out, using the gauge as a guide. Note the number of stitches at bottom, hip, waist, underarm, shoulders, etc., and divide by the number of stitches per inch. Compare blocking measurements to body measurements (making same allowance for style, as shown in picture). Make notes of adjustments that should be made.

Preparing Garment for Blocking: Conceal all ends of yarn by running them diagonally through several stithes on wrong side, using a tapestry needle or crochet ook. If yarn is particularly heavy, split it and run each nd separately through adjoining stitches to avoid bulk.

If washing is necessary, wash pieces separately. mooth out flat on Turkish towels, adjusting pieces so at they measure no more than finished measurements esired. Some knits stretch larger when wet so must be ushed into slight puckers (which will disappear as bric dries). Drying process may be hastened by placing wels on window screens raised so that air can circulate nderneath.

Special Considerations: Certain pattern stitches such ribbing, cables, lacy stitches or other patterns which quire stretching in width for proper effect should be ocked one to two inches wider to allow for shrinking ack; if wool contains 50% or more nylon, allow two three inches for shrinking back.

Some yarns have considerable "hang" and measure uch longer held up than lying flat on the table. The ount of "hang" should be taken into consideration d the garment should be blocked shorter and wider. his is true of extra heavy or loosely knitted garments. ohair needs a little extra stretching in length only; herwise it may buckle.

For the full-busted figure it is best to have an under- m bustline dart which can be sewn in when fabric is t bulky. Allowance must be made by stretching the ont longer at the sides to make room for dart; Figure 3. fabric is to be steamed, rather than pressed flat, dart owance can be accomplished by inserting a pad from e seam towards centre front, before seaming, to in- ease length at side.

Plan Seams: Consider what type of seam will be most itable. In most garments a running backstitch made th Coats Satinised sewing thread or fine yarn is best d will need an allowance of only one stitch from edge. machine zigzag stitch is to be used, allow $\frac{3}{8}''$ for ams. If fabric calls for overcast or woven seams, it is t necessary to make any allowances. Any jogs caused increases, bind-offs, or other shaping can be evened t in blocking and taken in in seams.

Basic Pattern: It is helpful to have a McCall's Basic y-On Pattern (McCall's Try-On Pattern 100, Misses' d Junior Sizes, and Pattern B-200, Half-Sizes, are ailable at pattern counters) to use as a blocking guide proper shaping of a skirt panel, cap of set-in sleeve, ape of basic collar and neckline, etc. Be sure to consi- seam allowances and darts in pattern. This pattern also useful for linings. Darts in basic pattern may be ned in and pads used for shaping the knitted fabric cordingly; or if more suitable for fabric to be blocked t, leave basic pattern as it is, and after blocking, shrink extra width allowed for darts.

Pinning: After writing down all measurements to be lowed in blocking, pin one section at a time on cking table, wrong side up (except ribbons). Fol- wing measurements, place pins in edge of section as se as necessary to obtain a perfectly even edge, never re than $\frac{1}{2}''$ apart; place into padding in opposite ection from fabric "stretch"; Figure 4.

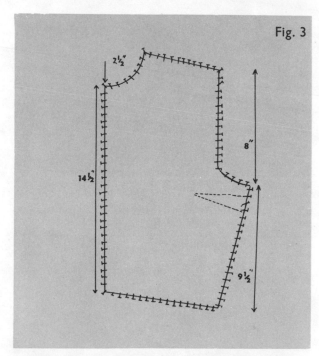

Side blocked $9\frac{1}{2}''$ is $8\frac{1}{2}''$ with $\frac{1}{2}''$ dart sewn in.

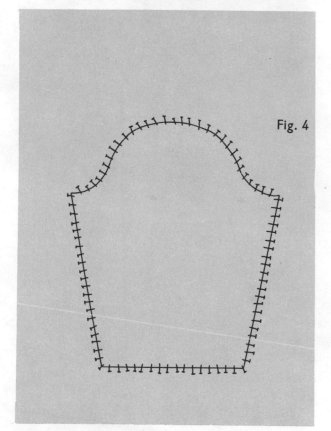

Placing of pins for blocking sleeve.

255

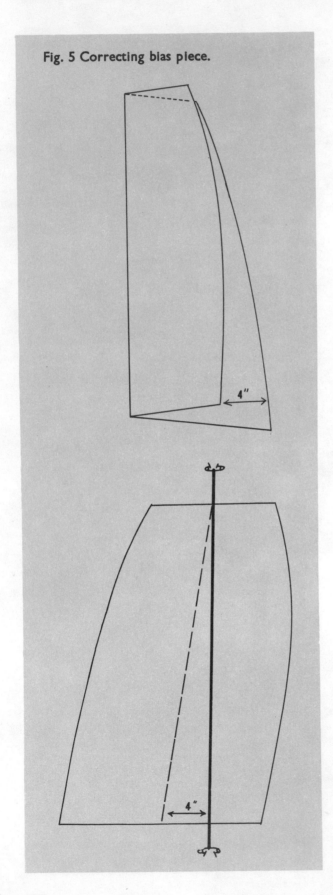

Fig. 5 Correcting bias piece.

Pressing: There are two methods of pressing knitte and crocheted pieces: flat pressing and steampressin. Consider the texture desired before touching iron t fabric. Some wools, such as mohair, should never I pressed flat as they would lose life and texture. If a so fluffy appearance is desirable, or if pattern stitch is ar type of raised stitch, it should not be pressed flat. If : doubt, try pressing a small piece flat in an inconspicuo section; then try another section steamed without pre sure and compare. Some materials, such as ribbon, ca be pressed flat and afterwards steamed up slight! before unpinning to obtain an attractive texture. there are cables separated by wide sections of pla knitting, you may wish to use a combination of tv techniques, pressing only plain section flat.

For steaming technique, support weight of iron your hand, hold as close as possible to fabric witho touching it and move slowly over entire pinned piec making certain that steam penetrates fabric. If yarn extra heavy, it may be necessary to use a spray iron a wet pressing cloth to provide extra steam.

To press sections flat, place organdie pressing cloth top of pinned piece and lower iron so that weight res on fabric. Raise and lower again over entire section; not use a back-and-forth ironing motion. With t transparent pressing cloth it is possible to see whe flat sections begin and end.

Leave pieces pinned to table until entirely dry. Dryi can be hastened by the use of a small electric fan hand dryer. If a piece has a duplicate, leave guide pi in the blocking table at intervals around the garme shape so that you have an outline for shaping the dup cate piece.

Wet Blocking: This may be desirable if the stitch us makes the finished pieces go strongly bias. Also, w blocking may be used for articles which have be washed. Wet or wash article thoroughly, squeeze o and roll in a Turkish towel, lay the individual pieces blocking table and pin to measurements using rustpro pins. Leave until thoroughly dry.

Bias Items: Some wools will work up straight wh knitted in garter stitch or pattern stitches with no pu ing, but will go strongly bias when knitted in stocki stitch. This may happen with some pattern stitches a some knitters, regardless of the wool used. Wet blocki will solve this problem, or if time and space do r permit, item can be straightened with steam blockir First mark centre stitch of item, then measure exac how much the bias amounts to and block it the sa amount in the opposite direction. Example: If the ite hangs 4" bias to the right, pin and block it 4" to the le and the blocked piece will hang straight; Figure 5.

THE CARE OF KNITTED GARMENTS

One question that is constantly asked by knitters "Ought I to have a knitted garment washed or c cleaned?" Unless you have used a yarn that definite specifies that the garment made in it should be c cleaned, washing is the answer every time.

This gives rise to the second question "Ought I to v

soap flakes or detergents?" You can use either, but you will find that if you live in a hard water area, detergents, providing they are recommended for wool or synthetic fibres, are easier to use. In soft water areas either soap flakes or detergents can be used quite satisfactorily. Certain yarns purchased to-day can be washed in home washing machines, but garments made in wool should always be hand-washed.

METHOD OF HAND-WASHING KNITTED GARMENTS

First of all mix your soap flakes or detergent in water hot enough to dip your hands in with complete comfort. When the solution is ready, place the knitted garment in the solution, making sure it is completely covered and leave it standing in the solution for three or four minutes. Leaving it standing in this way loosens the soiling and makes the washing operation itself easier in every way.

After the garment has stood for a few minutes, hand wash it by gently squeezing the garment, this will ease all the dirt out of it.

When the garment is completely clean rinse it thoroughly in water at approximately the same temperature it was washed in. Whether you use soap flakes or a detergent rinsing is essential. When the garment has been thoroughly rinsed remove it from the water, squeezing out as much of the surplus moisture as possible. Run the garment through a wringer and it will then be ready to dry.

The ideal method of drying garments is to lay them flat if possible. You can buy drying racks that can be placed on top of the bath.

If you cannot dry the garment flat, hang it lengthways over a clothes line or rack. Do not let the sleeves dangle as this will cause them to stretch. Lift the sleeves up and hang them over the line or rack again.

When the garment is almost dry take it down, turn it inside out, re-block it on your ironing sheet and lightly press under a dry cloth.

In storing woollen garments it is advisable to wrap them in a sheet of paper, placing one or two moth balls in the cupboard or drawer where they are stored.

There is one important point to remember if you are drying garments in the open air and that is to avoid drying them in direct sunlight. This is particularly applicable to white garments that are much better dried indoors than in the open air. Sunlight has a tendency to cause the whiteness to deteriorate, turning it in time to a creamy-yellow colour. It is not necessary to remove small buttons from knitted garments when they are washed, providing care is taken to see that the buttons are flat when running the damp garment through the wringer. If, however, the garment has large buttons, or buckles, or metal trimmings it is advisable to remove these before washing, sewing them on again after the garment has been re-blocked and pressed.

ASSEMBLY

Many dressmaking techniques are used in assembling knitted garments and the couturier types require a good knowledge of dressmaking techniques for a successful result. In assembling knitted garments there are no helpful notches to match as in dressmaking patterns. Everything has to be measured and marked with pins or chalk to take the place of notches. Careful and precise blocking will show its value here. Some garments have definite ribs or patterns that can be matched. Plain stitches must be measured and marked at intervals and the markings matched.

It is desirable to have a form with collapsible shoulders for fitting garments. A store would need several, in different sizes.

Preliminary Try-On: Baste pieces together with contrasting thread, taking in darts and seam allowances. Try garment on form. If you find something wrong other than seam adjustments, you can shrink or stretch for

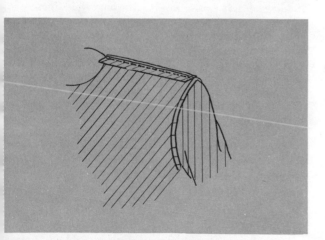

Fig. 6 Staying stitch for a shoulder seam.

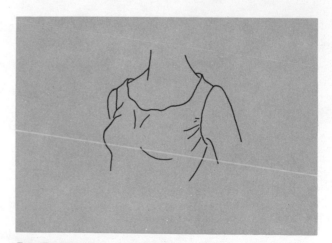

Fig. 7 Neckline is too big. Solution: Slip stitch, and adjust the fullness. Hold with the stitching. Armhole is too small. Solution: Release crocheted shrink edge, pin out and stretch armhole.

Fig. 8 Meshing crocheted box stitch patterns together: Join zigzag edges, sew back and forth holding pieces right side up.

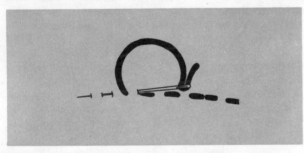

Fig. 9 Running Backstitch.

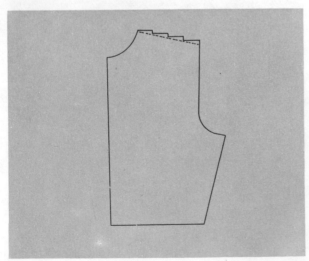

Fig. 10 Sewing shoulder seam to take in jogs of bind-offs.

desired fit. If it is necessary to stretch, the part to be stretched should be pinned to desired measurement and steam applied to just that portion. If shrinking is necessary, pin to desired measurement and form small puckers which will disappear with steam applied and a little coaxing with the fingers. The wide part of the sleeve board is useful for small adjustments which can be done without removing bastings. If garment fits form, sew the main seams. It is now ready for fitting. (If garment is to be lined, sew main seams of lining and try on at same fitting.)

Common Fitting Problems: Shoulder seams that sag can be held by a running backstitch of yarn through the seam, which is left in garment; Figure 6. Necklines can be adjusted and held by slip stitching with yarn; Figure 7

If fronts of jacket or coat hang away from each other, front edge is too long and should be shortened by a staying thread as described for shoulders and shrinking; or side seam is too tight and should be stretched. If front edges hang forward and overlap more at bottom than they should, front edges are too short and are drawing (common if edges are crocheted); or side seams are too loose. Solution: Stretch front edge if it has any curve, or restitch side seams more firmly.

If wide square neckline gapes or sags in front and slides on shoulders, take more seam allowance from shoulder neck edge to nothing more at shoulder tip. Sew $1\frac{1}{2}''$ wide folded piece of nylon tulle along square of neckline to hold it to desired shape. Also check bustline fit of garment, for if it is stretching through bustline, neckline will be affected.

If straight skirt ripples or flares at bottom, hips are too tight. It is best to pin zipper in place while garment is being tried on to prevent buckling of zipper. Mark positions of buttons and buttonholes, if they are to be made later.

If grosgrain or nylon tulle facings are to be applied to front edges or neckline, cut and pin them in place during try-on. Mark waistline if it is fitted and pin seam binding or soft elastic in place to hold waistline.

If it is necessary to cut fabric for major adjustments mark cutting line with chalk or basting and zigzag stitch on sewing machine $\frac{1}{4}''$ inside marked line (adjust size of zigzag stitch to fabric). Or sew by hand, being careful to catch every stitch. Then cut fabric. Raw edge can be crocheted if yarn is not too heavy, or overcast by hand. If garment is too long, excess can be removed by pulling a thread at desired length and binding off the open stitches with crochet hook in same tension as knitting.

Seams: Seams should be as nearly invisible as possible and, above all, straight and neat. They must be firm enough to hold, yet elastic enough to give with the fabric, having the same tension and resilience as the knitting. All patterns, stripes, tops of ribbed bands, coloured borders, etc., must be matched carefully. Seams may be sewn in various ways depending on type of knitted or crocheted fabric and stitch. Ribbons, unless edge patterns are to be meshed together as in Figure 8, can be sewn by machine. A zigzag stitch with Coats Satinised sewing cotton is best. Test for resilience after sewing a few stitches. A zigzag stitch will give with the fabric while a straight stitch is apt to break. Certain firm fabrics knitted of wool or other yarns also take to this machine stitching.

Hand-Sewn Seams: In every case sleeves should be set in and collars sewn on by hand. Hand sewing should be a running backstitch, Figure 9, taking in seam allowance planned, usually 1 stitch (2 stitches if finely knit). Sewing with wool makes a bulky seam which is hard to take out, if necessary, without cutting the wrong strand. However, if wool is desired, use very fine matching wool or split the original wool. Seams may also be woven or meshed when called for in a pattern. Be careful to take in bound-off stitches in seams; Figure 10.

Weaving Seams: (a) Lengthwise Woven Seam. Thread needle with matching wool. Lay the two pieces face up on a flat surface, edges meeting. Take a vertical stitch through one edge, then a vertical stitch through the other edge.

When wool is drawn sufficiently tight it will make a running stitch seam and each stitch will meet its neighbour in the proper order; Figure 11.

(b) Crosswise Woven Seam: Thread needle with matching yarn. Lay the two edges face up on a flat surface. Starting at right-hand side, take a small stitch through both edges; then insert needle into first stitch and up through next stitch on one edge, down through second stitch and up through next stitch on other edge. Working first in one edge and then the other, insert needle into last stitch in and bring it up through next stitch. Continue across in this manner; Figure 12.

Setting in Sleeves and Attaching Collars: Sleeves cannot be woven into place. Because the set of a sleeve is so important, it is best to baste it in place and try on before sewing in by hand.

It is not enough to match underarm seams; you must find the centre of sleeve cap and pin to shoulder seam. Then, starting at underarm, pin each side fitting sleeve carefully into armhole and ease in any slight fullness through top of sleeve cap; Figure 13. If there is too much fullness to be eased in, check cap measurements and armhole length with basic pattern and reshape if necessary. A small amount extra may be taken in when sewing sleeve in place without resorting to cutting the fabric.

Find centre back of collar and neck and pin together Pin front edges of collar in position; pin carefully and evenly between the pins placed at centre and front edges; Figure 14.

If collar is double, or faced with tulle, under-collar must be smaller to allow for turndown. This also applies to lapels for proper "roll".

Join the two collars at outer edges by sewing right sides together closely along edge (if fabric is not bulky) or by single crocheting, slip stitching or overcasting along stitches at edges through both thicknesses. Sew upper collar to neck edge, taking in small seam or overcasting edge stitches together, then roll collar over your hand and pin under-collar so that it covers seam and has proper roll without bulk underneath. Sew under-collar in place.

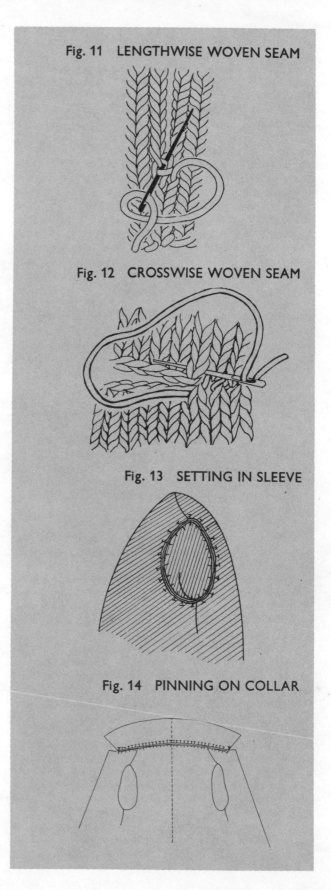

Fig. 11   LENGTHWISE WOVEN SEAM

Fig. 12   CROSSWISE WOVEN SEAM

Fig. 13   SETTING IN SLEEVE

Fig. 14   PINNING ON COLLAR

Finishing

Hems: If garment is to have a hem at bottom or on sleeves, these can be picked up before or after main seams are in and facings turned. Use a size smaller needle than used in garment and work in stocking stitch. With wrong side facing you, pick up and knit through the whole stitch at edge; pick up to within one stitch of side edges (seam allowance) and within one stitch of facing when turned.

If garment has cables starting at hemline, it is necessary to pick up hems in this way, picking up fewer stitches across cables so that hem will not buckle. This is also true of widely ribbed garments, if they need hems. If garment is finely ribbed at bottom or has a nonroll border, it does not need a hem. Another method used for hems when garment is clumsy to handle is to hem separately and single crochet, overcast or slip stitch to bottom edge of garment. Ribbing on bottom edges and cuffs should be flat seamed or woven together so that ribbing can be turned up without showing a "wrong side" seam.

Interfacing: Sometimes it is desirable to interface a collar with nylon tulle or Vilene. Cut interfacing to fit under-collar and catch stitch to entire under-collar before joining to upper collar; Figure 15. Interfacing should also be used along front edges of garments, especially tailored jackets and coats. Pin to piece to be interfaced and cut to fit.

Facing: Most facings are knitted but nylon tulle is good to use as a facing. It provides a base for sewing buttonholes, as well as a crisp front edge. Patch pockets will not sag if they are catch stitched throughout to nylon tulle. A strip of tulle will do wonders for a low neckline, the edges of slot pockets, or for cuffs. It is easy to work with, does not ravel, and is not as scratchy as coarse net.

If garment is too bulky for a knitted facing, French belting (grosgrain) can be used. This has a picot edge and can be steamed and stretched into a curve.

To face front edges of a cardigan with ribbon, wet and press ribbon before sewing to garment to preshrink it, or use nylon ribbon. Use matching grosgrain ribbon slightly narrower than front bands. If there are no front bands, use ribbon 1″ wide. Cut ribbon 1″ longer than edge to be faced. Place ribbon on wrong side of garment just inside edge; turn under top and bottom edges of ribbon; pin to neck and bottom edges of cardigan. Baste ribbon in place; whip edges of ribbon to cardigan with matching sewing thread. If cardigan does not have front band the inner edge of ribbon can be left free. Slash ribbon under buttonholes. Buttonhole-stitch or overcast around slashes. Or, if desired, hem edges of slashes around the buttonholes.

Buttonholes: Although buttonholes are usually knitted in, a neater buttonhole can be made by cutting and pulling a strand out for the required number of stitches; Figure 16. Either single crochet or slip stitch with yarn through the open stitches on both sides of buttonhole. This method is especially good for bulky yarns: split the yarn to be used for crocheting the open stitches.

If garment has a facing, the buttonhole must be opened in facing as well and matched to that on outside.

Except in the case of mohair or extremely bulky yarns, both buttonholes can be crocheted at the same time by inserting hook through loop of outside and inside stitches and working as one. In the above-mentioned yarns, or when facing is of a different colour than garment, work each buttonhole separately and tack loosely together with thread. Make long shanks when sewing the buttons on these bulkies.

Outlined buttonholes can be made by using a contrasting yarn to single crochet or slip stitch the buttonhole. Soutache can be used for slip stitching to give a trimmed or bound effect. If it would be best to have a vertical rather than a horizontal buttonhole, mark position and baste a piece of seam binding or narrow grosgrain ribbon slightly longer than buttonhole to wrong side of garment. Machine-stitch buttonhole using the zigzag machine. Cut with razor blade between lines of stitching and through seam binding. Work buttonhole stitch around opening with split yarn or buttonhole twist.

Buttons: Select attractive buttons that are light in weight, shank type for bulky yarns, sew-through type for fine yarns. Buttons can be made from plastic rings or button moulds. Directions for these are given under Crocheted Trimmings (see Index).

Belts: A self-belt should always have a buckle to avoid a homemade look. Covered rings can be used as buckles. If rings are not used, buckles of several sizes can be purchased and crocheted over with same yarn or ribbon used in belt. If knitted belt has a neat edge, overcast grosgrain to the wrong side along edges. If belt is wide, catchstitch grosgrain back and forth, in a wide zigzag pattern, through centre to hold firm and prevent rolling. Insert a strip of interfacing in extra wide belts. If edges of belt require smoothing, single crochet or slip stitch around entire belt before facing.

Skirt Tops: Tailored skirts are best fitted to waist and closed with a placket zipper. In yarn garments, single crochet around zipper opening before sewing in zipper. Ease fabric into zipper and sew by hand with small running backstitch. If skirt has knitted waistband, face with grosgrain, overlap at left side and fasten with snaps. If there is no waistband, sew 1½″ wide grosgrain, cut to waist measure, on inside of skirt. If a skirt has no zipper, a crocheted elastic edge is neater than the "beading" type. Use round millinery elastic with yarn. Work one round of single crochet on top of skirt, making sure skirt will go over shoulders. On next round, hold elastic along edge of skirt and single crochet over it. Next round, single crochet without elastic, and following round single crochet over elastic. Alternate rounds in this manner, having three or four with elastic.

Finishing Edges: In finishing edges by crocheting, do not use more than one row of single crochet plus one row of slip stitch, from wrong side, if required. Some bulky yarns require only a row of slip stitch done loosely from wrong side, while some garments look best with one row of single crochet done from right side. Other patterns (usually in two colours) require one row of slip stitch from the right side, plus one row of single crochet, also from right side. It is necessary to have the proper tension in all crocheting done along edges. There should be fewer single crochet stitches to the inch than knitted stitches; do not work into every stitch or row.

To turn an outside corner, work two or three stitches into corner stitch. To turn an inside corner, decrease two stitches by pulling through loops in corner, and one stitch each side of corner, and drawing yarn through all loops on hook tightly. This decrease should also be done at the end of any opening such as a zipper placket.

Pressing Seams: Give seams final pressing, using sleeve board and point of iron, taking care not to shrink or stretch seams.

Linings: It is desirable to have a lining in most coats, and in some jackets. Mohair in particular should be lined. Lightweight taffeta lining material is easy to work with and comes in a wide range of colours. Jap silk or sheath lining is recommended for ribbon sheath dresses and skirts. For detailed directions on lining a coat, see next page

In lining sheath dresses, the basic blocking pattern can be used to cut lining. Leave ample seam allowance, and slight ease at back of neck. Stitch main seams. Try dress on inside out wih lining on top. Pin along main seams and around neckline, turning in edges of lining at neckline and armholes or sleeve edges. Turn edges of lining

at zipper opening, and pin along zipper tape. Pin at waistline. Sew lining to dress at waistline, neck, and sleeve edges. Do not attach lining at lower seams of skirt.

Mounting on Tulle: Some ribbon dresses, especially those with full skirts, made of silk organdie ribbon in lacy patterns, are greatly enhanced by mounting entire dress on tulle, a painstaking process. Cut tulle to basic bodice pattern. Use dress as pattern for skirt panels, allowing $\frac{1}{2}''$ for overlap. Do not sew seams. Try on dress inside out. Pin tulle sections to dress while on, pinning in darts. Pin tulle to dress throughout bodice in diagonal crossbar design, overlapping tulle $\frac{1}{2}''$ at side seams and turning in $\frac{1}{2}''$ at zipper opening. Pin sections of tulle to skirt, overlapping $\frac{1}{2}''$ at waistline and wherever panels meet. Pin darts at waist for smooth fit. Turn $\frac{1}{2}''$ under and pin along zipper opening. Now pin tulle to entire skirt in diagonal crossbar design. Turn small hem under and pin to bottom of skirt.

Remove dress carefully. Catch stitch tulle to dress following pin lines, conforming as closely as possible to pattern stitch. Take only tiny catch stitches in dress; run thread between dress and lining for about $\frac{1}{2}''$, then catch stitch to lining with medium-size stitch. Hem around neckline, bottom edge, and zipper. Close overlapped sections of tulle with running backstitch.

Catch stitching interfacing to collar: cut interfacing to fit under–collar, join with catch stitch to entire under–collar before joining to upper–collar.

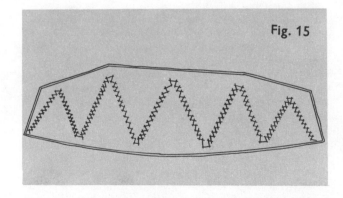

Fig. 15

Cutting strand for buttonhole: although buttonholes are normally knitted in, a neater buttonhole can be made by cutting and pulling a strand out for the required number of stitches.

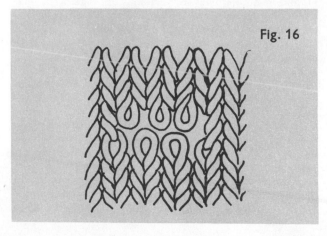

Fig. 16

Lining a handknitted or crocheted coat

The technique of lining a hand knitted or crocheted coat is more involved than that of lining a cloth coat, and requires considerably more work—nearly all by hand. One should allow two to three days to finish and line the coat. However, since there is so much to be gained in appearance, fit, and wear by lining the coat, it is well worth the extra work.

Lining Materials: Choose a lining material with "body" and slight stiffness. Taffeta, satin, Milium satin, or lightweight brocade of either rayon or silk are all suitable; choice depends on style of coat. Use lightweight Vilene for interfacing and collars.

Preparing Coat for Lining: The first step before blocking is to close and sew together any buttonholes; then judge the amount of "hang" of the pieces. Test for hang as follows: Lay back of coat smoothly on table and measure the length from neck to hem. Now fold in half lengthwise, armholes and shoulder seams together. Hold piece at back of neck and measure along fold while hanging in mid-air. The difference in measurement is the amount of "natural hang" before blocking. If there is a great amount of hang, the back and fronts of the coat should be blocked shorter and wider than the desired finished measurement. Width is lost to some extent, particularly at upper half of coat, as a result of hang in heavy or loosely worked pieces. One must consider also that the coat has to hang unsupported from the shoulders, unless it is to be tightly belted at the waist.

Blocking and Finishing: Block pieces following instruction on preceding pages. After the pieces have been blocked, make paper tracings of all pieces.

Sew shoulder seams, side seams, sleeve seams, and set sleeves in place. Always use matching thread and small, loose backstitches unless otherwise specified. Now hang coat on a dressmaker's form, pinning to form at neck and pinning and holding in slightly across shoulders to prevent weight of sleeves from stretching shoulder line and neck. Let hang at least over night.

After coat has hung overnight, check length and see that the front edges hang in a straight line following pattern stitch used. Make any necessary adjustments. If length is correct and coat has a separate hem, pin hem around bottom of coat with wrong sides together, being careful not to draw in or buckle bottom of coat. It is best to do this while garment is on the form. Allow for any facings at front of coat. Overcast hem in place with matching thread; sew upper edge loosely in place.

If coat has hung to a longer length than desired, mark length with pins. If coat is knitted, pull a strand of yarn at nearest place consistent with the pattern stitch used and cut, thus removing the excess length. With crochet hook and yarn, slip-stitch through the open stitches from the wrong side, being careful not to work too tightly. Pin and overcast the separate hem in place. If coat is crocheted, turn up excess and use for hem. If coat needs to be shortened and has a knitted-on hem, open stitches at desired length and also at the "turning row"

of hem to remove excess length. With wrong sides together, pin hem in place, having open stitches at bottom. With inside of coat facing, slip-stitch together with crochet hook and yarn through two open stitches (hem and coat edge), being careful to work with loose tension. Sew upper edge of hem loosely in place with matching thread.

Cutting: Cut out lining so that it will correspond to measurements of coat while it is hanging on form. Allow $1\frac{1}{2}''$ extra width for a $\frac{3}{4}''$ pleat at back of neck and $1''$ on each shoulder of back for $\frac{1}{2}''$ darts. If garment has set-in or dolman sleeves, allow $2\frac{1}{2}''$ for a $1\frac{1}{4}''$ dart on each shoulder of front; if raglan sleeves, allow $2''$ for $1''$ dart on each shoulder of front. Allow $\frac{1}{2}''$ extra length in sleeves for "elbow room". Allow $\frac{1}{2}''$ extension of lining on all edges, plus $3''$ at bottom edge for hem.

Sewing: Sew darts on shoulders: taper darts on back to nothing about $4''$ down; taper darts on set-in or dolman-sleeved coat fronts to nothing about $7''$ down; taper darts on raglan-sleeved coat fronts to nothing about $5''$ down. Sew seams of lining and press. Always press seams and joinings as in dressmaking. Press all knitted facings and hems which will not show on right side of coat as flat as possible before sewing to coat, to avoid undesirable bulk.

Interfacings: Cut neck interfacing from Vilene to conform to neck of coat. If coat is made of ribbon and yarn, use Vilene interfacing $3''$ wide at front edges as well.

Place coat on form wrong side out. Pin interfacing carefully in place and catch-stitch throughout in zigzag pattern.

Pinning Lining in Place: Remove coat and place lining on form wrong side out. Place coat right side out over lining. Pin coat to lining, starting at centre back of neck and pinning towards shoulders and along shoulder seam, allowing $\frac{1}{2}''$ to extend at neck edge and easing coat slightly across shoulder span for graceful drape. Pin side seam of lining to side seam of coat near underarm. Allowing $\frac{1}{2}''$ of lining to extend, pin lining to coat along both front edges while it is still hanging on form.

Place a few pins along upper half of armhole and along the shoulder darts. (If coat has a raglan sleeve, pins should be placed along seam line.) Tack lightly to lining where pinned. Baste $\frac{1}{4}''$ horizontal pleat in sleeve lining just below elbow (to be released later for ease). Pin lining to sleeve edge, allowing $\frac{1}{2}''$ to extend at bottom of sleeve.

Sew invisibly from right side along all pinned edges, $\frac{1}{4}''$ from edge of coat.

Lining must extend into and turn with all edges—except for bottom hem—for a tailored and neat look. Pin and sew bottom hem of lining in place.

Make holding bars for hem by crocheting a chain $1\frac{1}{2}''$ long with yarn. Slip stitch to seam of coat near bottom; sew other end to inside seam of lining.

Sleeves: If sleeves have hems, trim lining just inside edge of sleeves. Sew invisibly along turn of hem. Turn and press up. Sew upper edge in place, sewing through lining to catch outside of coat sleeve lightly; then release the basted "ease pleat."

If sleeves have no hems, turn edge of lining to inside (between lining and coat) and hem in place just inside edge of sleeve; lightly sew lining to sleeve at 1″ above, so that "elbow ease pleat", when released, will not cause lining to show at bottom.

Facings: If coat has separate facings, pin to front of coat, right sides together, while on form. Sew along front edges, taking in a small amount consistent with pattern stitch. Press seam open. Turn facings to inside. Press again. With inside of coat facing you, sew lightly along turned edge ¼″ to ½″ in from edge, taking small stitches and catching outside of coat invisibly. Take care not to draw front edge. Pin and sew inside edge of facings through lining and invisibly to front of coat.

If facings are knitted in one with front of coat, mark place where facings will turn and sew lining to coat along this line. Press lightly, trim edge of lining, and sew inside edge of facings in place in same way as separate facings. There will be a double thickness of lining inside facings.

If coat has no facings at all, trim extending edge of lining. Turn ½″ on edge of coat (more, if called for by pattern) after sewing along line of prospective turn in order to hold lining inside fold for sharp edge. Pin and sew turned edge in place, catching outside of coat invisibly.

If coat is collarless, or has a set-away collar, or stand-up band set away from neck edge, finish neck by turning extending edge of lining to inside; then turn ¼″ of neck edge to inside (over lining) and sew. If knitted or crocheted neck facing is provided, pin in place, then sew so that it joins turned edge of neck. Sew other edge lightly in place, catching through lining to interfacing.

Collars: If coat has a collar, face with Vilene, catch-stitching throughout in zigzag pattern. Cut lining, allowing ½″ to turn to inside at all edges, and sew to collar on three sides leaving neck edge open, except where knitted under-collar is provided. In this case, Vilene is catch-stitched to under-collar before sewing together with upper-collar. Always fold or roll collar in desired position (this applies also to lapels) before sewing under-collar or collar lining in place (under part will need to be smaller, to avoid buckling collar). Pin and sew upper part of collar to neck edge of coat, working from inside of coat. Press seam. Fold collar in position and sew under-collar or collar lining in place, covering seam. Catch-stitch invisibly through all thicknesses, 1″ from outside edges of collar, using zigzag pattern.

Helpful Suggestions Regarding Collars: Stand-up band collars, although worked straight, should be blocked longer at lower edge and held in slightly at upper edge in order to stand straight up when sewn to coat. These collars are usually set farthest away at shoulder seams. Set-away collars are sewn at neck edge of front, slightly down at back of neck, and farthest away at shoulder seams. Collar is completely finished before attaching to coat. Shawl colllars must be blocked considerably longer at the outside edge than at the neck edge, to prevent front of coat from pulling up. Stretch collar and under-collar at outside edge and ease at back edge. Notched collars should be woven to lapels with yarn, because edges seamed in the conventional way tend to be bulky.

Patch Pockets and Belts: If edges of pockets would not look well showing, a small amount can be turned to inside after lining. Cut Vilene to fit, and catchstitch in place throughout. Cut lining material extending ½″ at edges. Turn $1/2$″ of lining to inside and sew along edge (or turn 1 row or 1 stitch to inside for better appearance). Try on coat. Pin patch pockets in place, pinning through to lining. If coat has a back belt, interline and line it as for pockets; pin it in place at becoming position. After checking to see that lining is smooth underneath pockets, sew pockets in place through to lining from right side. This supports pockets and prevents sag. Run invisible stitches ½″ from edges of belt so that lining cannot show from right side. Separate cuffs are also handled this way.

Buttonholes: If buttonholes have been knitted or crocheted in, release basting used to close buttonholes. With crochet hook and yarn, work 1 row of slip stitch around buttonhole; sew buttonhole together at ends for neat corners. Slit lining material and turn under ⅛″ around buttonhole; sew in place, overcasting to buttonhole. If coat has a facing and has double buttonholes, finish each buttonhole separately with slip stitch. Slit lining and sew double buttonhole together, catching the lining material between for support. When sewing buttons in place, leave enough shank so that buttons do not dimple front of coat.

Glossary

Throughout this book, many stitches are taught and many needlework terms are explained in the section where they occur. In order to round out our information, we are adding seventeen stitches and giving a glossary of needlework terms, techniques, and materials which have not been fully explained elsewhere. If you are looking for any information not given here, consult the index.

---

afghan A knitted or crocheted coverlet.

afghan crochet A form of crochet made with a special afghan hook which has a long shaft of uniform thickness. A full row of stitches is worked on to the hook, then the stitches are worked off.

appliqué A form of embroidery. Material of one kind or colour is sewn to a background; stitching is usually of secondary importance. Sewn-on design can consist of cut-out design motifs, coloured shapes to form a new design, crocheted or tatted motifs, etc.

Aran The group of three islands at entrance to Ireland's Galway Bay have given their name to the knitting done by the inhabitants. Usually worked in unbleached wool, the knitting is characterised by raised pattern stitches.

argyle A knitting in a colourful diamond and plaid pattern worked with bobbins, commonly used in socks and sweaters; named for a branch of the Scottish Campbell clan, from whose tartan the design was originally adapted.

Assisi A form of old Italian embroidery; solid cross-stitch background emphasizing unworked design areas; traditionally scarlet or blue on creamy linen, sometimes black with black outline.

bangles Ornamental flat metallic shapes (round, oval, diamond, oblong, etc.) which have a hole near one edge for stitching to garment so that bangles hang loosely.

Bargello A form of embroidery; thread worked in upright stitches on canvas to form peaked, shaded, distinctive patterns; known also as "flame work", "Hungarian point," and "Florentine stitch."

beading needle A long, very thin needle with slender, long eye, fits through tiny hole of beads; used for bead embroidery and stringing.

bead work (a) American Indians decorated skins and later clothes with tiny beads strung on short threads, massed in short rows or as outlines. Designs were accented with shells, animal teeth, and silk ribbon appliqué. (b) Victorian needlewomen worked their popular "Berlin work" patterns in beads.

Berlin work A form of needlepoint very popular during Victorian era. Brilliantly coloured wools were worked in patterns on canvas; the best quality of both wool and canvas came from Berlin.

black work A form of embroidery in which designs (usually scrolls, grapes, leaves) were worked with fine black silk on white linen. First appeared in England at the time of Henry VIII. Known also as "Spanish work", it was probably introduced by Catherine of Aragon.

bobbin A core upon which yarn or thread is wound for pattern knitting or tatting; may be round, cylindrical or spindle-shaped depending upon its use.

bodkin A flat, blunt, large-eyed needle used to draw ribbon or tape through casings, or to turn cording right side out.

Bosnian An embroidery stitch used for filling; composed of straight (either vertical or horizontal) stitches and connecting diagonal stitches.

braid work The decorative application of braid, stitched in elaborate patterns to garments, pictures, or almost any article. Silk, cotton, linen, worsted, and mohair braids are used.

broderie Anglaise A simple type of cutwork embroidery consisting mostly of small oval and round eyelets; sometimes all are cut, sometimes some are worked solidly in satin stitch. Also called "Madeira".

bugle beads Small cylindrical glass or plastic beads used in decorative trimming.

bullion A cord formed by gold, silver, or metallic threads wound around wire or cotton; used generally for braids or fringes. Also, bullion stitch (see Index).

butt To join end-to-end without overlapping; used by braiders to form a perfect circle, oval, or square.

candlewicking (a) A form of embroidery especially popular in early American days. (b) A special heavy, soft thread used to make designs in running stitch, usually clipped to form tufts.

chain stitch embroidery One of the most ancient forms of embroidery. When worked with a hook and not with a needle, it became known as tambour work.

chenille A form of embroidery, fashionable in France during the 18th century, worked with "chenille"—the French word for caterpillar, which the thread resembles! There are two kinds: soft, unwired "chenille à broder" which can be worked to look like painting on velvet, and coarse "chenille ordinaire" used for couching or in satin stitch over large open-meshed canvas.

crêpe work The forming of imitation flowers or leaves of crêpe and sewing them to silk or satin backgrounds, or making them up on wire foundations as detached sprays.

crewel stitch One of the old embroidery stitches, the most used in crewel work, now called stem stitch.

crewel wool A fine, loosely-twisted 2-ply wool used in crewel embroidery.

crewelwork Embroidery worked in a variety of stitches with crewel wools on linen which was first in vogue during the reign of James I of England (1603–1625); also known as Jacobean work. Traditionally, designs consisted of a large stylized tree with numerous exotic fruits and flowers, sometimes with various animals and insects. From the main trunk grew curving, leafy branches to fill the required area.

cross-stitch A form of embroidery employing one simple stitch throughout; may be worked on fabric stamped with a transfer design or by counting threads. Commonly used for samplers, pictures, borders, and repeat patterns.

cut canvas work A kind of embroidery worked on coarse canvas with 4-thread soft wool, cut and combed to look like pile. (Tufts are tied and fastened to the canvas with fine thread.) Known also as "British raised work."

cutwork A form of embroidery which is worked by cutting out areas of the fabric. See also broderie Anglaise, hardanger, hedebo, reticella, Renaissance, Richelieu, Venetian, white work for specific types of cutwork.

darning on net Embroidering designs on a net background with darning stitches. See net embroidery.

double knitting A knitting stitch which results in a double stitch, tabular material; English 4-ply wool similar to knitting worsted.

drawn work A form of embroidery in which threads are drawn from the fabric and the open area is decoratively stitched. See also hardanger, hemstitching, and white work.

emboss A term employed in embroidery to signify the execution of a design in relief, either by stuffing with layers of thread or a succession of stitches underneath the embroidery, or else by working over a pad made with thick materials.

embroidery floss A soft, loosely-twisted, six-strand thread of mercerized cotton.

faggoting An insertion stitch used to join two pieces of material.

Fair Isle A form of knitting originated in one of the Shetland islands, which features horizontal pattern stripes worked in stocking stitch with two or more colours which are carried across back of work.

filet crochet A type of crochet featuring designs formed by solid "blocks" surrounded by openwork "spaces" which make up the background; originated to resemble filet lace.

filet lace An embroidery on netting background using variations of darning, buttonhole, backstitch, and filling stitches.

fish scale embroidery A kind of embroidery worked on silk, satin, or velvet foundations from flower patterns. Principal parts of the design, such as flowers, leaves, butterflies, are covered over with brightly tinted fish scales sewn to the foundation with coloured silks. Stems, vines, etc., are worked in satin stitch; centres, with French knots, beads, pearls, or spangles.

fishskin appliqué A form of embroidery practised by the Aleuts and other Eskimos. Translucent strips of dried seal intestine (or, away from the coastal areas, bear or deer intestine) were painted and appliquéd to garments. Beads, fringe, and fur tufts added further decoration.

foundation fabric The background material for embroidery, hooking, or knotting. For rug making, it is the material through which strips of yarn or fabric are worked. Depending upon the hooking technique employed, it may be burlap, rug canvas, warp cloth, monk's cloth, etc.

gauge In knitting and crochet, the number of stitches and rows per inch on which each set of directions is planned.

graph paper Paper marked into squares commonly ranging from 10-to-the-inch to 4-to-the-inch; usually the inch lines are accented. Available at art supply and some stationery stores.

gros point A form of needlepoint worked in tapestry yarn on 8- to 12-to-the-inch mesh canvas.

hairpin lace A form of crochet worked on a hairpin staple, known also as a fork or a loom, to produce an exceptionally lacy crochet.

half-pattern A pattern for one half of a symmetrical design; when "flopped" it forms a complete pattern.

hardanger A form of embroidery in which threads are drawn, satin stitch squares are embroidered, and threads are cut. See also cutwork and drawn work.

hatchment An embroidered panel of a coat-of-arms worked on a black background, usually square and hung cornerwise. Upon the death of the person so represented, the panel was hung upon the door to give notice to the public, as a wreath is now used.

hedebo A form of embroidery in which openwork parts are cut away and filled in with a variety of lace stitches, solid areas are worked with satin stitch, and edgings are button holed. See also cutwork.

hemstitching A decorative needlework for making hems and borders for which threads are drawn; the exposed threads are stitched together in groups forming various patterns. See also drawn work.

hooking A rug-making technique; strips of fabric or yarn are pulled with a hook through a foundation fabric at close intervals to solidly cover surface. A large crochet-type hook is used for the traditional hand-hooked type. See also punch needle and latch hook.

huck embroidery Darning stitches worked in formalized designs on linen or cotton towelling called huck which has pairs of raised threads on the wrong side. Also known as huck-a-back darning. Not to be confused with Swedish weaving.

interfacing A material set between surface fabric and facing to provide body and shape.

interlining A material set between surface fabric and lining to provide warmth and shaping.

Irish crochet A form of crochet consisting of a background of picot loops and raised motifs of flowers or fruit and leaves.

Jacobean Characteristic of the time of James I of England, who reigned from 1603 to 1625; often refers to crewelwork.

knitting The creating of fabric for garments, accessories, afghans, etc., by interlacing yarn or thread in series of connected loops using pointed needles.

lacer A blunt, needle-like device sometimes used for lacing braid to braid with carpet thread when making braided rugs.

laid work A form of embroidery in which large, bold designs are filled with threads laid across the surface and secured with surface stitches. Simply, quickly, and inexpensively worked, it is common to almost every needleworking locality, and is often known by different names.

latch hook or latchet hook A rug-hooking device used to knot short pieces of yarn on to canvas mesh; hook has a movable latch to facilitate the work.

loopers Jersey loops used for weaving on small hand looms.

macrame A form of needlework originally Arabic; threads are knotted, braided, and fringed to produce ornamental trims and fabrics. When made in fine thread, it is referred to as macrame lace.

Madeira A form of embroidery consisting of eyelet holes, the edges caught by simple overcast stitches; sometimes called "broderie Anglaise."

mesh Openings between threads; often used as size designation for the number of openings to the inch.

mesh sticks Flat sticks with rounded ends used in netting; available in widths from $\frac{1}{4}''$ to $\frac{3}{4}''$.

mitre A diagonal joining of material at a corner without overlapping.

Moravian work A name given to the gloomy memorial pictures so popular with American needleworkers in the 18th century. The fad for making them is supposed to

have originated with people of the Moravian sect, immigrants from Moravia.

motif A design element used singly or repeated.

Mountmellick work A form of bold, padded white work embroidery with no drawn or open spaces; stitches lie on the surface with little thread on the wrong side; derives its name from the Irish town where it originated.

multiple The number of stitches required to work one pattern.

nap Short fibres on fabric surface which have been brushed in one direction.

needle lace A lace made using only a needle and worked in buttonhole bars, picots, and knot stitches with a single thread.

needle gauge A piece of heavy cardboard or plastic with holes punched and numbered according to corresponding knitting needle sizes.

needlepoint An embroidery on canvas, worked to cover the area completely with even stitches to resemble tapestry.
Known through the ages, it has been called in successive periods "opus pulvinarium," "cushion style," "canvas work," and "Berlin work,"
As a general term, it includes petit point, needlepoint, gros point, and quick point, all of which are worked in the same manner, on canvas of various sizes of mesh. Today needlepoint, specifically, is done with tapestry yarn or crewel wool on 16- to 18-to-the-inch mesh canvas. See tent stitch (Index).

needleweaving A form of drawn work in which threads are woven back and forth over the exposed area; known also as woven hemstitching or Swedish weaving.

net embroidery An embroidered pattern in a variety of stitches worked on net, usually by counting holes (or the design may be on a piece of fabric basted under the net). See also darning on net.

ombré A colour term referring to yarn or fabric which is shaded from light to dark tones of one colour.

openwork A form of embroidery in which the design is outlined and then the background is "punched" with holes by pulling and stitching the threads apart.

paillettes A general term for shiny objects (spangles, sequins, beads, etc.) with a hole for sewing on; used as decorative trim.

patchwork The sewing together of small pieces of fabric, usually to form either an all over pattern or a pattern of blocks. Also known as "pieced work".

Penelope canvas A fine, double-thread canvas sometimes used for needlepoint; and, when basted to linen, as a guide for working cross-stitch (canvas threads are removed when embroidery is complete).

petit point A needlepoint worked in fine wool yarn, silk, or cotton on single-thread canvas, 20-to-the-inch mesh or smaller.

pile Raised loops or tufts which cover the surface of a fabric.

plush stitch One of the stitches on canvas; made with loops which are cut to form a plush-like surface, or left whole to form a border or fringe; also called raised stitch.

pompon A rounded tuft or ball made by tying together strands of yarn or thread.

pounce (a) To transfer a perforated design by forcing fine powder or charcoal through tiny holes. (b) The powder so used.

pouncer The tool used for pouncing.

pricking A pattern made by hand-pricking, transferred with pouncer.

punch needle A needle used for the traditional embroidered punch work which is fairly thick, round on top, and three-sided from the middle to the point.

punch work (a) Traditionally, a form of embroidery which is used chiefly for fillings and backgrounds. See openwork. (b) An embroidery worked with an automatic punch needle, which forms looped designs,

quick point Needlepoint worked in doubled tapestry wool or rug yarn on 5 mesh-per-inch canvas.

quill embroidery A form of embroidery worked by American Indians. Dyed porcupine quills were sewn on leather with a thin strip of sinew, or inserted through holes made in birch bark, or woven and wrapped.

quilting A decorative stitching together of two or more layers of fabric; extra padding or cording may be used for a more pronounced raised or puffed effect.

rabbet The inner edge of a picture frame into which the picture fits.

raised canvas work A form of embroidery executed from designs upon canvas with plush stitch; when completed, it is raised above the foundation and has the appearance of pile.

reticella work Another name for elaborate cutwork; also known as Renaissance work, having been extremely popular in that period.

ribbon work A form of embroidery in which narrow ribbon is stitched and gathered into shape on satin foundations for ornamentation.

Richelieu A form of cutwork embroidery in which picots and connecting buttonholed bars predominated.

rocailles Transparent glass seed beads.

sampler Originally, samples of fundamental embroidery stitches worked in a rather scattered pattern arrangement, which became more formalized by the end of the 17th century. Now cross-stitch is generally used for the pictorial samplers which typically include alphabet, numbers, names, and dates, etc.

sculpturing The scissors-trimming of pile to emphasize design areas.

seed beads Tiny round beads.

sequins Small metallic shapes with centre holes for thread; sewn, knitted, or crocheted on as decoration.

shuttle A thread-wound device used in tatting and weaving, etc.

smocking A decorative gathering of fabric worked in a number of stitches to form banded designs, usually worked in a combination of coloured threads.

soutache A narrow braid woven in a herringbone pattern.

spangle A flat metallic sequin-type paillette, often in a novelty shape.

splicing A method of joining strips used in rug braiding.

stab stitch A stitch made holding the needle at a right angle to the cloth; commonly used in quilting.

stump work An elaborate form of embroidery which flourished in the 17th century. Parts of the design were raised in high relief from the background by outlining and padding up with horsehair, wool, or pieces of wood. This was covered with thick silk or satin upon which embroidery stitches were worked.

tambour A form of embroidery worked with a special needle resembling a crochet hook with which thread is drawn in and out of the material in a chain-like stitch. Floral designs so stitched on fine net achieve the effect of lace.

taper (a) To become gradually narrower. (b) A long, waxed wick customarily used to light candles, sometimes used by embroiderers to singe wool fuzz from work.

tapestry wool A tightly twisted yarn used for working needlepoint.

Teneriffe embroidery Similar to needleweaving, but worked over embroidered bar stitches instead of through fabric as in drawn work or needleweaving.

ticking A strong, firm cotton fabric, usually striped, used for pillows, mattresses, etc.

tracing wheel A spiked rotating wheel on a handle; used with carbon to transfer dressmaker markings.

tramé Long laid threads indicating design and colour on needlepoint canvas; stitches are worked over these threads and the canvas beneath them.

transfer (a) To copy from one surface to another. (b) A commercial design printed in a special preparation which can be imprinted on fabric using a hot iron.

tubular knitting Knitting usually worked on four needles or a circular needle to produce tube-shaped material.

tuft A knotted cluster of short, soft threads.

Turkey work A form of needlework copying texture and designs of early Turkish rugs, made by knotting yarn on canvas or coarse cloth.

Venetian embroidery A kind of embroidery similar in appearance to Venetian lace, but worked with button-hole stitch outlines in high relief; backgrounds are filled with a variety of stitches and cutouts.

warp cloth A sturdy foundation fabric used for punch needle rugs.

warp thread Lengthwise threads in a woven fabric.

weft thread Crosswise (selvage-to-selvage) threads in a woven fabric.

welting A cord covered with bias fabric strips used as seam or edge trim.

white work Any embroidery worked in white on white. Most commonly, it refers to the especially delicate form of white work, in which drawn threads and cutwork are combined with a variety of stitches to add to the lacy effect.

An exotic flower embroidery of the early eighteenth century. Reproduced by courtesy of the Victoria and Albert museum.

Additional Embroidery Stitches

BOKHARA STITCH   One thread is laid across the area at a time, and couched in place as shown with small stitches, using the same thread. Good for filling large spaces.

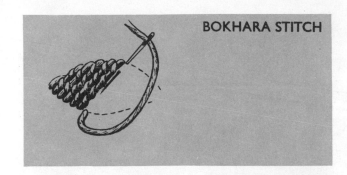

BOKHARA STITCH

BRAID STITCH   This stitch should be worked closely and kept rather small. Wrap thread around needle once as shown to make an inverted loop; insert needle in fabric from top to bottom, thus twisting thread. Bring thread under needle tip. Pull needle through and tighten stitch carefully. Do not pull too tightly, or braid effect will be lost.

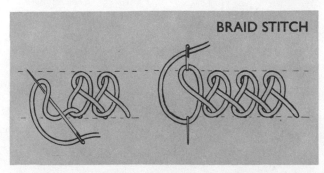

BRAID STITCH

BULLION STITCH   Insert point of needle in and out of fabric for length of stitch desired, do not pull needle through. Wrap thread around needle a number of times as shown, enough fo fill space of stitch. Hold wrapped needle and fabric firmly with thumb and finger of left hand and pull needle through, drawing the thread up; this will reverse direction of the stitch, so that it lies in the space of first stitch. Insert needle in fabric at end of stitch.

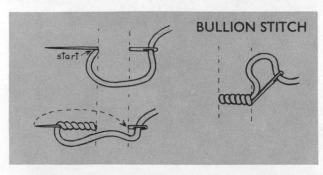

BULLION STITCH

CROWN STITCH   Make centre straight stitch with two slightly shorter stitches at either side as shown; bring needle to front of fabric above and to left of three stitches. Then pass needle under the three stitches, but not through fabric. Insert needle in fabric again above and to right.

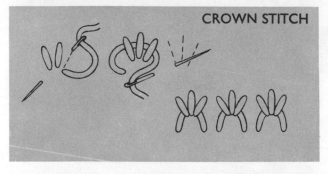

CROWN STITCH

DIAMOND STITCH   A good border decoration. Take a horizontal stitch from left to right and bring needle out just below as shown; pass needle under the stitch, under and over the thread and pull to make knot. Bring thread across and knot on opposite end of first stitch. Insert needle through fabric under knot and bring out a short distance below. Knot again at centre of last stitch as shown; insert needle at opposite side and bring out just below.

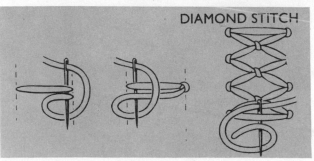

DIAMOND STITCH

INTERLACING STITCH

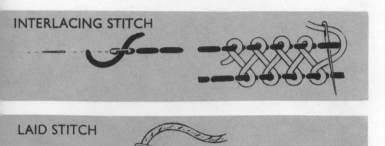

INTERLACING STITCH Make two rows of back stitch the distance apart desired, with stitches alternately spaced as shown. With a different colour thread, loop stitches under back stitches and over thread as shown, alternating on top and bottom rows.

LAID STITCH

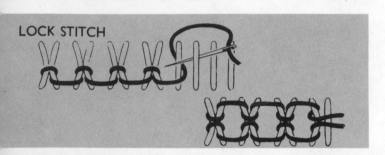

LAID STITCH Take stitches across the area to be filled, allowing a space between each, the size of another stitch. Fill these spaces with another series of stitches. This method conserves yarn and produces smooth, flat stitches, which may also be couched at intervals.

LOCK STITCH

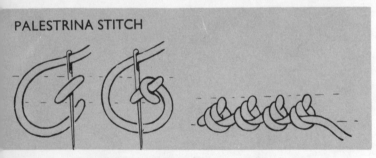

LOCK STITCH This stitch may be worked in one or two colours and is a good banding design. Take a number of vertical stitches spaced as desired, either close or wide apart. With another thread, work from left to right as shown, along bottom section of stitches. Repeat across top in same manner.

PALESTRINA STITCH

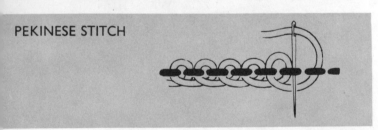

PALESTRINA STITCH To start, take a short diagonal stitch, bringing needle out below. Draw needle under stitch from top down and over thread as shown; pull up thread gently and repeat. For next stitch, insert needle to right from top to bottom, making a diagonal stitch and repeat. Keep stitches short and close together.

PEKINESE STITCH

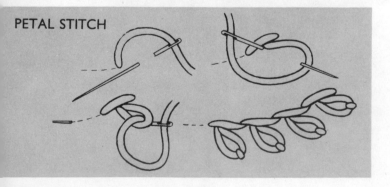

PEKINESE STITCH This is most effective when two colours or two different kinds of thread are used. First make a line of fairly large backstitches. Then make looped stitches through the backstitches.

PETAL STITCH

PETAL STITCH This is actually a combination of outline stitch and lazy daisy stitch, worked simultaneously. Take one stitch of outline, bringing needle back to middle of stitch; make lazy daisy to one side, then continue with another stitch of outline.

SCROLL STITCH Working from left to right, loop thread around as shown; take a tiny stitch to the right with needle over both top and bottom of loop. Pull up thread to make knot. Space the tiny stitches far enough apart so scroll effect is clearly defined.

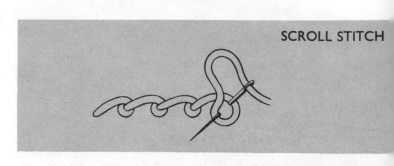

SCROLL STITCH

SIENESE STITCH When worked closely, this stitch makes a good border. Make first vertical stitch, bring needle out at bottom and to right. Loop thread around vertical stitch as shown; insert needle at top to the right and bring out at bottom, ready for next vertical stitch.

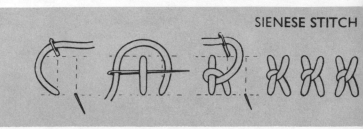

SIENESE STITCH

SORBELLO STITCH First take a horizontal stitch and bring needle out below and left. Loop thread around horizontal stitch twice as shown; insert needle below and right; bring out to right even with horizontal stitch for beginning of another stitch.

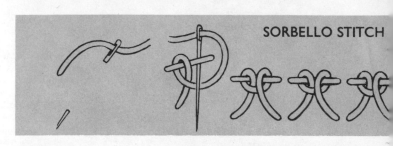

SORBELLO STITCH

SPLIT STITCH When a fine line is desired, this stitch may be used. Work as for outline stitch, bring needle out through thread as shown, thus splitting it in half.

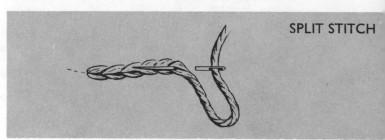

SPLIT STITCH

WHEAT-EAR STITCH First make two straight stitches forming a V; bring needle out below at centre. Pass needle under the two stitches and insert needle in fabric again at centre below, making a chain loop.

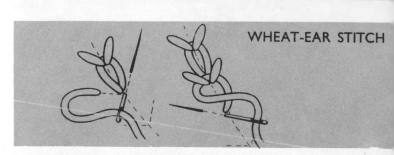

WHEAT-EAR STITCH

WOVEN BAND Make row of vertical foundation stitches evenly spaced. Use two needles and contrasting colour yarn. Work from top down, alternating threads. Each thread is brought over one foundation stitch and under next; threads twist over each other for each stitch as shown.

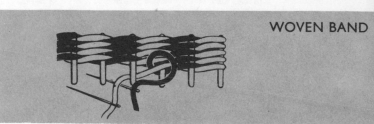

WOVEN BAND

Index

INDEX